DATE DUE

JUN 1 0 2009		

EVERYMAN,
I WILL GO WITH THEE,
AND BE THY GUIDE,
IN THY MOST NEED
TO GO BY THY SIDE

KAHLIL GIBRAN

THE
COLLECTED
WORKS

WITH EIGHTY-FOUR ILLUSTRATIONS
BY THE AUTHOR

EVERYMAN'S LIBRARY
Alfred A. Knopf   NewYork   London   Toronto

310

THIS IS A BORZOI BOOK
PUBLISHED BY ALFRED A. KNOPF

First included in Everyman's Library, 2007

US website: www.randomhouse.com/everymans

ISBN: 978-0-307-26707-8 (US)
1-84159-310-9 & 978-1-84159-310-4 (UK)

A CIP catalogue reference for this book is available from the
British Library

Book design by Barbara de Wilde and Carol Devine Carson

Typeset in the UK by AccComputing, North Barrow, Somerset

Printed and bound in Germany by GGP Media GmbH, Pössneck

CONTENTS

Kahlil Gibran was born on January 6, 1883, to a Maronite Catholic family in Bsharri, in what is now northern Lebanon. Gibran had an older half-brother named Peter and two younger sisters, Mariana and Sultana. When Gibran was eight years old, his father was sent to prison for tax evasion, and the family lost their home and went to live with relatives. Gibran's mother, Kamilah, soon decided that they should immigrate to the United States, following an uncle who had immigrated earlier. Gibran's father was released from prison but remained behind in Lebanon.

On June 25, 1895, the Gibrans left for the United States. They settled in Boston, which at the time contained the second-largest Lebanese and Syrian communities in the United States after New York. At school, Gibran was placed in a class for immigrant children who needed to learn English, and his birth name (Gibran Khalil Gibran) was shortened and the spelling of Khalil changed to Kahlil. Eventually, Gibran's sketches and drawings attracted the attention of his teachers, and he was introduced to Fred Holland Day, an artist who opened up Gibran's cultural horizons and encouraged and supported his artistic aspirations. In 1904, Gibran had his first art exhibition in Boston, which led to his meeting Mary Elizabeth Haskell, whose financial patronage and personal support would prove crucial throughout his career. From 1908 to 1910 he studied art in Paris and in 1912 he settled in New York, where he devoted himself to painting and, increasingly, to writing.

Gibran's early works were written in Arabic, but from 1918 on he published mostly in English. After *The Madman*, his first work in English, was rejected by several publishers, Gibran turned to Alfred A. Knopf, who had founded his company only a few years earlier and was willing to take a chance on the author. Knopf would go on to publish all Gibran's English-language books for the rest of his life, including his masterpiece, *The Prophet*, in 1923. Gibran continued to write in Arabic as well, but mostly on political or cultural subjects relating to the

Arab world. The works collected in this volume represent all twelve of his major books in English that were originally published by Alfred A. Knopf in the United States, including some earlier works written in Arabic and later translated.

Gibran died in 1931 in New York at the age of forty-eight. He was buried in his hometown of Bsharri in Lebanon.

THE MADMAN
HIS PARABLES AND POEMS

CONTENTS

YOU ASK ME how I became a madman. It happened thus: One day, long before many gods were born, I woke from a deep sleep and found all my masks were stolen, — the seven masks I have fashioned and worn in seven lives, — I ran maskless through the crowded streets shouting, "Thieves, thieves, the cursèd thieves."

Men and women laughed at me and some ran to their houses in fear of me.

And when I reached the market place, a youth standing on a house-top cried, "He is a madman." I looked up to behold him; the sun kissed my own naked face for the first time. For the first time the sun kissed my own naked face and my soul was inflamed with love for the sun, and I wanted my masks no more. And as if in a trance I cried, "Blessed, blessed are the thieves who stole my masks."

Thus I became a madman.

And I have found both freedom and safety in my madness; the freedom of loneliness and the safety from being understood, for those who understand us enslave something in us.

But let me not be too proud of my safety. Even a Thief in a jail is safe from another thief.

GOD

IN THE ANCIENT days, when the first quiver of speech came to my lips, I ascended the holy mountain and spoke unto God, saying, "Master, I am thy slave. Thy hidden will is my law and I shall obey thee for ever more."

But God made no answer, and like a mighty tempest passed away.

And after a thousand years I ascended the holy mountain and again spoke unto God, saying, "Creator, I am thy creation. Out of clay hast thou fashioned me and to thee I owe mine all."

And God made no answer, but like a thousand swift wings passed away.

And after a thousand years I climbed the holy mountain and spoke unto God again, saying, "Father, I am thy son. In pity and love thou hast given me birth, and through love and worship I shall inherit thy kingdom."

And God made no answer, and like the mist that veils the distant hills he passed away.

And after a thousand years I climbed the sacred mountain and again spoke unto God, saying, "My God, my aim and my fulfilment; I am thy yesterday and thou art my tomorrow. I am thy root in the earth and thou art my flower in the sky, and together we grow before the face of the sun."

Then God leaned over me, and in my ears whispered words of sweetness, and even as the sea that enfoldeth a brook that runneth down to her, he enfolded me.

And when I descended to the valleys and the plains God was there also.

MY FRIEND

MY FRIEND, I am not what I seem. Seeming is but a garment I wear — a care-woven garment that protects me from thy questionings and thee from my negligence.

The "I" in me, my friend, dwells in the house of silence, and therein it shall remain for ever more, unperceived, unapproachable.

I would not have thee believe in what I say nor trust in what I do — for my words are naught but thy own thoughts in sound and my deeds thy own hopes in action.

When thou sayest, "The wind bloweth eastward," I say, "Aye, it doth blow eastward"; for I would not have thee know that my mind doth not dwell upon the wind but upon the sea.

Thou canst not understand my seafaring thoughts, nor would I have thee understand. I would be at sea alone.

When it is day with thee, my friend, it is night with me; yet even then I speak of the noontide that dances upon the hills and of the purple shadow that steals its way across the valley; for thou canst not hear the songs of my darkness nor see my wings beating against the stars — and I fain would not have thee hear or see. I would be with night alone.

When thou ascendest to thy Heaven I descend to my Hell — even then thou callest to me across the unbridgeable gulf, "My companion, my comrade," and I call back to thee, "My comrade, my companion" — for I would not have thee see my Hell. The flame would burn thy eyesight and the smoke would crowd thy nostrils. And I love my Hell too well to have thee visit it. I would be in Hell alone.

Thou lovest Truth and Beauty and Righteousness; and I for thy sake say it is well and seemly to love these things. But in my heart I laugh at thy love. Yet I would not have thee see my laughter. I would laugh alone.

My friend, thou art good and cautious and wise; nay, thou art perfect — and I, too, speak with thee wisely and cautiously. And yet I am mad. But I mask my madness. I would be mad alone.

My friend, thou art not my friend, but how shall I make thee understand? My path is not thy path, yet together we walk, hand in hand.

THE SCARECROW

ONCE I SAID to a scarecrow, "You must be tired of standing in this lonely field."

And he said, "The joy of scaring is a deep and lasting one, and I never tire of it."

Said I, after a minute of thought, "It is true; for I too have known that joy."

Said he, "Only those who are stuffed with straw can know it."

Then I left him, not knowing whether he had complimented or belittled me.

A year passed, during which the scarecrow turned philosopher.

And when I passed by him again I saw two crows building a nest under his hat.

THE SLEEP-WALKERS

IN THE TOWN where I was born lived a woman and her daughter, who walked in their sleep.

One night, while silence enfolded the world, the woman and her daughter, walking, yet asleep, met in their mist-veiled garden.

And the mother spoke, and she said: "At last, at last, my enemy! You by whom my youth was destroyed – who have built up your life upon the ruins of mine. Would I could kill you!"

And the daughter spoke, and she said: "O hateful woman, selfish and old! Who stand between my freer self and me! Who would have my life an echo of your own faded life! Would you were dead!"

At that moment a cock crew, and both women awoke. The mother said gently, "Is that you, darling?" And the daughter answered gently, "Yes, dear."

THE WISE DOG

ONE DAY THERE passed by a company of cats a wise dog.

And as he came near and saw that they were very intent and heeded him not, he stopped.

Then there arose in the midst of the company a large, grave cat and looked upon them and said, "Brethren, pray ye; and when ye have prayed again and yet again, nothing doubting, verily then it shall rain mice."

And when the dog heard this he laughed in his heart and turned from them saying, "O blind and foolish cats, has it not been written and have I not known and my fathers before me, that that which raineth for prayer and faith and supplication is not mice but bones."

THE TWO HERMITS

UPON A LONELY mountain, there lived two hermits who worshipped God and loved one another.

Now these two hermits had one earthen bowl, and this was their only possession.

One day an evil spirit entered into the heart of the older hermit and he came to the younger and said, "It is long that we have lived together. The time has come for us to part. Let us divide our possessions."

Then the younger hermit was saddened and he said, "It grieves me, Brother, that thou shouldst leave me. But if thou must needs go, so be it," and he brought the earthen bowl and gave it to him saying, "We cannot divide it, Brother, let it be thine."

Then the older hermit said, "Charity I will not accept. I will take nothing but mine own. It must be divided."

And the younger one said, "If the bowl be broken, of what use would it be to thee or to me? If it be thy pleasure let us rather cast a lot."

But the older hermit said again, "I will have but justice and mine own, and I will not trust justice and mine own to vain chance. The bowl must be divided."

Then the younger hermit could reason no further and he said, "If it be indeed thy will, and if even so thou wouldst have it let us now break the bowl."

But the face of the older hermit grew exceeding dark, and he cried, "O thou cursed coward, thou wouldst not fight."

ON GIVING AND TAKING

ONCE THERE LIVED a man who had a valleyful of needles. And one day the mother of Jesus came to him and said: "Friend, my son's garment is torn and I must needs mend it before he goeth to the temple. Wouldst thou not give me a needle?"

And he gave her not a needle, but he gave her a learned discourse on Giving and Taking to carry to her son before he should go to the temple.

THE SEVEN SELVES

IN THE STILLEST hour of the night, as I lay half asleep, my seven selves sat together and thus conversed in whispers:

First Self: Here, in this madman, I have dwelt all these years, with naught to do but renew his pain by day and re-create his sorrow by night. I can bear my fate no longer, and now I rebel.

Second Self: Yours is a better lot than mine, brother, for it is given me to be this madman's joyous self. I laugh his laughter and sing his happy hours, and with thrice winged feet I dance his brighter thoughts. It is I that would rebel against my weary existence.

Third Self: And what of me, the love-ridden self, the flaming brand of wild passion and fantastic desires? It is I the love-sick self who would rebel against this madman.

Fourth Self: I, amongst you all, am the most miserable, for naught was given me but odious hatred and destructive loathing. It is I, the tempest-like self, the one born in the black caves of Hell, who would protest against serving this madman.

Fifth Self: Nay, it is I, the thinking self, the fanciful self, the self of hunger and thirst, the one doomed to wander without rest in search of unknown things and things not yet created; it is I, not you, who would rebel.

Sixth Self: And I, the working self, the pitiful labourer, who, with patient hands, and longing eyes, fashion the days into images and give the formless elements new and eternal forms – it is I, the solitary one, who would rebel against this restless madman.

Seventh Self: How strange that you all would rebel against this man, because each and every one of you has a preordained fate to fulfil. Ah! could I but be like one of you, a self with a determined lot! But I have none, I am the do-nothing self, the one who sits in the dumb, empty nowhere and nowhen, while you are busy re-creating life. Is it you or I, neighbours, who should rebel?

When the seventh self thus spake the other six selves looked with pity upon him but said nothing more; and as the night grew deeper one after the other went to sleep enfolded with a new and happy submission.

But the seventh self remained watching and gazing at nothingness, which is behind all things.

WAR

ONE NIGHT A feast was held in the palace, and there came a man and prostrated himself before the prince, and all the feasters looked upon him; and they saw that one of his eyes was out and that the empty socket bled. And the prince inquired of him, "What has befallen you?" And the man replied, "O prince, I am by profession a thief, and this night, because there was no moon, I went to rob the money-changer's shop, and as I climbed in through the window I made a mistake and entered the weaver's shop, and in the dark I ran into the weaver's loom and my eye was plucked out. And now, O prince, I ask for justice upon the weaver."

Then the prince sent for the weaver and he came, and it was decreed that one of his eyes should be plucked out.

"O prince," said the weaver, "the decree is just. It is right that one of my eyes be taken. And yet, alas! both are necessary to me in order that I may see the two sides of the cloth that I weave. But I have a neighbour, a cobbler, who has also two eyes, and in his trade both eyes are not necessary."

Then the prince sent for the cobbler. And he came. And they took out one of the cobbler's two eyes.

And justice was satisfied.

THE FOX

A FOX LOOKED at his shadow at sunrise and said, "I will have a camel for lunch today." And all morning he went about looking for camels. But at noon he saw his shadow again – and he said, "A mouse will do."

THE WISE KING

ONCE THERE RULED in the distant city of Wirani a king who was both mighty and wise. And he was feared for his might and loved for his wisdom.

Now, in the heart of that city was a well, whose water was cool and crystalline, from which all the inhabitants drank, even the king and his courtiers; for there was no other well.

One night when all were asleep, a witch entered the city, and poured seven drops of strange liquid into the well, and said, "From this hour he who drinks this water shall become mad."

Next morning all the inhabitants, save the king and his lord chamberlain, drank from the well and became mad, even as the witch had foretold.

And during that day the people in the narrow streets and in the market places did naught but whisper to one another, "The king is mad. Our king and his lord chamberlain have lost their reason. Surely we cannot be ruled by a mad king. We must dethrone him."

That evening the king ordered a golden goblet to be filled from the well. And when it was brought to him he drank deeply, and gave it to his lord chamberlain to drink.

And there was great rejoicing in that distant city of Wirani, because its king and its lord chamberlain had regained their reason.

AMBITION

THREE MEN MET at a tavern table. One was a weaver, another a carpenter and the third a ploughman.

Said the weaver, "I sold a fine linen shroud today for two pieces of gold. Let us have all the wine we want."

"And I," said the carpenter, "I sold my best coffin. We will have a great roast with the wine."

"I only dug a grave," said the ploughman, "but my patron paid me double. Let us have honey cakes too."

And all that evening the tavern was busy, for they called often for wine and meat and cakes. And they were merry.

And the host rubbed his hands and smiled at his wife; for his guests were spending freely.

When they left the moon was high, and they walked along the road singing and shouting together.

The host and his wife stood in the tavern door and looked after them.

"Ah!" said the wife, "these gentlemen! So freehanded and so gay! If only they could bring us such luck every day! Then our son need not be a tavern-keeper and work so hard. We could educate him, and he could become a priest."

THE NEW PLEASURE

LAST NIGHT I invented a new pleasure, and as I was giving it the first trial an angel and a devil came rushing toward my house. They met at my door and fought with each other over my newly created pleasure; the one crying, "It is a sin!" – the other, "It is a virtue!"

THE OTHER LANGUAGE

THREE DAYS AFTER I was born, as I lay in my silken cradle, gazing with astonished dismay on the new world round about me, my mother spoke to the wet-nurse, saying, "How does my child?"

And the wet-nurse answered, "He does well, madame, I have fed him three times; and never before have I seen a babe so young yet so gay."

And I was indignant; and I cried, "It is not true, mother; for my bed is hard, and the milk I have sucked is bitter to my mouth, and the odour of the breast is foul in my nostrils, and I am most miserable."

But my mother did not understand, nor did the nurse; for the language I spoke was that of the world from which I came.

And on the twenty-first day of my life, as I was being christened, the priest said to my mother, "You should indeed be happy, madame, that your son was born a christian."

And I was surprised, – and I said to the priest, "Then your mother in Heaven should be unhappy, for you were not born a christian."

But the priest too did not understand my language.

And after seven moons, one day a soothsayer looked at me, and he said to my mother, "Your son will be a statesman and a great leader of men."

But I cried out, – "That is a false prophecy; for I shall be a musician, and naught but a musician shall I be."

But even at that age my language was not understood – and great was my astonishment.

And after three and thirty years, during which my mother, and the nurse, and the priest have all died, (the shadow of God be upon their spirits) the soothsayer still lives. And yesterday I met him near the gate of the temple; and while we were talking together he said, "I have always known you would become a great musician. Even in your infancy I prophesied and foretold your future."

And I believed him – for now I too have forgotten the language of that other world.

THE POMEGRANATE

ONCE WHEN I was living in the heart of a pomegranate, I heard a seed saying, "Someday I shall become a tree, and the wind will sing in my branches, and the sun will dance on my leaves, and I shall be strong and beautiful through all the seasons."

Then another seed spoke and said, "When I was as young as you, I too held such views; but now that I can weigh and measure things, I see that my hopes were vain."

And a third seed spoke also, "I see in us nothing that promises so great a future."

And a fourth said, "But what a mockery our life would be, without a greater future!"

Said a fifth, "Why dispute what we shall be, when we know not even what we are."

But a sixth replied, "Whatever we are, that we shall continue to be."

And a seventh said, "I have such a clear idea how everything will be, but I cannot put it into words."

Then an eighth spoke – and a ninth – and a tenth – and then many – until all were speaking, and I could distinguish nothing for the many voices.

And so I moved that very day into the heart of a quince, where the seeds are few and almost silent.

THE TWO CAGES

IN MY FATHER'S garden there are two cages. In one is a lion, which my father's slaves brought from the desert of Ninavah; in the other is a songless sparrow.

Every day at dawn the sparrow calls to the lion, "Good morrow to thee, brother prisoner."

THE THREE ANTS

THREE ANTS MET on the nose of a man who was lying asleep in the sun. And after they had saluted one another, each according to the custom of his tribe, they stood there conversing.

The first ant said, "These hills and plains are the most barren I have known. I have searched all day for a grain of some sort, and there is none to be found."

Said the second ant, "I too have found nothing, though I have visited every nook and glade. This is, I believe, what my people call the soft, moving land where nothing grows."

Then the third ant raised his head and said, "My friends, we are standing now on the nose of the Supreme Ant, the mighty and infinite Ant, whose body is so great that we cannot see it, whose shadow is so vast that we cannot trace it, whose voice is so loud that we cannot hear it; and He is omnipresent."

When the third ant spoke thus the other ants looked at each other and laughed.

At that moment the man moved and in his sleep raised his hand and scratched his nose, and the three ants were crushed.

THE GRAVE-DIGGER

ONCE, AS I was burying one of my dead selves, the grave-digger came by and said to me, "Of all those who come here to bury, you alone I like."

Said I, "You please me exceedingly, but why do you like me?"

"Because," said he, "they come weeping and go weeping – you only come laughing and go laughing."

ON THE STEPS OF THE TEMPLE

YESTEREVE, ON THE marble steps of the Temple, I saw a woman sitting between two men. One side of her face was pale, the other was blushing.

THE BLESSED CITY

IN MY YOUTH I was told that in a certain city every one lived according to the Scriptures.

And I said, "I will seek that city and the blessedness thereof." And it was far. And I made great provision for my journey. And after forty days I beheld the city and on the forty-first day I entered into it.

And lo! the whole company of the inhabitants had each but a single eye and but one hand. And I was astonished and said to myself, "Shall they of this so holy city have but one eye and one hand?"

Then I saw that they too were astonished, for they were marvelling greatly at my two hands and my two eyes. And as they were speaking together I inquired of them saying, "Is this indeed the Blessed City, where each man lives according to the Scriptures?" And they said, "Yes, this is that city."

"And what," said I, "hath befallen you, and where are your right eyes and your right hands?"

And all the people were moved. And they said, "Come thou and see."

And they took me to the temple in the midst of the city. And in the temple I saw a heap of hands and eyes. All withered. Then said I, "Alas! what conqueror hath committed this cruelty upon you?"

And there went a murmur amongst them. And one of their elders stood forth and said, "This doing is of ourselves. God hath made us conquerors over the evil that was in us."

And he led me to a high altar, and all the people followed. And he showed me above the altar an inscription graven, and I read:

"If thy right eye offend thee, pluck it out and cast it from thee; for it is profitable for thee that one of thy members should perish, and not that thy whole body should be cast into hell. And if thy right hand offend thee, cut it off and cast it from thee; for it is profitable for thee that one of thy members should perish, and not that thy whole body should be cast into hell."

Then I understood. And I turned about to all the people and cried, "Hath no man or woman among you two eyes or two hands?"

And they answered me saying, "No, not one. There is none whole save such as are yet too young to read the Scripture and to understand its commandment."

And when we had come out of the temple, I straightway left that Blessed City; for I was not too young, and I could read the scripture.

THE GOOD GOD AND THE EVIL GOD

THE GOOD GOD and the Evil God met on the mountain top.

The Good God said, "Good day to you, brother."

The Evil God made no answer.

And the Good God said, "You are in a bad humour today."

"Yes," said the Evil God, "for of late I have been often mistaken for you, called by your name, and treated as if I were you, and it ill-pleases me."

And the Good God said, "But I too have been mistaken for you and called by your name."

The Evil God walked away cursing the stupidity of man.

"DEFEAT"

DEFEAT, MY DEFEAT, my solitude and my aloofness;
You are dearer to me than a thousand triumphs,
And sweeter to my heart than all world-glory.

Defeat, my Defeat, my self-knowledge and my defiance,
Through you I know that I am yet young and swift of foot
And not to be trapped by withering laurels.
And in you I have found aloneness
And the joy of being shunned and scorned.

Defeat, my Defeat, my shining sword and shield,
In your eyes I have read
That to be enthroned is to be enslaved,
And to be understood is to be levelled down,
And to be grasped is but to reach one's fulness
And like a ripe fruit to fall and be consumed.

Defeat, my Defeat, my bold companion,
You shall hear my songs and my cries and my silences,
And none but you shall speak to me of the beating of wings,
And urging of seas,
And of mountains that burn in the night,
And you alone shall climb my steep and rocky soul.

Defeat, my Defeat, my deathless courage,
You and I shall laugh together with the storm,
And together we shall dig graves for all that die in us,
And we shall stand in the sun with a will,
And we shall be dangerous.

NIGHT AND THE MADMAN

"I AM LIKE THEE, O, Night, dark and naked; I walk on the flaming path which is above my day-dreams, and whenever my foot touches earth a giant oaktree comes forth."

"Nay, thou art not like me, O, Madman, for thou still lookest backward to see how large a foot-print thou leavest on the sand."

"I am like thee, O, Night, silent and deep and in the heart of my loneliness lies a Goddess in child-bed; and in him who is being born Heaven touches Hell."

"Nay, thou art not like me, O, Madman, for thou shudderest yet before pain, and the song of the abyss terrifies thee."

"I am like thee, O, Night, wild and terrible; for my ears are crowded with cries of conquered nations and sighs for forgotten lands."

"Nay, thou art not like me, O, Madman, for thou still takest thy little-self for a comrade, and with thy monster-self thou canst not be friend."

"I am like thee, O, Night, cruel and awful; for my bosom is lit by burning ships at sea, and my lips are wet with blood of slain warriors."

"Nay, thou art not like me, O, Madman; for the desire for a sister-spirit is yet upon thee, and thou hast not become a law unto thyself."

"I am like thee, O, Night, joyous and glad; for he who dwells in my shadow is now drunk with virgin wine, and she who follows me is sinning mirthfully."

"Nay, thou art not like me, O, Madman, for thy soul is wrapped in the veil of seven folds and thou holdest not thy heart in thine hand."

"I am like thee, O, Night, patient and passionate; for in my breast a thousand dead lovers are buried in shrouds of withered kissses."

"Yea, Madman, art thou like me? Art thou like me? And canst thou ride the tempest as a steed, and grasp the lightning as a sword?"

"Like thee, O, Night, like thee, mighty and high, and my throne is built upon heaps of fallen Gods; and before me too pass the days to kiss the hem of my garment but never to gaze at my face."

"Art thou like me, child of my darkest heart? And dost thou think my untamed thoughts and speak my vast language?"

"Yea, we are twin brothers, O, Night; for thou revealest space and I reveal my soul."

FACES

I HAVE SEEN a face with a thousand countenances, and a face that was but a single countenance as if held in a mould.

I have seen a face whose sheen I could look through to the ugliness beneath, and a face whose sheen I had to lift to see how beautiful it was.

I have seen an old face much lined with nothing, and a smooth face in which all things were graven.

I know faces, because I look through the fabric my own eye weaves, and behold the reality beneath.

THE GREATER SEA

MY SOUL AND I went to the great sea to bathe. And when we reached the shore, we went about looking for a hidden and lonely place.

But as we walked, we saw a man sitting on a grey rock taking pinches of salt from a bag and throwing them into the sea.

"This is the pessimist," said my soul. "Let us leave this place. We cannot bathe here."

We walked on until we reached an inlet. There we saw, standing on a white rock, a man holding a bejewelled box, from which he took sugar and threw it into the sea.

"And this is the optimist," said my soul. "And he too must not see our naked bodies."

Further on we walked. And on a beach we saw a man picking up dead fish and tenderly putting them back into the water.

"And we cannot bathe before him," said my soul. "He is the humane philanthropist."

And we passed on.

Then we came where we saw a man tracing his shadow on the sand. Great waves came and erased it. But he went on tracing it again and again.

"He is the mystic," said my soul. "Let us leave him."

And we walked on, till in a quiet cove we saw a man scooping up the foam and putting it into an alabaster bowl.

"He is the idealist," said my soul. "Surely he must not see our nudity."

And on we walked. Suddenly we heard a voice crying, "This is the sea. This is the deep sea. This is the vast and mighty sea." And when we reached the voice it was a man whose back was turned to the sea, and at his ear he held a shell, listening to its murmur.

And my soul said, "Let us pass on. He is the realist, who turns his back on the whole he cannot grasp, and busies himself with a fragment."

So we passed on. And in a weedy place among the rocks was a man with his head buried in the sand. And I said to my soul, "We can bathe here, for he cannot see us."

"Nay," said my soul. "For he is the most deadly of them all. He is the puritan."

Then a great sadness came over the face of my soul, and into her voice.

"Let us go hence," she said, "for there is no lonely, hidden place where we can bathe. I would not have this wind lift my golden hair, or bare my white bosom in this air, or let the light disclose my sacred nakedness."

Then we left that sea to seek the Greater Sea.

CRUCIFIED

I CRIED TO MEN, "I would be crucified!"

And they said, "Why should your blood be upon our heads?"

And I answered, "How else shall you be exalted except by crucifying madmen?"

And they heeded and I was crucified. And the crucifixion appeased me.

And when I was hanged between earth and heaven they lifted up their heads to see me. And they were exalted, for their heads had never before been lifted.

But as they stood looking up at me one called out, "For what art thou seeking to atone?"

And another cried, "In what cause dost thou sacrifice thyself?"

And a third said, "Thinkest thou with this price to buy world glory?"

Then said a fourth, "Behold, how he smiles! Can such pain be forgiven?"

And I answered them all, and said:

"Remember only that I smiled. I do not atone – nor sacrifice – nor wish for glory; and I have nothing to forgive. I thirsted – and I besought you to give me my blood to drink. For what is there can quench a madman's thirst but his own blood? I was dumb – and I asked wounds of you for mouths. I was imprisoned in your days and nights – and I sought a door into larger days and nights.

"And now I go – as others already crucified have gone. And think not we are weary of crucifixion. For we must be crucified by larger and yet larger men, between greater earths and greater heavens."

THE ASTRONOMER

IN THE SHADOW of the temple my friend and I saw a blind man sitting alone. And my friend said, "Behold the wisest man of our land."

Then I left my friend and approached the blind man and greeted him. And we conversed.

After a while I said, "Forgive my question; but since when hast thou been blind?"

"From my birth," he answered.

Said I, "And what path of wisdom followest thou?"

Said he, "I am an astronomer."

Then he placed his hand upon his breast saying, "I watch all these suns and moons and stars."

THE GREAT LONGING

HERE I SIT between my brother the mountain and my sister the sea.

We three are one in loneliness, and the love that binds us together is deep and strong and strange. Nay, it is deeper than my sister's depth and stronger than my brother's strength, and stranger than the strangeness of my madness.

Æons upon æons have passed since the first grey dawn made us visible to one another; and though we have seen the birth and the fulness and the death of many worlds, we are still eager and young.

We are young and eager and yet we are mateless and unvisited, and though we lie in unbroken half embrace, we are uncomforted. And what comfort is there for controlled desire and unspent passion? Whence shall come the flaming god to warm my sister's bed? And what she-torrent shall quench my brother's fire? And who is the woman that shall command my heart?

In the stillness of the night my sister murmurs in her sleep the fire-god's unknown name, and my brother calls afar upon the cool and distant goddess. But upon whom I call in my sleep I know not.

*

Here I sit between my brother the mountain and my sister the sea. We three are one in loneliness, and the love that binds us together is deep and strong and strange.

SAID A BLADE OF GRASS

SAID A BLADE of grass to an autumn leaf, "You make such a noise falling! You scatter all my winter dreams."

Said the leaf indignant, "Low-born and low-dwelling! Songless, peevish thing! You live not in the upper air and you cannot tell the sound of singing."

Then the autumn leaf lay down upon the earth and slept. And when spring came she waked again – and she was a blade of grass.

And when it was autumn and her winter sleep was upon her, and above her through all the air the leaves were falling, she muttered to herself, "O these autumn leaves! They make such a noise! They scatter all my winter dreams."

THE EYE

SAID THE EYE one day, "I see beyond these valleys a mountain veiled with blue mist. Is it not beautiful?"

The Ear listened, and after listening intently awhile, said, "But where is any mountain? I do not hear it."

Then the Hand spoke and said, "I am trying in vain to feel it or touch it, and I can find no mountain."

And the Nose said, "There is no mountain, I cannot smell it."

Then the Eye turned the other way, and they all began to talk together about the Eye's strange delusion. And they said, "Something must be the matter with the Eye."

THE TWO LEARNED MEN

ONCE THERE LIVED in the ancient city of Afkar two learned men who hated and belittled each other's learning. For one of them denied the existence of the gods and the other was a believer.

One day the two met in the marketplace, and amidst their followers they began to dispute and to argue about the existence or the non-existence of the gods. And after hours of contention they parted.

That evening the unbeliever went to the temple and prostrated himself before the altar and prayed the gods to forgive his wayward past.

And the same hour the other learned man, he who had upheld the gods, burned his sacred books. For he had become an unbeliever.

WHEN MY SORROW WAS BORN

WHEN MY SORROW was born I nursed it with care, and watched over it with loving tenderness.

And my Sorrow grew like all living things, strong and beautiful and full of wondrous delights.

And we loved one another, my Sorrow and I, and we loved the world about us; for Sorrow had a kindly heart and mine was kindly with Sorrow.

And when we conversed, my Sorrow and I, our days were winged and our nights were girdled with dreams; for Sorrow had an eloquent tongue, and mine was eloquent with Sorrow.

And when we sang together, my Sorrow and I, our neighbours sat at their windows and listened; for our songs were deep as the sea and our melodies were full of strange memories.

And when we walked together, my Sorrow and I, people gazed at us with gentle eyes and whispered in words of exceeding sweetness. And there were those who looked with envy upon us, for Sorrow was a noble thing and I was proud with Sorrow.

But my Sorrow died, like all living things, and alone I am left to muse and ponder.

And now when I speak my words fall heavily upon my ears.

And when I sing my songs my neighbours come not to listen.

And when I walk the streets no one looks at me.

Only in my sleep I hear voices saying in pity, "See, there lies the man whose Sorrow is dead."

AND WHEN MY JOY WAS BORN

AND WHEN MY Joy was born, I held it in my arms and stood on the house-top shouting, "Come ye, my neighbours, come and see, for Joy this day is born unto me. Come and behold this gladsome thing that laugheth in the sun."

But none of my neighbours came to look upon my Joy, and great was my astonishment.

And every day for seven moons I proclaimed my Joy from the house-top – and yet no one heeded me. And my Joy and I were alone, unsought and unvisited.

Then my Joy grew pale and weary because no other heart but mine held its loveliness and no other lips kissed its lips.

Then my Joy died of isolation.

And now I only remember my dead Joy in remembering my dead Sorrow. But memory is an autumn leaf that murmurs a while in the wind and then is heard no more.

"THE PERFECT WORLD"

GOD OF LOST souls, thou who art lost amongst the gods, hear me:

Gentle Destiny that watchest over us, mad, wandering spirits, hear me:

I dwell in the midst of a perfect race, I the most imperfect.

I, a human chaos, a nebula of confused elements, I move amongst finished worlds – peoples of complete laws and pure order, whose thoughts are assorted, whose dreams are arranged, and whose visions are enrolled and registered.

Their virtues, O God, are measured, their sins are weighed, and even the countless things that pass in the dim twilight of neither sin nor virtue are recorded and catalogued.

Here days and nights are divided into seasons of conduct and governed by rules of blameless accuracy.

To eat, to drink, to sleep, to cover one's nudity, and then to be weary in due time.

To work, to play, to sing, to dance, and then to lie still when the clock strikes the hour.

To think thus, to feel thus much, and then to cease thinking and feeling when a certain star rises above yonder horizon.

To rob a neighbour with a smile, to bestow gifts with a graceful wave of the hand, to praise prudently, to blame cautiously, to destroy a soul with a word, to burn a body with a breath, and then to wash the hands when the day's work is done.

To love according to an established order, to entertain one's best self in a preconceived manner, to worship the gods becomingly, to intrigue the devils artfully – and then to forget all as though memory were dead.

To fancy with a motive, to contemplate with consideration, to be happy sweetly, to suffer nobly – and then to empty the cup so that tomorrow may fill it again.

All these things, O God, are conceived with forethought, born with determination, nursed with exactness, governed by rules, directed by reason, and then slain and buried after a prescribed method. And even their silent graves that lie within the human soul are marked and numbered.

It is a perfect world, a world of consummate excellence, a world of supreme wonders, the ripest fruit in God's garden, the master-thought of the universe.

But why should I be here, O God, I a green seed of unfulfilled passion, a mad tempest that seeketh neither east nor west, a bewildered fragment from a burnt planet?

Why am I here, O God of lost souls, thou who art lost amongst the gods?

THE FORERUNNER

HIS PARABLES AND POEMS

CONTENTS

THE FORERUNNER

YOU ARE YOUR own forerunner, and the towers you have builded are but the foundation of your giant-self. And that self too shall be a foundation.

And I too am my own forerunner, for the long shadow stretching before me at sunrise shall gather under my feet at the noon hour. Yet another sunrise shall lay another shadow before me, and that also shall be gathered at another noon.

Always have we been our own forerunners, and always shall we be. And all that we have gathered and shall gather shall be but seeds for fields yet unploughed. We are the fields and the ploughmen, the gatherers and the gathered.

When you were a wandering desire in the mist, I too was there, a wandering desire. Then we sought one another, and out of our eagerness dreams were born. And dreams were time limitless, and dreams were space without measure.

And when you were a silent word upon Life's quivering lips, I too was there, another silent word. Then Life uttered us and we came down the years throbbing with memories of yesterday and with longing for tomorrow, for yesterday was death conquered and tomorrow was birth pursued.

And now we are in God's hands. You are a sun in His right hand and I an earth in His left hand. Yet you are not more, shining, than I, shone upon.

And we, sun and earth, are but the beginning of a greater sun and a greater earth. And always shall we be the beginning.

*

You are your own forerunner, you the stranger passing by the gate of my garden.

And I too am my own forerunner, though I sit in the shadows of my trees and seem motionless.

GOD'S FOOL

ONCE THERE CAME from the desert to the great city of Sharia a man who was a dreamer, and he had naught but his garment and a staff.

And as he walked through the streets he gazed with awe and wonder at the temples and towers and palaces, for the city of Sharia was of surpassing beauty. And he spoke often to the passersby, questioning them about their city – but they understood not his language, nor he their language.

At the noon hour he stopped before a vast inn. It was built of yellow marble, and people were going in and coming out unhindered.

"This must be a shrine," he said to himself, and he too went in. But what was his surprise to find himself in a hall of great splendour and a large company of men and women seated about many tables. They were eating and drinking and listening to the musicians.

"Nay," said the dreamer. "This is no worshipping. It must be a feast given by the prince to the people, in celebration of a great event."

At that moment a man, whom he took to be the slave of the prince, approached him, and bade him be seated. And he was served with meat and wine and most excellent sweets.

When he was satisfied, the dreamer rose to depart. At the door he was stopped by a large man magnificently arrayed.

"Surely this is the prince himself," said the dreamer in his heart, and he bowed to him and thanked him.

Then the large man said in the language of the city:

"Sir, you have not paid for your dinner." And the dreamer did not understand, and again thanked him heartily. Then the large man bethought him, and he looked more closely upon the dreamer. And he saw that he was a stranger, clad in but a poor garment, and that indeed he had not wherewith to pay for his meal. Then the large man clapped his hands and called – and there came four watchmen of the city. And they listened to the large man. Then they took the dreamer between them, and they were two on each side of him. And the dreamer noted the ceremoniousness of their dress and of their manner and he looked upon them with delight.

"These," said he, "are men of distinction."

And they walked all together until they came to the House of Judgment and they entered.

The dreamer saw before him, seated upon a throne, a venerable man with flowing beard, robed majestically. And he thought he was the king. And he rejoiced to be brought before him.

Now the watchmen related to the judge, who was the venerable man, the charge against the dreamer; and the judge appointed two advocates, one to present the charge and the other to defend the stranger. And the advocates rose, the one after the other, and delivered each his argument. And the dreamer thought himself to be listening to addresses of welcome, and his heart filled with gratitude to the king and the prince for all that was done for him.

Then sentence was passed upon the dreamer, that upon a tablet hung about his neck his crime should be written, and that he should ride through the city on a naked horse, with a trumpeter and a drummer before him. And the sentence was carried out forthwith.

Now as the dreamer rode through the city upon the naked horse, with the trumpeter and the drummer before him, the inhabitants of the city came running forth at the sound of the noise, and when they saw him they laughed one and all, and the children ran after him in companies from street to street. And the dreamer's heart was filled with ecstasy, and his eyes shone upon them. For to him the tablet was a sign of the king's blessing and the procession was in his honour.

Now as he rode, he saw among the crowd a man who was from the desert like himself and his heart swelled with joy, and he cried out to him with a shout:

"Friend! Friend! Where are we? What city of the heart's desire is this? What race of lavish hosts? – who feast the chance

guest in their palaces, whose princes companion him, whose
king hangs a token upon his breast and opens to him the hospi-
tality of a city descended from heaven."

And he who was also of the desert replied not. He only smiled
and slightly shook his head. And the procession passed on.

And the dreamer's face was uplifted and his eyes were over-
flowing with light.

LOVE

THEY SAY THE jackal and the mole
Drink from the self-same stream
Where the lion comes to drink.

And they say the eagle and the vulture
Dig their beaks into the same carcass,
And are at peace, one with the other,
In the presence of the dead thing.

O love, whose lordly hand
Has bridled my desires,
And raised my hunger and my thirst
To dignity and pride,
Let not the strong in me and the constant
Eat the bread or drink the wine
That tempt my weaker self.
Let me rather starve,
And let my heart parch with thirst,
And let me die and perish,
Ere I stretch my hand
To a cup you did not fill,
Or a bowl you did not bless.

THE KING-HERMIT

THEY TOLD ME that in a forest among the mountains lives a young man in solitude who once was a king of a vast country beyond the Two Rivers. And they also said that he, of his own will, had left his throne and the land of his glory and come to dwell in the wilderness.

And I said, "I would seek that man, and learn the secret of his heart; for he who renounces a kingdom must needs be greater than a kingdom."

On that very day I went to the forest where he dwells. And I found him sitting under a white cypress, and in his hand a reed as if it were a sceptre. And I greeted him even as I would greet a king.

And he turned to me and said gently, "What would you in this forest of serenity? Seek you a lost self in the green shadows, or is it a home-coming in your twilight?"

And I answered, "I sought but you — for I fain would know that which made you leave a kingdom for a forest."

And he said, "Brief is my story, for sudden was the bursting of the bubble. It happened thus: One day as I sat at a window in my palace, my chamberlain and an envoy from a foreign land were walking in my garden. And as they approached my window, the lord chamberlain was speaking of himself and saying, 'I am like the king; I have a thirst for strong wine and a hunger for all games of chance. And like my lord the king I have storms of temper.' And the lord chamberlain and the envoy disappeared among the trees. But in a few minutes they returned, and this time the lord chamberlain was speaking of me, and he was saying, 'My lord the king is like myself — a good marksman; and like me he loves music and bathes thrice a day.'"

After a moment he added, "On the eve of that day I left my palace with but my garment, for I would no longer be ruler

over those who assume my vices and attribute to me their virtues."

And I said, "This is indeed a wonder, and passing strange."

And he said, "Nay, my friend, you knocked at the gate of my silences and received but a trifle. For who would not leave a kingdom for a forest where the seasons sing and dance ceaselessly? Many are those who have given their kingdom for less than solitude and the sweet fellowship of aloneness. Countless are the eagles who descend from the upper air to live with moles that they may know the secrets of the earth. There are those who renounce the kingdom of dreams that they may not seem distant from the dreamless. And those who renounce the kingdom of nakedness and cover their souls that others may not be ashamed in beholding truth uncovered and beauty unveiled. And greater yet than all of these is he who renounces the kingdom of sorrow that he may not seem proud and vainglorious."

Then rising he leaned upon his reed and said, "Go now to the great city and sit at its gate and watch all those who enter into it and those who go out. And see that you find him who, though born a king, is without kingdom; and him who though ruled in flesh rules in spirit – though neither he nor his subjects know this; and him also who but seems to rule yet is in truth slave of his own slaves."

After he had said these things he smiled on me, and there were a thousand dawns upon his lips. Then he turned and walked away into the heart of the forest.

And I returned to the city, and I sat at its gate to watch the passersby even as he had told me. And from that day to this numberless are the kings whose shadows have passed over me and few are the subjects over whom my shadow has passed.

THE LION'S DAUGHTER

FOUR SLAVES STOOD fanning an old queen who was asleep upon her throne. And she was snoring. And upon the queen's lap a cat lay purring and gazing lazily at the slaves.

The first slave spoke, and said, "How ugly this old woman is in her sleep. See her mouth droop; and she breathes as if the devil were choking her."

Then the cat said, purring, "Not half so ugly in her sleep as you in your waking slavery."

And the second slave said, "You would think sleep would smooth her wrinkles instead of deepening them. She must be dreaming of something evil."

And the cat purred, "Would that you might sleep also and dream of your freedom."

And the third slave said, "Perhaps she is seeing the procession of all those that she has slain."

And the cat purred, "Aye, she sees the procession of your forefathers and your descendants."

And the fourth slave said, "It is all very well to talk about her, but it does not make me less weary of standing and fanning."

And the cat purred, "You shall be fanning to all eternity; for as it is on earth so it is in heaven."

At this moment the old queen nodded in her sleep, and her crown fell to the floor.

And one of the slaves said, "That is a bad omen."

And the cat purred, "The bad omen of one is the good omen of another."

And the second slave said, "What if she should wake, and find her crown fallen! She would surely slay us."

And the cat purred, "Daily from your birth she has slain you and you know it not."

And the third slave said, "Yes, she would slay us and she would call it making sacrifice to the gods."

And the cat purred, "Only the weak are sacrificed to the gods."

And the fourth slave silenced the others, and softly he picked up the crown and replaced it, without waking her, on the old queen's head.

And the cat purred, "Only a slave restores a crown that has fallen."

And after a while the old queen woke, and she looked about her and yawned. Then she said, "Methought I dreamed, and I saw four caterpillars chased by a scorpion around the trunk of an ancient oaktree. I like not my dream."

Then she closed her eyes and went to sleep again. And she snored. And the four slaves went on fanning her.

And the cat purred, "Fan on, fan on, stupids. You fan but the fire that consumes you."

TYRANNY

THUS SINGS THE She-Dragon that guards the seven caves by the sea:

"My mate shall come riding on the waves. His thundering roar shall fill the earth with fear, and the flames of his nostrils shall set the sky afire. At the eclipse of the moon we shall be wedded, and at the eclipse of the sun I shall give birth to a Saint George, who shall slay me."

Thus sings the She-Dragon that guards the seven caves by the sea.

THE SAINT

IN MY YOUTH I once visited a saint in his silent grove beyond the hills; and as we were conversing upon the nature of virtue a brigand came limping wearily up the ridge. When he reached the grove he knelt down before the saint and said, "O saint, I would be comforted! My sins are heavy upon me."

And the saint replied, "My sins, too, are heavy upon me."

And the brigand said, "But I am a thief and a plunderer."

And the saint replied, "I too am a thief and a plunderer."

And the brigand said, "But I am a murderer, and the blood of many men cries in my ears."

And the saint replied, "I too am a murderer, and in my ears cries the blood of many men."

And the brigand said, "I have committed countless crimes."

And the saint replied, "I too have committed crimes without number."

Then the brigand stood up and gazed at the saint, and there was a strange look in his eyes. And when he left us he went skipping down the hill.

And I turned to the saint and said, "Wherefore did you accuse yourself of uncommitted crimes? See you not that this man went away no longer believing in you?"

And the saint answered, "It is true he no longer believes in me. But he went away much comforted."

At that moment we heard the brigand singing in the distance, and the echo of his song filled the valley with gladness.

THE PLUTOCRAT

IN MY WANDERINGS I once saw upon an island a man-headed, iron-hoofed monster who ate of the earth and drank of the sea incessantly. And for a long while I watched him. Then I approached him and said, "Have you never enough; is your hunger never satisfied and your thirst never quenched?"

And he answered saying, "Yes, I am satisfied, nay, I am weary of eating and drinking; but I am afraid that tomorrow there will be no more earth to eat and no more sea to drink."

THE GREATER SELF

THIS CAME TO PASS. After the coronation of Nufsibaäl, King of Byblus, he retired to his bed chamber – the very room which the three hermit-magicians of the mountain had built for him. He took off his crown and his royal raiment, and stood in the centre of the room thinking of himself, now the all-powerful ruler of Byblus.

Suddenly he turned; and he saw stepping out of the silver mirror which his mother had given him, a naked man.

The king was startled, and he cried out to the man, "What would you?"

And the naked man answered, "Naught but this: Why have they crowned you king?"

And the king answered, "Because I am the noblest man in the land."

Then the naked man said, "If you were still more noble, you would not be king."

And the king said, "Because I am the mightiest man in the land they crowned me."

And the naked man said, "If you were mightier yet, you would not be king."

Then the king said, "Because I am the wisest man they crowned me king."

And the naked man said, "If you were still wiser you would not choose to be king."

Then the king fell to the floor and wept bitterly.

The naked man looked down upon him. Then he took up the crown and with tenderness replaced it upon the king's bent head.

And the naked man, gazing lovingly upon the king, entered into the mirror.

And the king roused, and straightway he looked into the mirror. And he saw there but himself crowned.

WAR AND THE SMALL NATIONS

ONCE, HIGH ABOVE a pasture, where a sheep and a lamb were grazing, an eagle was circling and gazing hungrily down upon the lamb. And as he was about to descend and seize his prey, another eagle appeared and hovered above the sheep and her young with the same hungry intent. Then the two rivals began to fight filling the sky with their fierce cries.

The sheep looked up and was much astonished. She turned to the lamb and said,

"How strange, my child, that these two noble birds should attack one another. Is not the vast sky large enough for both of them? Pray, my little one, pray in your heart that God may make peace between your winged brothers."

And the lamb prayed in his heart.

CRITICS

ONE NIGHTFALL A man travelling on horseback toward the sea reached an inn by the roadside. He dismounted, and confident in man and night like all riders toward the sea, he tied his horse to a tree beside the door and entered into the inn.

At midnight, when all were asleep, a thief came and stole the traveller's horse.

In the morning the man awoke, and discovered that his horse was stolen. And he grieved for his horse, and that a man had found it in his heart to steal.

Then his fellow-lodgers came and stood around him and began to talk.

And the first man said, "How foolish of you to tie your horse outside the stable."

And the second said, "Still more foolish, without even hobbling the horse!"

And the third man said, "It is stupid at best to travel to the sea on horseback."

And the fourth said, "Only the indolent and the slow of foot own horses."

Then the traveller was much astonished. At last he cried, "My friends, because my horse is stolen, you have hastened one and all to tell me my faults and my shortcomings. But strange, not one word of reproach have you uttered about the man who stole my horse."

POETS

FOUR POETS WERE sitting around a bowl of punch that stood on a table.

Said the first poet, "Methinks I see with my third eye the fragrance of this wine hovering in space like a cloud of birds in an enchanted forest."

The second poet raised his head and said, "With my inner ear I can hear those mist-birds singing. And the melody holds my heart as the white rose imprisons the bee within her petals."

The third poet closed his eyes and stretched his arm upward, and said, "I touch them with my hand. I feel their wings, like the breath of a sleeping fairy, brushing against my fingers."

Then the fourth poet rose and lifted up the bowl, and he said, "Alas, friends! I am too dull of sight and of hearing and of touch. I cannot see the fragrance of this wine, nor hear its song, nor feel the beating of its wings. I perceive but the wine itself. Now therefore must I drink it, that it may sharpen my senses and raise me to your blissful heights."

And putting the bowl to his lips, he drank the punch to the very last drop.

The three poets, with their mouths open, looked at him aghast, and there was a thirsty yet unlyrical hatred in their eyes.

THE WEATHER-COCK

SAID THE WEATHER-COCK to the wind, "How tedious and monotonous you are! Can you not blow any other way but in my face? You disturb my God-given stability."

And the wind did not answer. It only laughed in space.

ONCE THE ELDERS of the city of Aradus presented themselves before the king, and besought of him a decree to forbid to men all wine and all intoxicants within their city.

And the king turned his back upon them and went out from them laughing.

Then the elders departed in dismay.

At the door of the palace they met the lord chamberlain. And the lord chamberlain observed that they were troubled, and he understood their case.

Then he said, "Pity, my friends! Had you found the king drunk, surely he would have granted you your petition."

OUT OF MY DEEPER HEART

OUT OF MY deeper heart a bird rose and flew skyward.

Higher and higher did it rise, yet larger and larger did it grow.

At first it was but like a swallow, then a lark, then an eagle, then as vast as a spring cloud, and then it filled the starry heavens.

Out of my heart a bird flew skyward. And it waxed larger as it flew. Yet it left not my heart.

*

O my faith, my untamed knowledge, how shall I fly to your height and see with you man's larger self pencilled upon the sky?

How shall I turn this sea within me into mist, and move with you in space immeasurable?

How can a prisoner within the temple behold its golden domes?

How shall the heart of a fruit be stretched to envelop the fruit also?

O my faith, I am in chains behind these bars of silver and ebony, and I cannot fly with you.

Yet out of my heart you rise skyward, and it is my heart that holds you, and I shall be content.

THE QUEEN OF Ishana was in travail of childbirth; and the King and the mighty men of his court were waiting in breathless anxiety in the great hall of the Winged Bulls.

At eventide there came suddenly a messenger in haste and prostrated himself before the King, and said, "I bring glad tidings unto my lord the King, and unto the kingdom and the slaves of the King. Mihrab the Cruel, thy life-long enemy, the King of Bethroun, is dead."

When the King and the mighty men heard this, they all rose and shouted for joy; for the powerful Mihrab, had he lived longer, had assuredly overcome Ishana and carried the inhabitants captive.

At this moment the court physician also entered the hall of Winged Bulls, and behind him came the royal midwives. And the physician prostrated himself before the King, and said, "My lord the King shall live for ever, and through countless generations shall he rule over the people of Ishana. For unto thee, O King, is born this very hour a son, who shall be thy heir."

Then indeed was the soul of the King intoxicated with joy, that in the same moment his foe was dead and the royal line was established.

Now in the City of Ishana lived a true prophet. And the prophet was young, and bold of spirit. And the King that very night ordered that the prophet should be brought before him. And when he was brought, the King said unto him, "Prophesy now, and foretell what shall be the future of my son who is this day born unto the kingdom."

And the prophet hesitated not, but said, "Hearken, O King, and I will indeed prophesy of the future of thy son, that is this day born. The soul of thy enemy, even of thy enemy King Mihrab, who died yestereve, lingered but a day upon the wind.

Then it sought for itself a body to enter into. And that which it entered into was the body of thy son that is born unto thee this hour."

Then the King was enraged, and with his sword he slew the prophet.

And from that day to this, the wise men of Ishana say one to another secretly, "Is it not known, and has it not been said from of old, that Ishana is ruled by an enemy."

KNOWLEDGE AND HALF-KNOWLEDGE

FOUR FROGS SAT upon a log that lay floating on the edge of a river. Suddenly the log was caught by the current and swept slowly down the stream. The frogs were delighted and absorbed, for never before had they sailed.

At length the first frog spoke, and said, "This is indeed a most marvellous log. It moves as if alive. No such log was ever known before."

Then the second frog spoke, and said, "Nay, my friend, the log is like other logs, and does not move. It is the river that is walking to the sea, and carries us and the log with it."

And the third frog spoke, and said, "It is neither the log nor the river that moves. The moving is in our thinking. For without thought nothing moves."

And the three frogs began to wrangle about what was really moving. The quarrel grew hotter and louder, but they could not agree.

Then they turned to the fourth frog, who up to this time had been listening attentively but holding his peace, and they asked his opinion.

And the fourth frog said, "Each of you is right, and none of you is wrong. The moving is in the log and the water and our thinking also."

And the three frogs became very angry, for none of them was willing to admit that his was not the whole truth, and that the other two were not wholly wrong.

Then the strange thing happened. The three frogs got together and pushed the fourth frog off the log into the river.

"SAID A SHEET OF SNOW-WHITE PAPER..."

SAID A SHEET of snow-white paper, "Pure was I created, and pure will I remain for ever. I would rather be burnt and turn to white ashes than suffer darkness to touch me or the unclean to come near me."

The ink-bottle heard what the paper was saying, and it laughed in its dark heart; but it never dared to approach her. And the multicoloured pencils heard her also, and they too never came near her.

And the snow-white sheet of paper did remain pure and chaste for ever – pure and chaste – and empty.

THE SCHOLAR AND THE POET

SAID THE SERPENT to the lark, "Thou flyest, yet thou canst not visit the recesses of the earth where the sap of life moveth in perfect silence."

And the lark answered, "Aye, thou knowest over much, nay thou art wiser than all things wise – pity thou canst not fly."

And as if he did not hear, the serpent said, "Thou canst not see the secrets of the deep, nor move among the treasures of the hidden empire. It was but yesterday I lay in a cave of rubies. It is like the heart of a ripe pomegranate, and the faintest ray of light turns it into a flame-rose. Who but me can behold such marvels?"

And the lark said, "None, none but thee can lie among the crystal memories of the cycles: pity thou canst not sing."

And the serpent said, "I know a plant whose root descends to the bowels of the earth, and he who eats of that root becomes fairer than Ashtarte."

And the lark said, "No one, no one but thee could unveil the magic thought of the earth – pity thou canst not fly."

And the serpent said, "There is a purple stream that runneth under a mountain, and he who drinketh of it shall become immortal even as the gods. Surely no bird or beast can discover that purple stream."

And the lark answered, "If thou willest thou canst become deathless even as the gods – pity thou canst not sing."

And the serpent said, "I know a buried temple, which I visit once a moon: It was built by a forgotten race of giants, and upon its walls are graven the secrets of time and space, and he who reads them shall understand that which passeth all understanding."

And the lark said, "Verily, if thou so desirest thou canst encircle with thy pliant body all knowledge of time and space – pity thou canst not fly."

Then the serpent was disgusted, and as he turned and entered into his hole he muttered, "Empty-headed songster!"

And the lark flew away singing, "Pity thou canst not sing. Pity, pity, my wise one, thou canst not fly."

VALUES

ONCE A MAN unearthed in his field a marble statue of great beauty. And he took it to a collector who loved all beautiful things and offered it to him for sale, and the collector bought it for a large price. And they parted.

And as the man walked home with his money he thought, and he said to himself, "How much life this money means! How can any one give all this for a dead carved stone buried and undreamed of in the earth for a thousand years?"

And now the collector was looking at his statue, and he was thinking, and he said to himself, "What beauty! What life! The dream of what a soul! – and fresh with the sweet sleep of a thousand years. How can any one give all this for money, dead and dreamless?"

OTHER SEAS

A FISH SAID to another fish, "Above this sea of ours there is another sea, with creatures swimming in it – and they live there even as we live here."

The fish replied, "Pure fancy! Pure fancy! When you know that everything that leaves our sea by even an inch, and stays out of it, dies. What proof have you of other lives in other seas?"

REPENTANCE

ON A MOONLESS night a man entered into his neighbour's garden and stole the largest melon he could find and brought it home.

He opened it and found it still unripe.

Then behold a marvel!

The man's conscience woke and smote him with remorse; and he repented having stolen the melon.

THE DYING MAN AND THE VULTURE

WAIT, WAIT YET awhile, my eager friend.
I shall yield but too soon this wasted thing,
Whose agony overwrought and useless
Exhausts your patience.
I would not have your honest hunger
Wait upon these moments:
But this chain, though made of a breath,
Is hard to break.
And the will to die,
Stronger than all things strong,
Is stayed by a will to live
Feebler than all things feeble.
Forgive me comrade; I tarry too long.
It is memory that holds my spirit;
A procession of distant days,
A vision of youth spent in a dream,
A face that bids my eyelids not to sleep,
A voice that lingers in my ears,
A hand that touches my hand.
Forgive me that you have waited too long.
It is over now, and all is faded: —
The face, the voice, the hand and the mist that brought
        them hither.
The knot is untied.
The cord is cleaved.
And that which is neither food nor drink is withdrawn.
Approach, my hungry comrade;
The board is made ready,
And the fare, frugal and spare,
Is given with love.
Come, and dig your beak here, into the left side,

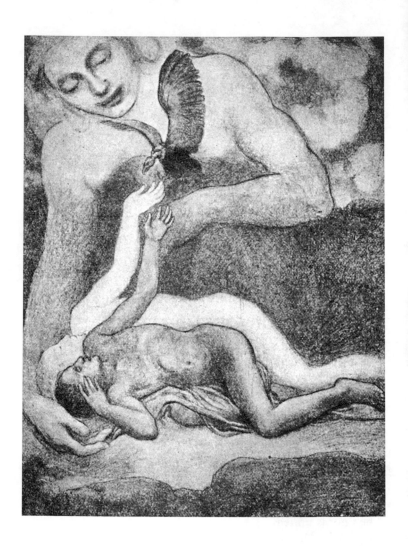

And tear out of its cage this smaller bird,
Whose wings can beat no more:
I would have it soar with you into the sky.
Come now, my friend, I am your host tonight,
And you my welcome guest.

BEYOND MY SOLITUDE

BEYOND MY SOLITUDE is another solitude, and to him who dwells therein my aloneness is a crowded market-place and my silence a confusion of sounds.

Too young am I and too restless to seek that above-solitude. The voices of yonder valley still hold my ears, and its shadows bar my way and I cannot go.

Beyond these hills is a grove of enchantment and to him who dwells therein my peace is but a whirlwind and my enchantment an illusion.

Too young am I and too riotous to seek that sacred grove. The taste of blood is clinging in my mouth, and the bow and the arrows of my fathers yet linger in my hand and I cannot go.

Beyond this burdened self lives my freer self; and to him my dreams are a battle fought in twilight and my desires the rattling of bones.

Too young am I and too outraged to be my freer self.

And how shall I become my freer self unless I slay my burdened selves, or unless all men become free?

How shall my leaves fly singing upon the wind unless my roots shall wither in the dark?

How shall the eagle in me soar against the sun until my fledglings leave the nest which I with my own beak have built for them?

THE LAST WATCH

AT THE HIGH-TIDE of night, when the first breath of dawn came upon the wind, the Forerunner, he who calls himself echo to a voice yet unheard, left his bed-chamber and ascended to the roof of his house. Long he stood and looked down upon the slumbering city. Then he raised his head, and even as if the sleepless spirits of all those asleep had gathered around him, he opened his lips and spoke, and he said:

"My friends and my neighbours and you who daily pass my gate, I would speak to you in your sleep, and in the valley of your dreams I would walk naked and unrestrained; far heedless are your waking hours and deaf are your sound-burdened ears.

"Long did I love you and overmuch.

"I love the one among you as though he were all, and all as if you were one. And in the spring of my heart I sang in your gardens, and in the summer of my heart I watched at your threshing-floors.

"Yea, I loved you all, the giant and the pigmy, the leper and the anointed, and him who gropes in the dark even as him who dances his days upon the mountains.

"You, the strong, have I loved, though the marks of your iron hoofs are yet upon my flesh; and you the weak, though you have drained my faith and wasted my patience.

"You the rich have I loved, while bitter was your honey to my mouth; and you the poor, though you knew my empty-handed shame.

"You the poet with the borrowed lute and blind fingers, you have I loved in self indulgence; and you the scholar, ever gathering rotted shrouds in potters' fields.

"You the priest I have loved, who sit in the silences of yesterday questioning the fate of my tomorrow; and you the worshippers of gods the images of your own desires.

"You the thirsting woman whose cup is ever full, I have loved you in understanding; and you the woman of restless nights, you too I have loved in pity.

"You the talkative have I loved, saying, 'Life hath much to say'; and you the dumb have I loved, whispering to myself, 'Says he not in silence that which I fain would hear in words?'

"And you the judge and the critic, I have loved also; yet when you have seen me crucified, you said, 'He bleeds rhythmically, and the pattern his blood makes upon his white skin is beautiful to behold.'

"Yea, I have loved you all, the young and the old, the trembling reed and the oak.

"But alas! it was the over-abundance of my heart that turned you from me. You would drink love from a cup, but not from a surging river. You would hear love's faint murmur, but when love shouts you would muffle your ears.

"And because I have loved you all you have said, 'Too soft and yielding is his heart, and too undiscerning is his path. It is the love of a needy one, who picks crumbs even as he sits at kingly feasts. And it is the love of a weakling, for the strong loves only the strong.'

"And because I have loved you overmuch you have said, 'It is but the love of a blind man who knows not the beauty of one nor the ugliness of another. And it is the love of the tasteless who drinks vinegar even as wine. And it is the love of the impertinent and the overweening, for what stranger could be our mother and father and sister and brother?'

"This you have said, and more. For often in the marketplace you pointed your fingers at me and said mockingly, 'There goes the ageless one, the man without seasons, who at the noon hour plays games with our children and at eventide sits with our elders and assumes wisdom and understanding.'

"And I said, 'I will love them more. Aye, even more. I will hide my love with seeming to hate, and disguise my tenderness as bitterness. I will wear an iron mask, and only when armed and mailed shall I seek them.'

"Then I laid a heavy hand upon your bruises, and like a tempest in the night I thundered in your ears.

"From the housetop I proclaimed you hypocrites, pharisees, tricksters, false and empty earth-bubbles.

"The short-sighted among you I cursed for blind bats, and those too near the earth I likened to soulless moles.

"The eloquent I pronounced fork-tongued, the silent, stone-lipped, and the simple and artless I called the dead never weary of death.

"The seekers after world knowledge I condemned as offenders of the holy spirit and those who would naught but the spirit I branded as hunters of shadows who cast their nets in flat waters and catch but their own images.

"Thus with my lips have I denounced you, while my heart, bleeding within me, called you tender names.

"It was love lashed by its own self that spoke. It was pride half slain that fluttered in the dust. It was my hunger for your love that raged from the housetop, while my own love, kneeling in silence, prayed your forgiveness.

"But behold a miracle!

"It was my disguise that opened your eyes, and my seeming to hate that woke your hearts.

"And now you love me.

"You love the swords that strike you and the arrows that crave your breast. For it comforts you to be wounded and only when you drink of your own blood can you be intoxicated.

"Like moths that seek destruction in the flame you gather daily in my garden: and with faces uplifted and eyes enchanted you watch me tear the fabric of your days. And in whispers you say the one to the other, 'He sees with the light of God. He speaks like the prophets of old. He unveils our souls and unlocks our hearts, and like the eagle that knows the way of foxes he knows our ways.'

"Aye, in truth, I know your ways, but only as an eagle knows the ways of his fledglings. And I fain would disclose my secret. Yet in my need for your nearness I feign remoteness, and in fear of the ebb-tide of your love I guard the floodgates of my love."

After saying these things the Forerunner covered his face with his hands and wept bitterly. For he knew in his heart that love humiliated in its nakedness is greater than love that seeks triumph in disguise; and he was ashamed.

But suddenly he raised his head, and like one waking from sleep he outstretched his arms and said, "Night is over, and we children of night must die when dawn comes leaping upon the hills; and out of our ashes a mightier love shall rise. And it shall laugh in the sun, and it shall be deathless."

THE PROPHET

CONTENTS

ALMUSTAFA, THE CHOSEN and the beloved, who was a dawn unto his own day, had waited twelve years in the city of Orphalese for his ship that was to return and bear him back to the isle of his birth.

And in the twelfth year, on the seventh day of Ielool, the month of reaping, he climbed the hill without the city walls and looked seaward; and he beheld his ship coming with the mist.

Then the gates of his heart were flung open, and his joy flew far over the sea. And he closed his eyes and prayed in the silences of his soul.

But as he descended the hill, a sadness came upon him, and he thought in his heart:

How shall I go in peace and without sorrow? Nay, not without a wound in the spirit shall I leave this city.

Long were the days of pain I have spent within its walls, and long were the nights of aloneness; and who can depart from his pain and his aloneness without regret?

Too many fragments of the spirit have I scattered in these streets, and too many are the children of my longing that walk naked among these hills, and I cannot withdraw from them without a burden and an ache.

It is not a garment I cast off this day, but a skin that I tear with my own hands.

Nor is it a thought I leave behind me, but a heart made sweet with hunger and with thirst.

Yet I cannot tarry longer.

The sea that calls all things unto her calls me, and I must embark.

For, to stay, though the hours burn in the night, is to freeze and crystallize and be bound in a mould.

Fain would I take with me all that is here. But how shall I?

A voice cannot carry the tongue and the lips that gave it wings. Alone must it seek the ether.

And alone and without his nest shall the eagle fly across the sun.

Now when he reached the foot of the hill, he turned again towards the sea, and he saw his ship approaching the harbour, and upon her prow the mariners, the men of his own land.

And his soul cried out to them, and he said:

Sons of my ancient mother, you riders of the tides,

How often have you sailed in my dreams. And now you come in my awakening, which is my deeper dream.

Ready am I to go, and my eagerness with sails full set awaits the wind.

Only another breath will I breathe in this still air, only another loving look cast backward,

And then I shall stand among you, a seafarer among seafarers.

And you, vast sea, sleepless mother,

Who alone are peace and freedom to the river and the stream,

Only another winding will this stream make, only another murmur in this glade,

And then shall I come to you, a boundless drop to a boundless ocean.

And as he walked he saw from afar men and women leaving their fields and their vineyards and hastening towards the city gates.

And he heard their voices calling his name, and shouting from field to field telling one another of the coming of his ship.

And he said to himself:

Shall the day of parting be the day of gathering?

And shall it be said that my eve was in truth my dawn?

And what shall I give unto him who has left his plough in mid-furrow, or to him who has stopped the wheel of his winepress?

Shall my heart become a tree heavy-laden with fruit that I may gather and give unto them?

And shall my desires flow like a fountain that I may fill their cups?

Am I a harp that the hand of the mighty may touch me, or a flute that his breath may pass through me?

A seeker of silences am I, and what treasure have I found in silences that I may dispense with confidence?

If this is my day of harvest, in what fields have I sowed the seed, and in what unremembered seasons?

If this indeed be the hour in which I lift up my lantern, it is not my flame that shall burn therein.

Empty and dark shall I raise my lantern,

And the guardian of the night shall fill it with oil and he shall light it also.

These things he said in words. But much in his heart remained unsaid. For he himself could not speak his deeper secret.

And when he entered into the city all the people came to meet him, and they were crying out to him as with one voice.

And the elders of the city stood forth and said:

Go not yet away from us.

A noontide have you been in our twilight, and your youth has given us dreams to dream.

No stranger are you among us, nor a guest, but our son and our dearly beloved.

Suffer not yet our eyes to hunger for your face.

And the priests and the priestesses said unto him:

Let not the waves of the sea separate us now, and the years you have spent in our midst become a memory.

You have walked among us a spirit, and your shadow has been a light upon our faces.

Much have we loved you. But speechless was our love, and with veils has it been veiled.

Yet now it cries aloud unto you, and would stand revealed before you.

And ever has it been that love knows not its own depth until the hour of separation.

*

And others came also and entreated him. But he answered them not. He only bent his head; and those who stood near saw his tears falling upon his breast.

And he and the people proceeded towards the great square before the temple.

And there came out of the sanctuary a woman whose name was Almitra. And she was a seeress.

And he looked upon her with exceeding tenderness, for it was she who had first sought and believed in him when he had been but a day in their city.

And she hailed him, saying:

Prophet of God, in quest of the uttermost, long have you searched the distances for your ship.

And now your ship has come, and you must needs go.

Deep is your longing for the land of your memories and the dwelling place of your greater desires; and our love would not bind you nor our needs hold you.

Yet this we ask ere you leave us, that you speak to us and give us of your truth.

And we will give it unto our children, and they unto their children, and it shall not perish.

In your aloneness you have watched with our days, and in your wakefulness you have listened to the weeping and the laughter of our sleep.

Now therefore disclose us to ourselves, and tell us all that has been shown you of that which is between birth and death.

And he answered,

People of Orphalese, of what can I speak save of that which is even now moving within your souls?

THEN SAID ALMITRA, Speak to us of Love.

And he raised his head and looked upon the people, and there fell a stillness upon them. And with a great voice he said:

When love beckons to you, follow him,

Though his ways are hard and steep.

And when his wings enfold you yield to him,

Though the sword hidden among his pinions may wound you.

And when he speaks to you believe in him,

Though his voice may shatter your dreams as the north wind lays waste the garden.

For even as love crowns you so shall he crucify you. Even as he is for your growth so is he for your pruning.

Even as he ascends to your height and caresses your tenderest branches that quiver in the sun,

So shall he descend to your roots and shake them in their clinging to the earth.

Like sheaves of corn he gathers you unto himself.

He threshes you to make you naked.

He sifts you to free you from your husks.

He grinds you to whiteness.

He kneads you until you are pliant;

And then he assigns you to his sacred fire, that you may become sacred bread for God's sacred feast.

All these things shall love do unto you that you may know the secrets of your heart, and in that knowledge become a fragment of Life's heart.

*

But if in your fear you would seek only love's peace and love's pleasure,

Then it is better for you that you cover your nakedness and pass out of love's threshing-floor,

Into the seasonless world where you shall laugh, but not all of your laughter, and weep, but not all of your tears.

Love gives naught but itself and takes naught but from itself.

Love possesses not nor would it be possessed;

For love is sufficient unto love.

When you love you should not say, "God is in my heart," but rather, "I am in the heart of God."

And think not you can direct the course of love, for love, if it finds you worthy, directs your course.

Love has no other desire but to fulfil itself.

But if you love and must needs have desires, let these be your desires:

To melt and be like a running brook that sings its melody to the night.

To know the pain of too much tenderness.

To be wounded by your own understanding of love;

And to bleed willingly and joyfully.

To wake at dawn with a winged heart and give thanks for another day of loving;

To rest at the noon hour and meditate love's ecstasy;

To return home at eventide with gratitude;

And then to sleep with a prayer for the beloved in your heart and a song of praise upon your lips.

THEN ALMITRA SPOKE again and said, And what of Marriage, master?

And he answered saying:

You were born together, and together you shall be forever-more.

You shall be together when the white wings of death scatter your days.

Ay, you shall be together even in the silent memory of God.

But let there be spaces in your togetherness,

And let the winds of the heavens dance between you.

Love one another, but make not a bond of love:

Let it rather be a moving sea between the shores of your souls.

Fill each other's cup but drink not from one cup.

Give one another of your bread but eat not from the same loaf.

Sing and dance together and be joyous, but let each one of you be alone,

Even as the strings of a lute are alone though they quiver with the same music.

Give your hearts, but not into each other's keeping.

For only the hand of Life can contain your hearts.

And stand together yet not too near together:

For the pillars of the temple stand apart,

And the oak tree and the cypress grow not in each other's shadow.

AND A WOMAN who held a babe against her bosom said, Speak to us of Children.

And he said:

Your children are not your children.

They are the sons and daughters of Life's longing for itself.

They come through you but not from you,

And though they are with you yet they belong not to you.

You may give them your love but not your thoughts,

For they have their own thoughts.

You may house their bodies but not their souls,

For their souls dwell in the house of tomorrow, which you cannot visit, not even in your dreams.

You may strive to be like them, but seek not to make them like you.

For life goes not backward nor tarries with yesterday.

You are the bows from which your children as living arrows are sent forth.

The archer sees the mark upon the path of the infinite, and He bends you with His might that His arrows may go swift and far.

Let your bending in the archer's hand be for gladness;

For even as He loves the arrow that flies, so He loves also the bow that is stable.

THEN SAID A rich man, Speak to us of Giving.

And he answered:

You give but little when you give of your possessions.

It is when you give of yourself that you truly give.

For what are your possessions but things you keep and guard for fear you may need them tomorrow?

And tomorrow, what shall tomorrow bring to the over-prudent dog burying bones in the trackless sand as he follows the pilgrims to the holy city?

And what is fear of need but need itself?

Is not dread of thirst when your well is full, the thirst that is unquenchable?

There are those who give little of the much which they have – and they give it for recognition and their hidden desire makes their gifts unwholesome.

And there are those who have little and give it all.

These are the believers in life and the bounty of life, and their coffer is never empty.

There are those who give with joy, and that joy is their reward.

And there are those who give with pain, and that pain is their baptism.

And there are those who give and know not pain in giving, nor do they seek joy, nor give with mindfulness of virtue;

They give as in yonder valley the myrtle breathes its fragrance into space.

Through the hands of such as these God speaks, and from behind their eyes He smiles upon the earth.

It is well to give when asked, but it is better to give unasked, through understanding;

And to the open-handed the search for one who shall receive is joy greater than giving.

And is there aught you would withhold?

All you have shall some day be given;

Therefore give now, that the season of giving may be yours and not your inheritors'.

You often say, "I would give, but only to the deserving."

The trees in your orchard say not so, nor the flocks in your pasture.

They give that they may live, for to withhold is to perish.

Surely he who is worthy to receive his days and his nights, is worthy of all else from you.

And he who has deserved to drink from the ocean of life deserves to fill his cup from your little stream.

And what desert greater shall there be, than that which lies in the courage and the confidence, nay the charity, of receiving?

And who are you that men should rend their bosom and unveil their pride, that you may see their worth naked and their pride unabashed?

See first that you yourself deserve to be giver, and an instrument of giving.

For in truth it is life that gives unto life – while you, who deem yourself a giver, are but a witness.

And you receivers – and you are all receivers – assume no weight of gratitude, lest you lay a yoke upon yourself and upon him who gives.

Rather rise together with the giver on his gifts as on wings;

For to be overmindful of your debt, is to doubt his generosity who has the free-hearted earth for mother, and God for father.

THEN AN OLD man, a keeper of an inn, said, Speak to us of Eating and Drinking.

And he said:

Would that you could live on the fragrance of the earth, and like an air plant be sustained by the light.

But since you must kill to eat, and rob the newly born of its mother's milk to quench your thirst, let it then be an act of worship.

And let your board stand an altar on which the pure and the innocent of forest and plain are sacrificed for that which is purer and still more innocent in man.

When you kill a beast say to him in your heart,

"By the same power that slays you, I too am slain; and I too shall be consumed.

For the law that delivered you into my hand shall deliver me into a mightier hand.

Your blood and my blood is naught but the sap that feeds the tree of heaven."

And when you crush an apple with your teeth, say to it in your heart,

"Your seeds shall live in my body,

And the buds of your tomorrow shall blossom in my heart,

And your fragrance shall be my breath,

And together we shall rejoice through all the seasons."

And in the autumn, when you gather the grapes of your vineyards for the winepress, say in your heart,

"I too am a vineyard, and my fruit shall be gathered for the winepress,

And like new wine I shall be kept in eternal vessels."

And in winter, when you draw the wine, let there be in your heart a song for each cup;

And let there be in the song a remembrance for the autumn days, and for the vineyard, and for the winepress.

THEN A PLOUGHMAN said, Speak to us of Work.

And he answered, saying:

You work that you may keep pace with the earth and the soul of the earth.

For to be idle is to become a stranger unto the seasons, and to step out of life's procession, that marches in majesty and proud submission towards the infinite.

When you work you are a flute through whose heart the whispering of the hours turns to music.

Which of you would be a reed, dumb and silent, when all else sings together in unison?

Always you have been told that work is a curse and labour a misfortune.

But I say to you that when you work you fulfil a part of earth's furthest dream, assigned to you when that dream was born,

And in keeping yourself with labour you are in truth loving life,

And to love life through labour is to be intimate with life's inmost secret.

But if you in your pain call birth an affliction and the support of the flesh a curse written upon your brow, then I answer that naught but the sweat of your brow shall wash away that which is written.

You have been told also that life is darkness, and in your weariness you echo what was said by the weary.

And I say that life is indeed darkness save when there is urge,

And all urge is blind save when there is knowledge,

And all knowledge is vain save when there is work,

And all work is empty save when there is love;

And when you work with love you bind yourself to yourself, and to one another, and to God.

And what is it to work with love?

It is to weave the cloth with threads drawn from your heart, even as if your beloved were to wear that cloth.

It is to build a house with affection, even as if your beloved were to dwell in that house.

It is to sow seeds with tenderness and reap the harvest with joy, even as if your beloved were to eat the fruit.

It is to charge all things you fashion with a breath of your own spirit,

And to know that all the blessed dead are standing about you and watching.

Often have I heard you say, as if speaking in sleep, "He who works in marble, and finds the shape of his own soul in the stone, is nobler than he who ploughs the soil.

And he who seizes the rainbow to lay it on a cloth in the likeness of man, is more than he who makes the sandals for our feet."

But I say, not in sleep but in the over-wakefulness of noon-tide, that the wind speaks not more sweetly to the giant oaks than to the least of all the blades of grass;

And he alone is great who turns the voice of the wind into a song made sweeter by his own loving.

Work is love made visible.

And if you cannot work with love but only with distaste, it is better that you should leave your work and sit at the gate of the temple and take alms of those who work with joy.

For if you bake bread with indifference, you bake a bitter bread that feeds but half man's hunger.

And if you grudge the crushing of the grapes, your grudge distils a poison in the wine.

And if you sing though as angels, and love not the singing, you muffle man's ears to the voices of the day and the voices of the night.

THEN A WOMAN said, Speak to us of Joy and Sorrow.

And he answered:

Your joy is your sorrow unmasked.

And the selfsame well from which your laughter rises was oftentimes filled with your tears.

And how else can it be?

The deeper that sorrow carves into your being, the more joy you can contain.

Is not the cup that holds your wine the very cup that was burned in the potter's oven?

And is not the lute that soothes your spirit, the very wood that was hollowed with knives?

When you are joyous, look deep into your heart and you shall find it is only that which has given you sorrow that is giving you joy.

When you are sorrowful look again in your heart, and you shall see that in truth you are weeping for that which has been your delight.

Some of you say, "Joy is greater than sorrow," and others say, "Nay, sorrow is the greater."

But I say unto you, they are inseparable.

Together they come, and when one sits alone with you at your board, remember that the other is asleep upon your bed.

Verily you are suspended like scales between your sorrow and your joy.

Only when you are empty are you at standstill and balanced.

When the treasure-keeper lifts you to weigh his gold and his silver, needs must your joy or your sorrow rise or fall.

THEN A MASON came forth and said, Speak to us of Houses.

And he answered and said:

Build of your imaginings a bower in the wilderness ere you build a house within the city walls.

For even as you have home-comings in your twilight, so has the wanderer in you, the ever distant and alone.

Your house is your larger body.

It grows in the sun and sleeps in the stillness of the night; and it is not dreamless. Does not your house dream? and dreaming, leave the city for grove or hill-top?

Would that I could gather your houses into my hand, and like a sower scatter them in forest and meadow.

Would the valleys were your streets, and the green paths your alleys, that you might seek one another through vineyards, and come with the fragrance of the earth in your garments.

But these things are not yet to be.

In their fear your forefathers gathered you too near together. And that fear shall endure a little longer. A little longer shall your city walls separate your hearths from your fields.

And tell me, people of Orphalese, what have you in these houses? And what is it you guard with fastened doors?

Have you peace, the quiet urge that reveals your power?

Have you remembrances, the glimmering arches that span the summits of the mind?

Have you beauty, that leads the heart from things fashioned of wood and stone to the holy mountain?

Tell me, have you these in your houses?

Or have you only comfort, and the lust for comfort, that

stealthy thing that enters the house a guest, and then becomes a host, and then a master?

Ay, and it becomes a tamer, and with hook and scourge makes puppets of your larger desires.

Though its hands are silken, its heart is of iron.

It lulls you to sleep only to stand by your bed and jeer at the dignity of the flesh.

It makes mock of your sound senses, and lays them in thistledown like fragile vessels.

Verily the lust for comfort murders the passion of the soul, and then walks grinning in the funeral.

But you, children of space, you restless in rest, you shall not be trapped nor tamed.

Your house shall be not an anchor but a mast.

It shall not be a glistening film that covers a wound, but an eyelid that guards the eye.

You shall not fold your wings that you may pass through doors, nor bend your heads that they strike not against a ceiling, nor fear to breathe lest walls should crack and fall down.

You shall not dwell in tombs made by the dead for the living.

And though of magnificence and splendour, your house shall not hold your secret nor shelter your longing.

For that which is boundless in you abides in the mansion of the sky, whose door is the morning mist, and whose windows are the songs and the silences of night.

AND THE WEAVER said, Speak to us of Clothes.

And he answered:

Your clothes conceal much of your beauty, yet they hide not the unbeautiful.

And though you seek in garments the freedom of privacy you may find in them a harness and a chain.

Would that you could meet the sun and the wind with more of your skin and less of your raiment,

For the breath of life is in the sunlight and the hand of life is in the wind.

Some of you say, "It is the north wind who has woven the clothes we wear."

And I say, Ay, it was the north wind,

But shame was his loom, and the softening of the sinews was his thread.

And when his work was done he laughed in the forest.

Forget not that modesty is for a shield against the eye of the unclean.

And when the unclean shall be no more, what were modesty but a fetter and a fouling of the mind?

And forget not that the earth delights to feel your bare feet and the winds long to play with your hair.

AND A MERCHANT said, Speak to us of Buying and Selling.

And he answered and said:

To you the earth yields her fruit, and you shall not want if you but know how to fill your hands.

It is in exchanging the gifts of the earth that you shall find abundance and be satisfied.

Yet unless the exchange be in love and kindly justice, it will but lead some to greed and others to hunger.

When in the market place you toilers of the sea and fields and vineyards meet the weavers and the potters and the gatherers of spices, –

Invoke then the master spirit of the earth, to come into your midst and sanctify the scales and the reckoning that weighs value against value.

And suffer not the barren-handed to take part in your transactions, who would sell their words for your labour.

To such men you should say,

"Come with us to the field, or go with our brothers to the sea and cast your net;

For the land and the sea shall be bountiful to you even as to us."

And if there come the singers and the dancers and the flute players, – buy of their gifts also.

For they too are gatherers of fruit and frankincense, and that which they bring, though fashioned of dreams, is raiment and food for your soul.

And before you leave the market place, see that no one has gone his way with empty hands.

For the master spirit of the earth shall not sleep peacefully upon the wind till the needs of the least of you are satisfied.

THEN ONE OF the judges of the city stood forth and said, Speak to us of Crime and Punishment.

And he answered, saying:

It is when your spirit goes wandering upon the wind,

That you, alone and unguarded, commit a wrong unto others and therefore unto yourself.

And for that wrong committed must you knock and wait a while unheeded at the gate of the blessed.

Like the ocean is your god-self;

It remains for ever undefiled.

And like the ether it lifts but the winged.

Even like the sun is your god-self;

It knows not the ways of the mole nor seeks it the holes of the serpent.

But your god-self dwells not alone in your being.

Much in you is still man, and much in you is not yet man,

But a shapeless pigmy that walks asleep in the mist searching for its own awakening.

And of the man in you would I now speak.

For it is he and not your god-self nor the pigmy in the mist, that knows crime and the punishment of crime.

Oftentimes have I heard you speak of one who commits a wrong as though he were not one of you, but a stranger unto you and an intruder upon your world.

But I say that even as the holy and the righteous cannot rise beyond the highest which is in each one of you,

So the wicked and the weak cannot fall lower than the lowest which is in you also.

And as a single leaf turns not yellow but with the silent knowledge of the whole tree,

So the wrong-doer cannot do wrong without the hidden will of you all.

Like a procession you walk together towards your god-self.

You are the way and the wayfarers.

And when one of you falls down he falls for those behind him, a caution against the stumbling stone.

Ay, and he falls for those ahead of him, who though faster and surer of foot, yet removed not the stumbling stone.

And this also, though the word lie heavy upon your hearts:

The murdered is not unaccountable for his own murder,

And the robbed is not blameless in being robbed.

The righteous is not innocent of the deeds of the wicked,

And the white-handed is not clean in the doings of the felon.

Yea, the guilty is oftentimes the victim of the injured,

And still more often the condemned is the burden bearer for the guiltless and unblamed.

You cannot separate the just from the unjust and the good from the wicked;

For they stand together before the face of the sun even as the black thread and the white are woven together.

And when the black thread breaks, the weaver shall look into the whole cloth, and he shall examine the loom also.

If any of you would bring to judgment the unfaithful wife,

Let him also weigh the heart of her husband in scales, and measure his soul with measurements.

And let him who would lash the offender look unto the spirit of the offended.

And if any of you would punish in the name of righteousness and lay the axe unto the evil tree, let him see to its roots;

And verily he will find the roots of the good and the bad, the fruitful and the fruitless, all entwined together in the silent heart of the earth.

And you judges who would be just,

What judgment pronounce you upon him who though honest in the flesh yet is a thief in spirit?

What penalty lay you upon him who slays in the flesh yet is himself slain in the spirit?

And how prosecute you him who in action is a deceiver and an oppressor,

Yet who also is aggrieved and outraged?

And how shall you punish those whose remorse is already greater than their misdeeds?

Is not remorse the justice which is administered by that very law which you would fain serve?

Yet you cannot lay remorse upon the innocent nor lift it from the heart of the guilty.

Unbidden shall it call in the night, that men may wake and gaze upon themselves.

And you who would understand justice, how shall you unless you look upon all deeds in the fullness of light?

Only then shall you know that the erect and the fallen are but one man standing in twilight between the night of his pigmy-self and the day of his god-self,

And that the corner-stone of the temple is not higher than the lowest stone in its foundation.

THEN A LAWYER said, But what of our Laws, master?

And he answered:

You delight in laying down laws,

Yet you delight more in breaking them.

Like children playing by the ocean who build sand-towers with constancy and then destroy them with laughter.

But while you build your sand-towers the ocean brings more sand to the shore,

And when you destroy them the ocean laughs with you.

Verily the ocean laughs always with the innocent.

But what of those to whom life is not an ocean, and man-made laws are not sand-towers,

But to whom life is a rock, and the law a chisel with which they would carve it in their own likeness?

What of the cripple who hates dancers?

What of the ox who loves his yoke and deems the elk and deer of the forest stray and vagrant things?

What of the old serpent who cannot shed his skin, and calls all others naked and shameless?

And of him who comes early to the wedding-feast, and when over-fed and tired goes his way saying that all feasts are violation and all feasters lawbreakers?

What shall I say of these save that they too stand in the sunlight, but with their backs to the sun?

They see only their shadows, and their shadows are their laws.

And what is the sun to them but a caster of shadows?

And what is it to acknowledge the laws but to stoop down and trace their shadows upon the earth?

But you who walk facing the sun, what images drawn on the earth can hold you?

You who travel with the wind, what weather-vane shall direct your course?

What man's law shall bind you if you break your yoke but upon no man's prison door?

What laws shall you fear if you dance but stumble against no man's iron chains?

And who is he that shall bring you to judgment if you tear off your garment yet leave it in no man's path?

People of Orphalese, you can muffle the drum, and you can loosen the strings of the lyre, but who shall command the skylark not to sing?

AND AN ORATOR said, Speak to us of Freedom.

And he answered:

At the city gate and by your fireside I have seen you prostrate yourself and worship your own freedom,

Even as slaves humble themselves before a tyrant and praise him though he slays them.

Ay, in the grove of the temple and in the shadow of the citadel I have seen the freest among you wear their freedom as a yoke and a handcuff.

And my heart bled within me; for you can only be free when even the desire of seeking freedom becomes a harness to you, and when you cease to speak of freedom as a goal and a fulfilment.

You shall be free indeed when your days are not without a care nor your nights without a want and a grief,

But rather when these things girdle your life and yet you rise above them naked and unbound.

And how shall you rise beyond your days and nights unless you break the chains which you at the dawn of your understanding have fastened around your noon hour?

In truth that which you call freedom is the strongest of these chains, though its links glitter in the sun and dazzle your eyes.

And what is it but fragments of your own self you would discard that you may become free?

If it is an unjust law you would abolish, that law was written with your own hand upon your own forehead.

You cannot erase it by burning your law books nor by washing the foreheads of your judges, though you pour the sea upon them.

And if it is a despot you would dethrone, see first that his throne erected within you is destroyed.

For how can a tyrant rule the free and the proud, but for a tyranny in their own freedom and a shame in their own pride?

And if it is a care you would cast off, that care has been chosen by you rather than imposed upon you.

And if it is a fear you would dispel, the seat of that fear is in your heart and not in the hand of the feared.

Verily all things move within your being in constant half embrace, the desired and the dreaded, the repugnant and the cherished, the pursued and that which you would escape.

These things move within you as lights and shadows in pairs that cling.

And when the shadow fades and is no more, the light that lingers becomes a shadow to another light.

And thus your freedom when it loses its fetters becomes itself the fetter of a greater freedom.

AND THE PRIESTESS spoke again and said: Speak to us of Reason and Passion.

And he answered, saying:

Your soul is oftentimes a battlefield, upon which your reason and your judgment wage war against your passion and your appetite.

Would that I could be the peacemaker in your soul, that I might turn the discord and the rivalry of your elements into oneness and melody.

But how shall I, unless you yourselves be also the peace-makers, nay, the lovers of all your elements?

Your reason and your passion are the rudder and the sails of your seafaring soul.

If either your sails or your rudder be broken, you can but toss and drift, or else be held at a standstill in mid-seas.

For reason, ruling alone, is a force confining; and passion, unattended, is a flame that burns to its own destruction.

Therefore let your soul exalt your reason to the height of passion, that it may sing;

And let it direct your passion with reason, that your passion may live through its own daily resurrection, and like the phœnix rise above its own ashes.

I would have you consider your judgment and your appetite even as you would two loved guests in your house.

Surely you would not honour one guest above the other; for he who is more mindful of one loses the love and the faith of both.

Among the hills, when you sit in the cool shade of the white poplars, sharing the peace and serenity of distant fields and meadows – then let your heart say in silence, "God rests in reason."

And when the storm comes, and the mighty wind shakes the forest, and thunder and lightning proclaim the majesty of the sky, – then let your heart say in awe, "God moves in passion."

And since you are a breath in God's sphere, and a leaf in God's forest, you too should rest in reason and move in passion.

AND A WOMAN spoke, saying, Tell us of Pain.

And he said:

Your pain is the breaking of the shell that encloses your understanding.

Even as the stone of the fruit must break, that its heart may stand in the sun, so must you know pain.

And could you keep your heart in wonder at the daily miracles of your life, your pain would not seem less wondrous than your joy;

And you would accept the seasons of your heart, even as you have always accepted the seasons that pass over your fields.

And you would watch with serenity through the winters of your grief.

Much of your pain is self-chosen.

It is the bitter potion by which the physician within you heals your sick self.

Therefore trust the physician, and drink his remedy in silence and tranquillity:

For his hand, though heavy and hard, is guided by the tender hand of the Unseen,

And the cup he brings, though it burn your lips, has been fashioned of the clay which the Potter has moistened with His own sacred tears.

AND A MAN said, Speak to us of Self-Knowledge.

And he answered, saying:

Your hearts know in silence the secrets of the days and the nights.

But your ears thirst for the sound of your heart's knowledge.

You would know in words that which you have always known in thought.

You would touch with your fingers the naked body of your dreams.

And it is well you should.

The hidden well-spring of your soul must needs rise and run murmuring to the sea;

And the treasure of your infinite depths would be revealed to your eyes.

But let there be no scales to weigh your unknown treasure;

And seek not the depths of your knowledge with staff or sounding line.

For self is a sea boundless and measureless.

Say not, "I have found the truth," but rather, "I have found a truth."

Say not, "I have found the path of the soul." Say rather, "I have met the soul walking upon my path."

For the soul walks upon all paths.

The soul walks not upon a line, neither does it grow like a reed.

The soul unfolds itself, like a lotus of countless petals.

THEN SAID A teacher, Speak to us of Teaching.

And he said:

No man can reveal to you aught but that which already lies half asleep in the dawning of your knowledge.

The teacher who walks in the shadow of the temple, among his followers, gives not of his wisdom but rather of his faith and his lovingness.

If he is indeed wise he does not bid you enter the house of his wisdom, but rather leads you to the threshold of your own mind.

The astronomer may speak to you of his understanding of space, but he cannot give you his understanding.

The musician may sing to you of the rhythm which is in all space, but he cannot give you the ear which arrests the rhythm nor the voice that echoes it.

And he who is versed in the science of numbers can tell of the regions of weight and measure, but he cannot conduct you thither.

For the vision of one man lends not its wings to another man.

And even as each one of you stands alone in God's knowledge, so must each one of you be alone in his knowledge of God and in his understanding of the earth.

AND A YOUTH said, Speak to us of Friendship.

And he answered, saying:

Your friend is your needs answered.

He is your field which you sow with love and reap with thanksgiving.

And he is your board and your fireside.

For you come to him with your hunger, and you seek him for peace.

When your friend speaks his mind you fear not the "nay" in your own mind, nor do you withhold the "ay".

And when he is silent your heart ceases not to listen to his heart;

For without words, in friendship, all thoughts, all desires, all expectations are born and shared, with joy that is unacclaimed.

When you part from your friend, you grieve not;

For that which you love most in him may be clearer in his absence, as the mountain to the climber is clearer from the plain.

And let there be no purpose in friendship save the deepening of the spirit.

For love that seeks aught but the disclosure of its own mystery is not love but a net cast forth: and only the unprofitable is caught.

And let your best be for your friend.

If he must know the ebb of your tide, let him know its flood also.

For what is your friend that you should seek him with hours to kill?

Seek him always with hours to live.

For it is his to fill your need, but not your emptiness.

And in the sweetness of friendship let there be laughter, and sharing of pleasures.

For in the dew of little things the heart finds its morning and is refreshed.

AND THEN A scholar said, Speak of Talking.

And he answered, saying:

You talk when you cease to be at peace with your thoughts;

And when you can no longer dwell in the solitude of your heart you live in your lips, and sound is a diversion and a pastime.

And in much of your talking, thinking is half murdered.

For thought is a bird of space, that in a cage of words may indeed unfold its wings but cannot fly.

There are those among you who seek the talkative through fear of being alone.

The silence of aloneness reveals to their eyes their naked selves and they would escape.

And there are those who talk, and without knowledge or forethought reveal a truth which they themselves do not understand.

And there are those who have the truth within them, but they tell it not in words.

In the bosom of such as these the spirit dwells in rhythmic silence.

When you meet your friend on the roadside or in the market place, let the spirit in you move your lips and direct your tongue.

Let the voice within your voice speak to the ear of his ear;

For his soul will keep the truth of your heart as the taste of the wine is remembered

When the colour is forgotten and the vessel is no more.

AND AN ASTRONOMER said, Master, what of Time?

And he answered:

You would measure time the measureless and the im-measurable.

You would adjust your conduct and even direct the course of your spirit according to hours and seasons.

Of time you would make a stream upon whose bank you would sit and watch its flowing.

Yet the timeless in you is aware of life's timelessness,

And knows that yesterday is but today's memory and to-morrow is today's dream.

And that that which sings and contemplates in you is still dwelling within the bounds of that first moment which scattered the stars into space.

Who among you does not feel that his power to love is boundless?

And yet who does not feel that very love, though boundless, encompassed within the centre of his being, and moving not from love thought to love thought, nor from love deeds to other love deeds?

And is not time even as love is, undivided and spaceless?

But if in your thought you must measure time into seasons, let each season encircle all the other seasons,

And let today embrace the past with remembrance and the future with longing.

AND ONE OF the elders of the city said, Speak to us of Good and Evil.

And he answered:

Of the good in you I can speak, but not of the evil.

For what is evil but good tortured by its own hunger and thirst?

Verily when good is hungry it seeks food even in dark caves, and when it thirsts it drinks even of dead waters.

You are good when you are one with yourself.

Yet when you are not one with yourself you are not evil.

For a divided house is not a den of thieves; it is only a divided house.

And a ship without rudder may wander aimlessly among perilous isles yet sink not to the bottom.

You are good when you strive to give of yourself.

Yet you are not evil when you seek gain for yourself.

For when you strive for gain you are but a root that clings to the earth and sucks at her breast.

Surely the fruit cannot say to the root, "Be like me, ripe and full and ever giving of your abundance."

For to the fruit giving is a need, as receiving is a need to the root.

You are good when you are fully awake in your speech,

Yet you are not evil when you sleep while your tongue staggers without purpose.

And even stumbling speech may strengthen a weak tongue.

*

You are good when you walk to your goal firmly and with bold steps.

Yet you are not evil when you go thither limping.

Even those who limp go not backward.

But you who are strong and swift, see that you do not limp before the lame, deeming it kindness.

You are good in countless ways, and you are not evil when you are not good,

You are only loitering and sluggard.

Pity that the stags cannot teach swiftness to the turtles.

In your longing for your giant self lies your goodness: and that longing is in all of you.

But in some of you that longing is a torrent rushing with might to the sea, carrying the secrets of the hillsides and the songs of the forest.

And in others it is a flat stream that loses itself in angles and bends and lingers before it reaches the shore.

But let not him who longs much say to him who longs little, "Wherefore are you slow and halting?"

For the truly good ask not the naked, "Where is your garment?" nor the houseless, "What has befallen your house?"

THEN A PRIESTESS said, Speak to us of Prayer.

And he answered, saying:

You pray in your distress and in your need; would that you might pray also in the fullness of your joy and in your days of abundance.

For what is prayer but the expansion of yourself into the living ether?

And if it is for your comfort to pour your darkness into space, it is also for your delight to pour forth the dawning of your heart.

And if you cannot but weep when your soul summons you to prayer, she should spur you again and yet again, though weeping, until you shall come laughing.

When you pray you rise to meet in the air those who are praying at that very hour, and whom save in prayer you may not meet.

Therefore let your visit to that temple invisible be for naught but ecstasy and sweet communion.

For if you should enter the temple for no other purpose than asking you shall not receive:

And if you should enter into it to humble yourself you shall not be lifted:

Or even if you should enter into it to beg for the good of others you shall not be heard.

It is enough that you enter the temple invisible.

I cannot teach you how to pray in words.

God listens not to your words save when He Himself utters them through your lips.

And I cannot teach you the prayer of the seas and the forests and the mountains.

But you who are born of the mountains and the forests and the seas can find their prayer in your heart,

And if you but listen in the stillness of the night you shall hear them saying in silence,

"Our God, who art our winged self, it is thy will in us that willeth.

It is thy desire in us that desireth.

It is thy urge in us that would turn our nights, which are thine, into days which are thine also.

We cannot ask thee for aught, for thou knowest our needs before they are born in us:

Thou art our need; and in giving us more of thyself thou givest us all."

THEN A HERMIT, who visited the city once a year, came forth and said, Speak to us of Pleasure.

And he answered, saying:

Pleasure is a freedom-song,

But it is not freedom.

It is the blossoming of your desires,

But it is not their fruit.

It is a depth calling unto a height,

But it is not the deep nor the high.

It is the caged taking wing,

But it is not space encompassed.

Ay, in very truth, pleasure is a freedom-song.

And I fain would have you sing it with fullness of heart; yet I would not have you lose your hearts in the singing.

Some of your youth seek pleasure as if it were all, and they are judged and rebuked.

I would not judge nor rebuke them. I would have them seek.

For they shall find pleasure, but not her alone;

Seven are her sisters, and the least of them is more beautiful than pleasure.

Have you not heard of the man who was digging in the earth for roots and found a treasure?

And some of your elders remember pleasures with regret like wrongs committed in drunkenness.

But regret is the beclouding of the mind and not its chastisement.

They should remember their pleasures with gratitude, as they would the harvest of a summer.

Yet if it comforts them to regret, let them be comforted.

*

And there are among you those who are neither young to seek nor old to remember;

And in their fear of seeking and remembering they shun all pleasures, lest they neglect the spirit or offend against it.

But even in their forgoing is their pleasure.

And thus they too find a treasure though they dig for roots with quivering hands.

But tell me, who is he that can offend the spirit?

Shall the nightingale offend the stillness of the night, or the firefly the stars?

And shall your flame or your smoke burden the wind?

Think you the spirit is a still pool which you can trouble with a staff?

Oftentimes in denying yourself pleasure you do but store the desire in the recesses of your being.

Who knows but that which seems omitted today, waits for tomorrow?

Even your body knows its heritage and its rightful need and will not be deceived.

And your body is the harp of your soul,

And it is yours to bring forth sweet music from it or confused sounds.

And now you ask in your heart, "How shall we distinguish that which is good in pleasure from that which is not good?"

Go to your fields and your gardens, and you shall learn that it is the pleasure of the bee to gather honey of the flower,

But it is also the pleasure of the flower to yield its honey to the bee.

For to the bee a flower is a fountain of life,

And to the flower a bee is a messenger of love,

And to both, bee and flower, the giving and the receiving of pleasure is a need and an ecstasy.

People of Orphalese, be in your pleasures like the flowers and the bees.

AND A POET said, Speak to us of Beauty.

And he answered:

Where shall you seek beauty, and how shall you find her unless she herself be your way and your guide?

And how shall you speak of her except she be the weaver of your speech?

The aggrieved and the injured say, "Beauty is kind and gentle. Like a young mother half-shy of her own glory she walks among us."

And the passionate say, "Nay, beauty is a thing of might and dread. Like the tempest she shakes the earth beneath us and the sky above us."

The tired and the weary say, "Beauty is of soft whisperings. She speaks in our spirit. Her voice yields to our silences like a faint light that quivers in fear of the shadow."

But the restless say, "We have heard her shouting among the mountains, And with her cries came the sound of hoofs, and the beating of wings and the roaring of lions."

At night the watchmen of the city say, "Beauty shall rise with the dawn from the east."

And at noontide the toilers and the wayfarers say, "We have seen her leaning over the earth from the windows of the sunset."

In winter say the snow-bound, "She shall come with the spring leaping upon the hills."

And in the summer heat the reapers say, "We have seen her dancing with the autumn leaves, and we saw a drift of snow in her hair."

All these things have you said of beauty,

Yet in truth you spoke not of her but of needs unsatisfied,

And beauty is not a need but an ecstasy.

It is not a mouth thirsting nor an empty hand stretched forth,

But rather a heart enflamed and a soul enchanted.

It is not the image you would see nor the song you would hear,

But rather an image you see though you close your eyes and a song you hear though you shut your ears.

It is not the sap within the furrowed bark, nor a wing attached to a claw,

But rather a garden for ever in bloom and a flock of angels for ever in flight.

People of Orphalese, beauty is life when life unveils her holy face.

But you are life and you are the veil.

Beauty is eternity gazing at itself in a mirror.

But you are eternity and you are the mirror.

AND AN OLD PRIEST said, Speak to us of Religion.

And he said:

Have I spoken this day of aught else?

Is not religion all deeds and all reflection,

And that which is neither deed nor reflection, but a wonder and a surprise ever springing in the soul, even while the hands hew the stone or tend the loom?

Who can separate his faith from his actions, or his belief from his occupations?

Who can spread his hours before him, saying, "This for God and this for myself; This for my soul, and this other for my body?"

All your hours are wings that beat through space from self to self.

He who wears his morality but as his best garment were better naked.

The wind and the sun will tear no holes in his skin.

And he who defines his conduct by ethics imprisons his song-bird in a cage.

The freest song comes not through bars and wires.

And he to whom worshipping is a window, to open but also to shut, has not yet visited the house of his soul whose windows are from dawn to dawn.

Your daily life is your temple and your religion.

Whenever you enter into it take with you your all.

Take the plough and the forge and the mallet and the lute,

The things you have fashioned in necessity or for delight.

For in reverie you cannot rise above your achievements nor fall lower than your failures.

And take with you all men:

For in adoration you cannot fly higher than their hopes nor humble yourself lower than their despair.

And if you would know God be not therefore a solver of riddles.

Rather look about you and you shall see Him playing with your children.

And look into space; you shall see Him walking in the cloud, outstretching His arms in the lightning and descending in rain.

You shall see Him smiling in flowers, then rising and waving His hands in trees.

THEN ALMITRA SPOKE, saying, We would ask now of Death.

And he said:

You would know the secret of death.

But how shall you find it unless you seek it in the heart of life?

The owl whose night-bound eyes are blind unto the day cannot unveil the mystery of light.

If you would indeed behold the spirit of death, open your heart wide unto the body of life.

For life and death are one, even as the river and the sea are one.

In the depth of your hopes and desires lies your silent knowledge of the beyond;

And like seeds dreaming beneath the snow your heart dreams of spring.

Trust the dreams, for in them is hidden the gate to eternity.

Your fear of death is but the trembling of the shepherd when he stands before the king whose hand is to be laid upon him in honour.

Is the shepherd not joyful beneath his trembling, that he shall wear the mark of the king?

Yet is he not more mindful of his trembling?

For what is it to die but to stand naked in the wind and to melt into the sun?

And what is it to cease breathing, but to free the breath from its restless tides, that it may rise and expand and seek God unencumbered?

Only when you drink from the river of silence shall you indeed sing.

And when you have reached the mountain top, then you shall begin to climb.

And when the earth shall claim your limbs, then shall you truly dance.

AND NOW IT was evening.

And Almitra the seeress said, Blessed be this day and this place and your spirit that has spoken.

And he answered, Was it I who spoke? Was I not also a listener?

Then he descended the steps of the Temple and all the people followed him. And he reached his ship and stood upon the deck.

And facing the people again, he raised his voice and said:

People of Orphalese, the wind bids me leave you.

Less hasty am I than the wind, yet I must go.

We wanderers, ever seeking the lonelier way, begin no day where we have ended another day; and no sunrise finds us where sunset left us.

Even while the earth sleeps we travel.

We are the seeds of the tenacious plant, and it is in our ripeness and our fullness of heart that we are given to the wind and are scattered.

Brief were my days among you, and briefer still the words I have spoken.

But should my voice fade in your ears, and my love vanish in your memory, then I will come again,

And with a richer heart and lips more yielding to the spirit will I speak.

Yea, I shall return with the tide,

And though death may hide me, and the greater silence enfold me, yet again will I seek your understanding.

And not in vain will I seek.

If aught I have said is truth, that truth shall reveal itself in a clearer voice, and in words more kin to your thoughts.

*

I go with the wind, people of Orphalese, but not down into emptiness;

And if this day is not a fulfilment of your needs and my love, then let it be a promise till another day.

Man's needs change, but not his love, nor his desire that his love should satisfy his needs.

Know therefore, that from the greater silence I shall return.

The mist that drifts away at dawn, leaving but dew in the fields, shall rise and gather into a cloud and then fall down in rain.

And not unlike the mist have I been.

In the stillness of the night I have walked in your streets, and my spirit has entered your houses,

And your heart-beats were in my heart, and your breath was upon my face, and I knew you all.

Ay, I knew your joy and your pain, and in your sleep your dreams were my dreams.

And oftentimes I was among you a lake among the mountains.

I mirrored the summits in you and the bending slopes, and even the passing flocks of your thoughts and your desires.

And to my silence came the laughter of your children in streams, and the longing of your youths in rivers.

And when they reached my depth the streams and the rivers ceased not yet to sing.

But sweeter still than laughter and greater than longing came to me.

It was the boundless in you;

The vast man in whom you are all but cells and sinews;

He in whose chant all your singing is but a soundless throbbing.

It is in the vast man that you are vast,

And in beholding him that I beheld you and loved you.

For what distances can love reach that are not in that vast sphere?

What visions, what expectations and what presumptions can outsoar that flight?

Like a giant oak tree covered with apple blossoms is the vast man in you.

His might binds you to the earth, his fragrance lifts you into space, and in his durability you are deathless.

You have been told that, even like a chain, you are as weak as your weakest link.

This is but half the truth. You are also as strong as your strongest link.

To measure you by your smallest deed is to reckon the power of ocean by the frailty of its foam.

To judge you by your failures is to cast blame upon the seasons for their inconstancy.

Ay, you are like an ocean,

And though heavy-grounded ships await the tide upon your shores, yet, even like an ocean, you cannot hasten your tides.

And like the seasons you are also,

And though in your winter you deny your spring,

Yet spring, reposing within you, smiles in her drowsiness and is not offended.

Think not I say these things in order that you may say the one to the other, "He praised us well. He saw but the good in us."

I only speak to you in words of that which you yourselves know in thought.

And what is word knowledge but a shadow of wordless knowledge?

Your thoughts and my words are waves from a sealed memory that keeps records of our yesterdays,

And of the ancient days when the earth knew not us nor herself,

And of nights when earth was upwrought with confusion.

Wise men have come to you to give you of their wisdom. I came to take of your wisdom:

And behold I have found that which is greater than wisdom.

It is a flame spirit in you ever gathering more of itself,

While you, heedless of its expansion, bewail the withering of your days.

It is life in quest of life in bodies that fear the grave.

*

There are no graves here.

These mountains and plains are a cradle and a stepping-stone.

Whenever you pass by the field where you have laid your ancestors look well thereupon, and you shall see yourselves and your children dancing hand in hand.

Verily you often make merry without knowing.

Others have come to you to whom for golden promises made unto your faith you have given but riches and power and glory.

Less than a promise have I given, and yet more generous have you been to me.

You have given me my deeper thirsting after life.

Surely there is no greater gift to a man than that which turns all his aims into parching lips and all life into a fountain.

And in this lies my honour and my reward, –

That whenever I come to the fountain to drink I find the living water itself thirsty;

And it drinks me while I drink it.

Some of you have deemed me proud and over-shy to receive gifts.

Too proud indeed am I to receive wages, but not gifts.

And though I have eaten berries among the hills when you would have had me sit at your board,

And slept in the portico of the temple when you would gladly have sheltered me,

Yet was it not your loving mindfulness of my days and my nights that made food sweet to my mouth and girdled my sleep with visions?

For this I bless you most:

You give much and know not that you give at all.

Verily the kindness that gazes upon itself in a mirror turns to stone,

And a good deed that calls itself by tender names becomes the parent to a curse.

*

And some of you have called me aloof, and drunk with my own aloneness,

And you have said, "He holds council with the trees of the forest, but not with men.

He sits alone on hill-tops and looks down upon our city."

True it is that I have climbed the hills and walked in remote places.

How could I have seen you save from a great height or a great distance?

How can one be indeed near unless he be far?

And others among you called unto me, not in words, and they said,

"Stranger, stranger, lover of unreachable heights, why dwell you among the summits where eagles build their nests?

Why seek you the unattainable?

What storms would you trap in your net,

And what vaporous birds do you hunt in the sky?

Come and be one of us.

Descend and appease your hunger with our bread and quench your thirst with our wine."

In the solitude of their souls they said these things;

But were their solitude deeper they would have known that I sought but the secret of your joy and your pain,

And I hunted only your larger selves that walk the sky.

But the hunter was also the hunted;

For many of my arrows left my bow only to seek my own breast.

And the flier was also the creeper;

For when my wings were spread in the sun their shadow upon the earth was a turtle.

And I the believer was also the doubter;

For often have I put my finger in my own wound that I might have the greater belief in you and the greater knowledge of you.

And it is with this belief and this knowledge that I say,

You are not enclosed within your bodies, nor confined to houses or fields.

That which is you dwells above the mountain and roves with the wind.

It is not a thing that crawls into the sun for warmth or digs holes into darkness for safety,

But a thing free, a spirit that envelops the earth and moves in the ether.

If these be vague words, then seek not to clear them.

Vague and nebulous is the beginning of all things, but not their end,

And I fain would have you remember me as a beginning.

Life, and all that lives, is conceived in the mist and not in the crystal.

And who knows but a crystal is mist in decay?

This would I have you remember in remembering me:

That which seems most feeble and bewildered in you is the strongest and most determined.

Is it not your breath that has erected and hardened the structure of your bones?

And is it not a dream which none of you remembers having dreamt, that builded your city and fashioned all there is in it?

Could you but see the tides of that breath you would cease to see all else,

And if you could hear the whispering of the dream you would hear no other sound.

But you do not see, nor do you hear, and it is well.

The veil that clouds your eyes shall be lifted by the hands that wove it,

And the clay that fills your ears shall be pierced by those fingers that kneaded it.

And you shall see

And you shall hear.

Yet you shall not deplore having known blindness, nor regret having been deaf.

For in that day you shall know the hidden purposes in all things,

And you shall bless darkness as you would bless light.

After saying these things he looked about him, and he saw the pilot of his ship standing by the helm and gazing now at the full sails and now at the distance.

And he said:

Patient, over patient, is the captain of my ship.

The wind blows, and restless are the sails;

Even the rudder begs direction;

Yet quietly my captain awaits my silence.

And these my mariners, who have heard the choir of the greater sea, they too have heard me patiently.

Now they shall wait no longer.

I am ready.

The stream has reached the sea, and once more the great mother holds her son against her breast.

Fare you well, people of Orphalese.

This day has ended.

It is closing upon us even as the water-lily upon its own tomorrow.

What was given us here we shall keep,

And if it suffices not, then again must we come together and together stretch our hands unto the giver.

Forget not that I shall come back to you.

A little while, and my longing shall gather dust and foam for another body.

A little while, a moment of rest upon the wind, and another woman shall bear me.

Farewell to you and the youth I have spent with you.

It was but yesterday we met in a dream.

You have sung to me in my aloneness, and I of your longings have built a tower in the sky.

But now our sleep has fled and our dream is over, and it is no longer dawn.

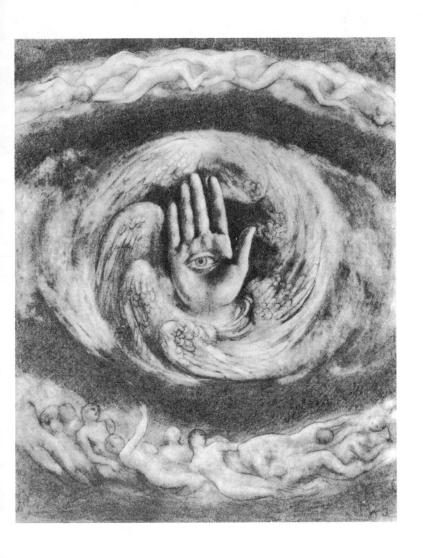

The noontide is upon us and our half waking has turned to fuller day, and we must part.

If in the twilight of memory we should meet once more, we shall speak again together and you shall sing to me a deeper song.

And if our hands should meet in another dream we shall build another tower in the sky.

So saying he made a signal to the seamen, and straightway they weighed anchor and cast the ship loose from its moorings, and they moved eastward.

And a cry came from the people as from a single heart, and it rose into the dusk and was carried out over the sea like a great trumpeting.

Only Almitra was silent, gazing after the ship until it had vanished into the mist.

And when all the people were dispersed she still stood alone upon the sea-wall, remembering in her heart his saying,

"A little while, a moment of rest upon the wind, and another woman shall bear me."

SAND AND FOAM
A BOOK OF APHORISMS

I am forever walking upon these shores,
Betwixt the sand and the foam.
The high tide will erase my foot-prints,
And the wind will blow away the foam.
But the sea and the shore will remain
Forever.

Once I filled my hand with mist.

Then I opened it and lo, the mist was a worm.

And I closed and opened my hand again, and behold there was a bird.

And again I closed and opened my hand, and in its hollow stood a man with a sad face, turned upward.

And again I closed my hand, and when I opened it there was naught but mist.

But I heard a song of exceeding sweetness.

It was but yesterday I thought myself a fragment quivering without rhythm in the sphere of life.

Now I know that I am the sphere, and all life in rhythmic fragments moves within me.

They say to me in their awakening, "You and the world you live in are but a grain of sand upon the infinite shore of an infinite sea."

And in my dream I say to them, "I am the infinite sea, and all worlds are but grains of sand upon my shore."

Only once have I been made mute. It was when a man asked me, "Who are you?"

The first thought of God was an angel.
The first word of God was a man.

We were fluttering, wandering, longing creatures a thousand thousand years before the sea and the wind in the forest gave us words.

Now how can we express the ancient of days in us with only the sounds of our yesterdays?

The Sphinx spoke only once, and the Sphinx said, "A grain of sand is a desert, and a desert is a grain of sand; and now let us all be silent again."

I heard the Sphinx, but I did not understand.

Once I saw the face of a woman, and I beheld all her children not yet born.

And a woman looked upon my face and she knew all my forefathers, dead before she was born.

Now would I fulfil myself. But how shall I unless I become a planet with intelligent lives dwelling upon it?

Is not this every man's goal?

A pearl is a temple built by pain around a grain of sand. What longing built our bodies and around what grains?

When God threw me, a pebble, into this wondrous lake I disturbed its surface with countless circles.

But when I reached the depths I became very still.

Give me silence and I will outdare the night.

I had a second birth when my soul and my body loved one another and were married.

Once I knew a man whose ears were exceedingly keen, but he was dumb. He had lost his tongue in a battle.

I know now what battles that man fought before the great silence came. I am glad he is dead.

The world is not large enough for two of us.

Long did I lie in the dust of Egypt, silent and unaware of the seasons.

Then the sun gave me birth, and I rose and walked upon the banks of the Nile,

Singing with the days and dreaming with the nights.

And now the sun treads upon me with a thousand feet that I may lie again in the dust of Egypt.

But behold a marvel and a riddle!

The very sun that gathered me cannot scatter me.

Still erect am I, and sure of foot do I walk upon the banks of the Nile.

Remembrance is a form of meeting.

Forgetfulness is a form of freedom.

We measure time according to the movement of countless suns; and they measure time by little machines in their little pockets.

Now tell me, how could we ever meet at the same place and the same time?

Space is not space between the earth and the sun to one who looks down from the windows of the Milky Way.

Humanity is a river of light running from ex-eternity to eternity.

Do not the spirits who dwell in the ether envy man his pain?

On my way to the Holy City I met another pilgrim and I asked him, "Is this indeed the way to the Holy City?"

And he said, "Follow me, and you will reach the Holy City in a day and a night."

And I followed him. And we walked many days and many nights, yet we did not reach the Holy City.

And what was to my surprise he became angry with me because he had misled me.

Make me, oh God, the prey of the lion, ere You make the rabbit my prey.

One may not reach the dawn save by the path of the night.

My house says to me, "Do not leave me, for here dwells your past."

And the road says to me, "Come and follow me, for I am your future."

And I say to both my house and the road, "I have no past, nor have I a future. If I stay here, there is a going in my staying; and if I go there is a staying in my going. Only love and death change all things."

How can I lose faith in the justice of life, when the dreams of those who sleep upon feathers are not more beautiful than the dreams of those who sleep upon the earth?

Strange, the desire for certain pleasures is a part of my pain.

Seven times have I despised my soul:

The first time when I saw her being meek that she might attain height.

The second time when I saw her limping before the crippled.

The third time when she was given to choose between the hard and the easy, and she chose the easy.

The fourth time when she committed a wrong, and comforted herself that others also commit wrong.

The fifth time when she forbore for weakness, and attributed her patience to strength.

The sixth time when she despised the ugliness of a face, and knew not that it was one of her own masks.

And the seventh time when she sang a song of praise, and deemed it a virtue.

I am ignorant of absolute truth. But I am humble before my ignorance and therein lies my honour and my reward.

There is a space between man's imagination and man's attainment that may only be traversed by his longing.

Paradise is there, behind that door, in the next room; but I have lost the key.

Perhaps I have only mislaid it.

You are blind and I am deaf and dumb, so let us touch hands and understand.

The significance of man is not in what he attains, but rather in what he longs to attain.

Some of us are like ink and some like paper.
And if it were not for the blackness of some of us, some of us would be dumb;
And if it were not for the whiteness of some of us, some of us would be blind.

Give me an ear and I will give you a voice.

Our mind is a sponge; our heart is a stream.
Is it not strange that most of us choose sucking rather than running?

When you long for blessings that you may not name, and when you grieve knowing not the cause, then indeed you are growing with all things that grow, and rising toward your greater self.

When one is drunk with a vision, he deems his faint expression of it the very wine.

You drink wine that you may be intoxicated; and I drink that it may sober me from that other wine.

When my cup is empty I resign myself to its emptiness; but when it is half full I resent its half-fulness.

The reality of the other person is not in what he reveals to you, but in what he cannot reveal to you.

Therefore, if you would understand him, listen not to what he says but rather to what he does not say.

Half of what I say is meaningless; but I say it so that the other half may reach you.

A sense of humour is a sense of proportion.

My loneliness was born when men praised my talkative faults and blamed my silent virtues.

When Life does not find a singer to sing her heart she produces a philosopher to speak her mind.

A truth is to be known always, to be uttered sometimes.

The real in us is silent; the acquired is talkative.

The voice of life in me cannot reach the ear of life in you; but let us talk that we may not feel lonely.

When two women talk they say nothing; when one woman speaks she reveals all of life.

Frogs may bellow louder than bulls, but they cannot drag the plough in the field nor turn the wheel of the winepress, and of their skins you cannot make shoes.

Only the dumb envy the talkative.

If winter should say, "Spring is in my heart," who would believe winter?

Every seed is a longing.

Should you really open your eyes and see, you would behold your image in all images.

And should you open your ears and listen, you would hear your own voice in all voices.

It takes two of us to discover truth: one to utter it and one to understand it.

Though the wave of words is forever upon us, yet our depth is forever silent.

Many a doctrine is like a window pane. We see truth through it but it divides us from truth.

Now let us play hide and seek. Should you hide in my heart it would not be difficult to find you. But should you hide behind your own shell, then it would be useless for anyone to seek you.

A woman may veil her face with a smile.

How noble is the sad heart who would sing a joyous song with joyous hearts.

He who would understand a woman, or dissect genius, or solve the mystery of silence is the very man who would wake from a beautiful dream to sit at a breakfast table.

I would walk with all those who walk. I would not stand still to watch the procession passing by.

You owe more than gold to him who serves you. Give him of your heart or serve him.

Nay, we have not lived in vain. Have they not built towers of our bones?

Let us not be particular and sectional. The poet's mind and the scorpion's tail rise in glory from the same earth.

Every dragon gives birth to a St George who slays it.

Trees are poems that the earth writes upon the sky. We fell them down and turn them into paper that we may record our emptiness.

Should you care to write (and only the saints know why you should) you must needs have knowledge and art and magic — the knowledge of the music of words, the art of being artless, and the magic of loving your readers.

They dip their pens in our hearts and think they are inspired.

Should a tree write its autobiography it would not be unlike the history of a race.

If I were to choose between the power of writing a poem and the ecstasy of a poem unwritten, I would choose the ecstasy. It is better poetry.

But you and all my neighbours agree that I always choose badly.

Poetry is not an opinion expressed. It is a song that rises from a bleeding wound or a smiling mouth.

Words are timeless. You should utter them or write them with a knowledge of their timelessness.

A poet is a dethroned king sitting among the ashes of his palace trying to fashion an image out of the ashes.

Poetry is a deal of joy and pain and wonder, with a dash of the dictionary.

In vain shall a poet seek the mother of the songs of his heart.

Once I said to a poet, "We shall not know your worth until you die."

And he answered saying, "Yes, death is always the revealer. And if indeed you would know my worth it is that I have more in my heart than upon my tongue, and more in my desire than in my hand."

If you sing of beauty though alone in the heart of the desert you will have an audience.

Poetry is wisdom that enchants the heart.

Wisdom is poetry that sings in the mind.

If we could enchant man's heart and at the same time sing in his mind,

Then in truth he would live in the shadow of God.

Inspiration will always sing; inspiration will never explain.

We often sing lullabies to our children that we ourselves may sleep.

All our words are but crumbs that fall down from the feast of the mind.

Thinking is always the stumbling stone to poetry.

A great singer is he who sings our silences.

How can you sing if your mouth be filled with food?

How shall your hand be raised in blessing if it is filled with gold?

They say the nightingale pierces his bosom with a thorn when he sings his love song.

So do we all. How else should we sing?

Genius is but a robin's song at the beginning of a slow spring.

Even the most winged spirit cannot escape physical necessity.

A madman is not less a musician than you or myself; only the instrument on which he plays is a little out of tune.

The song that lies silent in the heart of a mother sings upon the lips of her child.

No longing remains unfulfilled.

I have never agreed with my other self wholly. The truth of the matter seems to lie between us.

Your other self is always sorry for you. But your other self grows on sorrow; so all is well.

There is no struggle of soul and body save in the minds of those whose souls are asleep and whose bodies are out of tune.

When you reach the heart of life you shall find beauty in all things, even in the eyes that are blind to beauty.

We live only to discover beauty. All else is a form of waiting.

Sow a seed and the earth will yield you a flower. Dream your dream to the sky and it will bring you your beloved.

The devil died the very day you were born.
Now you do not have to go through hell to meet an angel.

Many a woman borrows a man's heart; very few could possess it.

If you would possess you must not claim.

When a man's hand touches the hand of a woman they both touch the heart of eternity.

Love is the veil between lover and lover.

Every man loves two women; the one is the creation of his imagination, and the other is not yet born.

Men who do not forgive women their little faults will never enjoy their great virtues.

Love that does not renew itself every day becomes a habit and in turn a slavery.

Lovers embrace that which is between them rather than each other.

Love and doubt have never been on speaking terms.

Love is a word of light, written by a hand of light, upon a page of light.

Friendship is always a sweet responsibility, never an opportunity.

If you do not understand your friend under all conditions you will never understand him.

Your most radiant garment is of the other person's weaving;
Your most savoury meal is that which you eat at the other person's table;
Your most comfortable bed is in the other person's house.
Now tell me, how can you separate yourself from the other person?

Your mind and my heart will never agree until your mind ceases to live in numbers and my heart in the mist.

We shall never understand one another until we reduce the language to seven words.

How shall my heart be unsealed unless it be broken?

Only great sorrow or great joy can reveal your truth.

If you would be revealed you must either dance naked in the sun, or carry your cross.

Should nature heed what we say of contentment no river would seek the sea, and no winter would turn to Spring. Should she heed all we say of thrift, how many of us would be breathing this air?

You see but your shadow when you turn your back to the sun.

You are free before the sun of the day, and free before the stars of the night;

And you are free when there is no sun and no moon and no star.

You are even free when you close your eyes upon all there is.

But you are a slave to him whom you love because you love him,

And a slave to him who loves you because he loves you.

We are all beggars at the gate of the temple, and each one of us receives his share of the bounty of the King when he enters the temple, and when he goes out.

But we are all jealous of one another, which is another way of belittling the King.

You cannot consume beyond your appetite. The other half of the loaf belongs to the other person, and there should remain a little bread for the chance guest.

If it were not for guests all houses would be graves.

Said a gracious wolf to a simple sheep, "Will you not honour our house with a visit?"

And the sheep answered: "We would have been honoured to visit your house if it were not in your stomach."

I stopped my guest on the threshold and said, "Nay, wipe not your feet as you enter, but as you go out."

Generosity is not in giving me that which I need more than you do, but it is in giving me that which you need more than I do.

You are indeed charitable when you give, and while giving, turn your face away so that you may not see the shyness of the receiver.

The difference between the richest man and the poorest is but a day of hunger and an hour of thirst.

We often borrow from our tomorrows to pay our debts to our yesterdays.

I too am visited by angels and devils, but I get rid of them. When it is an angel I pray an old prayer, and he is bored; When it is a devil I commit an old sin, and he passes me by.

After all this is not a bad prison; but I do not like this wall between my cell and the next prisoner's cell;

Yet I assure you that I do not wish to reproach the warder nor the Builder of the prison.

Those who give you a serpent when you ask for a fish, may have nothing but serpents to give. It is then generosity on their part.

Trickery succeeds sometimes, but it always commits suicide.

You are truly a forgiver when you forgive murderers who never spill blood, thieves who never steal, and liars who utter no falsehood.

He who can put his finger upon that which divides good from evil is he who can touch the very hem of the garment of God.

If your heart is a volcano how shall you expect flowers to bloom in your hands?

A strange form of self-indulgence! There are times when I would be wronged and cheated, that I may laugh at the expense of those who think I do not know I am being wronged and cheated.

What shall I say of him who is the pursuer playing the part of the pursued?

Let him who wipes his soiled hands with your garment take your garment. He may need it again; surely you would not.

It is a pity that money-changers cannot be good gardeners.

Please do not whitewash your inherent faults with your acquired virtues. I would have the faults; they are like mine own.

How often have I attributed to myself crimes I have never committed, so that the other person may feel comfortable in my presence.

Even the masks of life are masks of deeper mystery.

You may judge others only according to your knowledge of yourself.

Tell me now, who among us is guilty and who is unguilty?

The truly just is he who feels half guilty of your misdeeds.

Only an idiot and a genius break man-made laws; and they are the nearest to the heart of God.

It is only when you are pursued that you become swift.

I have no enemies, O God, but if I am to have an enemy
Let his strength be equal to mine,
That truth alone may be the victor.

You will be quite friendly with your enemy when you both die.

Perhaps a man may commit suicide in self-defence.

Long ago there lived a Man who was crucified for being too
loving and too lovable.

And strange to relate I met him thrice yesterday.

The first time He was asking a policeman not to take a prosti-
tute to prison; the second time He was drinking wine with an
outcast; and the third time He was having a fist-fight with a
promoter inside a church.

If all they say of good and evil were true, then my life is but
one long crime.

Pity is but half justice.

The only one who has been unjust to me is the one to whose brother I have been unjust.

When you see a man led to prison say in your heart, "Mayhap he is escaping from a narrower prison."

And when you see a man drunken say in your heart, "Mayhap he sought escape from something still more unbeautiful."

Oftentimes I have hated in self-defence; but if I were stronger I would not have used such a weapon.

How stupid is he who would patch the hatred in his eyes with the smile of his lips.

Only those beneath me can envy or hate me.
I have never been envied nor hated; I am above no one.
Only those above me can praise or belittle me.
I have never been praised nor belittled; I am below no one.

Your saying to me, "I do not understand you," is praise beyond my worth, and an insult you do not deserve.

How mean am I when life gives me gold and I give you silver, and yet I deem myself generous.

When you reach the heart of life you will find yourself not higher than the felon, and not lower than the prophet.

Strange that you should pity the slow-footed and not the slow-minded,
And the blind-eyed rather than the blind-hearted.

It is wiser for the lame not to break his crutches upon the head of his enemy.

How blind is he who gives you out of his pocket that he may take out of your heart.

Life is a procession. The slow of foot finds it too swift and he steps out;

And the swift of foot finds it too slow and he too steps out.

If there is such a thing as sin some of us commit it backward following our forefathers' footsteps;

And some of us commit it forward by overruling our children.

The truly good is he who is one with all those who are deemed bad.

We are all prisoners but some of us are in cells with windows and some without.

Strange that we all defend our wrongs with more vigour than we do our rights.

Should we all confess our sins to one another we would all laugh at one another for our lack of originality.

Should we all reveal our virtues we would also laugh for the same cause.

An individual is above man-made laws until he commits a crime against man-made conventions;
After that he is neither above anyone nor lower than anyone.

Government is an agreement between you and myself. You and myself are often wrong.

Crime is either another name of need or an aspect of a disease.

Is there a greater fault than being conscious of the other person's faults?

If the other person laughs at you, you can pity him; but if you laugh at him you may never forgive yourself.

If the other person injures you, you may forget the injury; but if you injure him you will always remember.

In truth the other person is your most sensitive self given another body.

How heedless you are when you would have men fly with your wings and you cannot even give them a feather.

Once a man sat at my board and ate my bread and drank my wine and went away laughing at me.

Then he came again for bread and wine, and I spurned him; And the angels laughed at me.

Hate is a dead thing. Who of you would be a tomb?

It is the honour of the murdered that he is not the murderer.

The tribune of humanity is in its silent heart never its talkative mind.

They deem me mad because I will not sell my days for gold;
And I deem them mad because they think my days have a price.

They spread before us their riches of gold and silver, of ivory and ebony, and we spread before them our hearts and our spirits;
And yet they deem themselves the hosts and us the guests.

I would be the least among men with dreams and the desire to fulfil them, rather than the greatest with no dreams and no desires.

The most pitiful among men is he who turns his dreams into silver and gold.

We are all climbing toward the summit of our hearts' desire. Should the other climber steal your sack and your purse and wax fat on the one and heavy on the other, you should pity him;

The climbing will be harder for his flesh, and the burden will make his way longer.

And should you in your leanness see his flesh puffing upward, help him a step; it will add to your swiftness.

You cannot judge any man beyond your knowledge of him, and how small is your knowledge.

I would not listen to a conqueror preaching to the conquered.

The truly free man is he who bears the load of the bond slave patiently.

A thousand years ago my neighbour said to me, "I hate life, for it is naught but a thing of pain."

And yesterday I passed by a cemetery and saw life dancing upon his grave.

Strife in nature is but disorder longing for order.

Solitude is a silent storm that breaks down all our dead branches;
Yet it sends our living roots deeper into the living heart of the living earth.

Once I spoke of the sea to a brook, and the brook thought me but an imaginative exaggerator;
And once I spoke of a brook to the sea, and the sea thought me but a depreciative defamer.

How narrow is the vision that exalts the busyness of the ant above the singing of the grasshopper.

The highest virtue here may be the least in another world.

The deep and the high go to the depth or to the height in a straight line; only the spacious can move in circles.

If it were not for our conception of weights and measures we would stand in awe of the firefly as we do before the sun.

A scientist without imagination is a butcher with dull knives and out-worn scales.

But what would you, since we are not all vegetarians?

When you sing the hungry hears you with his stomach.

Death is not nearer to the aged than to the new-born; neither is life.

If indeed you must be candid, be candid beautifully; otherwise keep silent, for there is a man in our neighbourhood who is dying.

Mayhap a funeral among men is a wedding feast among the angels.

A forgotten reality may die and leave in its will seven thousand actualities and facts to be spent in its funeral and the building of a tomb.

In truth we talk only to ourselves, but sometimes we talk loud enough that others may hear us.

The obvious is that which is never seen until someone expresses it simply.

If the Milky Way were not within me how should I have seen it or known it?

Unless I am a physician among physicians they would not believe that I am an astronomer.

Perhaps the sea's definition of a shell is the pearl.
Perhaps time's definition of coal is the diamond.

Fame is the shadow of passion standing in the light.

A root is a flower that disdains fame.

There is neither religion nor science beyond beauty.

Every great man I have known had something small in his make-up; and it was that small something which prevented inactivity or madness or suicide.

The truly great man is he who would master no one, and who would be mastered by none.

I would not believe that man is mediocre simply because he kills the criminals and the prophets.

Tolerance is love sick with the sickness of haughtiness.

Worms will turn; but is it not strange that even elephants will yield?

A disagreement may be the shortest cut between two minds.

I am the flame and I am the dry brush, and one part of me consumes the other part.

We are all seeking the summit of the holy mountain; but shall not our road be shorter if we consider the past a chart and not a guide?

Wisdom ceases to be wisdom when it becomes too proud to weep, too grave to laugh, and too self-ful to seek other than itself.

Had I filled myself with all that you know what room should I have for all that you do not know?

I have learned silence from the talkative, toleration from the intolerant, and kindness from the unkind; yet strange, I am ungrateful to these teachers.

A bigot is a stone-deaf orator.

The silence of the envious is too noisy.

When you reach the end of what you should know, you will be at the beginning of what you should sense.

An exaggeration is a truth that has lost its temper.

If you can see only what light reveals and hear only what sound announces,

Then in truth you do not see nor do you hear.

A fact is a truth unsexed.

You cannot laugh and be unkind at the same time.

The nearest to my heart are a king without a kingdom and a poor man who does not know how to beg.

A shy failure is nobler than an immodest success.

Dig anywhere in the earth and you will find a treasure, only you must dig with the faith of a peasant.

Said a hunted fox followed by twenty horsemen and a pack of twenty hounds, "Of course they will kill me. But how poor and how stupid they must be. Surely it would not be worth while for twenty foxes riding on twenty asses and accompanied by twenty wolves to chase and kill one man."

It is the mind in us that yields to the laws made by us, but never the spirit in us.

A traveller am I and a navigator, and every day I discover a new region within my soul.

A woman protested saying, "Of course it was a righteous war. My son fell in it."

I said to Life, "I would hear Death speak."
And Life raised her voice a little higher and said, "You hear him now."

When you have solved all the mysteries of life you long for death, for it is but another mystery of life.

Birth and death are the two noblest expressions of bravery.

My friend, you and I shall remain strangers unto life,
And unto one another, and each unto himself,
Until the day when you shall speak and and I shall listen
Deeming your voice my own voice;
And when I shall stand before you
Thinking myself standing before a mirror.

They say to me, "Should you know yourself you would know all men."
And I say, "Only when I seek all men shall I know myself."

Man is two men; one is awake in darkness, the other is asleep in light.

A hermit is one who renounces the world of fragments that he may enjoy the world wholly and without interruption.

There lies a green field between the scholar and the poet; should the scholar cross it he becomes a wise man; should the poet cross it, he becomes a prophet.

Yestereve I saw philosophers in the market-place carrying their heads in baskets, and crying aloud, "Wisdom! Wisdom for sale!"

Poor philosophers! They must needs sell their heads to feed their hearts.

Said a philosopher to a street sweeper, "I pity you. Yours is a hard and dirty task."

And the street sweeper said, "Thank you, sir. But tell me what is your task?"

And the philosopher answered saying, "I study man's mind, his deeds and his desires."

Then the street sweeper went on with his sweeping and said with a smile, "I pity you too."

He who listens to truth is not less than he who utters truth.

No man can draw the line between necessities and luxuries. Only the angels can do that, and the angels are wise and wistful. Perhaps the angels are our better thoughts in space.

He is the true prince who finds his throne in the heart of the dervish.

Generosity is giving more than you can, and pride is taking less than you need.

In truth you owe naught to any man. You owe all to all men.

All those who have lived in the past live with us now. Surely none of us would be an ungracious host.

He who longs the most lives the longest.

They say to me, "A bird in the hand is worth ten in the bush."
But I say, "A bird and a feather in the bush is worth more
than ten birds in the hand."

Your seeking after *that feather* is life with winged feet; nay, it
is life itself.

There are only two elements here, beauty and truth; beauty
in the hearts of lovers, and truth in the arms of the tillers of
the soil.

Great beauty captures me, but a beauty still greater frees me
even from itself.

Beauty shines brighter in the heart of him who longs for it
than in the eyes of him who sees it.

I admire the man who reveals his mind to me; I honour him
who unveils his dreams. But why am I shy, and even a little
ashamed before him who serves me?

The gifted were once proud in serving princes.
Now they claim honour in serving paupers.

The angels know that too many practical men eat their bread
with the sweat of the dreamer's brow.

Wit is often a mask. If you could tear it you would find either
a genius irritated or cleverness juggling.

The understanding attributes to me understanding and the
dull, dullness. I think they are both right.

Only those with secrets in their hearts could divine the secrets
in our hearts.

He who would share your pleasure but not your pain shall lose the key to one of the seven gates of Paradise.

Yes, there is a Nirvana; it is in leading your sheep to a green pasture, and in putting your child to sleep, and in writing the last line of your poem.

We choose our joys and our sorrows long before we experience them.

Sadness is but a wall between two gardens.

When either your joy or your sorrow becomes great the world becomes small.

Desire is half of life; indifference is half of death.

The bitterest thing in our today's sorrow is the memory of our yesterday's joy.

They say to me, "You must needs choose between the pleasures of this world and the peace of the next world."

And I say to them, "I have chosen both the delights of this world and the peace of the next. For I know in my heart that the Supreme Poet wrote but one poem, and it scans perfectly, and it also rhymes perfectly."

Faith is an oasis in the heart which will never be reached by the caravan of thinking.

When you reach your height you shall desire but only for desire; and you shall hunger, for hunger; and you shall thirst for greater thirst.

If you reveal your secrets to the wind you should not blame the wind for revealing them to the trees.

The flowers of spring are winter's dreams related at the breakfast table of the angels.

Said a skunk to a tube-rose, "See how swiftly I run, while you cannot walk nor even creep."

Said the tube-rose to the skunk, "Oh, most noble swift runner, please run swiftly!"

Turtles can tell more about the roads than hares.

Strange that creatures without backbones have the hardest shells.

The most talkative is the least intelligent, and there is hardly a difference between an orator and an auctioneer.

Be grateful that you do not have to live down the renown of a father nor the wealth of an uncle.

But above all be grateful that no one will have to live down either your renown or your wealth.

Only when a juggler misses catching his ball does he appeal to me.

The envious praises me unknowingly.

Long were you a dream in your mother's sleep, and then she woke to give you birth.

The germ of the race is in your mother's longing.

My father and mother desired a child and they begot me.
And I wanted a mother and a father and I begot night and the sea.

Some of our children are our justifications and some are but our regrets.

When night comes and you too are dark, lie down and be dark with a will.

And when morning comes and you are still dark stand up and say to the day with a will, "I am still dark."

It is stupid to play a rôle with the night and the day.

They would both laugh at you.

The mountain veiled in mist is not a hill; an oak tree in the rain is not a weeping willow.

Behold here is a paradox: the deep and high are nearer to one another than the mid-level to either.

When I stood a clear mirror before you, you gazed into me and saw your image.

Then you said, "I love you."

But in truth you loved yourself in me.

When you enjoy loving your neighbour it ceases to be a virtue.

Love which is not always springing is always dying.

You cannot have youth and the knowledge of it at the same time;

For youth is too busy living to know, and knowledge is too busy seeking itself to live.

You may sit at your window watching the passersby. And watching you may see a nun walking toward your right hand, and a prostitute toward your left hand.

And you may say in your innocence, "How noble is the one and how ignoble is the other."

But should you close your eyes and listen awhile you would hear a voice whispering in the ether, "One seeks me in prayer, and the other in pain. And in the spirit of each there is a bower for my spirit."

Once every hundred years Jesus of Nazareth meets Jesus of the Christian in a garden among the hills of Lebanon. And they talk long; and each time Jesus of Nazareth goes away saying to Jesus of the Christian, "My friend, I fear we shall never, never agree."

May God feed the over-abundant!

A great man has two hearts; one bleeds and the other forbears.

Should one tell a lie which does not hurt you nor anyone else, why not say in your heart that the house of his facts is too small for his fancies, and he had to leave it for larger space?

Behind every closed door is a mystery sealed with seven seals.

Waiting is the hoofs of time.

What if trouble should be a new window in the Eastern wall of your house?

You may forget the one with whom you have laughed, but never the one with whom you have wept.

There must be something strangely sacred in salt. It is in our tears and in the sea.

Our God in His gracious thirst will drink us all, the dewdrop and the tear.

You are but a fragment of your giant self, a mouth that seeks bread, and a blind hand that holds the cup for a thirsty mouth.

If you would rise but a cubit above race and country and self you would indeed become godlike.

If I were you I would not find fault with the sea at low tide.
It is a good ship and our Captain is able; it is only your stomach that is in disorder.

What we long for and cannot attain is dearer than what we have already attained.

Should you sit upon a cloud you would not see the boundary line between one country and another, nor the boundary stone between a farm and a farm.

It is a pity you cannot sit upon a cloud.

Seven centuries ago seven white doves rose from a deep valley flying to the snow-white summit of the mountain. One of the seven men who watched the flight said, "I see a black spot on the wing of the seventh dove."

Today the people in that valley tell of seven black doves that flew to the summit of the snowy mountain.

In the autumn I gathered all my sorrows and buried them in my garden.

And when April returned and spring came to wed the earth, there grew in my garden beautiful flowers unlike all other flowers.

And my neighbours came to behold them, and they all said to me, "When autumn comes again, at seeding time, will you not give us of the seeds of these flowers that we may have them in our gardens?"

It is indeed misery if I stretch an empty hand to men and receive nothing; but it is hopelessness if I stretch a full hand and find none to receive.

I long for eternity because there I shall meet my unwritten poems and my unpainted pictures.

Art is a step from nature toward the Infinite.

A work of art is a mist carved into an image.

Even the hands that make crowns of thorns are better than idle hands.

Our most sacred tears never seek our eyes.

Every man is the descendant of every king and every slave that ever lived.

If the great-grandfather of Jesus had known what was hidden within him, would he not have stood in awe of himself?

Was the love of Judas' mother for her son less than the love of Mary for Jesus?

There are three miracles of our Brother Jesus not yet recorded in the Book: the first that He was a man like you and me; the second that He had a sense of humour; and the third that He knew He was a conqueror though conquered.

Crucified One, you are crucified upon my heart; and the nails that pierce your hands pierce the walls of my heart.

And tomorrow when a stranger passes by this Golgotha he will not know that two bled here.

He will deem it the blood of one man.

You may have heard of the Blessed Mountain.

It is the highest mountain in our world.

Should you reach the summit you would have only one desire, and that to descend and be with those who dwell in the deepest valley.

That is why it is called the Blessed Mountain.

Every thought I have imprisoned in expression I must free by my deeds.

JESUS THE SON OF MAN

HIS WORDS AND HIS DEEDS AS TOLD AND
RECORDED BY THOSE WHO KNEW HIM

CONTENTS

UPON A DAY in the spring of the year Jesus stood in the market-place of Jerusalem and He spoke to the multitudes of the kingdom of heaven.

And He accused the scribes and the Pharisees of setting snares and digging pitfalls in the path of those who long after the kingdom; and He denounced them.

Now amongst the crowd was a company of men who defended the Pharisees and the scribes, and they sought to lay hands upon Jesus and upon us also.

But He avoided them and turned aside from them, and walked towards the north gate of the city.

And He said to us, "My hour has not yet come. Many are the things I have still to say unto you, and many are the deeds I shall yet perform ere I deliver myself up to the world."

Then He said, and there was joy and laughter in His voice, "Let us go into the North Country and meet the spring. Come with me to the hills, for winter is past and the snows of Lebanon are descending to the valleys to sing with the brooks.

"The fields and the vineyards have banished sleep and are awake to greet the sun with their green figs and tender grapes."

And He walked before us and we followed Him, that day and the next.

And upon the afternoon of the third day we reached the summit of Mount Hermon, and there He stood looking down upon the cities of the plains.

And His face shone like molten gold, and He outstretched His arms and He said to us, "Behold the earth in her green raiment, and see how the streams have hemmed the edges of her garments with silver.

"In truth the earth is fair and all that is upon her is fair.

"But there is a kingdom beyond all that you behold, and

therein I shall rule. And if it is your choice, and if it is indeed your desire, you too shall come and rule with me.

"My face and your faces shall not be masked; our hand shall hold neither sword nor sceptre, and our subjects shall love us in peace and shall not be in fear of us."

Thus spoke Jesus, and unto all the kingdoms of the earth I was blinded, and unto all the cities of walls and towers; and it was in my heart to follow the Master to His kingdom.

Then just at that moment Judas of Iscariot stepped forth. And he walked close up to Jesus, and spoke and said, "Behold, the kingdoms of the world are vast, and behold the cities of David and Solomon shall prevail against the Romans. If you will be the king of the Jews we shall stand beside you with sword and shield and we shall overcome the alien."

But when Jesus heard this He turned upon Judas, and His face was filled with wrath. And He spoke in a voice terrible as the thunder of the sky and He said, "Get you behind me, Satan. Think you that I came down the years to rule an ant-hill for a day?

"My throne is a throne beyond your vision. Shall he whose wings encircle the earth seek shelter in a nest abandoned and forgotten?

"Shall the living be honoured and exalted by the wearer of shrouds?

"My kingdom is not of this earth, and my seat is not builded upon the skulls of your ancestors.

"If you seek aught save the kingdom of the spirit then it were better for you to leave me here, and go down to the caves of your dead, where the crownèd heads of yore hold court in their tombs and may still be bestowing honours upon the bones of your forefathers.

"Dare you tempt me with a crown of dross, when my fore-head seeks the Pleiades, or else your thorns?

"Were it not for a dream dreamed by a forgotten race I would not suffer your sun to rise upon my patience, nor your moon to throw my shadow across your path.

"Were it not for a mother's desire I would have stripped me of the swaddling-clothes and escaped back to space.

"And were it not for sorrow in all of you I would not have stayed to weep.

"Who are you and what are you, Judas Iscariot? And why do you tempt me?

"Have you in truth weighed me in the scale and found me one to lead legions of pygmies, and to direct chariots of the shapeless against an enemy that encamps only in your hatred and marches nowhere but in your fear?

"Too many are the worms that crawl about my feet, and I will give them no battle. I am weary of the jest, and weary of pitying the creepers who deem me coward because I will not move among their guarded walls and towers.

"Pity it is that I must needs pity to the very end. Would that I could turn my steps towards a larger world where larger men dwell. But how shall I?

"Your priest and your emperor would have my blood. They shall be satisfied ere I go hence. I would not change the course of the law. And I would not govern folly.

"Let ignorance reproduce itself until it is weary of its own offspring.

"Let the blind lead the blind to the pitfall.

"And let the dead bury the dead till the earth be choked with its own bitter fruit.

"My kingdom is not of the earth. My kingdom shall be where two or three of you shall meet in love, and in wonder at the loveliness of life, and in good cheer, and in remembrance of me."

Then of a sudden He turned to Judas, and He said, "Get you behind me, man. Your kingdoms shall never be in my kingdom."

*

And now it was twilight, and He turned to us and said, "Let us go down. The night is upon us. Let us walk in light while the light is with us."

Then He went down from the hills and we followed Him. And Judas followed afar off.

And when we reached the lowland it was night.

And Thomas, the son of Diophanes, said unto Him, "Master,

it is dark now, and we can no longer see the way. If it is in your will, lead us to the lights of yonder village where we may find meat and shelter."

And Jesus answered Thomas, and He said, "I have led you to the heights when you were hungry, and I have brought you down to the plains with a greater hunger. But I cannot stay with you this night. I would be alone."

Then Simon Peter stepped forth, and said: "Master, suffer us not to go alone in the dark. Grant that we may stay with you even here on this byway. The night and the shadows of the night will not linger, and the morning shall soon find us if you will but stay with us."

And Jesus answered, "This night the foxes shall have their holes, and the birds of the air their nests, but the Son of Man has not where on earth to lay His head. And indeed I would now be alone. Should you desire me you will find me again by the lake where I found you."

Then we walked away from Him with heavy hearts, for it was not in our will to leave Him.

Many times did we stop and turn our faces towards Him, and we saw Him in lonely majesty, moving westward.

The only man among us who did not turn to behold Him in His aloneness was Judas Iscariot.

And from that day Judas became sullen and distant. And methought there was danger in the sockets of his eyes.

ANNA THE MOTHER OF MARY

JESUS THE SON of my daughter, was born here in Nazareth in the month of January. And the night that Jesus was born we were visited by men from the East. They were Persians who came to Esdraelon with the caravans of the Midianites on their way to Egypt. And because they did not find rooms at the inn they sought shelter in our house.

And I welcomed them and I said, "My daughter has given birth to a son this night. Surely you will forgive me if I do not serve you as it behooves a hostess."

Then they thanked me for giving them shelter. And after they had supped they said to me: "We would see the new-born."

Now the Son of Mary was beautiful to behold, and she too was comely.

And when the Persians beheld Mary and her babe, they took gold and silver from their bags, and myrrh and frankincense, and laid them all at the feet of the child.

Then they fell down and prayed in a strange tongue which we did not understand.

And when I led them to the bedchamber prepared for them they walked as if they were in awe at what they had seen.

When morning was come they left us and followed the road to Egypt.

But at parting they spoke to me and said: "The child is but a day old, yet we have seen the light of our God in His eyes and the smile of our God upon His mouth.

"We bid you protect Him that He may protect you all."

And so saying, they mounted their camels and we saw them no more.

Now Mary seemed not so much joyous in her first-born, as full of wonder and surprise.

She would look long upon her babe, and then turn her face

to the window and gaze far away into the sky as if she saw visions.

And there were valleys between her heart and mine.

And the child grew in body and spirit, and He was different from other children. He was aloof and hard to govern, and I could not lay my hand upon Him.

But He was beloved by everyone in Nazareth, and in my heart I knew why.

Oftentimes He would take away our food to give to the passerby. And He would give other children the sweetmeat I had given Him, before He had tasted it with His own mouth.

He would climb the trees of my orchard to get the fruits, but never to eat them Himself.

And He would race with other boys, and sometimes, because He was swifter of foot, He would delay so that they might pass the stake ere He should reach it.

And sometimes when I led Him to His bed He would say, "Tell my mother and the others that only my body will sleep. My mind will be with them till their mind come to my morning."

And many other wondrous words He said when He was a boy, but I am too old to remember.

Now they tell me I shall see Him no more. But how shall I believe what they say?

I still hear His laughter, and the sound of His running about my house. And whenever I kiss the cheek of my daughter His fragrance returns to my heart, and His body seems to fill my arms.

But is it not passing strange that my daughter does not speak of her first-born to me?

Sometimes it seems that my longing for Him is greater than hers. She stands as firm before the day as if she were a bronzen image, while my heart melts and runs into streams.

Perhaps she knows what I do not know. Would that she might tell me also.

ASSAPH CALLED THE ORATOR OF TYRE

WHAT SHALL I say of His speech? Perhaps something about His person lent power to His words and swayed those who heard Him. For He was comely, and the sheen of the day was upon His countenance.

Men and women gazed at Him more than they listened to His argument. But at times He spoke with the power of a spirit, and that spirit had authority over those who heard Him.

In my youth I had heard the orators of Rome and Athens and Alexandria. The young Nazarene was unlike them all.

They assembled their words with an art to enthral the ear, but when you heard Him your heart would leave you and go wandering into regions nor yet visited.

He would tell a story or relate a parable, and the like of His stories and parables had never been heard in Syria. He seemed to spin them out of the seasons, even as time spins the years and the generations.

He would begin a story thus: "The ploughman went forth to the field to sow his seeds."

Or, "Once there was a rich man who had many vineyards."

Or, "A shepherd counted his sheep at eventide and found that one sheep was missing."

And such words would carry His listeners into their simpler selves, and into the ancient of their days.

At heart we are all ploughmen, and we all love the vineyard. And in the pastures of our memory there is a shepherd and a flock and the lost sheep;

And there is the plough-share and the winepress and the threshing-floor.

He knew the source of our older self, and the persistent thread of which we are woven.

The Greek and the Roman orators spoke to their listeners of

life as it seemed to the mind. The Nazarene spoke of a longing that lodged in the heart.

They saw life with eyes only a little clearer than yours and mine. He saw life in the light of God.

I often think that He spoke to the crowd as a mountain would speak to the plain.

And in His speech there was a power that was not commanded by the orators of Athens or of Rome.

MARY MAGDALEN

IT WAS IN the month of June when I saw Him for the first time. He was walking in the wheatfield when I passed by with my handmaidens, and He was alone.

The rhythm of His step was different from other men's, and the movement of His body was like naught I had seen before.

Men do not pace the earth in that manner. And even now I do not know whether He walked fast or slow.

My handmaidens pointed their fingers at Him and spoke in shy whispers to one another. And I stayed my steps for a moment, and raised my hand to hail Him. But He did not turn His face, and He did not look at me. And I hated Him. I was swept back into myself and I was as cold as if I had been in a snow-drift. And I shivered.

That night I beheld Him in my dreaming; and they told me afterwards that I screamed in my sleep and was restless upon my bed.

It was in the month of August that I saw Him again, through my window. He was sitting in the shadow of the cypress tree across my garden, and He was as still as if He had been carved out of stone, like the statues in Antioch and other cities of the North Country.

And my slave, the Egyptian, came to me and said, "That man is here again. He is sitting there across your garden."

And I gazed at Him, and my soul quivered within me, for He was beautiful.

His body was single and each part seemed to love every other part.

Then I clothed myself with raiment of Damascus, and I left my house and walked towards Him.

Was it my aloneness, or was it His fragrance, that drew me to Him? Was it a hunger in my eyes that desired comeliness, or was it His beauty that sought the light of my eyes?

247

Even now I do not know.

I walked to Him with my scented garments and my golden sandals, the sandals the Roman captain had given me, even these sandals. And when I reached Him, I said, "Good-morrow to you."

And He said, "Good-morrow to you, Miriam."

And He looked at me, and His night-eyes saw me as no man had seen me. And suddenly I was as if naked, and I was shy.

Yet He had only said, "Good-morrow to you."

And then I said to Him, "Will you not come to my house?"

And He said, "Am I not already in your house?"

I did not know what He meant then, but I know now.

And I said, "Will you not have wine and bread with me?"

And He said, "Yes, Miriam, but not now."

Not now, not now, He said. And the voice of the sea was in those two words, and the voice of the wind and the trees. And when He said them unto me, life spoke to death.

For mind you, my friend, I was dead. I was a woman who had divorced her soul. I was living apart from this self which you now see. I belonged to all men, and to none. They called me harlot, and a woman possessed of seven devils. I was cursed, and I was envied.

But when His dawn-eyes looked into my eyes all the stars of my night faded away, and I became Miriam, only Miriam, a woman lost to the earth she had known, and finding herself in new places.

And now again I said to Him, "Come into my house and share bread and wine with me."

And He said, "Why do you bid me to be your guest?"

And I said, "I beg you to come into my house." And it was all that was sod in me, and all that was sky in me calling unto Him.

Then He looked at me, and the noontide of His eyes was upon me, and He said, "You have many lovers, and yet I alone love you. Other men love themselves in your nearness. I love you in your self. Other men see a beauty in you that shall fade away sooner than their own years. But I see in you a beauty that shall not fade away, and in the autumn of your days that beauty shall not be afraid to gaze at itself in the mirror, and it shall not be offended.

"I alone love the unseen in you."

Then He said in a low voice, "Go away now. If this cypress tree is yours and you would not have me sit in its shadow, I will walk my way."

And I cried to Him and I said, "Master, come to my house. I have incense to burn for you, and a silver basin for your feet. You are a stranger and yet not a stranger. I entreat you, come to my house."

Then He stood up and looked at me even as the seasons might look down upon the field, and He smiled. And He said again: "All men love you for themselves. I love you for yourself."

And then He walked away.

But no other man ever walked the way He walked. Was it a breath born in my garden that moved to the east? Or was it a storm that would shake all things to their foundations?

I knew not, but on that day the sunset of His eyes slew the dragon in me, and I became a woman, I became Miriam, Miriam of Mijdel.

PHILEMON, A GREEK APOTHECARY

THE NAZARENE WAS the Master Physician of His people. No other man knew so much of our bodies and of their elements and properties.

He made whole those who were afflicted with diseases unknown to the Greeks and the Egyptians. They say He even called back the dead to life. And whether this be true or not true, it declares His power; for only to him who has wrought great things is the greatest ever attributed.

They say also that Jesus visited India and the Country between the Two Rivers, and that there the priests revealed to Him the knowledge of all that is hidden in the recesses of our flesh.

Yet that knowledge may have been given Him direct by the gods, and not through the priests. For that which has remained unknown to all men for an æon may be disclosed to one man in but a moment. And Apollo may lay his hand on the heart of the obscure and make it wise.

Many doors were open to the Tyrians and the Thebans, and to this man also certain sealed doors were opened. He entered the temple of the soul, which is the body; and He beheld the evil spirits that conspire against our sinews, and also the good spirits that spin the threads thereof.

Methinks it was by the power of opposition and resistance that He healed the sick, but in a manner unknown to our philosophers. He astonished fever with His snowlike touch and it retreated; and He surprised the hardened limbs with His own calm and they yielded to Him and were at peace.

He knew the ebbing sap within the furrowed bark – but how He reached the sap with His fingers I do not know. He knew the sound steel underneath the rust – but how He freed the sword and made it shine no man can tell.

Sometimes it seems to me that He heard the murmuring pain

of all things that grow in the sun, and that then He lifted them up and supported them, not only by His own knowledge, but also by disclosing to them their own power to rise and become whole.

Yet He was not much concerned with Himself as a physician. He was rather preoccupied with the religion and the politics of this land. And this I regret, for first of all things we must needs be sound of body.

But these Syrians, when they are visited by an illness, seek an argument rather than medicine.

And pity it is that the greatest of all their physicians chose rather to be but a maker of speeches in the market-place.

SIMON WHO WAS CALLED PETER

I WAS ON the shore of the Lake of Galilee when I first beheld Jesus my Lord and my Master.

My brother Andrew was with me and we were casting our net into the waters.

The waves were rough and high and we caught but few fish. And our hearts were heavy.

Suddenly Jesus stood near us, as if He had taken form that very moment, for we had not seen Him approaching.

He called us by our names, and He said, "If you will follow me I will lead you to an inlet where the fishes are swarming."

And as I looked at His face the net fell from my hands, for a flame kindled within me and I recognized Him.

And my brother Andrew spoke and said, "We know all the inlets upon these shores, and we know also that on a windy day like this the fish seek a depth beyond our nets."

And Jesus answered, "Follow me to the shores of a greater sea. I shall make you fishers of men. And your net shall never be empty."

And we abandoned our boat and our net and followed Him.

I myself was drawn by a power, viewless, that walked beside His person.

I walked near Him, breathless and full of wonder, and my brother Andrew was behind us, bewildered and amazed.

And as we walked on the sand I made bold and said unto Him, "Sir, I and my brother will follow your footsteps, and where you go we too will go. But if it please you to come to our house this night, we shall be graced by your visit. Our house is not large and our ceiling not high, and you will sit at but a frugal meal. Yet if you will abide in our hovel it will be to us a palace. And would you break bread with us, we in your presence were to be envied by the princes of the land."

And He said, "Yea, I will be your guest this night."

And I rejoiced in my heart. And we walked behind Him in silence until we reached our house.

And as we stood at the threshold Jesus said, "Peace be to this house, and to those who dwell in it."

Then He entered and we followed Him.

My wife and my wife's mother and my daughter stood before Him and they worshipped Him; then they knelt before Him and kissed the hem of His sleeve.

They were astonished that He, the chosen and the well beloved, had come to be our guest; for they had already seen Him by the River Jordan when John the Baptist had proclaimed Him before the people.

And straightway my wife and my wife's mother began to prepare the supper.

My brother Andrew was a shy man, but his faith in Jesus was deeper than my faith.

And my daughter, who was then but twelve years old, stood by Him and held His garment as if she were in fear He would leave us and go out again into the night. She clung to Him like a lost sheep that has found its shepherd.

Then we sat at the board, and He broke the bread and poured the wine; and He turned to us saying, "My friends, grace me now in sharing this food with me, even as the Father has graced us in giving it unto us."

These words He said ere He touched a morsel, for He wished to follow an ancient custom that the honoured guest becomes the host.

And as we sat with Him around the board we felt as if we were sitting at the feast of the great King.

My daughter Petronelah, who was young and unknowing, gazed at His face and followed the movements of His hands. And I saw a veil of tears in her eyes.

When He left the board we followed Him and sat about Him in the vine-arbour.

And He spoke to us and we listened, and our hearts fluttered within us like birds.

He spoke of the second birth of man, and of the opening of the gates of the heavens; and of angels descending and bringing peace and good cheer to all men, and of angels ascending to the throne bearing the longings of men to the Lord God.

Then He looked into my eyes and gazed into the depths of my heart. And He said, "I have chosen you and your brother, and you must needs come with me. You have laboured and you have been heavy-laden. Now I shall give you rest. Take up my yoke and learn of me, for in my heart is peace, and your soul shall find abundance and a home-coming."

When He spoke thus I and my brother stood up before Him, and I said to Him, "Master, we will follow you to the ends of the earth. And if our burden were as heavy as the mountain we would bear it with you in gladness. And should we fall by the wayside we shall know that we have fallen on the way to heaven, and we shall be satisfied."

And my brother Andrew spoke and said, "Master, we would be threads between your hands and your loom. Weave us into the cloth if you will, for we would be in the raiment of the Most High."

And my wife raised her face, and the tears were upon her cheeks and she spoke with joy, and she said, "Blessed are you who come in the name of the Lord. Blessed is the womb that carried you, and the breast that gave you milk."

And my daughter, who was but twelve years old, sat at His feet and she nestled close to Him.

And the mother of my wife, who sat at the threshold, said not a word. She only wept in silence and her shawl was wet with her tears.

Then Jesus walked over to her and He raised her face to His face and He said to her, "You are the mother of all these. You weep for joy, and I will keep your tears in my memory."

And now the old moon rose above the horizon. And Jesus gazed upon it for a moment, and then He turned to us and said, "It is late. Seek your beds, and may God visit your repose. I will be here in this arbour until dawn. I have cast my net this day and I have caught two men; I am satisfied, and now I bid you good-night."

Then my wife's mother said, "But we have laid your bed in the house, I pray you enter and rest."

And He answered her saying, "I would indeed rest, but not under a roof. Suffer me to lie this night under the canopy of the grapes and the stars."

And she made haste and brought out the mattress and the pillows and the coverings. And He smiled on her and He said, "Behold, I shall lie down upon a bed twice made."

Then we left Him and entered into the house, and my daughter was the last one to enter. And her eyes were upon Him until I had closed the door.

Thus for the first time I knew my Lord and Master.

And though it was many years ago, it still seems but of today.

CAIAPHAS THE HIGH PRIEST

IN SPEAKING OF that man Jesus and of His death let us consider two salient facts: the Torah must needs be held in safety by us, and this kingdom must needs be protected by Rome.

Now that man was defiant to us and to Rome. He poisoned the mind of the simple people, and He led them as if by magic against us and against Cæsar.

My own slaves, both men and women, after hearing Him speak in the market-place, turned sullen and rebellious. Some of them left my house and escaped to the desert whence they came.

Forget not that the Torah is our foundation and our tower of strength. No man shall undermine us while we have this power to restrain his hand, and no man shall overthrow Jerusalem so long as its walls stand upon the ancient stone that David laid.

If the seed of Abraham is indeed to live and thrive this soil must remain undefiled.

And that man Jesus was a defiler and a corrupter. We slew Him with a conscience both deliberate and clean. And we shall slay all those who would debase the laws of Moses or seek to befoul our sacred heritage.

We and Pontius Pilatus knew the danger in that man, and that it was wise to bring Him to an end.

I shall see that His followers come to the same end, and the echo of His word to the same silence.

If Judea is to live all men who oppose her must be brought down to the dust. And ere Judea shall die I will cover my grey head with ashes even as did Samuel the prophet, and I will tear off this garment of Aaron and clothe me in sackcloth until I go hence for ever.

JESUS WAS NEVER married but He was a friend of women, and He knew them as they would be known in sweet comradeship.

And He loved children as they would be loved in faith and understanding.

In the light of His eyes there was a father and a brother and a son.

He would hold a child upon His knees and say, "Of such is your might and your freedom; and of such is the kingdom of the spirit."

They say that Jesus heeded not the law of Moses, and that He was over-forgiving to the prostitutes of Jerusalem and the countryside.

I myself at that time was deemed a prostitute, for I loved a man who was not my husband, and he was a Sadducee.

And on a day the Sadducees came upon me in my house when my lover was with me, and they seized me and held me, and my lover walked away and left me.

Then they led me to the market-place where Jesus was teaching.

It was their desire to hold me up before Him as a test and a trap for Him.

But Jesus judged me not. He laid shame upon those who would have had me shamed, and He reproached them.

And He bade me go my way.

And after that all the tasteless fruit of life turned sweet to my mouth, and the scentless blossoms breathed fragrance into my nostrils. I became a woman without a tainted memory, and I was free, and my head was no longer bowed down.

THIS HAPPENED BEFORE He was known to the people.

I was in my mother's garden tending the rose-bushes, when He stopped at our gate.

And He said, "I am thirsty. Will you give me water from your well?"

And I ran and brought the silver cup, and filled it with water; and I poured into it a few drops from the jasmine vial.

And He drank deep and was pleased.

Then He looked into my eyes and said, "My blessing shall be upon you."

When He said that I felt as it were a gust of wind rushing through my body. And I was no longer shy; and I said, "Sir, I am betrothed to a man of Cana in Galilee. And I shall be married on the fourth day of the coming week. Will you not come to my wedding and grace my marriage with your presence?"

And He answered, "I will come, my child."

Mind you, He said, "My child," yet He was but a youth, and I was nearly twenty.

Then He walked on down the road.

And I stood at the gate of our garden until my mother called me into the house.

On the fourth day of the following week I was taken to the house of my bridegroom and given in marriage.

And Jesus came, and with Him His mother and His brother James.

And they sat around the wedding-board with our guests whilst my maiden comrades sang the wedding-songs of Solomon the King. And Jesus ate our food and drank our wine and smiled upon me and upon the others.

And He heeded all the songs of the lover bringing his beloved into his tent; and of the young vineyard-keeper who loved the

daughter of the lord of the vineyard and led her to his mother's house; and of the prince who met the beggar maiden and bore her to his realm and crowned her with the crown of his fathers.

And it seemed as if He were listening to yet other songs also, which I could not hear.

At sundown the father of my bridegroom came to the mother of Jesus and whispered saying, "We have no more wine for our guests. And the day is not yet over."

And Jesus heard the whispering, and He said, "The cup bearer knows that there is still more wine."

And so it was indeed — and as long as the guests remained there was fine wine for all who would drink.

Presently Jesus began to speak with us. He spoke of the wonders of earth and heaven; of sky flowers that bloom when night is upon the earth, and of earth flowers that blossom when the day hides the stars.

And He told us stories and parables, and His voice enchanted us so that we gazed upon Him as if seeing visions, and we forgot the cup and the plate.

And as I listened to Him it seemed as if I were in a land distant and unknown.

After a while one of the guests said to the father of my bridegroom, "You have kept the best wine till the end of the feast. Other hosts do not so."

And all believed that Jesus had wrought a miracle, that they should have more wine and better at the end of the wedding-feast than at the beginning.

I too thought that Jesus had poured the wine, but I was not astonished; for in His voice I had already listened to miracles.

And afterwards indeed, His voice remained close to my heart, even until I had been delivered of my first-born child.

And now even to this day in our village and in the villages near by, the word of our guest is still remembered. And they say, "The spirit of Jesus of Nazareth is the best and the oldest wine."

A PERSIAN PHILOSOPHER IN DAMASCUS

I CANNOT TELL the fate of this man, nor can I say what shall befall His disciples.

A seed hidden in the heart of an apple is an orchard invisible. Yet should that seed fall upon a rock, it will come to naught.

But this I say: The ancient God of Israel is harsh and relentless. Israel should have another God; one who is gentle and forgiving, who would look down upon them with pity; one who would descend with the rays of the sun and walk on the path of their limitations, rather than sit for ever in the judgment seat to weigh their faults and measure their wrongdoings.

Israel should bring forth a God whose heart is not a jealous heart, and whose memory of their shortcomings is brief; one who would not avenge Himself upon them even to the third and the fourth generation.

Man here in Syria is like man in all lands. He would look into the mirror of his own understanding and therein find his deity. He would fashion the gods after his own likeness, and worship that which reflects his own image.

In truth man prays to his deeper longing, that it may rise and fulfil the sum of his desires.

There is no depth beyond the soul of man, and the soul is the deep that calls unto itself; for there is no other voice to speak and there are no other ears to hear.

Even we in Persia would see our faces in the disc of the sun and our bodies dancing in the fire that we kindle upon the altars.

Now the God of Jesus, whom He called Father, would not be a stranger unto the people of Jesus, and He would fulfil their desires.

The gods of Egypt have cast off their burden of stones and fled to the Nubian desert, to be free among those who are still free from knowing.

The gods of Greece and Rome are vanishing into their own sunset. They were too much like men to live in the ecstasy of men. The groves in which their magic was born have been cut down by the axes of the Athenians and the Alexandrians.

And in this land also the high places are made low by the lawyers of Beirut and the young hermits of Antioch.

Only the old women and the weary men seek the temples of their forefathers; only the exhausted at the end of the road seek its beginning.

But this man Jesus, this Nazarene, He has spoken of a God too vast to be unlike the soul of any man, too knowing to punish, too loving to remember the sins of His creatures. And this God of the Nazarene shall pass over the threshold of the children of the earth, and He shall sit at their hearth, and He shall be a blessing within their walls and a light upon their path.

But my God is the God of Zoroaster, the God who is the sun in the sky and fire upon the earth and light in the bosom of man. And I am content. I need no other God.

I DID NOT know the meaning of His discourses or His parables until He was no longer among us. Nay, I did not understand until His words took living forms before my eyes and fashioned themselves into bodies that walk in the procession of my own day.

Let me tell you this: On a night as I sat in my house pondering, and remembering His words and His deeds that I might inscribe them in a book, three thieves entered my house. And though I knew they came to rob me of my goods, I was too mindful of what I was doing to meet them with the sword, or even to say, "What do you here?"

But I continued writing my remembrances of the Master.

And when the thieves had gone then I remembered His saying, "He who would take your cloak, let him take your other cloak also."

And I understood.

As I sat recording His words no man could have stopped me even were he to have carried away all my possessions.

For though I would guard my possessions and also my person, I know where lies the greater treasure.

LUKE

JESUS DESPISED AND scorned the hypocrites, and His wrath was like a tempest that scourged them. His voice was thunder in their ears and He cowed them.

In their fear of Him they sought His death; and like moles in the dark earth they worked to undermine His footsteps. But He fell not into their snares.

He laughed at them, for well He knew that the spirit shall not be mocked, nor shall it be taken in the pitfall.

He held a mirror in His hand and therein He saw the sluggard and the limping and those who stagger and fall by the roadside on the way to the summit.

And He pitied them all. He would even have raised them to His stature and He would have carried their burden. Nay, He would have bid their weakness lean on His strength.

He did not utterly condemn the liar or the thief or the murderer, but He did utterly condemn the hypocrite whose face is masked and whose hand is gloved.

Often have I pondered on the heart that shelters all who come from the wasteland to its sanctuary, yet against the hypocrite is closed and sealed.

On a day as we rested with Him in the Garden of Pomegranates, I said to Him, "Master, you forgive and console the sinner and all the weak and the infirm save only the hypocrite alone."

And He said, "You have chosen your words well when you called sinners weak and infirm. I do forgive them their weakness of body and their infirmity of spirit. For their failings have been laid upon them by their forefathers, or by the greed of their neighbours.

"But I tolerate not the hypocrite, because he himself lays a yoke upon the guileless and the yielding.

"Weaklings, whom you call sinners, are like the featherless young that fall from the nest. The hypocrite is the vulture waiting upon a rock for the death of the prey.

"Weaklings are men lost in a desert. But the hypocrite is not lost. He knows the way yet he laughs between the sand and the wind.

"For this cause I do not receive him."

Thus our Master spoke, and I did not understand. But I understand now.

Then the hypocrites of the land laid hands upon Him and they judged Him; and in so doing they deemed themselves justified. For they cited the law of Moses in the Sanhedrin in witness and evidence against Him.

And they who break the law at the rise of every dawn and break it again at sunset, brought about His death.

MATTHEW

ONE HARVEST DAY Jesus called us and His other friends to the hills. The earth was fragrant, and like the daughter of a king at her wedding-feast, she wore all her jewels. And the sky was her bridegroom.

When we reached the heights Jesus stood still in the grove of laurels, and He said, "Rest here, quiet your mind and tune your heart, for I have much to tell you."

Then we reclined on the grass, and the summer flowers were all about us, and Jesus sat in our midst.

And Jesus said:

"Blessed are the serene in spirit.

"Blessed are they who are not held by possessions, for they shall be free.

"Blessed are they who remember their pain, and in their pain await their joy.

"Blessed are they who hunger after truth and beauty, for their hunger shall bring bread, and their thirst cool water.

"Blessed are the kindly, for they shall be consoled by their own kindliness.

"Blessed are the pure in heart, for they shall be one with God.

"Blessed are the merciful, for mercy shall be in their portion.

"Blessed are the peacemakers, for their spirit shall dwell above the battle, and they shall turn the potter's field into a garden.

"Blessed are they who are hunted, for they shall be swift of foot and they shall be winged.

"Rejoice and be joyful, for you have found the kingdom of heaven within you. The singers of old were persecuted when they sang of that kingdom. You too shall be persecuted, and therein lies your honour, and therein your reward.

"You are the salt of the earth; should the salt lose its savour wherewith shall the food of man's heart be salted?

"You are the light of the world. Put not that light under a bushel. Let it shine rather from the summit, to those who seek the City of God.

"Think not I came to destroy the laws of the scribes and the Pharisees; for my days among you are numbered and my words are counted, and I have but hours in which to fulfil another law and reveal a new covenant.

"You have been told that you shall not kill, but I say unto you, you shall not be angry without a cause.

"You have been charged by the ancients to bring your calf and your lamb and your dove to the temple, and to slay them upon the altar, that the nostrils of God may feed upon the odour of their fat, and that you may be forgiven your failings.

"But I say unto you, would you give God that which was His own from the beginning; and would you appease Him whose throne is above the silent deep and whose arms encircle space?

"Rather, seek out your brother and be reconciled unto him ere you seek the temple; and be a loving giver unto your neighbour. For in the soul of these God has builded a temple that shall not be destroyed, and in their heart He has raised an altar that shall never perish.

"You have been told, an eye for an eye and a tooth for a tooth. But I say unto you: Resist not evil, for resistance is food unto evil and makes it strong. And only the weak would revenge themselves. The strong of soul forgive, and it is honour in the injured to forgive.

"Only the fruitful tree is shaken or stoned for food.

"Be not heedful of the morrow, but rather gaze upon today, for sufficient for today is the miracle thereof.

"Be not over-mindful of yourself when you give but be mindful of the necessity. For every giver himself receives from the Father, and that much more abundantly.

"And give to each according to his need; for the Father gives not salt to the thirsty, nor a stone to the hungry, nor milk to the weaned.

"And give not that which is holy to dogs; nor cast your pearls before swine. For with such gifts you mock them; and they also shall mock your gift, and in their hate would fain destroy you.

"Lay not up for yourselves treasures that corrupt or that thieves may steal away. Lay up rather treasure which shall not corrupt nor be stolen, and whose loveliness increases when many eyes behold it. For where your treasure is, your heart is also.

"You have been told that the murderer shall be put to the sword, that the thief shall be crucified, and the harlot stoned. But I say unto you that you are not free from the wrongdoing of the murderer and the thief and the harlot, and when they are punished in the body your own spirit is darkened.

"Verily no crime is committed by one man or one woman. All crimes are committed by all. And he who pays the penalty may be breaking a link in the chain that hangs upon your own ankles. Perhaps he is paying with his sorrow the price for your passing joy."

Thus spake Jesus, and it was in my desire to kneel down and worship Him, yet in my shyness I could not move nor speak a word.

But at last I spoke; and I said, "I would pray this moment, yet my tongue is heavy. Teach me to pray."

And Jesus said, "When you would pray, let your longing pronounce the words. It is in my longing now to pray thus:

"Our Father in earth and heaven, sacred is Thy name.
Thy will be done with us, even as in space.
Give us of Thy bread sufficient for the day.
In Thy compassion forgive us and enlarge us to forgive one
    another.
Guide us towards Thee and stretch down Thy hand to us in
    darkness.
For Thine is the kingdom, and in Thee is our power and our
    fulfilment."

And it was now evening, and Jesus walked down from the hills, and all of us followed Him. And as I followed I was repeating His prayer, and remembering all that He had said; for I knew that the words that had fallen like flakes that day must set and grow firm like crystals, and that the wings that had fluttered above our heads were to beat the earth like iron hoofs.

JOHN THE SON OF ZEBEDEE

YOU HAVE REMARKED that some of us call Jesus *the Christ*, and some *the Word*, and others call Him the *Nazarene*, and still others the *Son of Man*.

I will try to make these names clear in the light that is given me.

The Christ, He who was in the ancient of days, is the flame of God that dwells in the spirit of man. He is the breath of life that visits us, and takes unto Himself a body like our bodies.

He is the will of the Lord.

He is the first Word, which would speak with our voice and live in our ear that we may heed and understand.

And the Word of the Lord our God built a house of flesh and bones, and was man like unto you and myself.

For we could not hear the song of the bodiless wind nor see our greater self walking in the mist.

Many times the Christ has come to the world, and He has walked many lands. And always He has been deemed a stranger and a madman.

Yet the sound of His voice descended never to emptiness, for the memory of man keeps that which his mind takes no care to keep.

This is the Christ, the innermost and the height, who walks with man towards eternity.

Have you not heard of Him at the cross-roads of India? And in the land of the Magi, and upon the sands of Egypt?

And here in your North Country your bards of old sang of Prometheus, the fire-bringer, he who was the desire of man fulfilled, the caged hope made free; and of Orpheus, who came with a voice and a lyre to quicken the spirit in beast and man.

And know you not of Mithra the king, and of Zoroaster the prophet of the Persians, who woke from man's ancient sleep and stood at the bed of our dreaming?

We ourselves become man anointed when we meet in the Temple Invisible, once every thousand years. Then comes one forth embodied, and at His coming our silence turns to singing.

Yet our ears turn not always to listening nor our eyes to seeing.

Jesus the Nazarene was born and reared like ourselves; His mother and father were like our parents, and He was a man.

But the Christ, the Word, who was in the beginning, the Spirit who would have us live our fuller life, came unto Jesus and was with Him.

And the Spirit was the versed hand of the Lord, and Jesus was the harp.

The Spirit was the psalm, and Jesus was the tune thereof.

And Jesus, the Man of Nazareth, was the host and the mouth-piece of the Christ, who walked with us in the sun and who called us His friends.

In those days the hills of Galilee and her valleys heard naught but His voice. And I was a youth then, and trod in His path and pursued His footprints.

I pursued His footprints and trod in His path, to hear the words of the Christ from the lips of Jesus of Galilee.

Now you would know why some of us call Him the Son of Man.

He Himself desired to be called by that name, for He knew the hunger and the thirst of man, and He beheld man seeking after His greater self.

The Son of Man was Christ the Gracious, who would be with us all.

He was Jesus the Nazarene who would lead all His brothers to the Anointed One, even to the Word which was in the beginning with God.

In my heart dwells Jesus of Galilee, the Man above men, the Poet who makes poets of us all, the Spirit who knocks at our door that we may wake and rise and walk out to meet truth naked and unencumbered.

A YOUNG PRIEST OF CAPERNAUM

HE WAS A magician, warp and woof, and a sorcerer, a man who bewildered the simple by charms and incantations. And He juggled with the words of our prophets and with the sanctities of our forefathers.

Aye, He even bade the dead be His witnesses, and the voiceless graves His forerunners and authority.

He sought the women of Jerusalem and the women of the countryside with the cunning of the spider that seeks the fly; and they were caught in His web.

For women are weak and empty-headed, and they follow the man who would comfort their unspent passion with soft and tender words. Were it not for these women, infirm and possessed by His evil spirit, His name would have been erased from the memory of man.

And who were the men who followed Him?

They were of the horde that are yoked and trodden down. In their ignorance and fear they would never have rebelled against their rightful masters. But when He promised them high stations in His kingdom of mirage, they yielded to His fantasy as clay yields to the potter.

Know you not, the slave in his dreaming would always be master; and the weakling would be a lion?

The Galilean was a conjuror and a deceiver, a man who forgave the sins of all the sinners that He might hear *Hail* and *Hosanna* from their unclean mouths; and who fed the faint heart of the hopeless and the wretched that He might have ears for His voice and a retinue at His command.

He broke the sabbath with those who break that He might gain the support of the lawless; and He spoke ill of our high priests that He might win attention in the Sanhedrin, and by opposition increase His fame.

I have said often that I hated that man. Ay, I hate Him more than I hate the Romans who govern our country. Even His coming was from Nazareth, a town cursed by our prophets, a dunghill of the Gentiles, from which no good shall ever proceed.

A RICH LEVITE IN THE NEIGHBOURHOOD OF NAZARETH

HE WAS A good carpenter. The doors he fashioned were never unlocked by thieves, and the windows he made were always ready to open to the east wind and to the west.

And He made chests of cedar wood, polished and enduring, and ploughs and pitchforks strong and yielding to the hand.

And He carved lecterns for our synagogues. He carved them out of the golden mulberry; and on both sides of the support, where the sacred book lies, He chiselled wings outspreading; and under the support, heads of bulls and doves, and large-eyed deer.

All this He wrought in the manner of the Chaldeans and the Greeks. But there was that in His skill which was neither Chaldean nor Greek.

Now this my house was builded by many hands thirty years ago. I sought builders and carpenters in all the towns of Galilee. They had each the skill and the art of building, and I was pleased and satisfied with all that they did.

But come now, and behold two doors and a window that were fashioned by Jesus of Nazareth. They in their stability mock at all else in my house.

See you not that these two doors are different from all other doors? And this window opening to the east, is it not different from other windows?

All my doors and windows are yielding to the years save these which He made. They alone stand strong against the elements.

And see those cross-beams, how he placed them; and these nails, how they are driven from one side of the board, and then caught and fastened so firmly upon the other side.

And what is passing strange is that that labourer who was worthy the wages of two men received but the wage of one man; and that same labourer now is deemed a prophet in Israel.

Had I known then that this youth with saw and plane was a prophet, I would have begged Him to speak rather than work, and then I would have over-paid Him for his words.

And now I still have many men working in my house and fields. How shall I know the man whose own hand is upon his tool, from the man upon whose hand God lays His hand?

Yea, how shall I know God's hand?

IT WAS LATE summer when He and three other men first walked upon that road yonder. It was evening, and He stopped and stood there at the end of the pasture.

I was playing upon my flute, and my flock was grazing all around me. When He stopped I rose and walked over and stood before Him.

And He asked me, "Where is the grave of Elijah? Is it not somewhere near this place?"

And I answered Him, "It is there, Sir, underneath that great heap of stones. Even unto this day every passerby brings a stone and places it upon the heap."

And He thanked me and walked away, and His friends walked behind Him.

And after three days Gamaliel, who was also a shepherd, said to me that the man who had passed by was a prophet in Judea; but I did not believe him. Yet I thought of that man for many a moon.

When spring came Jesus passed once more by this pasture, and this time He was alone.

I was not playing on my flute that day for I had lost a sheep and I was bereaved, and my heart was downcast within me.

And I walked towards Him and stood still before Him, for I desired to be comforted.

And He looked at me and said, "You do not play upon your flute this day. Whence is the sorrow in your eyes?"

And I answered, "A sheep from among my sheep is lost. I have sought her everywhere but I find her not. And I know not what to do."

And He was silent for a moment. Then He smiled upon me and said, "Wait here awhile and I will find your sheep." And He walked away and disappeared among the hills.

After an hour He returned, and my sheep was close beside Him. And as He stood before me, the sheep looked up into His face even as I was looking. Then I embraced her in gladness.

And He put His hand upon my shoulder and said, "From this day you shall love this sheep more than any other in your flock, for she was lost and now she is found."

And again I embraced my sheep in gladness, and she came close to me, and I was silent.

But when I raised my head to thank Jesus, He was already walking afar off, and I had not the courage to follow Him.

JOHN THE BAPTIST

I AM NOT silent in this foul hole while the voice of Jesus is heard on the battlefield. I am not to be held nor confined while He is free.

They tell me the vipers are coiling round His loins, but I answer: The vipers shall awaken His strength, and He shall crush them with His heel.

I am only the thunder of His lightning. Though I spoke first, His was the word and the purpose.

They caught me unwarned. Perhaps they will lay hands on Him also. Yet not before He has pronounced His word in full. And He shall overcome them.

His chariot shall pass over them, and the hoofs of His horses shall trample them, and He shall be triumphant.

They shall go forth with lance and sword, but He shall meet them with the power of the Spirit.

His blood shall run upon the earth, but they themselves shall know the wounds and the pain thereof, and they shall be baptized in their tears until they are cleansed of their sins.

Their legions shall march towards His cities with rams of iron, but on their way they shall be drowned in the River Jordan.

And His walls and His towers shall rise higher, and the shields of His warriors shall shine brighter in the sun.

They say I am in league with Him, and that our design is to urge the people to rise and revolt against the kingdom of Judea.

I answer, and would that I had flames for words: if they deem this pit of iniquity a kingdom, let it then fall into destruction and be no more. Let it go the way of Sodom and Gomorrah, and let this race be forgotten by God, and this land be turned to ashes.

Aye, behind these prison walls I am indeed an ally to Jesus of Nazareth, and He shall lead my armies, horse and foot. And

I myself, though a captain, am not worthy to loose the strings of His sandals.

Go to Him and repeat my words, and then in my name beg Him for comfort and blessing.

I shall not be here long. At night 'twixt waking and waking I feel slow feet with measured steps treading above this body. And when I hearken, I hear the rain falling upon my grave.

Go to Jesus, and say that John of Kedron whose soul is filled with shadows and then emptied again, prays for Him, while the grave-digger stands close by, and the swordsman outstretches his hand for his wages.

JOSEPH OF ARIMATHÆA

YOU WOULD KNOW the primal aim of Jesus, and I would fain tell you. But none can touch with fingers the life of the blessed vine, nor see the sap that feeds the branches.

And though I have eaten of the grapes and have tasted the new vintage at the winepress, I cannot tell you all.

I can only relate what I know of Him.

Our Master and our Beloved lived but three prophet's seasons. They were the spring of His song, the summer of His ecstasy, and the autumn of His passion; and each season was a thousand years.

The spring of His song was spent in Galilee. It was there that He gathered His lovers about Him, and it was on the shores of the blue lake that He first spoke of the Father, and of our release and our freedom.

By the Lake of Galilee we lost ourselves to find our way to the Father; and oh, the little, little loss that turned to such gain.

It was there the angels sang in our ears and bade us leave the arid land for the garden of heart's desire.

He spoke of fields and green pastures; of the slopes of Lebanon where the white lilies are heedless of the caravans passing in the dust of the valley.

He spoke of the wild brier that smiles in the sun and yields its incense to the passing breeze.

And He would say, "The lilies and the brier live but a day, yet that day is eternity spent in freedom."

And one evening as we sat beside the stream He said, "Behold the brook and listen to its music. Forever shall it seek the sea, and though it is for ever seeking, it sings its mystery from noon to noon.

"Would that you seek the Father as the brook seeks the sea."

Then came the summer of His ecstasy, and the June of His love was upon us. He spoke of naught then but the other man – the neighbour, the road-fellow, the stranger, and our childhood's playmates.

He spoke of the traveller journeying from the east to Egypt, of the ploughman coming home with his oxen at eventide, of the chance guest led by dusk to our door.

And He would say, "Your neighbour is your unknown self made visible. His face shall be reflected in your still waters, and if you gaze therein you shall behold your own countenance.

"Should you listen in the night, you shall hear him speak, and his words shall be the throbbing of your own heart.

"Be unto him that which you would have him be unto you.

"This is my law, and I shall say it unto you, and unto your children, and they unto their children until time is spent and generations are no more.

And on another day He said, "You shall not be yourself alone. You are in the deeds of other men, and they though unknowing are with you all your days.

"They shall not commit a crime and your hand not be with their hand.

"They shall not fall down but that you shall also fall down; and they shall not rise but that you shall rise with them.

"Their road to the sanctuary is your road, and when they seek the wasteland you too seek with them.

"You and your neighbour are two seeds sown in the field. Together you grow and together you shall sway in the wind. And neither of you shall claim the field. For a seed on its way to growth claims not even its own ecstasy.

"Today I am with you. Tomorrow I go westward; but ere I go, I say unto you that your neighbour is your unknown self made visible. Seek him in love that you may know yourself, for only in that knowledge shall you become my brothers."

Then came the autumn of His passion.

And He spoke to us of freedom, even as He had spoken in Galilee in the spring of His song; but now His words sought our deeper understanding.

He spoke of leaves that sing only when blown upon the wind; and of man as a cup filled by the ministering angel of the day to quench the thirst of another angel. Yet whether that cup is full or empty it shall stand crystalline upon the board of the Most High.

He said, "You are the cup and you are the wine. Drink of yourselves to the dregs; or else remember me and you shall be quenched."

And on our way to the southward He said, "Jerusalem, which stands in pride upon the height, shall descend to the depth of Jahannum the dark valley, and in the midst of her desolation I shall stand alone.

"The temple shall fall to dust, and around the portico you shall hear the cry of widows and orphans; and men in their haste to escape shall not know the faces of their brothers, for fear shall be upon them all.

"But even there, if two of you shall meet and utter my name and look to the west, you shall see me, and these my words shall again visit your ears."

And when we reached the hill of Bethany, He said, "Let us go to Jerusalem. The city awaits us. I will enter the gate riding upon a colt, and I will speak to the multitude.

"Many are there who would chain me, and many who would put out my flame, but in my death you shall find life and you shall be free.

"They shall seek the breath that hovers betwixt heart and mind as the swallow hovers between the field and his nest. But my breath has already escaped them, and they shall not overcome me.

"The walls that my Father has built around me shall not fall down, and the acre He has made holy shall not be profaned.

"When the dawn shall come, the sun will crown my head and I shall be with you to face the day. And that day shall be long, and the world shall not see its eventide.

"The scribes and the Pharisees say the earth is thirsty for my blood. I would quench the thirst of the earth with my blood. But the drops shall rise oak trees and maple, and the east wind shall carry the acorns to other lands."

And then He said, "Judea would have a king, and she would march against the legions of Rome.

"I shall not be her king. The diadems of Zion were fashioned for lesser brows. And the ring of Solomon is small for this finger.

"Behold my hand. See you not that it is overstrong to hold a sceptre, and over-sinewed to wield a common sword?

"Nay, I shall not command Syrian flesh against Roman. But you with my words shall wake that city, and my spirit shall speak to her second dawn.

"My words shall be an invisible army with horses and chariots, and without axe or spear I shall conquer the priests of Jerusalem, and the Cæsars.

"I shall not sit upon a throne where slaves have sat and ruled other slaves. Nor will I rebel against the sons of Italy.

"But I shall be a tempest in their sky, and a song in their soul.

"And I shall be remembered.

"They shall call me Jesus the Anointed."

These things He said outside the walls of Jerusalem before He entered the city.

And His words are graven as with chisels.

NATHANIEL

THEY SAY THAT Jesus of Nazareth was humble and meek.

They say that though He was a just man and righteous, He was a weakling, and was often confounded by the strong and the powerful; and that when He stood before men of authority He was but a lamb among lions.

But I say that Jesus had authority over men, and that He knew His power and proclaimed it among the hills of Galilee, and in the cities of Judea and Phœnicia.

What man yielding and soft would say, "I am life, and I am the way to truth"?

What man meek and lowly would say, "I am in God, our Father; and our God, the Father, is in me"?

What man unmindful of His own strength would say, "He who believes not in me believes not in this life nor in the life everlasting"?

What man uncertain of tomorrow would proclaim, "Your world shall pass away and be naught but scattered ashes ere my words shall pass away"?

Was He doubtful of Himself when He said to those who would confound Him with a harlot, "He who is without sin, let him cast a stone"?

Did He fear authority when He drove the money-changers from the court of the temple, though they were licensed by the priests?

Were His wings shorn when He cried aloud, "My kingdom is above your earthly kingdoms"?

Was He seeking shelter in words when He repeated again and yet again, "Destroy this temple and I will rebuild it in three days"?

Was it a coward who shook His hand in the face of the authorities and pronounced them "liars, low, filthy, and degenerate"?

Shall a man bold enough to say these things to those who ruled Judea be deemed meek and humble?

Nay. The eagle builds not his nest in the weeping willow. And the lion seeks not his den among the ferns.

I am sickened and the bowels within me stir and rise when I hear the faint-hearted call Jesus humble and meek, that they may justify their own faint-heartedness; and when the down-trodden, for comfort and companionship, speak of Jesus as a worm shining by their side.

Yea, my heart is sickened by such men. It is the mighty hunter I would preach, and the mountainous spirit unconquerable.

THIS DAY I heard Saul of Tarsus preaching the Christ unto the Jews of this city.

He calls himself Paul now, the apostle to the Gentiles.

I knew him in my youth, and in those days he persecuted the friends of the Nazarene. Well do I remember his satisfaction when his fellows stoned the radiant youth called Stephen.

This Paul is indeed a strange man. His soul is not the soul of a free man.

At times he seems like an animal in the forest, hunted and wounded, seeking a cave wherein he would hide his pain from the world.

He speaks not of Jesus, nor does he repeat His words. He preaches the Messiah whom the prophets of old had foretold.

And though he himself is a learned Jew he addresses his fellow Jews in Greek; and his Greek is halting, and he ill chooses his words.

But he is a man of hidden powers and his presence is affirmed by those who gather round him. And at times he assures them of what he himself is not assured.

*

We who knew Jesus and heard His discourses say that He taught man how to break the chains of his bondage that he might be free from his yesterdays.

But Paul is forging chains for the man of tomorrow. He would strike with his own hammer upon the anvil in the name of one whom he does not know.

The Nazarene would have us live the hour in passion and ecstasy.

The man of Tarsus would have us be mindful of laws recorded in the ancient books.

Jesus gave His breath to the breathless dead. And in my lone nights I believe and I understand.

When He sat at the board, He told stories that gave happiness to the feasters, and spiced with His joy the meat and the wine.

But Paul would prescribe our loaf and our cup.

Suffer me now to turn my eyes the other way.

SALOME TO A WOMAN FRIEND

HE WAS LIKE poplars shimmering in the sun;
And like a lake among the lonely hills,
Shining in the sun;
And like snow upon the mountain heights,
White, white in the sun.

Yea, He was like unto all these,
And I loved Him.
Yet I feared His presence.
And my feet would not carry my burden of love
That I might girdle His feet with my arms.

I would have said to Him,
"I have slain your friend in an hour of passion.
Will you forgive me my sin?
And will you not in mercy release my youth
From its blind deed,
That it may walk in your light?"

I know He would have forgiven my dancing
For the saintly head of His friend.
I know He would have seen in me
An object of His own teaching.
For there was no valley of hunger He could not bridge,
And no desert of thirst He could not cross.
Yea, He was even as the poplars,
And as the lakes among the hills,
And like the snow upon Lebanon.
And I would have cooled my lips in the folds of His garment.

But He was far from me,
And I was ashamed.
And my mother held me back
When the desire to seek Him was upon me.

Whenever He passed by, my heart ached for his loveliness,
But my mother frowned at Him in contempt,
And would hasten me from the window
To my bedchamber.
And she would cry aloud saying,
"Who is He but another locust-eater from the desert?

What is He but a scoffer and a renegade.
A seditious riot-monger, who would rob us of sceptre and
    crown,
And bid the foxes and the jackals of His accursed land
Howl in our halls and sit upon our throne?
Go hide your face from this day,
And await the day when His head shall fall down,
But not upon your platter."
These things my mother said.
But my heart would not keep her words.
I loved Him in secret,
And my sleep was girdled with flames.

He is gone now.
And something that was in me is gone also.
Perhaps it was my youth
That would not tarry here,
Since the God of youth was slain.

RACHAEL, A WOMAN DISCIPLE

I OFTEN WONDER whether Jesus was a man of flesh and blood like ourselves, or a thought without a body, in the mind, or an idea that visits the vision of man.

Often it seems to me that He was but a dream dreamed by countless men and women at the same time in a sleep deeper than sleep and a dawn more serene than all dawns.

And it seems that in relating the dream, the one to the other, we began to deem it a reality that had indeed come to pass; and in giving it body of our fancy and a voice of our longing we made it a substance of our own substance.

But in truth He was not a dream. We knew Him for three years and beheld Him with our open eyes in the high tide of noon.

We touched His hands, and we followed Him from one place to another. We heard His discourses and witnessed His deeds. Think you that we were a thought seeking after more thought, or a dream in the region of dreams?

Great events always seem alien to our daily lives, though their nature may be rooted in our nature. But though they appear sudden in their coming and sudden in their passing, their true span is for years and for generations.

Jesus of Nazareth was Himself the Great Event. That man whose father and mother and brothers we know, was Himself a miracle wrought in Judea. Yea, all His own miracles, if placed at His feet, would not rise to the height of His ankles.

And all the rivers of all the years shall not carry away our remembrance of Him.

He was a mountain burning in the night, yet He was a soft glow beyond the hills. He was a tempest in the sky, yet He was a murmur in the mist of daybreak.

He was a torrent pouring from the heights to the plains to

destroy all things in its path. And He was like the laughter of children.

Every year I had waited for spring to visit this valley. I had waited for the lilies and the cyclamen, and then every year my soul had been saddened within me; for ever I longed to rejoice with the spring, yet I could not.

But when Jesus came to my seasons He was indeed a spring, and in Him was the promise of all the years to come. He filled my heart with joy; and like the violets I grew, a shy thing, in the light of His coming.

And now the changing seasons of worlds not yet ours shall not erase His loveliness from this our world.

Nay, Jesus was not a phantom, nor a conception of the poets. He was man like yourself and myself. But only to sight and touch and hearing; in all other ways He was unlike us.

He was a man of joy; and it was upon the path of joy that He met the sorrows of all men. And it was from the high roofs of His sorrows that He beheld the joy of all men.

He saw visions that we did not see, and heard voices that we did not hear; and He spoke as if to invisible multitudes, and ofttimes He spoke through us to races yet unborn.

And Jesus was often alone. He was among us yet not one with us. He was upon the earth, yet He was of the sky. And only in our aloneness may we visit the land of His aloneness.

He loved us with tender love. His heart was a winepress. You and I could approach with a cup and drink therefrom.

One thing I did not use to understand in Jesus: He would make merry with His listeners; He would tell jests and play upon words, and laugh with all the fullness of His heart, even when there were distances in His eyes and sadness in His voice. But I understand now.

I often think of the earth as a woman heavy with her first child. When Jesus was born, He was the first child. And when He died, He was the first man to die.

For did it not appear to you that the earth was stilled on that dark Friday, and the heavens were at war with the heavens?

And felt you not when His face disappeared from our sight as if we were naught but memories in the mist?

CLEOPAS OF BETHROUNE

WHEN JESUS SPOKE the whole world was hushed to listen. His words were not for our ears but rather for the elements of which God made this earth.

He spoke to the sea, our vast mother, that gave us birth. He spoke to the mountain, our elder brother whose summit is a promise.

And He spoke to the angels beyond the sea and the mountain to whom we entrusted our dreams ere the clay in us was made hard in the sun.

And still His speech slumbers within our breast like a love-song half forgotten, and sometimes it burns itself through to our memory.

His speech was simple and joyous, and the sound of His voice was like cool water in a land of drought.

Once He raised His hand against the sky, and His fingers were like the branches of a sycamore tree; and He said with a great voice:

"The prophets of old have spoken to you, and your ears are filled with their speech. But I say unto you, empty your ears of what you have heard."

And these words of Jesus, "*But I say unto you*," were not uttered by a man of our race nor of our world; but rather by a host of seraphim marching across the sky of Judea.

Again and yet again He would quote the law and the prophets, and then He would say, "*But I say unto you*."

Oh, what burning words, what waves of seas unknown to the shores of our mind, "*But I say unto you*."

What stars seeking the darkness of the soul, and what sleepless souls awaiting the dawn.

*

To tell of the speech of Jesus one must needs have His speech or the echo thereof.

I have neither the speech nor the echo.

I beg you to forgive me for beginning a story that I cannot end. But the end is not yet upon my lips. It is still a love song in the wind.

HIS DISCIPLES ARE dispersed. He gave them the legacy of pain ere He Himself was put to death. They are hunted like the deer, and the foxes of the fields, and the quiver of the hunter is yet full of arrows.

But when they are caught and led to death, they are joyous, and their faces shine like the face of the bridegroom at the wedding-feast. For He gave them also the legacy of joy.

I had a friend from the North Country, and his name was Stephen; and because he proclaimed Jesus as the Son of God, he was led to the market-place and stoned.

And when Stephen fell to earth he outstretched his arms as if he would die as his Master had died. His arms were spread like wings ready for flight. And when the last gleam of light was fading in his eyes, with my own eyes I saw a smile upon his lips. It was a smile like the breath that comes before the end of winter for a pledge and a promise of spring.

How shall I describe it?

It seemed that Stephen was saying, "If I should go to another world, and other men should lead me to another market-place to stone me, even then I would proclaim Him for the truth which was in Him, and for that same truth which is in me now."

And I noticed that there was a man standing near, and looking with pleasure upon the stoning of Stephen.

His name was Saul of Tarsus, and it was he who had yielded Stephen to the priests and the Romans and the crowd, for stoning.

Saul was bald of head and short of stature. His shoulders were crooked and his features ill-sorted; and I liked him not.

I have been told that he is now preaching Jesus from the housetops. It is hard to believe.

But the grave halts not Jesus' walking to the enemies' camp to tame and take captive those who had opposed Him.

Still I do not like that man of Tarsus, though I have been told that after Stephen's death he was tamed and conquered on the road to Damascus. But his head is too large for his heart to be that of a true disciple.

And yet perhaps I am mistaken. I am often mistaken.

THOMAS

MY GRANDFATHER WHO was a lawyer once said, "Let us observe truth, but only when truth is made manifest unto us."

When Jesus called me I heeded Him, for His command was more potent than my will; yet I kept my counsel.

When He spoke and the others were swayed like branches in the wind, I listened immovable. Yet I loved Him.

Three years ago He left us, a scattered company to sing His name, and to be His witnesses unto the nations.

At that time I was called Thomas the Doubter. The shadow of my grandfather was still upon me, and always I would have truth made manifest.

I would even put my hand in my own wound to feel the blood ere I would believe in my pain.

Now a man who loves with his heart yet holds a doubt in his mind, is but a slave in a galley who sleeps at his oar and dreams of his freedom, till the lash of the master wakes him.

I myself was that slave, and I dreamed of freedom, but the sleep of my grandfather was upon me. My flesh needed the whip of my own day.

Even in the presence of the Nazarene I had closed my eyes to see my hands chained to the oar.

Doubt is a pain too lonely to know that faith is his twin brother.

Doubt is a foundling unhappy and astray, and though his own mother who gave him birth should find him and enfold him, he would withdraw in caution and in fear.

For Doubt will not know truth till his wounds are healed and restored.

I doubted Jesus until He made Himself manifest to me, and thrust my own hand into His very wounds.

Then indeed I believed, and after that I was rid of my yesterday and the yesterdays of my forefathers.

The dead in me buried their dead; and the living shall live for the Anointed King, even for Him who was the Son of Man.

Yesterday they told me that I must go and utter His name among the Persians and the Hindus.

I shall go. And from this day to my last day, at dawn and at eventide, I shall see my Lord rising in majesty and I shall hear Him speak.

ELMADAM THE LOGICIAN

YOU BID ME speak of Jesus the Nazarene, and much have I to tell, but the time has not come. Yet whatever I say of Him now is the truth; for all speech is worthless save when it discloses the truth.

Behold a man disorderly, against all order; a mendicant, opposed to all possessions; a drunkard who would only make merry with rogues and castaways.

He was not the proud son of the State, nor was He the protected citizen of the Empire; therefore He had contempt for both State and Empire.

He would live as free and dutiless as the fowls of the air, and for this the hunters brought Him to earth with arrows.

No man shall ram the towers of yesterday and escape the falling stones.

No one shall open the floodgates of his ancestors without drowning. It is the law. And because that Nazarene broke the law, He and His witless followers were brought to naught.

And there lived many others like Him, men who would change the course of our destiny.

They themselves were changed, and they were the losers.

There is a grapeless vine that grows by the city walls. It creeps upward and clings to the stones. Should that vine say in her heart, "With my might and my weight I shall destroy these walls," what would the other plants say? Surely they would laugh at her foolishness.

Now sir, I cannot but laugh at this man and His ill-advised disciples.

ONE OF THE MARYS

HIS HEAD WAS always high, and the flame of God was in His eyes.

He was often sad, but His sadness was tenderness shown to those in pain, and comradeship given to the lonely.

When He smiled His smile was as the hunger of those who long after the unknown. It was like the dust of stars falling upon the eyelids of children. And it was like a morsel of bread in the throat.

He was sad, yet it was a sadness that would rise to the lips and become a smile.

It was like a golden veil in the forest when autumn is upon the world. And sometimes it seemed like moonlight upon the shores of the lake.

He smiled as if His lips would sing at the wedding-feast.

Yet He was sad with the sadness of the winged who will not soar above his comrade.

RUMANOUS, A GREEK POET

HE WAS A POET. He saw for our eyes and heard for our ears, and our silent words were upon His lips; and His fingers touched what we could not feel.

Out of His heart there flew countless singing birds to the north and to the south, and the little flowers on the hill-sides stayed His steps towards the heavens.

Oftentimes I have seen Him bending down to touch the blades of grass. And in my heart I have heard Him say: "Little green things, you shall be with me in my kingdom, even as the oaks of Besan, and the cedars of Lebanon."

He loved all things of loveliness, the shy faces of children, and the myrrh and frankincense from the south.

He loved a pomegranate or a cup of wine given Him in kindness; it mattered not whether it was offered by a stranger in the inn or by a rich host.

And He loved the almond blossoms. I have seen Him gathering them into His hands and covering His face with the petals, as though He would embrace with His love all the trees in the world.

He knew the sea and the heavens; and He spoke of pearls which have light that is not of this light, and of stars that are beyond our night.

He knew the mountains as eagles know them, and the valleys as they are known by the brooks and the streams. And there was a desert in His silence and a garden in His speech.

Aye, He was a poet whose heart dwelt in a bower beyond the heights, and His songs though sung for our ears, were sung for other ears also, and to men in another land where life is for ever young and time is always dawn.

Once I too deemed myself a poet, but when I stood before Him in Bethany, I knew what it is to hold an instrument with but a single string before one who commands all instruments. For in His voice there was the laughter of thunder and the tears of rain, and the joyous dancing of trees in the wind.

And since I have known that my lyre has but one string, and that my voice weaves neither the memories of yesterday nor the hopes of tomorrow, I have put aside my lyre and I shall keep silence. But always at twilight I shall hearken, and I shall listen to the Poet who is the sovereign of all poets.

LEVI, A DISCIPLE

UPON AN EVENTIDE He passed by my house, and my soul was quickened within me.

He spoke to me and said, "Come, Levi, and follow me."

And I followed Him that day.

And at the eventide of the next day I begged Him to enter my house and be my guest. And He and His friends crossed my threshold and blessed me and my wife and my children.

And I had other guests. They were publicans and men of learning, but they were against Him in their hearts.

And when we were sitting about the board, one of the publicans questioned Jesus, saying, "Is it true that you and your disciples break the law, and make fire on the sabbath day?"

And Jesus answered Him saying, "We do indeed make fire on the sabbath day. We would inflame the sabbath day, and we would burn with our torch the dry stubble of all the days."

And another publican said, "It was brought to us that you drink wine with the unclean at the inn."

And Jesus answered, "Aye, these also we would comfort. Came we here except to share the loaf and the cup with the uncrowned and the unshod amongst you?

"Few, aye too few are the featherless who dare the wind, and many are the winged and full-fledged yet in the nest.

"And we would feed them all with our beak, both the sluggish and the swift."

And another publican said, "Have I not been told that you would protect the harlots of Jerusalem?"

Then in the face of Jesus I saw, as it were, the rocky heights of Lebanon, and He said, "It is true.

"On the day of reckoning these women shall rise before the throne of my Father, and they shall be made pure by their own tears. But you shall be held down by the chains of your own judgment.

"Babylon was not put to waste by her prostitutes; Babylon fell to ashes that the eyes of her hypocrites might no longer see the light of day."

And other publicans would have questioned Him, but I made a sign and bade them be silent, for I knew He would confound them; and they too were my guests, and I would not have them put to shame.

When it was midnight the publicans left my house, and their souls were limping.

Then I closed my eyes and I saw, as if in a vision, seven women in white raiment standing about Jesus. Their arms were crossed upon their bosoms, and their heads were bent down, and I looked deep into the mist of my dream and beheld the face of one of the seven women, and it shone in my darkness.

It was the face of a harlot who lived in Jerusalem.

Then I opened my eyes and looked at Him, and He was smiling at me and at the others who had not left the board.

And I closed my eyes again, and I saw in a light seven men in white garments standing around Him. And I beheld the face of one of them.

It was the face of the thief who was crucified afterwards at His right hand.

And later Jesus and His comrades left my house for the road.

A WIDOW IN GALILEE

MY SON WAS my first and my only born. He laboured in our field and he was contented until he heard the man called Jesus speaking to the multitude.

Then my son suddenly became different, as if a new spirit, foreign and unwholesome, had embraced his spirit.

He abandoned the field and the garden; and he abandoned me also. He became worthless, a creature of the highways.

That man Jesus of Nazareth was evil, for what good man would separate a son from his mother?

The last thing my child said to me was this: "I am going with one of His disciples to the North Country. My life is established upon the Nazarene. You have given me birth, and for that I am grateful to you. But I needs must go. Am I not leaving with you our rich land, and all our silver and gold? I shall take naught but this garment and this staff."

Thus my son spoke, and departed.

And now the Romans and the priests have laid hold upon Jesus and crucified Him; and they have done well.

A man who would part mother and son could not be godly.

The man who sends our children to the cities of the Gentiles cannot be our friend.

I know my son will not return to me. I saw it in his eyes. And for this I hate Jesus of Nazareth who caused me to be alone in this unploughed field and this withered garden.

And I hate all those who praise Him.

Not many days ago they told me that Jesus once said, "My father and my mother and my brethren are those who hear my word and follow me."

But why should sons leave their mothers to follow His footsteps?

And why should the milk of my breast be forgotten for a

fountain not yet tasted? And the warmth of my arms be forsaken for the Northland, cold and unfriendly?

Aye, I hate the Nazarene, and I shall hate Him to the end of my days, for He has robbed me of my first-born, my only son.

UPON A NIGHT in the month of August we were with the Master on a heath not far from the lake. The heath was called by the ancients the Meadow of Skulls.

And Jesus was reclining on the grass and gazing at the stars.

And of a sudden two men came rushing towards us breathless. They were as if in agony, and they fell prostrate at the feet of Jesus.

And Jesus stood up and He said, "Whence came you?"

And one of the men answered, "From Machærus."

And Jesus looked upon him and was troubled, and He said, "What of John?"

And the man said, "He was slain this day. He was beheaded in his prison cell."

Then Jesus lifted up His head. And then He walked a little way from us. After a while He stood again in our midst.

And He said, "The king could have slain the prophet ere this day. Verily the king has tried the pleasure of His subjects. Kings of yore were not so slow in giving the head of a prophet to the head-hunters.

"I grieve not for John, but rather for Herod, who let fall the sword. Poor king, like an animal caught and led with a ring and a rope.

"Poor petty tetrarchs lost in their own darkness, they stumble and fall down. And what would you of the stagnant sea but dead fishes?

"I hate not kings. Let them rule men, but only when they are wiser than men."

And the Master looked at the two sorrowful faces and then He looked at us, and He spoke again and said, "John was born wounded, and the blood of his wound streamed forth with his words. He was freedom not yet free from itself, and patient only with the straight and the just.

"In truth he was a voice crying in the land of the deaf; and I loved him in his pain and his aloneness.

"And I loved his pride that would give its head to the sword ere it would yield it to the dust.

"Verily I say unto you that John, the son of Zachariah, was the last of his race, and like his forefathers he was slain between the threshold of the temple and the altar."

And again Jesus walked away from us.

Then He returned and He said, "Forever it has been that those who rule for an hour would slay the rules of years. And forever they would hold a trial and pronounce condemnation upon a man not yet born, and decree his death ere he commits the crime.

"The son of Zachariah shall live with me in my kingdom and his day shall be long."

Then He turned to the disciples of John and said, "Every deed has its morrow. I myself may be the morrow of this deed. Go back to my friend's friends, and tell them I shall be with them."

And the two men walked away from us, and they seemed less heavy-hearted.

Then Jesus laid Himself down again upon the grass and out-stretched His arms, and again He gazed at the stars.

Now it was late. And I lay not far from Him, and I would fain have rested, but there was a hand knocking upon the gate of my sleep, and I lay awake until Jesus and the dawn called me again to the road.

THE MAN FROM THE DESERT

I WAS A STRANGER in Jerusalem. I had come to the Holy City to behold the great temple, and to sacrifice upon the altar, for my wife had given twin sons to my tribe.

And after I had made my offering, I stood in the portico of the temple looking down upon the money-changers and those who sold doves for sacrifice, and listening to the great noise in the court.

And as I stood there came of a sudden a man into the midst of the money-changers and those who sold doves.

He was a man of majesty, and He came swiftly.

In His hand He held a rope of goat's hide; and He began to overturn the tables of the money-changers and to beat the pedlars of birds with the rope.

And I heard Him saying with a loud voice, "Render these birds unto the sky which is their nest."

Men and women fled from before His face, and He moved amongst them as the whirling wind moves on the sand-hills.

All this came to pass in but a moment, and then the court of the Temple was emptied of the money-changers. Only the man stood there alone, and His followers stood at a distance.

Then I turned my face and I saw another man in the portico of the temple. And I walked towards him and said, "Sir, who is this man who stands alone, even like another temple?" And he answered me, "This is Jesus of Nazareth, a prophet who has appeared of late in Galilee. Here in Jerusalem all men hate Him."

And I said, "My heart was strong enough to be with His whip, and yielding enough to be at His feet."

And Jesus turned towards His followers who were awaiting Him. But before He reached them, three of the temple doves flew back, and one alighted upon His left shoulder and the other two at His feet. And He touched each one tenderly. Then He walked on, and there were leagues in every step of His steps.

Now tell me, what power had He to attack and disperse hundreds of men and women without opposition? I was told that they all hate Him, yet no one stood before Him on that day. Had He plucked out the fangs of hate on His way to the court of the temple?

PETER

ONCE AT SUNDOWN Jesus led us into the village of Bethsaida. We were a tired company, and the dust of the road was upon us.

And we came to a great house in the midst of a garden, and the owner stood at the gate.

And Jesus said to him, "These men are weary and footsore. Let them sleep in your house. The night is cold and they are in need of warmth and rest."

And the rich man said, "They shall not sleep in my house."

And Jesus said, "Suffer them then to sleep in your garden."

And the man answered, "Nay, they shall not sleep in my garden."

Then Jesus turned to us and said, "This is what your tomorrow will be, and this present is like your future. All doors shall be closed in your face, and not even the gardens that lie under the stars may be your couch.

"Should your feet indeed be patient with the road and follow me, it may be you will find a basin and a bed, and perhaps bread and wine also. But if it should be that you find none of these things, forget not then that you have crossed one of my deserts.

"Come, let us go forth."

And the rich man was disturbed, and his face was changed, and he muttered to himself words that I did not hear; and he shrank away from us and turned into his garden.

And we followed Jesus upon the road.

MELACHI OF BABYLON, AN ASTRONOMER

YOU QUESTION ME concerning the miracles of Jesus.

Every thousand thousand years the sun and the moon and this earth and all her sister planets meet in a straight line, and they confer for a moment together.

Then they slowly disperse and await the passing of another thousand thousand years.

There are no miracles beyond the seasons, yet you and I do not know all the seasons. And what if a season shall be made manifest in the shape of a man?

In Jesus the elements of our bodies and our dreams came together according to law. All that was timeless before Him became timeful in Him.

They say He gave sight to the blind and walking to the paralysed, and that He drove devils out of madmen.

Perchance blindness is but a dark thought that can be overcome by a burning thought. Perchance a withered limb is but idleness that can be quickened by energy. And perhaps the devils, these restless elements in our life, are driven out by the angels of peace and serenity.

They say He raised the dead to life. If you can tell me *what is death*, then I will tell you *what is life*.

In a field I have watched an acorn, a thing so still and seemingly useless. And in the spring I have seen that acorn take roots and rise, the beginning of an oak tree, towards the sun.

Surely you would deem this a miracle, yet that miracle is wrought a thousand thousand times in the drowsiness of every autumn and the passion of every spring.

Why shall it not be wrought in the heart of man? Shall not the seasons meet in the hand or upon the lips of a Man Anointed?

If our God has given to earth the art to nestle seed whilst the seed is seemingly dead, why shall He not give to the heart of man to breathe life into another heart, even a heart seemingly dead?

I have spoken of these miracles which I deem but little beside the greater miracle, which is the man Himself, the Wayfarer, the man who turned my dross into gold, who taught me how to love those who hate me, and in so doing brought me comfort and gave sweet dreams to my sleep.

This is the miracle in my own life.

My soul was blind, my soul was lame. I was possessed by restless spirits, and I was dead.

But now I see clearly, and I walk erect. I am at peace, and I live to witness and proclaim my own being every hour of the day.

And I am not one of His followers. I am but an old astronomer who visits the fields of space once a season, and who would be heedful of the law and the miracles thereof.

And I am at the twilight of my time, but whenever I would seek its dawning, I seek the youth of Jesus.

And for ever shall age seek youth. In me now it is knowledge that is seeking vision.

A PHILOSOPHER

WHEN HE WAS with us He gazed at us and at our world with eyes of wonder, for His eyes were not veiled with the veil of years, and all that He saw was clear in the light of His youth.

Though He knew the depth of beauty, He was for ever surprised by its peace and its majesty; and He stood before the earth as the first man had stood before the first day.

We whose senses have been dulled, we gaze in full daylight and yet we do not see. We would cup our ears, but we do not hear; and stretch forth our hands, but we do not touch. And though all the incense of Arabia is burned, we go our way and do not smell.

We see not the ploughman returning from his field at eventide; nor hear the shepherd's flute when he leads his flock to the fold; nor do we stretch our arms to touch the sunset; and our nostrils hunger no longer for the roses of Sharon.

Nay, we honour no kings without kingdoms; nor hear the sound of harps save when the strings are plucked by hands; nor do we see a child playing in our olive grove as if he were a young olive tree. And all words must needs rise from lips of flesh, or else we deem each other dumb and deaf.

In truth we gaze but do not see, and hearken but do not hear; we eat and drink but do not taste. And there lies the difference between Jesus of Nazareth and ourselves.

His senses were all continually made new, and the world to Him was always a new world.

To Him the lisping of a babe was not less than the cry of all mankind, while to us it is only lisping.

To Him the root of a buttercup was a longing towards God, while to us it is naught but a root.

URIAH, AN OLD MAN OF NAZARETH

HE WAS A STRANGER in our midst, and His life was hidden with dark veils.

He walked not the path of our God, but followed the course of the foul and the infamous.

His childhood revolted, and rejected the sweet milk of our nature.

His youth was inflamed like dry grass that burns in the night.

And when He became man, He took arms against us all.

Such men are conceived in the ebb tide of human kindness, and born in unholy tempests. And in tempests they live a day and then perish forever.

Do you not remember Him, a boy overweening, who would argue with our learned elders, and laugh at their dignity?

And remember you not His youth, when He lived by the saw and the chisel? He would not accompany our sons and daughters on their holidays. He would walk alone.

And He would not return the salutation of those who hailed Him, as though He were above us.

I myself met Him once in the field and greeted Him, and He only smiled, and in His smile I beheld arrogance and insult.

Not long afterwards my daughter went with her companions to the vineyards to gather the grapes, and she too spoke to Him and He did not answer her.

He spoke only to the whole company of grape-gatherers, as if my daughter had not been among them.

When He abandoned His people and turned vagabond He became naught but a babbler. His voice was like a claw in our flesh, and the sound of His voice is still a pain in our memory.

He would utter only evil of us and of our fathers and fore-fathers. And His tongue sought our bosoms like a poisoned arrow.

Such was Jesus.

If He had been my son, I would have committed Him with the Roman legions to Arabia, and I would have begged the captain to place Him in the forefront of the battle, so that the archer of the foe might mark Him, and free me of His insolence.

But I have no son. And mayhap I should be grateful. For what if my son had been an enemy of his own people, and my grey hairs were now seeking the dust with shame, my white beard humbled?

MANY ARE THE fools who say that Jesus stood in His own path and opposed Himself; that He knew not His own mind, and in the absence of that knowledge confounded Himself.

Many indeed are the owls who know no song unlike their own hooting.

You and I know the jugglers of words who would honour only a greater juggler, men who carry their heads in baskets to the market-place and sell them to the first bidder.

We know the pygmies who abuse the sky-man. And we know what the weed would say of the oak tree and the cedar.

I pity them that they cannot rise to the heights.

I pity the shrivelling thorn envying the elm that dares the seasons.

But pity, though enfolded by the regret of all the angels, can bring them no light.

I know the scarecrow whose rotting garments flutter in the corn, yet he himself is dead to the corn and to the singing wind.

I know the wingless spider that weaves a net for all who fly.

I know the crafty, the blowers of horns and the beaters of drums, who in the abundance of their own noise cannot hear the skylark nor the east wind in the forest.

I know him who paddles against all streams, but never finds the source, who runs with all rivers, but never dares to the sea.

I know him who offers his unskilled hands to the builder of the temple, and when his unskilled hands are rejected, says in the darkness of his heart, "I will destroy all that shall be builded."

I know all these. They are the men who object that Jesus said on a certain day, "I bring peace unto you," and on another day, "I bring a sword."

They cannot understand that in truth he said, "I bring peace unto men of goodwill, and I lay a sword between him who would peace and him who would a sword."

They wonder that He who said, "My kingdom is not of this earth," said also, "Render unto Cæsar that which is Cæsar's"; and know not that if they would indeed be free to enter the kingdom of their passion, they must not resist the gate-keeper of their necessities. It behooves them gladly to pay that dole to enter into that city.

These are the men who say, "He preached tenderness and kindliness and filial love, yet He would not heed His mother and His brothers when they sought Him in the streets of Jerusalem."

They do not know that His mother and brothers in their loving fear would have had Him return to the bench of the carpenter, whereas He was opening our eyes to the dawn of a new day.

His mother and His brothers would have had Him live in the shadow of death, but He Himself was challenging death upon yonder hill that He might live in our sleepless memory.

I know these moles that dig paths to nowhere. Are they not the ones who accuse Jesus of glorifying Himself in that He said to the multitude, "I am the path and the gate to salvation," and even called Himself the life and the resurrection.

But Jesus was not claiming more than the month of May claims in her high tide.

Was He not to tell the shining truth because it was so shining?

He indeed said that He was the way and the life and the resurrection of the heart; and I myself am a testimony to His truth.

Do you not remember me, Nicodemus, who believed in naught but the laws and decrees and was in continual subjection to observances?

And behold me now, a man who walks with life and laughs with the sun from the first moment it smiles upon the mountain until it yields itself to bed behind the hills.

Why do you halt before the word *salvation*? I myself through Him have attained my salvation.

I care not for what shall befall me tomorrow, for I know that Jesus quickened my sleep and made my distant dreams my companions and my roadfellows.

Am I less man because I believe in a greater man?

The barriers of flesh and bone fell down when the Poet of Galilee spoke to me; and I was held by a spirit, and was lifted to the heights, and in mid-air my wings gathered the song of passion.

And when I dismounted from the wind and in the Sanhedrin my pinions were shorn, even then my ribs, my featherless wings, kept and guarded the song. And all the poverties of the lowlands cannot rob me of my treasure.

I have said enough. Let the deaf bury the humming of life in their dead ears. I am content with the sound of His lyre, which He held and struck while the hands of His body were nailed and bleeding.

THERE WERE TWO streams running in the heart of the Nazarene: the stream of kinship to God whom He called Father, and the stream of rapture which He called the kingdom of the Above-world.

And in my solitude I thought of Him and I followed these two streams in His heart. Upon the banks of the one I met my own soul; and sometimes my soul was a beggar and a wanderer, and sometimes it was a princess in her garden.

Then I followed the other stream in His heart, and on my way I met one who had been beaten and robbed of his gold, and he was smiling. And farther on I saw the robber who had robbed him, and there were unshed tears upon his face.

Then I heard the murmur of these two streams in my own bosom also, and I was gladdened.

When I visited Jesus the day before Pontius Pilatus and the elders laid hands on Him, we talked long, and I asked Him many questions, and He answered my questionings with graciousness; and when I left Him I knew He was the Lord and Master of this our earth.

It is long since the cedar tree has fallen, but its fragrance endures, and will forever seek the four corners of the earth.

HE AND HIS friends were in the grove of pines beyond my hedge, and He was talking to them.

I stood near the hedge and listened. And I knew who He was, for His fame had reached these shores ere He Himself visited them.

When He ceased speaking I approached Him, and I said, "Sir, come with these men and honour me and my roof."

And He smiled upon me and said, "Not this day, my friend. Not this day."

And there was a blessing in His words, and His voice enfolded me like a garment on a cold night.

Then He turned to His friends and said, "Behold a man who deems us not strangers, and though He has not seen us ere this day, he bids us to His threshold.

"Verily in my kingdom there are no strangers. Our life is but the life of all other men, given us that we may know all men, and in that knowledge love them.

"The deeds of all men are but our deeds, both the hidden and the revealed.

"I charge you not to be one self but rather many selves, the householder and the homeless, the ploughman and the sparrow that picks the grain ere it slumber in the earth, the giver who gives in gratitude, and the receiver who receives in pride and recognition.

"The beauty of the day is not only in what you see, but in what other men see.

"For this I have chosen you from among the many who have chosen me."

Then He turned to me again and smiled and said, "I say these things to you also, and you also shall remember them."

Then I entreated Him and said, "Master, will you not visit in my house?"

And He answered, "I know your heart, and I have visited your larger house."

And as He walked away with His disciples He said, "Good-night, and may your house be large enough to shelter all the wanderers of the land."

MARY MAGDALEN

HIS MOUTH WAS like the heart of a pomegranate, and the shadows in His eyes were deep.

And He was gentle, like a man mindful of his own strength.

In my dreams I beheld the kings of the earth standing in awe in His presence.

I would speak of His face, but how shall I?

It was like night without darkness, and like day without the noise of day.

It was a sad face, and it was a joyous face.

And well I remember how once He raised His hand towards the sky, and His parted fingers were like the branches of an elm.

And I remember Him pacing the evening. He was not walking. He Himself was a road above the road; even as a cloud above the earth that would descend to refresh the earth.

But when I stood before Him and spoke to Him, He was a man, and His face was powerful to behold. And He said to me, "What would you, Miriam?"

I did not answer Him, but my wings enfolded my secret, and I was made warm.

And because I could bear His light no more, I turned and walked away, but not in shame. I was only shy, and I would be alone, with His fingers upon the strings of my heart.

JOTHAM OF NAZARETH TO A ROMAN

MY FRIEND, YOU like all other Romans would conceive life rather than live it. You would rule lands rather than be ruled by the spirit.

You would conquer races and be cursed by them rather than stay in Rome and be blest and happy.

You think but of armies marching and of ships launched into the sea.

How shall you then understand Jesus of Nazareth, a man simple and alone, who came without armies or ships, to establish a kingdom in the heart and an empire in the free spaces of the soul?

How shall you understand this man who was not a warrior, but who came with the power of the mighty ether?

He was not a god, He was a man like unto ourselves; but in Him the myrrh of the earth rose to meet the frankincense of the sky; and in His words our lisping embraced the whispering of the unseen; and in His voice we heard a song unfathomable.

Aye, Jesus was a man and not a god, and therein lies our wonder and our surprise.

But you Romans wonder not save at the gods, and no man shall surprise you. Therefore you understand not the Nazarene.

He belonged to the youth of the mind and you belong to its old age.

You govern us today; but let us wait another day.

Who knows but that this man with neither armies nor ships shall govern tomorrow?

We who follow the spirit shall sweat blood while journeying after Him. But Rome shall lie a white skeleton in the sun.

We shall suffer much, yet we shall endure and we shall live. But Rome must needs fall into the dust.

Yet if Rome, when humbled and made low, shall pronounce

His name, He will heed her voice. And He will breathe new life into her bones that she may rise again, a city among the cities of the earth.

But this He shall do without legions, nor with slaves to oar His galleys. He will be alone.

EPHRAIM OF JERICHO

WHEN HE CAME again to Jericho I sought Him out and said to Him, "Master, on the morrow my son will take a wife. I beg you come to the wedding-feast and do us honour, even as you honoured the wedding at Cana of Galilee."

And He answered, "It is true that I was once a guest at a wedding-feast, but I shall not be a guest again. I am myself now the Bridegroom."

And I said, "I entreat you, Master, come to the wedding-feast of my son."

And He smiled as though He would rebuke me, and said, "Why do you entreat me? Have you not wine enough?"

And I said, "My jugs are full, Master; yet I beseech you, come to my son's wedding-feast."

Then He said, "Who knows? I may come, I may surely come, if your heart is an altar in your temple."

Upon the morrow my son was married, but Jesus came not to the wedding-feast. And though we had many guests, I felt that no one had come.

In very truth, I myself who welcomed the guests, was not there.

Perhaps my heart had not been an altar when I invited Him. Perhaps I desired another miracle.

BARCA, A MERCHANT OF TYRE

I BELIEVE THAT neither the Romans nor the Jews understood Jesus of Nazareth, nor did His disciples who now preach His name.

The Romans slew Him and that was a blunder. The Galileans would make a god of Him and that is a mistake.

Jesus was of the heart of man.

I have sailed the Seven Seas with my ships, and bartered with kings and princes and with cheats and the wily in the market-places of distant cities; but never have I seen a man who understood merchants as He did.

I heard Him once tell this parable:

"A merchant left his country for a foreign land. He had two servants, and he gave each a handful of gold, saying: 'Even as I go abroad, you also shall go forth and seek profit. Make just exchange, and see that you serve in giving and taking.'

"And after a year the merchant returned.

"And he asked his two servants what they had done with his gold.

"The first servant said, 'Behold, Master, I have bought and sold, and I have gained.'

"And the merchant answered, 'The gain shall be yours, for you have done well, and have been faithful to me and to yourself.'

"Then the other servant stood forth and said, 'Sir, I feared the loss of your money; and I did not buy nor sell. Behold, it is all here in this purse.'

"And the merchant took the gold, and said, 'Little is your faith. To barter and lose is better than not to go forth. For even as the wind scatters her seed and waits for the fruit, so must all merchants. It were fitter for you henceforth to serve others.' "

When Jesus spoke thus, though He was no merchant, He disclosed the secret of commerce.

Moreover, His parables often brought to my mind lands more distant than my journeys, and yet nearer than my house and my goods.

But the young Nazarene was not a god; and it is a pity His followers seek to make a god of such a sage.

PHUMIAH THE HIGH PRIESTESS OF SIDON

TAKE YOUR HARPS and let me sing.
Beat your strings, the silver and the gold;
For I would sing the dauntless Man
Who slew the dragon of the valley,
Then gazèd down with pity
Upon the thing He had slain.

Take your harps and sing with me
The lofty Oak upon the height,
The sky-hearted and the ocean-handed Man,
Who kissed the pallid lips of death,
Yet quivers now upon the mouth of life.

Take your harps and let us sing
The fearless Hunter on the hill,
Who marked the beast, and shot His viewless arrow,
And brought the horn and tusk
Down to the earth.

Take your harps and sing with me
The valiant Youth who conquered the mountain cities,
And the cities of the plain that coiled like serpents in the sand.
He fought not against pygmies but against gods
Who hungered for our flesh and thirsted for our blood.

And like the first Golden Hawk
He would rival only eagles;
For His wings were vast and proud
And would not outwing the less wingèd.

Take your harps and sing with me
The joyous song of sea and cliff.
The gods are dead,
And they are lying still
In the forgotten isle of a forgotten sea.
And He who slew them sits upon His throne.

He was but a youth.
Spring had not yet given Him full beard,
And His summer was still young in His field.

Take your harps and sing with me
The tempest in the forest
That breaks the dry branch and the leafless twig,
Yet sends the living root to nestle deeper at the breast of earth.

Take your harps and sing with me
The deathless song of our Belovèd.
Nay, my maidens, stay your hands.
Lay by your harps.
We cannot sing Him now.
The faint whisper of our song cannot reach His tempest,
Nor pierce the majesty of His silence.

Lay by your harps and gather close around me.
I would repeat His words to you,
And I would tell you of His deeds,
For the echo of His voice is deeper than our passion.

IT HAS BEEN said that Jesus was the enemy of Rome and Judea.

But I say that Jesus was the enemy of no man and no race.

I have heard Him say, "The birds of the air and the mountain tops are not mindful of the serpents in their dark holes.

"Let the dead bury their dead. Be you yourself among the living, and soar high."

I was not one of His disciples. I was but one of the many who went after Him to gaze at His face.

He looked upon Rome and upon us who are the slaves of Rome, as a father looks upon his children playing with toys and fighting among themselves for the larger toy. And He laughed from His height.

He was greater than State and race; He was greater than revolution.

He was single and alone, and He was an awakening.

He wept all our unshed tears and smiled all our revolts.

We knew it was in His power to be born with all who are not yet born, and to bid them see, not with their eyes but with His vision.

Jesus was the beginning of a new kingdom upon the earth, and that kingdom shall remain.

He was the son and the grandson of all the kings who builded the kingdom of the spirit.

And only the kings of spirit have ruled our world.

YOU BELIEVE IN what you hear said. Believe in the unsaid, for the silence of men is nearer the truth than their words.

You ask if Jesus could have escaped His shameful death and saved His followers from persecution.

I answer, He could indeed have escaped had He chosen, but He did not seek safety nor was He mindful of protecting His flock from wolves of the night.

He knew His fate and the morrow of His constant lovers. He foretold and prophesied what should befall every one of us. He sought not His death; but He accepted death as a husbandman shrouding his corn with earth, accepts the winter, and then awaits the spring and harvest; and as a builder lays the largest stone in the foundation.

We were men of Galilee and from the slopes of Lebanon. Our Master could have led us back to our country, to live with His youth in our gardens until old age should come and whisper us back into the years.

Was anything barring His path back to the temples of our villages where others were reading the prophets and then disclosing their hearts?

Could He not have said, "Now I go east with the west wind," and so saying dismiss us with a smile upon His lips?

Aye, He could have said, "Go back to your kin. The world is not ready for me. I shall return a thousand years hence. Teach your children to await my return."

He could have done this had He so chosen.

But He knew that to build the temple invisible He must needs lay Himself the corner-stone, and lay us around as little pebbles cemented close to Himself.

He knew that the sap of His sky-tree must rise from its roots, and He poured His blood upon its roots; and to Him it was not sacrifice but rather gain.

Death is the revealer. The death of Jesus revealed His life.

Had He escaped you and His enemies, you would have been the conquerors of the world. Therefore He did not escape.

Only He who desires all shall give all.

Aye, Jesus could have escaped His enemies and lived to old age. But He knew the passing of the seasons, and He would sing His song.

What man facing the armed world would not be conquered for the moment that he might overcome the ages?

And now you ask who, in very truth, slew Jesus, the Romans or the priests of Jerusalem?

Neither the Romans slew Him, nor the priests. The whole world stood to honour Him upon that hill.

JONATHAN

UPON A DAY my belovèd and I were rowing upon the lake of
sweet waters. And the hills of Lebanon were about us.

We moved beside the weeping willows, and the reflections of
the willows were deep around us.

And while I steered the boat with an oar, my belovèd took
her lute and sang thus:

What flower save the lotus knows the waters and the sun?
What heart save the lotus heart shall know both earth and sky?
Behold my love, the golden flower that floats 'twixt deep
    and high
Even as you and I float betwixt a love that has for ever been
And shall for ever be.

Dip your oar, my love,
And let me touch my strings.
Let us follow the willows, and let us leave not the
    water-lilies.
In Nazareth there lives a Poet, and His heart is like the lotus.
He has visited the soul of woman,
He knows her thirst growing out of the waters,
And her hunger for the sun, though all her lips are fed.
They say He walks in Galilee.
I say He is rowing with us.
Can you not see His face, my love?
Can you not see, where the willow bough and its reflection
    meet,
He is moving as we move?

Belovèd, it is good to know the youth of life.
It is good to know its singing joy.

Would that you might always have the oar
And I my stringèd lute,
Where the lotus laughs in the sun,
And the willow is dipping to the waters,
And His voice is upon my strings.

Dip your oar, my belovèd,
And let me touch my strings.
There is a Poet in Nazareth
Who knows and loves us both.
Dip your oar, my lover,
And let me touch my strings.

HANNAH OF BETHSAIDA

THE SISTER OF my father had left us in her youth to dwell in a hut beside her father's ancient vineyard.

She lived alone, and the people of the countryside sought her in their maladies, and she healed them with green herbs, and with roots and flowers dried in the sun.

And they deemed her a seeress; but there were those also who called her witch and sorceress.

One day my father said to me, "Take these loaves of wheaten bread to my sister, and take this jug of wine and this basket of raisins."

And it was all put upon the back of a colt, and I followed the road until I reached the vineyard, and the hut of my father's sister. And she was gladdened.

Now as we sat together in the cool of the day, a man came by upon the road, and He greeted the sister of my father, saying: "Good-even to you, and the blessing of the night be upon you."

Then she rose up; and she stood as in awe before Him and said, "Good-even to you, master of all good spirits, and conqueror of all evil spirits."

The man looked at her with tender eyes, and then He passed on by.

But I laughed in my heart. Methought my father's sister was mad. But now I know that she was not mad. It was I who did not understand.

She knew of my laughter, though it was hidden.

And she spoke, but not in anger. She said, "Listen, my daughter, and hearken and keep my word in remembrance: the man who but now passed by, like the shadow of a bird flying between the sun and the earth, shall prevail against the Cæsars and the empire of the Cæsars. He shall wrestle with the crowned bull of Chaldea, and the man-headed lion of Egypt, and He shall overcome them; and He shall rule the world.

"But this land that now He walks shall come to naught; and Jerusalem, which sits proudly upon the hill, shall drift away in smoke upon the wind of desolation."

When she spoke thus, my laughter turned to stillness and I was quiet. Then I said, "Who is this man, and of what country and tribe does He come? And how shall He conquer the great kings and the empires of the great kings?"

And she answered, "He is one born here in this land, but we have conceived Him in our longing from the beginning of years. He is of all tribes and yet of none. He shall conquer by the word of His mouth and by the flame of His spirit."

Then suddenly she rose and stood up like a pinnacle of rock; and she said, "May the angel of the Lord forgive me for pronouncing this word also: He shall be slain, and His youth shall be shrouded, and He shall be laid in silence beside the tongueless heart of the earth. And the maidens of Judea shall weep for Him."

Then she lifted her hand skyward and spoke again, and she said, "But He shall be slain only in the body.

"In the spirit He shall rise and go forth leading His host from this land where the sun is born, to the land where the sun is slain at eventide.

"And His name shall be first among men."

She was an aged seeress when she said these things, and I was but a girl, a field unploughed, a stone not yet in a wall.

But all that she beheld in the mirror of her mind has come to pass even in my day.

Jesus of Nazareth rose from the dead and led men and women unto the people of the sunset. The city that yielded Him to judgment was given unto destruction; and in the Judgment Hall where He was tried and sentenced, the owl hoots a dirge while the night weeps the dew of her heart upon the fallen marble.

And I am an old woman, and the years bend me down. My people are no more and my race is vanished.

I saw Him but once again after that day, and once again heard His voice. It was upon a hill-top when He was talking to His friends and followers.

And now I am old and alone, yet still He visits my dreams.

He comes like a white angel with pinions; and with His grace He hushes my dread of darkness. And He uplifts me to dreams yet more distant.

I am still a field unploughed, a ripe fruit that would not fall. The most that I possess is the warmth of the sun, and the memory of that man.

I know that among my people there shall not rise again king nor prophet nor priest, even as the sister of my father foretold.

We shall pass with the flowing of the rivers, and we shall be nameless.

But those who crossed Him in mid-stream shall be remembered for crossing Him in mid-stream.

MANASSEH, A LAWYER IN JERUSALEM

YES, I USED to hear Him speak. There was always a ready word upon His lips.

But I admired Him as a man rather than as a leader. He preached something beyond my liking, perhaps beyond my reason. And I would have no man preach to me.

I was taken by His voice and His gestures, but not by the substance of His speech. He charmed me but never convinced me; for He was too vague, too distant and obscure to reach my mind.

I have known other men like Him. They are never constant nor are they consistent. It is with eloquence not with principles that they hold your ear and your passing thought, but never the core of your heart.

What a pity that His enemies confronted Him and forced the issue. It was not necessary. I believe their hostility will add to His stature and turn His mildness to power.

For is it not strange that in opposing a man you give Him courage? And in staying His feet you give Him wings?

I know not His enemies, yet I am certain that in their fear of a harmless man they have lent Him strength and made Him dangerous.

JEPHTHA OF CÆSAREA

THIS MAN WHO fills your day and haunts your night is repellent to me. Yet you would tire my ears with His sayings and my mind with His deeds.

I am weary of His words, and all that He did. His very name offends me, and the name of His countryside. I will none of Him.

Why make you a prophet of a man who was but a shadow? Why see a tower in this sand-dune, or imagine a lake in the raindrops gathered together in this hoof-print?

I scorn not the echo of caves in valleys nor the long shadows of the sunset; but I would not listen to the deceptions that hum in your head, nor study the reflections in your eyes.

What word did Jesus utter that Halliel had not spoken? What wisdom did He reveal that was not of Gamaliel? What are His lispings to the voice of Philo? What cymbals did He beat that were not beaten ere ever He lived?

I hearken to the echo from the caves into the silent valleys, and I gaze upon the long shadows of sunset; but I would not have this man's heart echo the sound of another heart, nor would I have a shadow of the seers call himself a prophet.

What man shall speak since Isaiah has spoken? Who dares sing since David? And shall wisdom be born now, after Solomon has been gathered to his fathers?

And what of our prophets, whose tongues were swords and their lips flames?

Left they a straw behind for this gleaner of Galilee? Or a fallen fruit for the beggar from the North Country? There was naught for Him save to break the loaf already baked by our ancestors, and to pour the wine which their holy feet had already pressed from the grapes of old.

It is the potter's hand I honour not the man who buys the ware.

I honour those who sit at the loom rather than the boor who wears the cloth.

Who was this Jesus of Nazareth, and what is He? A man who dared not live His mind. Therefore He faded into oblivion and that is His end.

I beg you, charge not my ears with His words or His deeds. My heart is overfull with the prophets of old, and that is enough.

YOU WOULD HAVE me speak of Jesus, but how can I lure the passion-song of the world into a hollowed reed?

In every aspect of the day Jesus was aware of the Father. He beheld Him in the clouds and in the shadows of the clouds that pass over the earth. He saw the Father's face reflected in the quiet pools, and the faint print of His feet upon the sand; and He often closed His eyes to gaze into the Holy Eyes.

The night spoke to Him with the voice of the Father, and in solitude He heard the angel of the Lord calling to Him. And when He stilled Himself to sleep He heard the whispering of the heavens in His dreams.

He was often happy with us, and He would call us brothers.

Behold, He who was the first Word called us brothers, though we were but syllables uttered yesterday.

You ask why I call Him the first Word.

Listen, and I will answer:

In the beginning God moved in space, and out of His measureless stirring the earth was born and the seasons thereof.

Then God moved again, and life streamed forth, and the longing of life sought the height and the depth and would have more of itself.

Then God spoke, and His words were man, and man was a spirit begotten by God's Spirit.

And when God spoke thus, the Christ was His first Word and that Word was perfect; and when Jesus of Nazareth came to the world the first Word was uttered unto us and the sound was made flesh and blood.

Jesus the Anointed was the first Word of God uttered unto man, even as if an apple tree in an orchard should bud and blossom a day before the other trees. And in God's orchard that day was an æon.

We are all sons and daughters of the Most High, but the Anointed One was His first-born, who dwelt in the body of Jesus of Nazareth, and He walked among us and we beheld Him.

All this I say that you may understand not only in the mind but rather in the spirit. The mind weighs and measures but it is the spirit that reaches the heart of life and embraces the secret; and the seed of the spirit is deathless.

The wind may blow and then cease, and the sea shall swell and then weary, but the heart of life is a sphere quiet and serene, and the star that shines therein is fixed for evermore.

THE JEWS, LIKE their neighbours the Phœnicians and the Arabs, will not suffer their gods to rest for a moment upon the wind.

They are over-thoughtful of their deity, and over-observant of one another's prayer and worship and sacrifice.

While we Romans build marble temples to our gods, these people would discuss their god's nature. When we are in ecstasy we sing and dance round the altars of Jupiter and Juno, of Mars and Venus; but they in their rapture wear sackcloth and cover their heads with ashes — and even lament the day that gave them birth.

And Jesus, the man who revealed God as a being of joy, they tortured Him, and then put Him to death.

These people would not be happy with a happy god. They know only the gods of their pain.

Even Jesus' friends and disciples who knew His mirth and heard His laughter, make an image of His sorrow, and they worship that image.

And in such worship they rise not to their deity; they only bring their deity down to themselves.

I believe however that this philosopher, Jesus, who was not unlike Socrates, will have power over His race and mayhap over other races.

For we are all creatures of sadness and of small doubts. And when a man says to us, "Let us be joyous with the gods," we cannot but heed his voice. Strange that the pain of this man has been fashioned into a rite.

These peoples would discover another Adonis, a god slain in the forest, and they would celebrate his slaying. It is a pity they heed not His laughter.

But let us confess, as Roman to Greek. Do even we ourselves hear the laughter of Socrates in the streets of Athens? Is it ever in us to forget the cup of hemlock, even at the theatre of Dionysus?

Do not rather our fathers still stop at the street corners to chat of troubles and to have a happy moment remembering the doleful end of all our great men?

PONTIUS PILATUS

MY WIFE SPOKE of Him many times ere He was brought before me, but I was not concerned.

My wife is a dreamer, and she is given, like so many Roman women of her rank, to Eastern cults and rituals. And these cults are dangerous to the Empire; and when they find a path to the hearts of our women they become destructive.

Egypt came to an end when the Hyksos of Arabia brought to her the one God of their desert. And Greece was overcome and fell to dust when Ashtarte and her seven maidens came from the Syrian shores.

As for Jesus, I never saw the man before He was delivered up to me as a malefactor, as an enemy of His own nation and also of Rome.

He was brought into the Hall of Judgment with His arms bound to His body with ropes.

I was sitting upon the dais, and He walked towards me with long, firm steps; then He stood erect and His head was held high.

And I cannot fathom what came over me at that moment; but it was suddenly my desire, though not my will, to rise and go down from the dais and fall before Him.

I felt as if Cæsar had entered the Hall, a man greater than even Rome herself.

But this lasted only a moment. And then I saw simply a man who was accused of treason by His own people. And I was His governor and His judge.

I questioned Him but He would not answer. He only looked at me. And in His look was pity, as if it were He who was my governor and my judge.

Then there rose from without the cries of the people. But

He remained silent, and still He was looking at me with pity in His eyes.

And I went out upon the steps of the palace, and when the people saw me they ceased to cry out. And I said, "What would you with this man?"

And they shouted as if with one throat, "We would crucify Him. He is our enemy and the enemy of Rome."

And some called out, "Did He not say He would destroy the temple? And was it not He who claimed the kingdom? We will have no king but Cæsar."

Then I left them and went back into the Judgment Hall again, and I saw Him still standing there alone, and His head was still high.

And I remembered what I had read that a Greek philosopher said: "The lonely man is the strongest man." At that moment the Nazarene was greater than His race.

And I did not feel clement towards Him. He was beyond my clemency.

I asked Him then, "Are you the King of the Jews?"

And He said not a word.

And I asked Him again, "Have you not said that you are the King of the Jews?"

And He looked upon me.

Then He answered with a quiet voice, "You yourself proclaimed me king. Perhaps to this end I was born, and for this cause came to bear witness unto truth."

Behold a man speaking of *truth* at such a moment.

In my impatience I said aloud, to myself as much as to Him, "What is truth? And what is truth to the guiltless when the hand of the executioner is already upon him?"

Then Jesus said with power, "None shall rule the world save with the Spirit and truth."

And I asked Him saying, "Are you of the Spirit?"

He answered, "So are you also, though you know it not."

And what was the Spirit and what was truth, when I, for the sake of the State, and they from jealousy for their ancient rites, delivered an innocent man unto His death?

No man, no race, no empire would halt before a truth on its way towards self-fulfilment.

And I said again, "Are you the King of the Jews?"

And He answered, "You yourself say this. I have conquered the world ere this hour."

And this alone of all that He said was unseemly, inasmuch as only Rome had conquered the world.

But now the voices of the people rose again, and the noise was greater than before.

And I descended from my seat and said to Him, "Follow me."

And again I appeared upon the steps of the palace, and He stood there beside me.

When the people saw Him they roared like the roaring thunder. And in their clamour I heard naught save "Crucify Him, crucify Him."

Then I yielded Him to the priests who had yielded Him to me and I said to them, "Do what you will with this just man. And if it is in your desire, take with you soldiers of Rome to guard Him."

Then they took Him, and I decreed that there be written upon the cross above His head, "Jesus of Nazareth, King of the Jews." I should have said instead, "Jesus of Nazareth, a King."

And the man was stripped and flogged and crucified.

It would have been within my power to save Him, but saving Him would have caused a revolution; and it is always wise for the governor of a Roman province not to be intolerant of the religious scruples of a conquered race.

I believe unto this hour that the man was more than an agitator. What I decreed was not my will, but rather for the sake of Rome.

Not long after, we left Syria, and from that day my wife has been a woman of sorrow. Sometimes even here in this garden I see a tragedy in her face.

I am told she talks much of Jesus to other women of Rome.

Behold, the man whose death I decreed returns from the world of shadows and enters into my own house.

And within myself I ask again and again, What is truth and what is not truth?

Can it be that the Syrian is conquering us in the quiet hours of the night?

It should not indeed be so.

For Rome must needs prevail against the nightmares of our wives.

BARTHOLOMEW IN EPHESUS

THE ENEMIES OF Jesus say that He addressed His appeal to slaves and outcasts, and would have incited them against their lords. They say that because He was of the lowly He invoked His own kind, yet that He sought to conceal His own origin.

But let us consider the followers of Jesus, and His leadership.

In the beginning He chose for companions a few men from the North Country, and they were freemen. They were strong of body and bold of spirit, and in these past twoscore years they have had the courage to face death with willingness and defiance.

Think you that these men were slaves or outcasts?

And think you that the proud princes of Lebanon and Armenia have forgotten their station in accepting Jesus as a prophet of God?

Or think you the high-born men and women of Antioch and Byzantium and Athens and Rome could be held by the voice of a leader of slaves?

Nay, the Nazarene was not with the servant against his master; neither was He with the master against his servant. He was with no man against another man.

He was a man above men, and the streams that ran in His sinews sang together with passion and with might.

If nobility lies in being protective, He was the noblest of all men. If freedom is in thought and word and action, He was the freest of all men. If high birth is in pride that yields only to love and in aloofness that is ever gentle and gracious, then He was of all men the highest born.

Forget not that only the strong and the swift shall win the race and the laurels, and that Jesus was crowned by those who loved Him, and also by His enemies though they knew it not.

Even now He is crowned every day by the priestess of Artemis in the secret places of her temple.

MATTHEW

UPON AN EVENING Jesus passed by a prison that was in the Tower of David. And we were walking after Him.

Of a sudden He tarried and laid His cheek against the stones of the prison wall. And thus He spoke:

"Brothers of my ancient day, my heart beats with your hearts behind the bars. Would that you could be free in my freedom and walk with me and my comrades.

"You are confined, but not alone. Many are the prisoners who walk the open streets. Their wings are not shorn, but like the peacock they flutter yet cannot fly.

"Brothers of my second day, I shall soon visit you in your cells and yield my shoulder to your burden. For the innocent and the guilty are not parted, and like the two bones of the forearm they shall never be cleaved.

"Brothers of this day, which is my day, you swam against the current of their reasoning and you were caught. They say I too swim against that current. Perhaps I shall soon be with you, a law-breaker among law-breakers.

"Brothers of a day not yet come, these walls shall fall down, and out of the stones other shapes shall be fashioned by Him whose mallet is light, and whose chisel is the wind, and you shall stand free in the freedom of my new day."

Thus spoke Jesus and He walked on, and His hand was upon the prison wall until He passed by the Tower of David.

ANDREW

THE BITTERNESS OF death is less bitter than life without Him. The days were hushed and made still when He was silenced. Only the echo in my memory repeats His words. But not His voice.

Once I heard Him say: "Go forth in your longing to the fields, and sit by the lilies, and you shall hear them humming in the sun. They weave not cloth for raiment, nor do they raise wood or stone for shelter; yet they sing.

"He who works in the night fulfils their needs and the dew of His grace is upon their petals.

"And are not you also His care who never wearies nor rests?"

And once I heard Him say, "The birds of the sky are counted and enrolled by your Father even as the hairs of your head are numbered. Not a bird shall lie at the archer's feet, neither shall a hair of your head turn grey or fall into the emptiness of age without His will."

And once again He said, "I have heard you murmur in your hearts: 'Our God shall be more merciful unto us, children of Abraham, than unto those who knew Him not in the beginning.'

"But I say unto you that the owner of the vineyard who calls a labourer in the morning to reap, and calls another at sundown, and yet renders wages to the last even as to the first, that man is indeed justified. Does he not pay out of his own purse and with his own will?

"So shall my Father open the gate of His mansion at the knocking of the Gentiles even as at your knocking. For His ear heeds the new melody with the same love that it feels for the oft-heard song. And with a special welcome because it is the youngest string of His heart."

And once again I heard Him say, "Remember this: a thief is a man in need, a liar is a man in fear; the hunter who is hunted by the watchman of your night is also hunted by the watchman of his own darkness.

"I would have you pity them all.

"Should they seek your house, see that you open your door and bid them sit at your board. If you do not accept them you shall not be free from whatever they have committed."

And on a day I followed Him to the market-place of Jerusalem as the others followed Him. And He told us the parable of the prodigal son, and the parable of the merchant who sold all his possessions that he might buy a pearl.

But as He was speaking the Pharisees brought into the midst of the crowd a woman whom they called a harlot. And they confronted Jesus and said to Him, "She defiled her marriage vow, and she was taken in the act."

And He gazed at her; and He placed His hand upon her forehead and looked deep into her eyes.

Then He turned to the men who had brought her to Him, and He looked long at them; and He leaned down and with His finger He began to write upon the earth.

He wrote the name of every man, and beside the name He wrote the sin that every man had committed.

And as He wrote they escaped in shame into the streets.

And ere He had finished writing only that woman and ourselves stood before Him.

And again He looked into her eyes, and He said, "You have loved overmuch. They who brought you here loved but little. But they brought you as a snare for my ensnaring.

"And now go in peace.

"None of them is here to judge you. And if it is in your desire to be wise even as you are loving, then seek me; for the Son of Man will not judge you."

And I wondered then whether He said this to her because He Himself was not without sin.

But since that day I have pondered long, and I know now that only the pure of heart forgive the thirst that leads to dead waters.

And only the sure of foot can give a hand to him who stumbles.

And again and yet again I say, the bitterness of death is less bitter than life without Him.

A RICH MAN

HE SPOKE ILL of rich men. And upon a day I questioned Him saying, "Sir, what shall I do to attain the peace of the spirit?"

And He bade me give my possessions to the poor and follow Him.

But He possessed nothing; therefore He knew not the assurance and the freedom of possessions, nor the dignity and the self-respect that lie within.

In my household there are sevenscore slaves and stewards; some labour in my groves and vineyards, and some direct my ships to distant isles.

Now had I heeded Him and given my possessions to the poor, what would have befallen my slaves and my servants and their wives and children? They too would have become beggars at the gate of the city or the portico of the temple.

Nay that good man did not fathom the secret of possessions. Because He and His followers lived on the bounty of others He thought all men should live likewise.

Behold a contradiction and a riddle: Should rich men bestow their riches upon the poor, and must the poor have the cup and the loaf of the rich man ere they welcome him to their board?

And must needs the holder of the tower be host to his tenants ere he calls himself lord of his own land?

The ant that stores food for the winter is wiser than a grasshopper that sings one day and hungers another.

Last sabbath one of His followers said in the market-place, "At the threshold of heaven where Jesus may leave His sandals, no other man is worthy to lay his head."

But I ask, at the threshold of whose house that honest vagabond could have left His sandals? He Himself never had a house nor a threshold; and often He went without sandals.

JOHN AT PATMOS

ONCE MORE I would speak of Him.

God gave me the voice and the burning lips though not the speech.

And unworthy am I for the fuller word, yet I would summon my heart to my lips.

Jesus loved me and I knew not why.

And I loved Him because He quickened my spirit to heights beyond my stature, and to depths beyond my sounding.

Love is a sacred mystery.

To those who love, it remains forever wordless;

But to those who do not love, it may be but a heartless jest.

Jesus called me and my brother when we were labouring in the field.

I was young then and only the voice of dawn had visited my ears.

But His voice and the trumpet of His voice was the end of my labour and the beginning of my passion.

And there was naught for me then but to walk in the sun and worship the loveliness of the hour.

Could you conceive a majesty too kind to be majestic? And a beauty too radiant to seem beautiful?

Could you hear in your dreams a voice shy of its own rapture?

He called me and I followed Him.

That evening I returned to my father's house to get my other cloak.

And I said to my mother, "Jesus of Nazareth would have me in His company."

And she said, "Go His way, my son, even like your brother."

And I accompanied Him.

His fragrance called me and commanded me, but only to release me.

Love is a gracious host to his guests though to the unbidden his house is a mirage and a mockery.

*

Now you would have me explain the miracles of Jesus.

We are all the miraculous gesture of the moment; our Lord and Master was the centre of that moment.

Yet it was not in His desire that His gestures be known.

I have heard Him say to the lame, "Rise and go home, but say not to the priest that I have made you whole."

And Jesus' mind was not with the cripple; it was rather with the strong and the upright.

His mind sought and held other minds and His complete spirit visited other spirits.

And in so doing His spirit changed these minds and these spirits.

It seemed miraculous, but with our Lord and Master it was simply like breathing the air of every day.

*

And now let me speak of other things.

On a day when He and I were alone walking in a field, we were both hungry, and we came to a wild apple tree.

There were only two apples hanging on the bough.

And He held the trunk of the tree with His arm and shook it, and the two apples fell down.

He picked them both up and gave one to me. The other He held in His hand.

In my hunger I ate the apple, and I ate it fast.

Then I looked at Him and I saw that He still held the other apple in His hand.

And He gave it to me saying, "Eat this also."

And I took the apple, and in my shameless hunger I ate it.

And as we walked on I looked upon His face.

But how shall I tell you of what I saw?

A night where candles burn in space,
A dream beyond our reaching;

A noon where all shepherds are at peace and happy that their
    flocks are grazing;
An eventide, and a stillness, and a home-coming;
Then a sleep and a dream.
All these things I saw in His face.

He had given me the two apples. And I knew He was hungry
even as I was hungry.

But I now know that in giving them to me He had been
satisfied. He Himself ate of other fruit from another tree.

I would tell you more of Him, but how shall I?

When love becomes vast love becomes wordless.

And when memory is overladen it seeks the silent deep.

PETER

ONCE IN CAPERNAUM my Lord and Master spoke thus:

"Your neighbour is your other self dwelling behind a wall. In understanding, all walls shall fall down.

"Who knows but that your neighbour is your better self wearing another body? See that you love him as you would love yourself.

"He too is a manifestation of the Most High, whom you do not know.

"Your neighbour is a field where the springs of your hope walk in their green garments, and where the winters of your desire dream of snowy heights.

"Your neighbour is a mirror wherein you shall behold your countenance made beautiful by a joy which you yourself did not know, and by a sorrow you yourself did not share.

"I would have you love your neighbour even as I have loved you."

Then I asked Him saying, "How can I love a neighbour who loves me not, and who covets my property? One who would steal my possessions?"

And He answered, "When you are ploughing and your man-servant is sowing the seed behind you, would you stop and look backward and put to flight a sparrow feeding upon a few of your seeds? Should you do this, you were not worthy of the riches of your harvest."

When Jesus had said this, I was ashamed and I was silent. But I was not in fear, for He smiled upon me.

A COBBLER IN JERUSALEM

I LOVED HIM not, yet I did not hate Him. I listened to Him not to hear His words but rather the sound of His voice; for His voice pleased me.

All that He said was vague to my mind, but the music thereof was clear to my ear.

Indeed were it not for what others have said to me of His teaching, I should not have known even so much as whether He was with Judea or against it.

SUSANNAH OF NAZARETH

I KNEW MARY the mother of Jesus, before she became the wife of Joseph the carpenter, when we were both still unwedded.

In those days Mary would behold visions and hear voices, and she would speak of heavenly ministers who visited her dreams.

And the people of Nazareth were mindful of her, and they observed her going and her coming. And they gazed upon her with kindly eyes, for there were heights in her brows and spaces in her steps.

But some said she was possessed. They said this because she would go only upon her own errands.

I deemed her old while she was young, for there was a harvest in her blossoming and ripe fruit in her spring.

She was born and reared amongst us yet she was like an alien from the North Country. In her eyes there was always the astonishment of one not yet familiar with our faces.

And she was as haughty as Miriam of old who marched with her brothers from the Nile to the wilderness.

Then Mary was betrothed to Joseph the carpenter.

*

When Mary was big with Jesus she would walk among the hills and return at eventide with loveliness and pain in her eyes.

And when Jesus was born I was told that Mary said to her mother, "I am but a tree unpruned. See you to this fruit." Martha the midwife heard her.

After three days I visited her. And there was wonder in her eyes, and her breasts heaved, and her arm was around her firstborn like the shell that holds the pearl.

We all loved Mary's babe and we watched Him, for there was a warmth in His being and He throbbed with the pace of His life.

367

The seasons passed, and He became a boy full of laughter and little wanderings. None of us knew what He would do for He seemed always outside of our race. But He was never rebuked though He was venturous and over-daring.

He played with the other children rather than they with Him.

When He was twelve years old, one day He led a blind man across the brook to the safety of the open road.

And in gratitude the blind man asked Him, "Little boy, who are you?"

And He answered, "I am not a little boy. I am Jesus."

And the blind man said, "Who is your father?"

And He answered, "God is my Father."

And the blind man laughed and replied, "Well said, my little boy. But who is your mother?"

And Jesus answered, "I am not your little boy. And my mother is the earth."

And the blind man said, "Then behold, I was led by the Son of God and the earth across the stream."

And Jesus answered, "I will lead you wherever you would go, and my eyes will accompany your feet."

And He grew like a precious palm tree in our gardens.

When He was nineteen He was as comely as a hart, and His eyes were like honey and full of the surprise of day.

And upon His mouth there was the thirst of the desert flock for the lake.

He would walk the fields alone and our eyes would follow Him, and the eyes of all the maidens of Nazareth. But we were shy of Him.

Love is forever shy of beauty, yet beauty shall forever be pursued by love.

Then the years bade Him speak in the temple and in the gardens of Galilee.

And at times Mary followed Him to listen to His words and to hear the sound of her own heart. But when He and those who loved Him went down to Jerusalem she would not go.

For we of the North Country are often mocked in the streets

of Jerusalem, even when we go carrying our offerings to the temple.

And Mary was too proud to yield to the South Country.

*

And Jesus visited other lands in the east and in the west. We knew not what lands He visited, yet our hearts followed Him.

But Mary awaited Him upon her threshold, and every eventide her eyes sought the road for His home-coming.

Yet upon His return she would say to us, "He is too vast to be my Son, too eloquent for my silent heart. How shall I claim Him?"

It seemed to us that Mary could not believe that the plain had given birth to the mountain; in the whiteness of her heart she did not see that the ridge is a pathway to the summit.

She knew the man, but because He was her Son she dared not know Him.

And on a day when Jesus went to the lake to be with the fishermen she said to me, "What is man but this restless being that would rise from the earth, and who is man but a longing that desires the stars?

"My son is a longing. He is all of us longing for the stars.

"Did I say my son? May God forgive me. Yet in my heart I would be His mother."

Now, it is hard to tell more of Mary and her Son, but though there shall be husks in my throat, and my words shall reach you like cripples on crutches, I must needs relate what I have seen and heard.

It was in the youth of the year when the red anemones were upon the hills that Jesus called His disciples saying to them, "Come with me to Jerusalem and witness the slaying of the lamb for the passover."

Upon that selfsame day Mary came to my door and said, "He is seeking the Holy City. Will you come and follow Him with me and the other women?"

And we walked the long road behind Mary and her son till we reached Jerusalem. And there a company of men and women hailed us at the gate, for His coming had been heralded to those who loved Him.

But upon that very night Jesus left the city with His men.

We were told that He had gone to Bethany.

And Mary stayed with us in the inn, awaiting His return.

Upon the eve of the following Thursday He was caught without the walls, and was held prisoner.

And when we heard He was a prisoner, Mary uttered not a word, but there appeared in her eyes the fulfilment of that promised pain and joy which we had beheld when she was but a bride in Nazareth.

She did not weep. She only moved among us like the ghost of a mother who would not bewail the ghost of her son.

We sat low upon the floor hut she was erect walking up and down the room.

She would stand beside the window and gaze eastward, and then with the fingers of her two hands brush back her hair.

At dawn she was still standing among us, like a lone banner in the wilderness wherein there are no hosts.

We wept because we knew the morrow of her son; but she did not weep for she knew also what would befall Him.

Her bones were of bronze and her sinews of the ancient elms, and her eyes were like the sky, wide and daring.

Have you heard a thrush sing while its nest burns in the wind?

Have you seen a woman whose sorrow is too much for tears, or a wounded heart that would rise beyond its own pain?

You have not seen such a woman, for you have not stood in the presence of Mary; and you have not been enfolded by the Mother Invisible.

In that still moment when the muffled hoofs of silence beat upon the breasts of the sleepless, John the young son of Zebedee, came and said: "Mary Mother, Jesus is going forth. Come, let us follow Him."

And Mary laid her hand upon John's shoulder and they went out, and we followed them.

When we came to the Tower of David we saw Jesus carrying His cross. And there was a great crowd about Him.

And two other men were also carrying their crosses.

And Mary's head was held high, and she walked with us after her son. And her step was firm.

And behind her walked Zion and Rome, ay, the whole world, to revenge itself upon one free Man.

When we reached the hill, He was raised high upon the cross.

And I looked at Mary. And her face was not the face of a woman bereaved. It was the countenance of the fertile earth, forever giving birth, forever burying her children.

Then to her eyes came the remembrance of His childhood, and she said aloud, "My son, who is not my son; man who once visited my womb, I glory in your power. I know that every drop of blood that runs down from your hands shall be the well-stream of a nation.

"You die in this tempest even as my heart once died in the sunset, and I shall not sorrow."

At that moment I desired to cover my face with my cloak and run away to the North Country. But of a sudden I heard Mary say, "My son, who is not my son, what have you said to the man at your right hand that has made him happy in his agony? The shadow of death is light upon his face, and he cannot turn his eyes from you.

"Now you smile upon me, and because you smile I know you have conquered."

And Jesus looked upon His mother and said, "Mary, from this hour be you the mother of John."

And to John He said, "Be a loving son unto this woman. Go to her house and let your shadow cross the threshold where I once stood. Do this in remembrance of me."

And Mary raised her right hand towards Him, and she was like a tree with one branch. And again she cried, "My son, who is not my son, if this be of God may God give us patience and the knowledge thereof. And if it be of man may God forgive him forevermore.

"If it be of God, the snow of Lebanon shall be your shroud; and if it be only of these priests and soldiers, then I have this garment for your nakedness.

"My son, who is not my son, that which God builds here

shall not perish; and that which man would destroy shall remain builded, but not in his sight."

And at that moment the heavens yielded Him to the earth, a cry and a breath.

And Mary yielded Him also unto man, a wound and a balsam.

And Mary said, "Now behold, He is gone. The battle is over. The star has shone forth. The ship has reached the harbour. He who once lay against my heart is throbbing in space."

And we came close to her, and she said to us, "Even in death He smiles. He has conquered. I would indeed be the mother of a conqueror."

And Mary returned to Jerusalem leaning upon John the young disciple.

And she was a woman fulfilled.

And when we reached the gate of the city, I gazed upon her face and I was astonished, for on that day the head of Jesus was the highest among men, yet Mary's head was not less high.

All this came to pass in the spring of the year.

And now it is autumn. And Mary the mother of Jesus has come again to her dwelling-place, and she is alone.

Two sabbaths ago my heart was as a stone in my breast, for my son had left me for a ship in Tyre. He would be a sailor.

And he said he would return no more.

And upon an evening I sought Mary.

When I entered her house she was sitting at her loom, but she was not weaving. She was looking into the sky beyond Nazareth.

And I said to her, "Hail, Mary."

And she stretched out her arm to me, and said, "Come and sit beside me, and let us watch the sun pour its blood upon the hills."

And I sat beside her on the bench and we gazed into the west through the window.

And after a moment Mary said, "I wonder who is crucifying the sun this eventide."

Then I said, "I came to you for comfort. My son has left me for the sea and I am alone in the house across the way."

Then Mary said, "I would comfort you but how shall I?"

And I said, "If you will only speak of your son I shall be comforted."

And Mary smiled upon me, and she laid her hand about my shoulder and she said, "I will speak of Him. That which will console you will give me consolation."

Then she spoke of Jesus, and she spoke long of all that was in the beginning.

And it seemed to me that in her speech she would have no difference between her son and mine.

For she said to me, "My son is also a seafarer. Why would you not trust your son to the waves even as I have trusted Him?

"Woman shall be forever the womb and the cradle but never the tomb. We die that we may give life unto life even as our fingers spin the thread for the raiment that we shall never wear.

"And we cast the net for the fish that we shall never taste.

"And for this we sorrow, yet in all this is our joy."

Thus spoke Mary to me.

And I left her and came to my house, and though the light of the day was spent I sat at my loom to weave more of the cloth.

JOSEPH SURNAMED JUSTUS

THEY SAY HE was vulgar, the common offspring of common seed, a man uncouth and violent.

They say that only the wind combed His hair, and only the rain brought His clothes and His body together.

They deem Him mad, and they attribute His words to demons.

Yet behold, the Man despised sounded a challenge and the sound thereof shall never cease.

He sang a song and none shall arrest that melody. It shall hover from generation to generation and it shall rise from sphere to sphere remembering the lips that gave it birth and the ears that cradled it.

He was a stranger. Aye, He was a stranger, a wayfarer on His way to a shrine, a visitor who knocked at our door, a guest from a far country.

And because He found not a gracious host, He has returned to His own place.

PHILIP

WHEN OUR BELOVED died, all mankind died and all things for a space were still and grey. Then the east was darkened, and a tempest rushed out of it and swept the land. The eyes of the sky opened and shut, and the rain came down in torrents and carried away the blood that streamed from His hands and His feet.

I too died. But in the depth of my oblivion I heard Him speak and say, "Father forgive them, for they know not what they do."

And His voice sought my drowned spirit and I was brought back to the shore.

And I opened my eyes and I saw His white body hanging against the cloud, and His words that I had heard took shape within me and became a new man. And I sorrowed no more.

Who would sorrow for a sea that is unveiling its face, or for a mountain that laughs in the sun?

Was it ever in the heart of man, when that heart was pierced, to say such words?

What other judge of men has released His judges? And did ever love challenge hate with power more certain of itself?

Was ever such a trumpet heard 'twixt heaven and earth?

Was it known before that the murdered had compassion on his murderers? Or that the meteor stayed his footsteps for the mole?

The seasons shall tire and the years grow old, ere they exhaust these words: "*Father forgive them, for they know not what they do.*"

And you and I, though born again and again, shall keep them.

And now I would go into my house, and stand an exalted beggar, at His door.

JESUS WAS PATIENT with the dullard and the stupid, even as the winter awaits the spring.

He was patient like a mountain in the wind.

He answered with kindliness the harsh questionings of His foes.

He could even be silent to cavil and dispute, for He was strong and the strong can be forbearing.

But Jesus was also impatient.

He spared not the hypocrite.

He yielded not to men of cunning nor to the jugglers of words.

And He would not be governed.

He was impatient with those who believed not in light because they themselves dwelt in shadow; and with those who sought after signs in the sky rather than in their own hearts.

He was impatient with those who weighed and measured the day and the night before they would trust their dreams to dawn or eventide.

Jesus was patient.

Yet He was the most impatient of men.

He would have you weave the cloth though you spend years between the loom and the linen.

But He would have none tear an inch off the woven fabric.

PILATE'S WIFE TO A ROMAN LADY

I WAS WALKING with my maidens in the groves outside of Jerusalem when I saw Him with a few men and women sitting about Him; and He was speaking to them in a language which I only half understood.

But one needs not a language to perceive a pillar of light or a mountain of crystal. The heart knows what the tongue may never utter and the ears may never hear.

He was speaking to His friends of love and strength. I know He spoke of love because there was melody in His voice; and I know He spoke of strength because there were armies in His gestures. And He was tender, though even my husband could not have spoken with such authority.

When He saw me passing by He stopped speaking for a moment and looked kindly upon me. And I was humbled; and in my soul I knew I had passed by a god.

After that day His image visited my privacy when I would not be visited by man or woman; and His eyes searched my soul when my own eyes were closed. And His voice governs the stillness of my nights.

I am held fast forevermore; and there is peace in my pain, and freedom in my tears.

Beloved friend, you have never seen that man, and you will never see Him.

He is gone beyond our senses, but of all men He is now the nearest to me.

A MAN OUTSIDE OF JERUSALEM

JUDAS CAME TO my house that Friday, upon the eve of the Passover; and he knocked at my door with force.

When he entered I looked at him, and his face was ashen. His hands trembled like dry twigs in the wind, and his clothes were as wet as if he had stepped out from a river; for on that evening there were great tempests.

He looked at me, and the sockets of his eyes were like dark caves and his eyes were blood-sodden.

And he said, "I have delivered Jesus of Nazareth to His enemies and to my enemies."

Then Judas wrung his hands and he said, "Jesus declared that He would overcome all His foes and the foes of our people. And I believed and I followed Him.

"When first He called us to Him He promised us a kingdom mighty and vast, and in our faith we sought His favour that we might have honourable stations in His court.

"We beheld ourselves princes dealing with these Romans as they have dealt with us. And Jesus said much about His kingdom, and I thought He had chosen me a captain of His chariots, and a chief man of His warriors. And I followed His footsteps willingly.

"But I found it was not a kingdom that Jesus sought, nor was it from the Romans He would have had us free. His kingdom was but the kingdom of the heart. I heard Him talk of love and charity and forgiveness, and the wayside women listened gladly, but my heart grew bitter and I was hardened.

"My promised king of Judea seemed suddenly to have turned flute-player, to soothe the mind of wanderers and vagabonds.

"I had loved Him as others of my tribe had loved Him. I had beheld in Him a hope and a deliverance from the yoke of the aliens. But when He would not utter a word or move a hand to

free us from that yoke, and when He would even have rendered unto Cæsar that which is Cæsar's, then despair filled me and my hopes died. And I said, 'He who murders my hopes shall be murdered, for my hopes and expectations are more precious than the life of any man.'"

Then Judas gnashed his teeth; and he bent down his head. And when he spoke again, he said, "I have delivered Him up. And He was crucified this day. . . . Yet when He died upon the cross, He died a king. He died in the tempest as deliverers die, like vast men who live beyond the shroud and the stone.

"And all the while He was dying, He was gracious, and He was kindly; and His heart was full of pity. He felt pity even for me who had delivered Him up."

And I said, "Judas, you have committed a grave wrong."

And Judas answered, "But He died a king. Why did He not live a king?"

And I said again, "You have committed a grave crime."

And he sat down there, upon that bench, and he was as still as a stone.

But I walked to and fro in the room, and once more I said, "You have committed a great sin."

But Judas said not a word. He remained as silent as the earth.

And after a while he stood up and faced me and he seemed taller, and when he spoke his voice was like the sound of a cracked vessel; and he said, "Sin was not in my heart. This very night I shall seek His kingdom, and I shall stand in His presence and beg His forgiveness.

"He died a king, and I shall die a felon. But in my heart I know He will forgive me."

After saying these words he folded his wet cloak around him and he said, "It was good that I came to you this night even though I have brought you trouble. Will you also forgive me?

"Say to your sons and to your sons' sons: 'Judas Iscariot delivered Jesus of Nazareth to His enemies because he believed Jesus was an enemy to His own race.'

"And say also that Judas upon the selfsame day of his great error followed the King to the steps of His throne to deliver up his own soul and to be judged.

"I shall tell Him that my blood also was impatient for the sod, and my crippled spirit would be free."

Then Judas leaned his head back against the wall and he cried out, "O God whose dreaded name no man shall utter ere his lips are touched by the fingers of death, why did you burn me with a fire that had no light?

"Why did you give the Galilean a passion for a land unknown and burden me with desire that would not escape kin or hearth? And who is this man Judas, whose hands are dipped in blood?

"Lend me a hand to cast him off, an old garment and a tattered harness.

"Help me to do this tonight.

"And let me stand again outside of these walls.

"I am weary of this wingless liberty. I would a larger dungeon.

"I would flow a stream of tears to the bitter sea. I would be a man of your mercy rather than one knocking at the gate of his own heart."

Thus Judas spoke, and thereupon he opened the door and went out again into the tempest.

Three days afterwards I visited Jerusalem and heard of all that had come to pass. And I also heard that Judas had flung himself from the summit of the High Rock.

I have pondered long since that day, and I understand Judas. He fulfilled his little life, which hovered like a mist on this land enslaved by the Romans, while the great prophet was ascending the heights.

One man longed for a kingdom in which he was to be a prince.

Another man desired a kingdom in which all men shall be princes.

SARKIS, AN OLD GREEK SHEPHERD, CALLED THE MADMAN

IN A DREAM I saw Jesus and my god Pan sitting together in the heart of the forest.

They laughed at each other's speech, with the brook that ran near them, and the laughter of Jesus was the merrier. And they conversed long.

Pan spoke of earth and her secrets, and of his hoofed brothers and his horned sisters; and of dreams. And he spoke of roots and their nestlings, and of the sap that wakes and rises and sings to summer.

And Jesus told of the young shoots in the forest, and of flowers and fruit, and the seed that they shall bear in a season not yet come.

He spoke of birds in space and their singing in the upper world.

And He told of white harts in the desert wherein God shepherds them.

And Pan was pleased with the speech of the new God, and his nostrils quivered.

And in the same dream I beheld Pan and Jesus grow quiet and still in the stillness of the green shadows.

And then Pan took his reeds and played to Jesus.

The trees were shaken and the ferns trembled, and there was a fear upon me.

And Jesus said, "Good brother, you have the glade and the rocky height in your reeds."

Then Pan gave the reeds to Jesus and said, "You play now. It is your turn."

And Jesus said, "These reeds are too many for my mouth. I have this flute."

And He took His flute and He played.

And I heard the sound of rain in the leaves, and the singing

383

of streams among the hills, and the falling of snow on the mountain-top.

The pulse of my heart, that had once beaten with the wind, was restored again to the wind, and all the waves of my yesterdays were upon my shore, and I was again Sarkis the shepherd, and the flute of Jesus became the pipes of countless shepherds calling to countless flocks.

Then Pan said to Jesus, "Your youth is more kin to the reed than my years. And long ere this in my stillness I have heard your song and the murmur of your name.

"Your name has a goodly sound; well shall it rise with the sap to the branches, and well shall it run with the hoofs among the hills.

"And it is not strange to me, though my father called me not by that name. It was your flute that brought it back to my memory.

"And now let us play our reeds together."

And they played together.

And their music smote heaven and earth, and a terror struck all living things.

I heard the bellow of beasts and the hunger of the forest. And I heard the cry of lonely men, and the plaint of those who long for what they know not.

I heard the sighing of the maiden for her lover, and the panting of the luckless hunter for his prey.

And then there came peace into their music, and the heavens and the earth sang together.

All this I saw in my dream, and all this I heard.

HE WAS OF the rabble, a brigand, a mountebank and a self-trumpeter. He appealed only to the unclean and the disinherited, and for this He had to go the way of all the tainted and the defiled.

He made sport of us and of our laws; He mocked at our honour and jeered at our dignity. He even said He would destroy the temple and desecrate the holy places. He was shameless, and for this He had to die a shameful death.

He was a man from Galilee of the Gentiles, an alien, from that North Country where Adonis and Ashtarte still claim power against Israel and the God of Israel.

He whose tongue halted when He spoke the speech of our prophets was loud and ear-splitting when He spoke the bastard language of the lowborn and the vulgar.

What else was there for me but to decree His death?

Am I not a guardian of the temple? Am I not a keeper of the law? Could I have turned my back on Him, saying in all tranquillity: "He is a madman among madmen. Let Him alone to exhaust Himself raving; for the mad and the crazed and those possessed with devils shall be naught in the path of Israel"?

Could I have been deaf unto Him when He called us liars, hypocrites, wolves, vipers, and the sons of vipers?

Nay I could not be deaf to Him, for He was not a madman. He was self-possessed; and in His big-sounding sanity He denounced and challenged us all.

For this I had Him crucified, and His crucifixion was a signal and warning unto the others who are stamped with the same damned seal.

I know well I have been blamed for this, even by some of the elders in the Sanhedrin. But I was mindful then as I am mindful now, that one man should die for the people rather than the people be led astray by one man.

Judea was conquered by an enemy from without. I shall see that Judea is not conquered again, by an enemy from within.

No man from the cursed North shall reach our Holy of Holies nor lay His shadow across the Ark of the Covenant.

A WOMAN, ONE OF MARY'S NEIGHBOURS

ON THE FORTIETH day after His death, all the women neighbours came to the house of Mary to console her and to sing threnodies.
And one of the women sang this song:

Whereto my Spring, whereto?
And to what other space your perfume ascending?
In what other fields shall you walk?
And to what sky shall you lift up your head to speak
    your heart?

These valleys shall be barren,
And we shall have naught but dried fields and arid.
All green things will parch in the sun,
And our orchards will bring forth sour apples,
And our vineyards bitter grapes.
We shall thirst for your wine,
And our nostrils will long for your fragrance.

Whereto Flower of our first spring, whereto?
And will you return no more?
Will not your jasmine visit us again,
And your cyclamen stand by our wayside
To tell us that we too have our roots deep in earth,
And that our ceaseless breath would forever climb the sky?

Whereto Jesus, whereto,
Son of my neighbour Mary,
And comrade to my son?
Whither, our first Spring, and to what other fields?
Will you return to us again?
Will you in your love-tide visit the barren shores of
    our dreams?

WELL DO I remember the last time I saw Jesus the Nazarene. Judas had come to me at the noon hour of that Thursday, and bidden me prepare supper for Jesus and His friends.

He gave me two silver pieces and said, "Buy all that you deem needful for the meal."

And after He was gone my wife said to me, "This is indeed a distinction." For Jesus had become a prophet and He had wrought many miracles.

At twilight He came and His followers, and they sat in the upper chamber around the board, but they were silent and quiet.

Last year also and the year before they had come and then they had been joyous. They broke the bread and drank the wine and sang our ancient strains; and Jesus would talk to them till midnight.

After that they would leave Him alone in the upper chamber and go to sleep in other rooms; for after midnight it was His desire to be alone.

And He would remain awake; I would hear His steps as I lay upon my bed.

But this last time He and His friends were not happy.

My wife had prepared fishes from the Lake of Galilee, and pheasants from Houran stuffed with rice and pomegranate seeds, and I had carried them a jug of my cypress wine.

And then I had left them for I felt that they wished to be alone.

They stayed until it was full dark, and then they all descended together from the upper chamber, but at the foot of the stairs Jesus tarried awhile. And He looked at me and my wife, and He placed His hand upon the head of my daughter and He said, "Good night to you all. We shall come back again to your upper chamber, but we shall not leave you at this early hour. We shall stay until the sun rises above the horizon.

"In a little while we shall return and ask for more bread and more wine. You and your wife have been good hosts to us, and we shall remember you when we come to our mansion and sit at our own board."

And I said, "Sir, it was an honour to serve you. The other inn-keepers envy me because of your visits, and in my pride I smile at them in the market-place. Sometimes I even make a grimace."

And He said, "All innkeepers should be proud in serving. For he who gives bread and wine is the brother of him who reaps and gathers the sheaves for the threshing-floor, and of him who crushes the grapes at the winepress. And you are all kindly. You give of your bounty even to those who come with naught but hunger and thirst."

Then He turned to Judas Iscariot who kept the purse of the company, and He said, "Give me two shekels."

And Judas gave Him two shekels saying: "These are the last silver pieces in my purse."

Jesus looked at him and said, "Soon, over-soon, your purse shall be filled with silver."

Then He put the two pieces into my hand and said, "With these buy a silken girdle for your daughter and bid her wear it on the day of the passover in remembrance of me."

And looking again into the face of my daughter, He leaned down and kissed her brow. And then He said once more, "Good-night to you all."

And He walked away.

I have been told that what He said to us has been recorded upon a parchment by one of His friends, but I repeat it to you even as I heard it from His own lips.

Never shall I forget the sound of His voice as He said those words, "Good-night to you all."

If you would know more of Him, ask my daughter. She is a woman now, but she cherishes the memory of her girlhood. And her words are more ready than mine.

BARABBAS

THEY RELEASED ME and chose Him. Then He rose and I fell down.

And they held Him a victim and a sacrifice for the Passover.

I was freed from my chains, and walked with the throng behind Him, but I was a living man going to my own grave.

I should have fled to the desert where shame is burned out by the sun.

Yet I walked with those who had chosen Him to bear my crime.

When they nailed Him on His cross I stood there.

I saw and I heard but I seemed outside of my body.

The thief who was crucified on His right said to Him, "Are you bleeding with me, even you, Jesus of Nazareth?"

And Jesus answered and said, "Were it not for this nail that stays my hand I would reach forth and clasp your hand.

"We are crucified together. Would they had raised your cross nearer to mine."

Then He looked down and gazed upon His mother and a young man who stood beside her.

He said, "Mother, behold your son standing beside you.

"Woman, behold a man who shall carry these drops of my blood to the North Country."

And when He heard the wailing of the women of Galilee He said: "Behold, they weep and I thirst.

"I am held too high to reach their tears.

"I will not take vinegar and gall to quench this thirst."

Then His eyes opened wide to the sky, and He said: "Father, why hast Thou forsaken us?"

And then He said in compassion, "Father, forgive them, for they know not what they do."

When He uttered these words methought I saw all men prostrated before God beseeching forgiveness for the crucifixion of this one man.

Then again He said with a great voice: "Father, into Thy hand I yield back my spirit."

And at last He lifted up His head and said, "Now it is finished, but only upon this hill."

And He closed His eyes.

Then lightning cracked the dark skies, and there was a great thunder.

I know now that those who slew Him in my stead achieved my endless torment.

His crucifixion endured but for an hour.

But I shall be crucified unto the end of my years.

CLAUDIUS, A ROMAN SENTINEL

AFTER HE WAS taken, they entrusted Him to me. And I was ordered by Pontius Pilatus to keep Him in custody until the following morning.

My soldiers led Him prisoner, and He was obedient to them.

At midnight I left my wife and children and visited the arsenal. It was my habit to go about and see that all was well with my battalions in Jerusalem; and that night I visited the arsenal where He was held.

My soldiers and some of the young Jews were making sport of Him. They had stripped Him of His garment, and they had put a crown of last year's brier-thorns upon His head.

They had seated Him against a pillar, and they were dancing and shouting before Him.

And they had given Him a reed to hold in His hand.

As I entered someone shouted: "Behold, O Captain, the King of the Jews."

I stood before Him and looked at Him, and I was ashamed. I knew not why.

I had fought in Gallia and in Spain, and with my men I had faced death. Yet never had I been in fear, nor been a coward. But when I stood before that man and He looked at me I lost heart. It seemed as though my lips were sealed, and I could utter no word.

And straightway I left the arsenal.

This chanced thirty years ago. My sons who were babes then are men now. And they are serving Cæsar and Rome.

But often in counselling them I have spoken of Him, a man facing death with the sap of life upon His lips, and with compassion for His slayers in His eyes.

And now I am old. I have lived the years fully. And I think

truly that neither Pompey nor Cæsar was so great a commander as that Man of Galilee.

For since His unresisting death an army has risen out of the earth to fight for Him. . . . And He is better served by them, though dead, than ever Pompey or Cæsar was served, though living.

JAMES THE BROTHER OF THE LORD

A THOUSAND TIMES I have been visited by the memory of that night. And I know now that I shall be visited a thousand times again.

The earth shall forget the furrows ploughed upon her breast, and a woman the pain and joy of childbirth, ere I shall forget that night.

In the afternoon we had been outside the walls of Jerusalem, and Jesus had said, "Let us go into the city now and take supper at the inn."

It was dark when we reached the inn, and we were hungry. The innkeeper greeted us and led us to an upper chamber.

And Jesus bade us sit around the board, but He Himself remained standing, and His eyes rested upon us.

And He spoke to the keeper of the inn and said, "Bring me a basin and a pitcher full of water, and a towel."

And He looked at us again and said gently, "Cast off your sandals."

We did not understand, but at His command we cast them off.

Then the keeper of the inn brought the basin and the pitcher; and Jesus said, "Now I will wash your feet. For I must needs free your feet from the dust of the ancient road, and give them the freedom of the new way."

And we were all abashed and shy.

Then Simon Peter stood up and said: "How shall I suffer my Master and my Lord to wash my feet?"

And Jesus answered, "I will wash your feet that you may remember that he who serves men shall be the greatest among men."

Then He looked at each one of us and He said: "The Son of

Man who has chosen you for His brethren, He whose feet were anointed yesterday with myrrh of Arabia and dried with a woman's hair, desires now to wash your feet."

And He took the basin and the pitcher and kneeled down and washed our feet, beginning with Judas Iscariot.

Then He sat down with us at the board; and His face was like the dawn rising upon a battlefield after a night of strife and blood-shedding.

And the keeper of the inn came with his wife, bringing food and wine.

And though I had been hungry before Jesus knelt at my feet, now I had no stomach for food. And there was a flame in my throat which I would not quench with wine.

Then Jesus took a loaf of bread and gave to us, saying, "Perhaps we shall not break bread again. Let us eat this morsel in remembrance of our days in Galilee."

And He poured wine from the jug into a cup, and He drank, and gave to us, and He said, "Drink this in remembrance of a thirst we have known together. And drink it also in hope for the new vintage. When I am enfolded and am no more among you, and when you meet here or elsewhere, break the bread and pour the wine, and eat and drink even as you are doing now. Then look about you; and perchance you may see me sitting with you at the board."

After saying this He began to distribute among us morsels of fish and pheasant, like a bird feeding its fledglings.

We ate little yet we were filled; and we drank but a drop, for we felt that the cup was like a space between this land and another land.

Then Jesus said, "Ere we leave this board let us rise and sing the joyous hymns of Galilee."

And we rose and sang together, and His voice was above our voices, and there was a ringing in every word of His words.

And He looked at our faces, each and every one, and He said, "Now I bid you farewell. Let us go beyond these walls. Let us go unto Gethsemane."

And John the son of Zebedee said, "Master, why do you say farewell to us this night?"

And Jesus said, "Let not your heart be troubled. I only leave you to prepare a place for you in my Father's house. But if you shall be in need of me, I will come back to you. Where you call me, there I shall hear you, and wherever your spirit shall seek me, there I will be.

"Forget not that thirst leads to the winepress, and hunger to the wedding-feast.

"It is in your longing that you shall find the Son of Man. For longing is the fountain-head of ecstasy, and it is the path to the Father."

And John spoke again and said, "If you would indeed leave us, how shall we be of good cheer? And why speak you of separation?"

And Jesus said, "The hunted stag knows the arrow of the hunter before he feels it in his breast; and the river is aware of the sea ere it comes to her shore. And the Son of Man has travelled the ways of men.

"Before another almond tree renders her blossoms to the sun, my roots shall be reaching into the heart of another field."

Then Simon Peter said: "Master, leave us not now, and deny us not the joy of your presence. Where you go we too will go; and wherever you abide there we will be also."

And Jesus put His hand upon Simon Peter's shoulder, and smiled upon him, and He said, "Who knows but that you may deny me before this night is over, and leave me before I leave you?"

Then of a sudden He said, "Now let us go hence."

And He left the inn and we followed Him. But when we reached the gate of the city, Judas of Iscariot was no longer with us. And we crossed the Valley of Jahannam. Jesus walked far ahead of us, and we walked close to one another.

When He reached an olive grove He stopped and turned towards us saying, "Rest here for an hour."

The evening was cool, though it was full spring with the mulberries unfolding their shoots and the apple trees in bloom. And the gardens were sweet.

Each one of us sought the trunk of a tree, and we lay down. I myself gathered my cloak around me and lay under a pine tree.

But Jesus left us and walked by Himself in the olive grove. And I watched Him while the others slept.

He would suddenly stand still, and again He would walk up and down. This He did many times.

Then I saw Him lift His face towards the sky and outstretch His arms to east and west.

Once He had said, "Heaven and earth, and hell too, are of man." And now I remembered His saying, and I knew that He who was pacing the olive grove was heaven made man; and I bethought me that the womb of the earth is not a beginning nor an end, but rather a chariot, a pause; and a moment of wonder and surprise; and hell I saw also, in the valley called Jahannam, which lay between Him and the Holy City.

And as He stood there and I lay wrapped in my garment, I heard His voice speaking. But He was not speaking to us. Thrice I heard Him pronounce the word *Father*. And that was all I heard.

After a while His arms dropped down, and He stood still like a cypress tree between my eyes and the sky.

At last He came over among us again, and He said to us, "Wake and rise. My hour has come. The world is already upon us, armed for battle."

And then He said, "A moment ago I heard the voice of my Father. If I see you not again, remember that the conqueror shall not have peace until he is conquered."

And when we had risen and come close to Him, His face was like the starry heaven above the desert.

Then He kissed each one of us upon the cheek. And when His lips touched my cheek, they were hot, like the hand of a child in fever.

Suddenly we heard a great noise in the distance, as of numbers, and when it came near it was a company of men approaching with lanterns and staves. And they came in haste.

As they reached the hedge of the grove Jesus left us and went forth to meet them. And Judas of Iscariot was leading them.

There were Roman soldiers with swords and spears, and men of Jerusalem with clubs and pickaxes.

And Judas came up to Jesus and kissed Him. And then he said to the armed men, "This is the Man."

And Jesus said to Judas, "Judas, you were patient with me. This could have been yesterday."

Then He turned to the armed men and said: "Take me now. But see that your cage is large enough for these wings."

Then they fell upon Him and held Him, and they were all shouting.

But we in our fear ran away and sought to escape. I ran alone through the olive groves, nor had I power to be mindful, nor did any voice speak in me except my fear.

Through the two or three hours that remained of that night I was fleeing and hiding, and at dawn I found myself in a village near Jericho.

Why had I left Him? I do not know. But to my sorrow I did leave Him. I was a coward and I fled from the face of His enemies.

Then I was sick and ashamed at heart, and I returned to Jerusalem, but He was a prisoner, and no friend could have speech with Him.

He was crucified, and His blood has made new clay of the earth.

And I am living still; I am living upon the honeycomb of His sweet life.

SIMON THE CYRENE

I WAS ON my way to the fields when I saw Him carrying His cross; and multitudes were following Him.

Then I too walked beside Him.

His burden stopped Him many a time, for His body was exhausted.

Then a Roman soldier approached me, saying, "Come, you are strong and firm built; carry the cross of this man."

When I heard these words my heart swelled within me and I was grateful.

And I carried His cross.

It was heavy, for it was made of poplar soaked through with the rains of winter.

And Jesus looked at me. And the sweat of His forehead was running down upon His beard.

Again He looked at me and He said, "Do you too drink this cup? You shall indeed sip its rim with me to the end of time."

So saying He placed His hand upon my free shoulder. And we walked together towards the Hill of the Skull.

But now I felt not the weight of the cross. I felt only His hand. And it was like the wing of a bird upon my shoulder.

Then we reached the hill top, and there they were to crucify Him.

And then I felt the weight of the tree.

He uttered no word when they drove the nails into His hands and feet, nor made He any sound.

And His limbs did not quiver under the hammer.

It seemed as if His hands and feet had died and would only live again when bathed in blood. Yet it seemed also as if He sought the nails as the prince would seek the sceptre; and that He craved to be raised to the heights.

And my heart did not think to pity Him, for I was too filled with wonder.

Now, the man whose cross I carried has become my cross.

Should they say to me again, "Carry the cross of this man," I would carry it till my road ended at the grave.

But I would beg Him to place His hand upon my shoulder.

This happened many years ago; and still whenever I follow the furrow in the field, and in that drowsy moment before sleep, I think always of that Beloved Man.

And I feel His winged hand, here, on my left shoulder.

MY SON WAS a good man and upright. He was tender and kind to me, and he loved his kin and his countrymen. And he hated our enemies, the cursed Romans, who wear purple cloth though they spin no thread nor sit at any loom; and who reap and gather where they have not ploughed nor sowed the seed.

My son was but seventeen when he was caught shooting arrows at the Roman legion passing through our vineyard.

Even at that age he would speak to the other youths of the glory of Israel, and he would utter many strange things that I did not understand.

He was my son, my only son.

He drank life from these breasts now dry, and he took his first steps in this garden, grasping these fingers that are now like trembling reeds.

With these selfsame hands, young and fresh then like the grapes of Lebanon, I put away his first sandals in a linen kerchief that my mother had given me. I still keep them there in that chest, beside the window.

He was my first-born, and when he took his first step, I too took my first step. For women travel not save when led by their children.

And now they tell me he is dead by his own hand; that he flung himself from the High Rock in remorse because he had betrayed his friend Jesus of Nazareth.

I know my son is dead. But I know he betrayed no one; for he loved his kin and hated none but the Romans.

My son sought the glory of Israel, and naught but that glory was upon his lips and in his deeds.

When he met Jesus on the highway he left me to follow Him. And in my heart I knew that he was wrong to follow any man.

When he bade me farewell I told him that he was wrong, but he listened not.

Our children do not heed us; like the high tide of today, they take no counsel with the high tide of yesterday.

I beg you question me no further about my son.

I loved him and I shall love him forevermore.

If love were in the flesh I would burn it out with hot irons and be at peace. But it is in the soul, unreachable.

And now I would speak no more. Go question another woman more honoured than the mother of Judas.

Go to the mother of Jesus. The sword is in her heart also; she will tell you of me, and you will understand.

THE WOMAN OF BYBLOS

WEEP WITH ME, ye daughters of Ashtarte, and all ye lovers
    of Tamouz.
Bid your heart melt and rise and run blood-tears,
For He who was made of gold and ivory is no more.
In the dark forest the boar overcame Him,
And the tusks of the boar pierced His flesh.
Now He lies stained with the leaves of yesteryear,
And no longer shall His footsteps wake the seeds that sleep in
    the bosom of spring.
His voice will not come with the dawn to my window,
And I shall be forever alone.

Weep with me, ye daughters of Ashtarte, and all ye lovers
    of Tamouz,
For my Belovèd has escaped me;
He who spoke as the rivers speak;
He whose voice and time were twins;
He whose mouth was a red pain made sweet;
He on whose lips gall would turn to honey.

Weep with me, daughters of Ashtarte, and ye lovers of Tamouz.
Weep with me around His bier as the stars weep,
And as the moon-petals fall upon His wounded body.
Wet with your tears the silken covers of my bed,
Where my Belovèd once lay in my dream,
And was gone away in my awakening.

I charge ye, daughters of Ashtarte, and all ye lovers of Tamouz,
Bare your breasts and weep and comfort me,
For Jesus of Nazareth is dead.

ONCE AGAIN I say that with death Jesus conquered death, and rose from the grave a spirit and a power. And He walked in our solitude and visited the gardens of our passion.

He lies not there in that cleft rock behind the stone.

We who love Him beheld Him with these our eyes which He made to see; and we touched Him with these our hands which He taught to reach forth.

I know you who believe not in Him. I was one of you, and you are many; but your number shall be diminished.

Must you break your harp and your lyre to find the music therein?

Or must you fell a tree ere you can believe it bears fruit?

You hate Jesus because someone from the North Country said He was the Son of God. But you hate one another because each of you deems himself too great to be the brother of the next man.

You hate Him because someone said He was born of a virgin, and not of man's seed.

But you know not the mothers who go to the tomb in virginity, nor the men who go down to the grave choked with their own thirst.

You know not that the earth was given in marriage to the sun, and that earth it is who sends us forth to the mountain and the desert.

There is a gulf that yawns between those who love Him and those who hate Him, between those who believe and those who do not believe.

But when the years have bridged that gulf you shall know that He who lived in us is deathless, that He was the Son of God even as we are the children of God; that He was born of a virgin even as we are born of the husbandless earth.

It is passing strange that the earth gives not to the unbelievers the roots that would suck at her breast nor the wings wherewith to fly high and drink, and be filled with the dews of her space.

But I know what I know, and it is enough.

A MAN FROM LEBANON

MASTER, MASTER SINGER,
Master of words unspoken,
Seven times was I born, and seven times have I died
Since your hasty visit and our brief welcome.
And behold I live again,
Remembering a day and a night among the hills,
When your tide lifted us up.
Thereafter many lands and many seas did I cross,
And wherever I was led by saddle or sail
Your name was prayer or argument.
Men would bless you or curse you;
The curse, a protest against failure,
The blessing, a hymn of the hunter
Who comes back from the hills
With provision for his mate.

*

Your friends are yet with us for comfort and support,
And your enemies also, for strength and assurance.
Your mother is with us;
I have beheld the sheen of her face in the countenance of all
    mothers;
Her hand rocks cradles with gentleness,
Her hand folds shrouds with tenderness.
And Mary Magdalen is yet in our midst,
She who drank the vinegar of life, and then its wine.
And Judas, the man of pain and small ambitions,
He too walks the earth;
Even now he preys upon himself when his hunger finds
    naught else,
And seeks his larger self in self-destruction.

*

And John, he whose youth loved beauty, is here,
And he sings though unheeded.
And Simon Peter the impetuous, who denied you that he
    might live longer for you,
He too sits by our fire.
He may deny you again ere the dawn of another day,
Yet he would be crucified for your purpose, and deem himself
    unworthy of the honour.
And Caiaphas and Annas still live their day,
And judge the guilty and the innocent.
They sleep upon their feathered bed
Whilst he whom they have judged is whipped with the rods.

*

And the woman who was taken in adultery,
She too walks the streets of our cities,
And hungers for bread not yet baked,
And she is alone in an empty house.
And Pontius Pilatus is here also:
He stands in awe before you,
And still questions you,
But he dares not risk his station or defy an alien race;
And he is still washing his hands.
Even now Jerusalem holds the basin and Rome the ewer,
And betwixt the two a thousand thousand hands would be
    washed to whiteness.

*

Master, Master Poet,
Master of words sung and spoken,
They have builded temples to house your name,
And upon every height they have raised your cross,
A sign and a symbol to guide their wayward feet,
But not unto your joy.
Your joy is a hill beyond their vision,
And it does not comfort them.
They would honour the man unknown to them.
And what consolation is there in a man like themselves, a man
    whose kindliness is like their own kindliness,

408

A god whose love is like their own love,
And whose mercy is in their own mercy?
They honour not the man, the living man,
The first man who opened His eyes and gazed at the sun
With eyelids unquivering.
Nay, they do not know Him, and they would not be
    like Him.

They would be unknown, walking in the procession of
    the unknown.
They would bear sorrow, their sorrow,
And they would not find comfort in your joy.
Their aching heart seeks not consolation in your words and
    the song thereof.
And their pain, silent and unshapen,
Makes them creatures lonely and unvisited.
Though hemmed about by kin and kind,
They live in fear, uncomraded;
Yet they would not be alone.
They would bend eastward when the west wind blows.
They call you king,
And they would be in your court.
They pronounce you the Messiah,
And they would themselves be anointed with the holy oil.
Yea, they would live upon your life.

*

Master, Master Singer,
Your tears were like the showers of May,
And your laughter like the waves of the white sea.
When you spoke your words were the far-off whisper of their
    lips when those lips should be kindled with fire;
You laughed for the marrow in their bones that was not yet
    ready for laughter;
And you wept for their eyes that yet were dry.
Your voice fathered their thoughts and their understanding.
Your voice mothered their words and their breath.

*

Seven times was I born and seven times have I died,
And now I live again, and I behold you,
The fighter among fighters,
The poet of poets,
King above all kings,
A man half-naked with your road-fellows.
Every day the bishop bends down his head
When he pronounces your name.
And every day the beggars say:
"For Jesus' sake
Give us a penny to buy bread."
We call upon each other,
But in truth we call upon you,
Like the flood tide in the spring of our want and desire,
And when our autumn comes, like the ebb tide.
High or low, your name is upon our lips,
The Master of infinite compassion.

*

Master, Master of our lonely hours,
Here and there, betwixt the cradle and the coffin, I meet your
    silent brothers,
The free men, unshackled,
Sons of your mother earth and space.
They are like the birds of the sky,
And like the lilies of the field.
They live your life and think your thoughts,
And they echo your song.
But they are empty-handed,
And they are not crucified with the great crucifixion.
And therein is their pain.
The world crucifies them every day,
But only in little ways.
The sky is not shaken,
And the earth travails not with her dead.
They are crucified and there is none to witness their agony.
They turn their face to right and left
And find not one to promise them a station in his kingdom.

Yet they would be crucified again and yet again,
That your God may be their God,
And your Father their Father.

*

Master, Master Lover,
The Princess awaits your coming in her fragrant chamber,
And the married unmarried woman in her cage;
The harlot who seeks bread in the streets of her shame,
And the nun in her cloister who has no husband;
The childless woman too at her window,
Where frost designs the forest on the pane,
She finds you in that symmetry,
And she would mother you, and be comforted.

*

Master, Master Poet,
Master of our silent desires,
The heart of the world quivers with the throbbing of
    your heart,
But it burns not with your song.
The world sits listening to your voice in tranquil delight,
But it rises not from its seat
To scale the ridges of your hills.
Man would dream your dream but he would not wake to
    your dawn
Which is his greater dream.
He would see with your vision,
But he would not drag his heavy feet to your throne.
Yet many have been enthroned in your name
And mitred with your power,
And have turned your golden visit
Into crowns for their head and sceptres for their hand.

*

Master, Master of Light,
Whose eye dwells in the seeking fingers of the blind,
You are still despised and mocked,
A man too weak and infirm to be God,
A God too much man to call forth adoration.

Their mass and their hymn,
Their sacrament and their rosary, are for their imprisoned self.
You are their yet distant self, their far-off cry, and their
  passion.

*

But Master, Sky-heart, Knight of our fairer dream,
You do still tread this day;
Nor bows nor spears shall stay your steps.
You walk through all our arrows.
You smile down upon us,
And though you are the youngest of us all
You father us all.

Poet, Singer, Great Heart,
May our God bless your name,
And the womb that held you, and the breasts that gave
  you milk.
And may God forgive us all.

THE EARTH GODS

WHEN THE NIGHT of the twelfth æon fell,
And silence, the high tide of night, swallowed the hills,
The three earth-born gods, the Master Titans of life,
Appeared upon the mountains.

Rivers ran about their feet;
The mist floated across their breasts,
And their heads rose in majesty above the world.

Then they spoke, and like distant thunder
Their voices rolled over the plains.

FIRST GOD

The wind blows eastward;
I would turn my face to the south,
For the wind crowds my nostrils with the odours of dead
    things.

SECOND GOD

It is the scent of burnt flesh, sweet and bountiful.
I would breathe it.

FIRST GOD

It is the odour of mortality parching upon its own faint flame.
Heavily does it hang upon the air,
And like foul breath of the pit
It offends my senses.
I would turn my face to the scentless north.

415

SECOND GOD

It is the inflamed fragrance of brooding life
That I would breathe now and forever.
Gods live upon sacrifice,
Their thirst quenched by blood,
Their hearts appeased with young souls,
Their sinews strengthened by the deathless sighs
Of those who dwell with death;
Their thrones are built upon the ashes of generations.

FIRST GOD

Weary is my spirit of all there is.
I would not move a hand to create a world
Nor to erase one.

I would not live could I but die,
For the weight of æons is upon me,
And the ceaseless moan of the seas exhausts my sleep.
Could I but lose the primal aim
And vanish like a wasted sun;
Could I but strip my divinity of its purpose
And breathe my immortality into space,
And be no more;
Could I but be consumed and pass from time's memory
Into the emptiness of nowhere!

THIRD GOD

Listen my brothers, my ancient brothers.
A youth in yonder vale
Is singing his heart to the night.
His lyre is gold and ebony.
His voice is silver and gold.

SECOND GOD

I would not be so vain as to be no more.
I could not but choose the hardest way;
To follow the seasons and support the majesty of the years;
To sow the seed and to watch it thrust through the soil;
To call the flower from its hiding place
And give it strength to nestle its own life,
And then to pluck it when the storm laughs in the forest;
To raise man from secret darkness,
Yet keep his roots clinging to the earth;
To give him thirst for life, and make death his cup-bearer;
To endow him with love that waxeth with pain,
And exalts with desire, and increases with longing,
And fadeth away with the first embrace;
To girdle his nights with dreams of higher days,
And infuse his days with visions of blissful nights,
And yet to confine his days and his nights
To their immutable resemblance;
To make his fancy like the eagle of the mountain,
And his thought as the tempests of the seas,
And yet to give him hands slow in decision,
And feet heavy with deliberation;
To give him gladness that he may sing before us,
And sorrow that he may call unto us,
And then to lay him low,
When the earth in her hunger cries for food;
To raise his soul high above the firmament
That he may foretaste our tomorrow,
And to keep his body grovelling in the mire
That he may not forget his yesterday.

Thus shall we rule man unto the end of time,
Governing the breath that began with his mother's crying,
And ends with the lamentation of his children.

FIRST GOD

My heart thirsts, yet I would not drink the faint blood of a
    feeble race,
For the cup is tainted, and the vintage therein is bitter to
    my mouth.
Like thee I have kneaded the clay and fashioned it to breathing
    forms
That crept out of my dripping fingers unto the marshes and
    the hills.
Like thee I have kindled the dark depths of beginning life
And watched it crawl from caves to rocky heights.
Like thee I have summoned spring and laid the beauty thereof
For a lure that seizes youth and binds it to generate and
    multiply.
Like thee I have led man from shrine to shrine,
And turned his mute fear of things unseen
To tremulous faith in us, the unvisited and the unknown.
Like thee I have ridden the wild tempest over his head
That he might bow before us,
And shaken the earth beneath him until he cried unto us;
And like thee, led the savage ocean against his nested isle,
Till he hath died calling upon us.
All this have I done, and more.
And all that I have done is empty and vain.
Vain is the waking and empty is the sleep,
And thrice empty and vain is the dream.

THIRD GOD

Brothers, my august brothers,
Down in the myrtle grove
A girl is dancing to the moon,
A thousand dew-stars are in her hair,
About her feet a thousand wings.

SECOND GOD

We have planted man, our vine, and tilled the soil
In the purple mist of the first dawn.
We watched the lean branches grow,
And through the days of seasonless years
We nursed the infant leaves.
From the angry element we shielded the bud,
And against all dark spirits we guarded the flower.
And now that our vine hath yielded the grape
You will not take it to the winepress and fill the cup.
Whose mightier hand than yours shall reap the fruit?
And what nobler end than your thirst awaits the wine?
Man is food for the gods,
And the glory of man begins
When his aimless breath is sucked by gods' hallowed lips.
All that is human counts for naught if human it remain;
The innocence of childhood, and the sweet ecstasy of youth,
The passion of stern manhood, and the wisdom of old age;
The splendour of kings and the triumph of warriors,
The fame of poets and the honour of dreamers and saints;
All these and all that lieth therein is bred for gods.
And naught but bread ungraced shall it be
If the gods raise it not to their mouths.
And as the mute grain turns to love songs when swallowed by
    the nightingale,
Even so as bread for gods shall man taste godhead.

FIRST GOD

Aye, man is meat for gods!
And all that is man shall come upon the gods' eternal board!
The pain of child-bearing and the agony of child-birth,
The blind cry of the infant that pierces the naked night,
And the anguish of the mother wrestling with the sleep
    she craves,
To pour life exhausted from her breast;
The flaming breath of youth tormented,

And the burdened sobs of passion unspent;
The dripping brows of manhood tilling the barren land,
And the regret of pale old age when life against life's will
Calls to the grave.
Behold this is man!
A creature bred on hunger and made food for hungry gods.
A vine that creeps in dust beneath the feet of deathless death.
The flower that blooms in nights of evil shadows;
The grape of mournful days, and days of terror and shame.
And yet you would have me eat and drink.
You would bid me sit amongst shrouded faces
And draw my life from stony lips
And from withered hands receive my eternity.

THIRD GOD

Brothers, my dreaded brothers,
Thrice deep the youth is singing,
And thrice higher is his song.
His voice shakes the forest
And pierces the sky,
And scatters the slumbering of earth.

SECOND GOD (*Always unhearing*)

The bee hums harshly in your ears,
And foul is the honey to your lips.
Fain would I comfort you,
But how shall I?
Only the abyss listens when gods call unto gods,
For measureless is the gulf that lies between divinities,
And windless is the space.
Yet I would comfort you,
I would make serene your clouded sphere;
And though equal we are in power and judgment,
I would counsel you.
    When out of chaos came the earth, and we, sons of the
beginning, beheld each other in the lustless light, we breathed

the first hushed, tremulous sound that quickened the currents of air and sea.

Then we walked, hand in hand, upon the grey infant world, and out of the echoes of our first drowsy steps time was born, a fourth divinity, that sets his feet upon our footprints, shadowing our thoughts and desires, and seeing only with our eyes.

And unto earth came life, and unto life came the spirit, the winged melody of the universe. And we ruled life and spirit, and none save us knew the measure of the years nor the weight of years' nebulous dreams, till we, at noontide of the seventh æon, gave the sea in marriage to the sun.

And from the inner chamber of their nuptial ecstasy, we brought man, a creature who, though yielding and infirm, bears ever the marks of his parentage.

Through man who walks earth with eyes upon the stars, we find pathways to earth's distant regions; and of man, the humble reed growing beside dark waters, we make a flute through whose hollowed heart we pour our voice to the silence-bound world.
From the sunless north to the sun-smitten sand of the south.
From the lotus land where days are born
To perilous isles where days are slain,
Man, the faint hearted, overbold by our purpose,
Ventures with lyre and sword.
Ours is the will he heralds,
And ours the sovereignty he proclaims,
And his love trodden courses are rivers, to the sea of our desires.
We, upon the heights, in man's sleep dream our dreams.
We urge his days to part from the valley of twilights
And seek their fullness upon the hills.
Our hands direct the tempests that sweep the world
And summon man from sterile peace to fertile strife,
And on to triumph.
In our eyes is the vision that turns man's soul to flame,
And leads him to exalted loneliness and rebellious prophecy,
And on to crucifixion.
Man is born to bondage,
And in bondage is his honour and his reward.
In man we seek a mouthpiece,

THE EARTH GODS

And in his life our self fulfilment.
Whose heart shall echo our voice if the human heart is
    deafened with dust?
Who shall behold our shining if man's eye is blinded with night?
And what would you do with man, child of our earliest heart,
    our own self image?

THIRD GOD

Brothers, my mighty brothers,
The dancer's feet are drunk with songs.
They set the air a-throbbing,
And like doves her hands fly upward.

FIRST GOD

The lark calls to the lark,
But upward the eagle soars,
Nor tarries to hear the song.
You would teach me self love fulfilled in man's worship,
And content with man's servitude.
But my self love is limitless and without measure.
I would rise beyond my earthbound mortality
And throne me upon the heavens.
My arms would girdle space and encompass the spheres.
I would take the starry way for a bow,
And the comets for arrows,
And with the infinite would I conquer the infinite.

But you would not do this, were it in your power.
For even as man is to man,
So are gods to gods.
Nay, you would bring to my weary heart
Remembrance of cycles spent in mist,
When my soul sought itself among the mountains
And mine eyes pursued their own image in slumbering waters;
Though my yesterday died in child-birth
And only silence visits her womb,
And the wind strewn sand nestles at her breast.

Oh yesterday, dead yesterday,
Mother of my chained divinity,
What super-god caught you in your flight
And made you breed in the cage?
What giant sun warmed your bosom
To give me birth?
I bless you not, yet I would not curse you;
For even as you have burdened me with life
So I have burdened man.
But less cruel have I been.
I, immortal, made man a passing shadow;
And you, dying, conceived me deathless.

Yesterday, dead yesterday,
Shall you return with distant tomorrow,
That I may bring you to judgment?
And will you wake with life's second dawn
That I may erase your earth-clinging memory from the earth?
Would that you might rise with all the dead of yore,
Till the land choke with its own bitter fruit,
And all the seas be stagnant with the slain,
And woe upon woe exhaust earth's vain fertility.

THIRD GOD

Brother, my sacred brothers,
The girl has heard the song,
And now she seeks the singer.
Like a fawn in glad surprise
She leaps over rocks and streams
And turns her to every side.
Oh, the joy in mortal intent,
The eye of purpose half-born;
The smile on lips that quiver
With foretaste of promised delight!
What flower has fallen from heaven,
What flame has risen from hell,
That startled the heart of silence

To this breathless joy and fear?
What dream dreamt we upon the height,
What thought gave we to the wind
That woke the drowsing valley
And made watchful the night?

SECOND GOD

The sacred loom is given you,
And the art to weave the fabric.
The loom and the art shall be yours forevermore,
And yours the dark thread and the light,
And yours the purple and the gold.
Yet you would grudge yourself a raiment.
Your hands have spun man's soul
From living air and fire,
Yet now you would break the thread,
And lend your versèd fingers to an idle eternity.

FIRST GOD

Nay, unto eternity unmoulded I would give my hands,
And to untrodden fields assign my feet.
What joy is there in songs oft heard,
Whose tune the remembering ear arrests
Ere the breath yields it to the wind?
My heart longs for what my heart conceives not,
And unto the unknown where memory dwells not
I would command my spirit.
Oh, tempt me not with glory possessed,
And seek not to comfort me with your dream or mine,
For all that I am, and all that there is on earth,
And all that shall be, inviteth not my soul.
    Oh my soul, Silent is thy face,
    And in thine eyes the shadows of night are sleeping.
    But terrible is thy silence,
    And thou art terrible.

THIRD GOD

Brothers, my solemn brothers,
The girl has found the singer.
She sees his raptured face.
Panther-like she slips with subtle steps
Through rustling vine and fern.
And now amid his ardent cries
He gazes full on her.

Oh my brothers, my heedless brothers,
Is it some other god in passion
Who has woven this web of scarlet and white?
What unbridled star has gone astray?
Whose secret keepeth night from morning?
And whose hand is upon our world?

FIRST GOD

Oh my soul, my soul,
Thou burning sphere that girdles me,
How shall I guide thy course,
And unto what space direct thy eagerness?

Oh my mateless soul,
In thy hunger thou preyest upon thyself,
And with thine own tears thou wouldst quench thy thirst;
For night gathers not her dew into thy cup,
And the day brings thee no fruit.
Oh my soul, my soul,
Thou grounded ship laden with desire,
Whence shall come the wind to fill thy sail,
And what higher tide shall release thy rudder?
Weighed is thine anchor and thy wings would spread,
But the skies are silent above thee,
And the still sea mocks at thy immobility.

*

And what hope is there for thee and me?
What shifting of worlds, what new purpose in the heavens,
That shall claim thee?
Does the womb of the virgin infinite
Bear the seed of thy Redeemer,
One mightier than thy vision
Whose hand shall deliver thee from thy captivity?

SECOND GOD

Hold your importunate cry,
And the breath of your burning heart,
For deaf is the ear of the infinite,
And heedless is the sky.
We are the beyond and we are the Most High,
And between us and boundless eternity
Is naught save our unshaped passion
And the motive thereof.

You invoke the unknown,
And the unknown clad with moving mist
Dwells in your own soul.
Yea, in your own soul your Redeemer lies asleep,
And in sleep sees what your waking cyc docs not see.
And that is the secret of our being.
Would you leave the harvest ungathered,
In haste to sow again the dreaming furrow?
And wherefore spread you your cloud in trackless fields
    and desolate,
When your own flock is seeking you,
And would fain gather in your shadow?
Forbear and look down upon the world.
Behold the unweaned children of your love.
The earth is your abode, and the earth is your throne;
And high beyond man's furtherest hope
Your hand upholds his destiny.
You would not abandon him
Who strives to reach you through gladness and through pain.
You would not turn away your face from the need in his eye.

THE EARTH GODS

FIRST GOD

Does dawn hold the heart of night unto her heart?
Or shall the sea heed the bodies of her dead?
Like dawn my soul rises within me
Naked and unencumbered.
And like the unresting sea
My heart casts out a perishing wrack of man and earth.
I would not cling to that that clings to me.
But unto that that rises beyond my reach I would arise.

THIRD GOD

Brothers, behold, my brothers,
They meet, two star-bound spirits in the sky encountering.
In silence they gaze the one upon the other.
He sings no more,
And yet his sunburnt throat throbs with the song;
And in her limbs the happy dance is stayed
But not asleep.

Brothers, my strange brothers,
The night waxeth deep,
And brighter is the moon,
And 'twixt the meadow and the sea
A voice in rapture calleth you and me.

SECOND GOD

To be, to rise, to burn before the burning sun,
To live, and to watch the nights of the living
As Orion watches us!
To face the four winds with a head crowned and high,
And to heal the ills of man with our tideless breath!
The tentmaker sits darkly at his loom,
And the potter turns his wheel unaware;
But we, the sleepless and the knowing,
We are released from guessing and from chance.

We pause not nor do we wait for thought.
We are beyond all restless questioning.
Be content and let the dreaming go.
Like rivers let us flow to ocean
Unwounded by the edges of the rocks;
And when we reach her heart and are merged,
No more shall we wrangle and reason of tomorrow.

FIRST GOD

Oh, this ache of ceaseless divining,
This vigil of guiding the day unto twilight,
And the night unto dawn;
This tide of ever remembering and forgetting;
This ever sowing destinies and reaping but hopes;
This changeless lifting of self from dust to mist,
Only to long for dust, and to fall down with longing
    unto dust,
And still with greater longing to seek the mist again.
And this timeless measuring of time.
Must my soul needs to be a sea whose currents forever
    confound one another,
Or the sky where the warring winds turn hurricane?

Were I man, a blind fragment,
I could have met it with patience.
Or if I were the Supreme Godhead,
Who fills the emptiness of man and of gods,
I would be fulfilled.
But you and I are neither human,
Nor the Supreme above us.
We are but twilights ever rising and ever fading
Between horizon and horizon.
We are but gods holding a world and held by it,
Fates that sound the trumpets
Whilst the breath and the music come from beyond.
And I rebel.
I would exhaust myself to emptiness.

I would dissolve myself afar from your vision,
And from the memory of this silent youth, our younger
   brother,
Who sits beside us gazing into yonder valley,
And though his lips move, utters not a word.

THIRD GOD

I speak, my unheeding brothers,
I do indeed speak,
But you hear only your own words.
I bid you see your glory and mine,
But you turn, and close your eyes,
And rock your thrones.
Ye sovereigns who would govern the above world and the
   world beneath,
Gods self-bent, whose yesterday is ever jealous of your
   tomorrow,
Self-weary, who would unleash your temper with speech
And lash our orb with thunderings!
Your feud is but the sounding of an Ancient Lyre
Whose strings have been half forgotten by His fingers
Who has Orion for a harp and the Pleiades for cymbals.
Even now, while you are muttering and rumbling,
His harp rings, His cymbals clash,
And I beseech you hear His song.

   Behold, man and woman,
   Flame to flame,
   In white ecstasy.
Roots that suck at the breast of purple earth,
Flame flowers at the breasts of the sky.
And we are the purple breast,
And we are the enduring sky.
Our soul, even the soul of life, your soul and mine,
Dwells this night in a throat enflamed,
And garments the body of a girl with beating waves.
Your sceptre cannot sway this destiny,

THE EARTH GODS

Your weariness is but ambition.
This and all is wiped away
In the passion of a man and a maid.

SECOND GOD

Yea, what of this love of man and woman?
See how the east wind dances with her dancing feet,
And the west wind rises singing with his song.
Behold our sacred purpose now enthroned,
In the yielding of a spirit that sings to a body that dances.

FIRST GOD

I will not turn my eyes downward to the conceit of earth,
Nor to her children in their slow agony that you call love.
And what is love,
But the muffled drum and leads the long procession of sweet
    uncertainty
To another slow agony?
I will not look downward.
What is there to behold
Save a man and a woman in the forest that grew to trap them
That they might renounce self
And parent creatures for our unborn tomorrow?

THIRD GOD

Oh, the affliction of knowing,
The starless veil of prying and questioning
Which we have laid upon the world;
And the challenge to human forbearance!
We would lay under a stone a waxen shape
And say, It is a thing of clay,
And in clay let it find its end.
We would hold in our hands a white flame
And say in our heart,
It is a fragment of ourselves returning,

437

THE EARTH GODS

    A breath of our breath that had escaped,
And now haunts our hands and lips for more fragrance.
Earth gods, my brothers,
High upon the mountain,
We are still earth-bound,
Through man desiring the golden hours of man's destiny.
Shall our wisdom ravish beauty from his eyes?
Shall our measures subdue his passion to stillness,
Or to our own passion?

What would your armies of reasoning
Where love encamps his host?
They who are conquered by love,
And upon whose bodies love's chariot ran
From sea to mountain
And again from mountain to the sea,
Stand even now in a shy half-embrace.
Petal unto petal they breathe the sacred perfume,
Soul to soul they find the soul of life,
And upon their eyelids lies a prayer
Unto you and unto me.
Love is a night bent down to a bower anointed,
A sky turned meadow, and all the stars to fireflies.
True it is, we are the beyond,
And we are the most high.
But love is beyond our questioning,
And love outsoars our song.

SECOND GOD

Seek you a distant orb,
And would not consider this star
Where your sinews are planted?
There is no centre in space
Save where self is wedded to self,
And beauty is the witness and the priest.
And see and behold beauty scattered about our feet,
And beauty filling our hands to shame our lips.

439

THE EARTH GODS

The most distant is the most near.
And where beauty is, there are all things.

Oh, lofty dreaming brother,
Return to us from time's dim borderland!
Unlace your feet from no-where and no-when,
And dwell with us in this security
Which your hand interwined with ours
Has builded stone upon stone.
Cast off your mantle of brooding,
And comrade us, masters of the young earth green and warm.

FIRST GOD

Eternal Altar! Wouldst thou indeed this night
A god for sacrifice?
Now then, I come, and coming I offer up
My passion and my pain.
Lo, there is the dancer, carved out of our ancient eagerness,
And the singer is crying mine own songs unto the wind.
And in that dancing and in that singing
A god is slain within me.
My god-heart within my human ribs
Shouts to my god-heart in mid-air.
The human pit that wearied me calls to divinity.
The beauty that we have sought from the beginning
Calls unto divinity.
I heed, and I have measured the call,
And now I yield.
Beauty is a path that leads to self self-slain.
Beat your strings.
I will to walk the path.
It stretches ever to another dawn.

THIRD GOD

Love triumphs.
The white and green of love beside a lake,

And the proud majesty of love in tower or balcony;
Love in a garden or in the desert untrodden,
Love is our lord and master.
It is not a wanton decay of the flesh,
Nor the crumbling of desire
When desire and self are wrestling;
Nor is it flesh that takes arms against the spirit.
Love rebels not.
It only leaves the trodden way of ancient destinies for the
    sacred grove,
To sing and dance its secret to eternity.
Love is youth with chains broken,
Manhood made free from the sod,
And womanhood warmed by the flame
And shining with the light of heaven deeper than our heaven.
Love is a distant laughter in the spirit.
It is a wild assault that hushes you to your awakening.
It is a new dawn upon the earth,
A day not yet achieved in your eyes or mine,
But already achieved in its own greater heart.

Brothers, my brothers,
The bride comes from the heart of dawn,
And the bridegroom from the sunset.
There is a wedding in the valley.
A day too vast for recording.

SECOND GOD

Thus has it been since the first morn
Discharged the plains to hill and vale,
And thus shall it be to the last even-tide.
Our roots have brought forth the dancing branches in
    the valley,
And we are the flowering of the song-scent that rises to
    the heights.
Immortal and mortal, twin rivers calling to the sea.
There is no emptiness between call and call,

But only in the ear.
Time maketh our listening more certain,
And giveth it more desire.
Only doubt in mortal hushes the sound.
We have outsoared the doubt.
Man is a child of our younger heart.
Man is god in slow arising;
And betwixt his joy and his pain
Lies our sleeping, and the dreaming thereof.

FIRST GOD

Let the singer cry, and let the dancer whirl her feet
And let me be content awhile.
Let my soul be serene this night.
Perchance I may drowse, and drowsing
Behold a brighter world
And creatures more starry supple to my mind.

THIRD GOD

Now I will rise and strip me of time and space,
And I will dance in that field untrodden,
And the dancer's feet will move with my feet;
And I will sing in that higher air,
And a human voice will throb within my voice.

We shall pass into the twilight;
Perchance to wake to the dawn of another world.
But love shall stay,
And his finger-marks shall not be erased.

The blessed forge burns,
The sparks rise, and each spark is a sun.
Better it is for us, and wiser,
To seek a shadowed nook and sleep in our earth divinity,
And let love, human and frail, command the coming day.

THE WANDERER
HIS PARABLES AND HIS SAYINGS

CONTENTS

THE WANDERER

I MET HIM at the crossroads, a man with but a cloak and a staff, and a veil of pain upon his face. And we greeted one another, and I said to him, "Come to my house and be my guest."

And he came.

My wife and my children met us at the threshold, and he smiled at them, and they loved his coming.

Then we all sat together at the board and we were happy with the man for there was a silence and a mystery in him.

And after supper we gathered to the fire and I asked him about his wanderings.

He told us many a tale that night and also the next day, but what I now record was born out of the bitterness of his days though he himself was kindly, and these tales are of the dust and patience of his road.

And when he left us after three days we did not feel that a guest had departed but rather that one of us was still out in the garden and had not yet come in.

GARMENTS

UPON A DAY Beauty and Ugliness met on the shore of a sea. And they said to one another, "Let us bathe in the sea."

Then they disrobed and swam in the waters. And after a while Ugliness came back to shore and garmented himself with the garments of Beauty and walked his way.

And Beauty too came out of the sea, and found not her raiment, and she was too shy to be naked, therefore she dressed herself with the raiment of Ugliness. And Beauty walked her way.

And to this very day men and women mistake the one for the other.

Yet some there are who have beheld the face of Beauty, and they know her notwithstanding her garments. And some there be who know the face of Ugliness, and the cloth conceals him not from their eyes.

THE EAGLE AND THE SKYLARK

A SKYLARK AND an eagle met on a rock upon a high hill. The skylark said, "Good morrow to you, Sir." And the eagle looked down upon him and said faintly, "Good morrow."

And the skylark said, "I hope all things are well with you, Sir."

"Aye," said the eagle, "all is well with us. But do you not know that we are the king of birds, and that you shall not address us before we ourselves have spoken?"

Said the skylark, "Methinks we are of the same family."

The eagle looked upon him with disdain and he said, "Who ever has said that you and I are of the same family?"

Then said the skylark, "But I would remind you of this, I can fly even as high as you, and I can sing and give delight to the other creatures of this earth. And you give neither pleasure nor delight."

Then the eagle was angered, and he said, "Pleasure and delight! You little presumptuous creature! With one thrust of my beak I could destroy you. You are but the size of my foot."

Then the skylark flew up and alighted upon the back of the eagle and began to pick at his feathers. The eagle was annoyed, and he flew swift and high that he might rid himself of the little bird. But he failed to do so. At last he dropped back to that very rock upon the high hill, more fretted than ever, with the little creature still upon his back, and cursing the fate of the hour.

Now at that moment a small turtle came by and laughed at the sight, and laughed so hard that she almost turned upon her back.

And the eagle looked down upon the turtle and he said, "You slow creeping thing, ever one with the earth, what are you laughing at?"

453

And the turtle said, "Why, I see that you are turned horse, and that you have a small bird riding you, but the small bird is the better bird."

And the eagle said to her, "Go you about your business. This is a family affair between my brother, the lark, and myself."

THE LOVE SONG

A POET ONCE wrote a love song and it was beautiful. And he made many copies of it, and sent them to his friends and his acquaintances, both men and women, and even to a young woman whom he had met but once, who lived beyond the mountains.

And in a day or two a messenger came from the young woman bringing a letter. And in the letter she said, "Let me assure you, I am deeply touched by the love song that you have written to me. Come now, and see my father and my mother, and we shall make arrangements for the betrothal."

And the poet answered the letter, and he said to her, "My friend, it was but a song of love out of a poet's heart, sung by every man to every woman."

And she wrote again to him saying, "Hypocrite and liar in words! From this day unto my coffin-day I shall hate all poets for your sake."

UPON THE BANK of the Nile at eventide, a hyena met a crocodile and they stopped and greeted one another.

The hyena spoke and said, "How goes the day with you, Sir?"

And the crocodile answered saying, "It goes badly with me. Sometimes in my pain and sorrow I weep, and then the creatures always say, 'They are but crocodile tears.' And this wounds me beyond all telling."

Then the hyena said, 'You speak of your pain and your sorrow, but think of me also, for a moment. I gaze at the beauty of the world, its wonders and its miracles, and out of sheer joy I laugh even as the day laughs. And then the people of the jungle say, 'It is but the laughter of a hyena.' "

THERE CAME TO the Fair a girl from the countryside, most comely. There was a lily and a rose in her face. There was sunset in her hair, and dawn smiled upon her lips.

No sooner did the lovely stranger appear in their sight than the young men sought her and surrounded her. One would dance with her, and another would cut a cake in her honour. And they all desired to kiss her cheek. For after all, was it not the Fair?

But the girl was shocked and startled, and she thought ill of the young men. She rebuked them, and she even struck one or two of them in the face. Then she ran away from them.

And on her way home that evening she was saying in her heart, "I am disgusted. How unmannerly and ill bred are these men. It is beyond all patience."

A year passed during which that very comely girl thought much of Fairs and men. Then she came again to the Fair with the lily and the rose in her face, the sunset in her hair and the smile of dawn upon her lips.

But now the young men, seeing her, turned from her. And all the day long she was unsought and alone.

And at eventide as she walked the road toward her home she cried in her heart, "I am disgusted. How unmannerly and ill bred are these youths. It is beyond all patience."

THE TWO PRINCESSES

IN THE CITY of Shawakis lived a prince, and he was loved by everyone, men and women and children. Even the animals of the field came unto him in greeting.

But all the people said that his wife, the princess, loved him not; nay, that she even hated him.

And upon a day the princess of a neighbouring city came to visit the princess of Shawakis. And they sat and talked together, and their words led to their husbands.

And the princess of Shawakis said with passion, "I envy your happiness with the prince, your husband, though you have been married these many years. I hate my husband. He belongs not to me alone, and I am indeed a woman most unhappy."

Then the visiting princess gazed at her and said, "My friend, the truth is that you love your husband. Aye, and you still have for him a passion unspent, and that is life in woman like unto Spring in a garden. But pity me, and my husband, for we do but endure one another in silent patience. And yet you and others deem this happiness."

THE LIGHTNING FLASH

THERE WAS A Christian bishop in his cathedral on a stormy day, and an un-Christian woman came and stood before him, and she said, "I am not a Christian. Is there salvation for me from hell-fire?"

And the bishop looked upon the woman, and he answered her saying, "Nay, there is salvation for those only who are baptized of water and of the spirit."

And even as he spoke a bolt from the sky fell with thunder upon the cathedral and it was filled with fire.

And the men of the city came running, and they saved the woman, but the bishop was consumed, food of the fire.

THE HERMIT AND THE BEASTS

ONCE THERE LIVED among the green hills a hermit. He was pure of spirit and white of heart. And all the animals of the land and all the fowls of the air came to him in pairs and he spoke unto them. They heard him gladly, and they would gather near unto him, and would not go until nightfall, when he would send them away, entrusting them to the wind and the woods with his blessing.

Upon an evening as he was speaking of love, a leopard raised her head and said to the hermit, "You speak to us of loving. Tell us, Sir, where is your mate?"

And the hermit said, "I have no mate."

Then a great cry of surprise rose from the company of beasts and fowls, and they began to say among themselves, "How can he tell us of loving and mating when he himself knows naught thereof?" And quietly and in disdain they left him alone.

That night the hermit lay upon his mat with his face earthward, and he wept bitterly and beat his hands upon his breast.

THE PROPHET AND THE CHILD

ONCE ON A day the prophet Sharia met a child in a garden. The child ran to him and said, "Good morrow to you, Sir," and the prophet said, "Good morrow to you, Sir." And in a moment, "I see that you are alone."

Then the child said, in laughter and delight, "It took a long time to lose my nurse. She thinks I am behind those hedges; but can't you see that I am here?" Then he gazed at the prophet's face and spoke again. "You are alone, too. What did you do with your nurse?"

The prophet answered and said, "Ah, that is a different thing. In very truth I cannot lose her oftentimes. But now, when I came into this garden, she was seeking after me behind the hedges."

The child clapped his hands and cried out, "So you are lost like me! Isn't it good to be lost?" And then he said, "Who are you?"

And the man answered, "They call me the prophet Sharia. And tell me, who are you?"

"I am only myself," said the child, "and my nurse is seeking after me, and she does not know where I am."

Then the prophet gazed into space saying, "I too have escaped my nurse for a while, but she will find me out."

And the child said, "I know mine will find me out too."

At that moment a woman's voice was heard calling the child's name. "See," said the child, "I told you she would be finding me."

And at the same moment another voice was heard, "Where art thou, Sharia?"

And the prophet said, "See, my child, they have found me also."

And turning his face upward, Sharia answered, "Here am I."

THE PEARL

SAID ONE OYSTER to a neighbouring oyster, "I have a very great pain within me. It is heavy and round and I am in distress."

And the other oyster replied with haughty complacence, "Praise be to the heavens and to the sea, I have no pain within me. I am well and whole both within and without."

At that moment a crab was passing by and heard the two oysters, and he said to the one who was well and whole both within and without, "Yes, you are well and whole; but the pain that your neighbour bears is a pearl of exceeding beauty."

A MAN AND a woman sat by a window that opened upon Spring. They sat close one unto the other. And the woman said, "I love you. You are handsome, and you are rich, and you are always well-attired."

And the man said, "I love you. You are a beautiful thought, a thing too apart to hold in the hand, and a song in my dreaming."

But the woman turned from him in anger, and she said, "Sir, please leave me now. I am not a thought, and I am not a thing that passes in your dreams. I am a woman. I would have you desire me, a wife, and the mother of unborn children."

And they parted.

And the man was saying in his heart, "Behold another dream is even now turned into the mist."

And the woman was saying, "Well, what of a man who turns me into a mist and a dream?"

THE KING

THE PEOPLE OF the Kingdom of Sadik surrounded the palace of their king shouting in rebellion against him. And he came down the steps of the palace carrying his crown in one hand and his sceptre in the other. The majesty of his appearance silenced the multitude, and he stood before them and said, "My friends, who are no longer my subjects, here I yield my crown and sceptre unto you. I would be one of you. I am only one man, but as a man I would work together with you that our lot may be made better. There is no need for a king. Let us go therefore to the fields and the vineyards and labour hand with hand. Only you must tell me to what field or vineyard I should go. All of you now are king."

And the people marvelled, and stillness was upon them, for the king whom they had deemed the source of their discontent now yielded his crown and sceptre to them and became as one of them.

Then each and every one of them went his way, and the king walked with one man to a field.

But the Kingdom of Sadik fared not better without a king, and the mist of discontent was still upon the land. The people cried out in the market places saying that they would be governed, and that they would have a king to rule them. And the elders and the youths said as if with one voice, "We will have our king."

And they sought the king and found him toiling in the field, and they brought him to his seat, and yielded unto him his crown and his sceptre. And they said, "Now rule us, with might and with justice."

And he said, "I will indeed rule you with might, and may the gods of the heaven and the earth help me that I may also rule with justice."

Now, there came to his presence men and women and spoke unto him of a baron who mistreated them, and to whom they were but serfs. And straightway the king brought the baron before him and said, "The life of one man is as weighty in the scales of God as the life of another. And because you know not how to weigh the lives of those who work in your fields and your vineyards, you are banished, and you shall leave this kingdom forever."

The following day came another company to the king and spoke of the cruelty of a countess beyond the hills, and how she brought them down to misery. Instantly the countess was brought to court, and the king sentenced her also to banishment, saying, "Those who till our fields and care for our vineyards are nobler than we who eat the bread they prepare and drink the wine of their wine-press. And because you know not this, you shall leave this land and be afar from this kingdom."

Then came men and women who said that the bishop made them bring stones and hew the stones for the cathedral, yet he gave them naught, though they knew the bishop's coffer was full of gold and silver while they themselves were empty with hunger.

And the king called for the bishop, and when the bishop came the king spoke and said unto him, "That cross you wear upon your bosom should mean giving life unto life. But you have taken life from life and you have given none. Therefore you shall leave this kingdom never to return."

Thus each day for a full moon men and women came to the king to tell him of the burdens laid upon them. And each and every day for a full moon some oppressor was exiled from the land.

And the people of Sadik were amazed, and there was cheer in their heart.

And upon a day the elders and the youths came and surrounded the tower of the king and called for him. And he came down holding his crown with one hand and his sceptre with the other.

And he spoke unto them and said, "Now, what would you of me? Behold, I yield back to you that which you desired me to hold."

But they cried, "Nay, nay, you are our rightful king. You have made clean the land of vipers, and you have brought the wolves to naught, and we come to sing our thanksgiving unto you. The crown is yours in majesty and the sceptre is yours in glory."

Then the king said, "Not I, not I. You yourselves are king. When you deemed me weak and a misruler, you yourselves were weak and misruling. And now the land fares well because it is in your will. I am but a thought in the mind of you all, and I exist not save in your actions. There is no such person as governor. Only the governed exist to govern themselves."

And the king re-entered his tower with his crown and his sceptre. And the elders and the youths went their various ways and they were content.

And each and every one thought of himself as king with a crown in one hand and a sceptre in the other.

UPON THE SAND

SAID ONE MAN to another, "At the high tide of the sea, long ago, with the point of my staff I wrote a line upon the sand; and the people still pause to read it, and they are careful that naught shall erase it."

And the other man said, "And I too wrote a line upon the sand, but it was at low tide, and the waves of the vast sea washed it away. But tell me, what did you write?"

And the first man answered and said, "I wrote this: 'I am he who is.' But what did you write?"

And the other man said, "This I wrote: 'I am but a drop of this great ocean.'"

THE THREE GIFTS

ONCE IN THE city of Becharrè there lived a gracious prince who was loved and honoured by all his subjects.

But there was one exceedingly poor man who was bitter against the prince, and who wagged continually a pestilent tongue in his dispraise.

The prince knew this, yet he was patient.

But at last he bethought him; and upon a wintry night there came to the door of the man a servant of the prince, bearing a sack of flour, a bag of soap and a cone of sugar.

And the servant said, "The prince sends you these gifts in token of remembrance."

The man was elated, for he thought the gifts were an homage from the prince. And in his pride he went to the bishop and told him what the prince had done, saying, "Can you not see how the prince desires my goodwill?"

But the bishop said, "Oh, how wise a prince, and how little you understand. He speaks in symbols. The flour is for your empty stomach; the soap is for your dirty hide; and the sugar is to sweeten your bitter tongue."

From that day forward the man became shy even of himself. His hatred of the prince was greater than ever, and even more he hated the bishop who had revealed the prince unto him.

But thereafter he kept silent.

THREE DOGS WERE basking in the sun and conversing.

The first dog said dreamily, "It is indeed wondrous to be living in this day of dogdom. Consider the ease with which we travel under the sea, upon the earth and even in the sky. And meditate for a moment upon the inventions brought forth for the comfort of dogs, even for our eyes and ears and noses."

And the second dog spoke and he said, "We are more heedful of the arts. We bark at the moon more rhythmically than did our forefathers. And when we gaze at ourselves in the water we see that our features are clearer than the features of yesterday."

Then the third dog spoke and said, "But what interests me most and beguiles my mind is the tranquil understanding existing between dogdoms."

At that very moment they looked, and lo, the dog-catcher was approaching.

The three dogs sprang up and scampered down the street; and as they ran the third dog said, "For God's sake, run for your lives. Civilization is after us."

THE DANCER

ONCE THERE CAME to the court of the Prince of Birkasha a dancer with her musicians. And she was admitted to the court, and she danced before the prince to the music of the lute and the flute and the zither.

She danced the dance of flames, and the dance of swords and spears; she danced the dance of stars and the dance of space. And then she danced the dance of flowers in the wind.

After this she stood before the throne of the prince and bowed her body before him. And the prince bade her to come nearer, and he said unto her, "Beautiful woman, daughter of grace and delight, whence comes your art? And how is it that you command all the elements in your rhythms and your rhymes?"

And the dancer bowed again before the prince, and she answered, "Mighty and gracious Majesty, I know not the answer to your questionings. Only this I know: The philosopher's soul dwells in his head, the poet's soul is in his heart; the singer's soul lingers about his throat, but the soul of the dancer abides in all her body."

THE TWO GUARDIAN ANGELS

ON AN EVENING two angels met at the city gate, and they greeted one another, and they conversed.

The one angel said, "What are you doing these days, and what work is given you?"

And the other answered, "It has been assigned me to be the guardian of a fallen man who lives down in the valley, a great sinner, most degraded. Let me assure you it is an important task, and I work hard."

The first angel said, "That is an easy commission. I have often known sinners, and have been their guardian many a time. But it has now been assigned me to be the guardian of the good saint who lives in a bower out yonder. And I assure you that is an exceedingly difficult work, and most subtle."

Said the first angel, "This is but assumption. How can guarding a saint be harder than guarding a sinner?"

And the other answered, "What impertinence, to call me assumptious! I have stated but the truth. Methinks it is you who are assumptious!"

Then the angels wrangled and fought, first with words and then with fists and wings.

While they were fighting an archangel came by. And he stopped them, and said, "Why do you fight? And what is it all about? Know you not that it is most unbecoming for guardian angels to fight at the city gate? Tell me, what is your disagreement?"

Then both angels spoke at once, each claiming that the work given him was the harder, and that he deserved the greater recognition.

The archangel shook his head and bethought him.

Then he said, "My friends, I cannot say now which one of you has the greater claim upon honour and reward. But since the power is bestowed in me, therefore for peace's sake and for good guardianship, I give to each of you the other's occupation, since each of you insists that the other's task is the easier one. Now go hence and be happy at your work."

The angels thus ordered went their ways. But each one looked backward with greater anger at the archangel. And in his heart each was saying, "Oh, these archangels! Every day they make life harder and still harder for us angels!"

But the archangel stood there, and once more he bethought him. And he said in his heart, "We have, indeed, to be watchful and to keep guard over our guardian angels."

THE STATUE

ONCE THERE LIVED a man among the hills who possessed a statue wrought by an ancient master. It lay at his door face downward and he was not mindful of it.

One day there passed by his house a man from the city, a man of knowledge, and seeing the statue he inquired of the owner if he would sell it.

The owner laughed and said, "And pray who would want to buy that dull and dirty stone?"

The man from the city said, "I will give you this piece of silver for it."

And the other man was astonished and delighted.

The statue was removed to the city, upon the back of an elephant. And after many moons the man from the hills visited the city, and as he walked the streets he saw a crowd before a shop, and a man with a loud voice was crying, "Come ye in and behold the most beautiful, the most wonderful statue in all the world. Only two silver pieces to look upon this most marvellous work of a master."

Thereupon the man from the hills paid two silver pieces and entered the shop to see the statue that he himself had sold for one piece of silver.

THE EXCHANGE

ONCE UPON A crossroad a poor Poet met a rich Stupid, and they conversed. And all that they said revealed but their discontent.

Then the Angel of the Road passed by, and he laid his hand upon the shoulder of the two men. And behold, a miracle: The two men had now exchanged their possessions.

And they parted. But strange to relate, the Poet looked and found naught in his hand but dry moving sand; and the Stupid closed his eyes and felt naught but moving cloud in his heart.

LOVE AND HATE

A WOMAN SAID unto a man, "I love you." And the man said, "It is in my heart to be worthy of your love."

And the woman said, "You love me not?" And the man only gazed upon her and said nothing.

Then the woman cried aloud, "I hate you." And the man said, "Then it is also in my heart to be worthy of your hate."

DREAMS

A MAN DREAMED a dream, and when he awoke he went to his soothsayer and desired that his dream be made plain unto him.

And the soothsayer said to the man, "Come to me with the dreams that you behold in your wakefulness and I will tell you their meaning. But the dreams of your sleep belong neither to my wisdom nor to your imagination."

THE MADMAN

IT WAS IN the garden of a madhouse that I met a youth with a face pale and lovely and full of wonder.

And I sat beside him upon the bench, and I said, "Why are you here?"

And he looked at me in astonishment, and he said, "It is an unseemly question, yet I will answer you. My father would make of me a reproduction of himself; so also would my uncle. My mother would have me the image of her illustrious father. My sister would hold up her seafaring husband as the perfect example for me to follow. My brother thinks I should be like him, a fine athlete.

"And my teachers also, the doctor of philosophy, and the music-master, and the logician, they too were determined, and each would have me but a reflection of his own face in a mirror.

"Therefore I came to this place. I find it more sane here. At least, I can be myself."

Then of a sudden he turned to me and he said, "But tell me, were you also driven to this place by education and good counsel?"

And I answered, "No, I am a visitor."

And he said, "Oh, you are one of those who live in the madhouse on the other side of the wall."

THE FROGS

UPON A SUMMER day a frog said to his mate, "I fear those people living in that house on the shore are disturbed by our night-songs."

And his mate answered and said, "Well, do they not annoy our silence during the day with their talking?"

The frog said, "Let us not forget that we may sing too much in the night."

And his mate answered, "Let us not forget that they chatter and shout overmuch during the day."

Said the frog, "How about the bullfrog who disturbs the whole neighbourhood with his God-forbidden booming?"

And his mate replied, "Aye, and what say you of the politician and the priest and the scientist who come to these shores and fill the air with noisy and rhymeless sound?"

Then the frog said, "Well, let us be better than these human beings. Let us be quiet at night, and keep our songs in our hearts, even though the moon calls for our rhythm and the stars for our rhyme. At least, let us be silent for a night or two, or even for three nights."

And his mate said, "Very well, I agree. We shall see what your bountiful heart will bring forth."

That night the frogs were silent; and they were silent the following night also, and again upon the third night.

And strange to relate, the talkative woman who lived in the house beside the lake came down to breakfast on that third day and shouted to her husband, "I have not slept these three nights. I was secure with sleep when the noise of the frogs was in my ear. But something must have happened. They have not sung now for three nights; and I am almost maddened with sleeplessness."

The frog heard this and turned to his mate and said, winking his eye, "And we were almost maddened with our silence, were we not?"

And his mate answered, "Yes, the silence of the night was heavy upon us. And I can see now that there is no need for us to cease our singing for the comfort of those who must needs fill their emptiness with noise."

And that night the moon called not in vain for their rhythm nor the stars for their rhyme.

LAWS AND LAW-GIVING

AGES AGO THERE was a great king, and he was wise. And he desired to lay laws unto his subjects.

He called upon one thousand wise men of one thousand different tribes to come to his capital and lay down the laws.

And all this came to pass.

But when the thousand laws written upon parchment were put before the king and he read them, he wept bitterly in his soul, for he had not known that there were one thousand forms of crime in his kingdom.

Then he called his scribe, and with a smile upon his mouth he himself dictated laws. And his laws were but seven.

And the one thousand wise men left him in anger and returned to their tribes with the laws they had laid down. And every tribe followed the laws of its wise men.

Therefore they have a thousand laws even to our own day.

It is a great country, but it has one thousand prisons, and the prisons are full of women and men, breakers of a thousand laws.

It is indeed a great country, but the people thereof are descendants of one thousand law-givers and of only one wise king.

I SAID TO my friend, "You see her leaning upon the arm of that man. It was but yesterday that she leaned thus upon my arm."

And my friend said, "And tomorrow she will lean upon mine."

I said, "Behold her sitting close at his side. It was but yesterday she sat close beside me."

And he answered, "Tomorrow she will sit beside me."

I said, "See, she drinks wine from his cup, and yesterday she drank from mine."

And he said, "Tomorrow, from my cup."

Then I said, "See how she gazes at him with love, and with yielding eyes. Yesterday she gazed thus upon me."

And my friend said, "It will be upon me she gazes tomorrow."

I said, "Do you not hear her now murmuring songs of love into his ears? Those very songs of love she murmured but yesterday into my ears."

And my friend said, "And tomorrow she will murmur them in mine."

I said, "Why see, she is embracing him. It was but yesterday that she embraced me."

And my friend said, "She will embrace me tomorrow."

Then I said, "What a strange woman."

But he answered, "She is like unto life, possessed by all men; and like death, she conquers all men; and like eternity, she enfolds all men."

THE PHILOSOPHER AND THE COBBLER

THERE CAME TO a cobbler's shop a philosopher with worn shoes. And the philosopher said to the cobbler, "Please mend my shoes."

And the cobbler said, "I am mending another man's shoes now, and there are still other shoes to patch before I can come to yours. But leave your shoes here, and wear this other pair today, and come tomorrow for your own."

Then the philosopher was indignant, and he said, "I wear no shoes that are not mine own."

And the cobbler said, "Well then, are you in truth a philosopher, and cannot enfold your feet with the shoes of another man? Upon this very street there is another cobbler who understands philosophers better than I do. Go you to him for mending."

BUILDERS OF BRIDGES

IN ANTIOCH WHERE the river Assi goes to meet the sea, a bridge was built to bring one half of the city nearer to the other half. It was built of large stones carried down from among the hills, on the backs of the mules of Antioch.

When the bridge was finished, upon a pillar thereof was engraven in Greek and in Aramaic, "This bridge was builded by King Antiochus II."

And all the people walked across the good bridge over the goodly river Assi.

And upon an evening, a youth, deemed by some a little mad, descended to the pillar where the words were engraven, and he covered over the graving with charcoal, and above it he wrote, "The stones of this bridge were brought down from the hills by the mules. In passing to and fro over it you are riding upon the backs of the mules of Antioch, builders of this bridge."

And when the people read what the youth had written, some of them laughed and some marvelled. And some said, "Ah yes, we know who has done this. Is he not a little mad?"

But one mule said, laughing, to another mule, "Do you not remember that we did carry those stones? And yet until now it has been said that the bridge was builded by King Antiochus."

THE FIELD OF ZAAD

UPON THE ROAD of Zaad a traveller met a man who lived in a nearby village, and the traveller, pointing with his hand to a vast field, asked the man saying, "Was not this the battle-ground where King Ahlam overcame his enemies?"

And the man answered and said, "This has never been a battle-ground. There once stood on this field the great city of Zaad, and it was burnt down to ashes. But now it is a good field, is it not?"

And the traveller and the man parted.

Not a half mile farther the traveller met another man, and pointing to the field again, he said, "So that is where the great city of Zaad once stood?"

And the man said, "There has never been a city in this place. But once there was a monastery here, and it was destroyed by the people of the South Country."

Shortly after, on that very road of Zaad, the traveller met a third man, and pointing once more to the vast field he said, "Is it not true that this is the place where once there stood a great monastery?"

But the man answered, "There has never been a monastery in this neighbourhood, but our fathers and our forefathers have told us that once there fell a great meteor on this field."

Then the traveller walked on, wondering in his heart. And he met a very old man, and saluting him he said, "Sir, upon this road I have met three men who live in the neighbourhood and I have asked each of them about this field, and each one denied what the other had said, and each one told me a new tale that the other had not told."

Then the old man raised his head, and answered, "My friend, each and every one of these men told you what was indeed so; but few of us are able to add fact to different fact and make a truth thereof."

THE GOLDEN BELT

ONCE UPON A day two men who met on the road were walking together toward Salamis, the City of Columns. In mid-afternoon they came to a wide river and there was no bridge to cross it. They must needs swim, or seek another road unknown to them.

And they said to one another, "Let us swim. After all, the river is not so wide." And they threw themselves into the water and swam.

And one of the men who had always known rivers and the ways of rivers, in mid-stream suddenly began to lose himself, and to be carried away by the rushing waters; while the other who had never swum before crossed the river straightway and stood upon the farther bank. Then seeing his companion still wrestling with the stream, he threw himself again into the waters and brought him also safely to the shore.

And the man who had been swept away by the current said, "But you told me you could not swim. How then did you cross that river with such assurance?"

And the second man answered, "My friend, do you see this belt which girdles me? It is full of golden coins that I have earned for my wife and my children, a full year's work. It is the weight of this belt of gold that carried me across the river, to my wife and my children. And my wife and my children were upon my shoulders as I swam."

And the two men walked on together toward Salamis.

THE RED EARTH

SAID A TREE to a man, "My roots are in the deep red earth, and I shall give you of my fruit."

And the man said to the tree, "How alike we are. My roots are also deep in the red earth. And the red earth gives you power to bestow upon me of your fruit, and the red earth teaches me to receive from you with thanksgiving."

THE FULL MOON

THE FULL MOON rose in glory upon the town, and all the dogs of that town began to bark at the moon.

Only one dog did not bark, and he said to them in a grave voice, "Awake not stillness from her sleep, nor bring you the moon to the earth with your barking."

Then all the dogs ceased barking, in awful silence. But the dog who had spoken to them continued barking for silence, the rest of the night.

THE HERMIT PROPHET

ONCE THERE LIVED a hermit prophet, and thrice a moon he would go down to the great city and in the market places he would preach giving and sharing to the people. And he was eloquent, and his fame was upon the land.

Upon an evening three men came to his hermitage and he greeted them. And they said, "You have been preaching giving and sharing, and you have sought to teach those who have much to give unto those who have little; and we doubt not that your fame has brought you riches. Now come and give us of your riches, for we are in need."

And the hermit answered and said, "My friends, I have naught but this bed and this mat and this jug of water. Take them if it is in your desire. I have neither gold nor silver."

Then they looked down with disdain upon him, and turned their faces from him; and the last man stood at the door for a moment, and said, "Oh, you cheat! You fraud! You teach and preach that which you yourself do not perform."

THE OLD, OLD WINE

ONCE THERE LIVED a rich man who was justly proud of his cellar and the wine therein. And there was one jug of ancient vintage kept for some occasion known only to himself.

The governor of the state visited him, and he bethought him and said, "That jug shall not be opened for a mere governor."

And a bishop of the diocese visited him, but he said to himself, "Nay, I will not open that jug. He would not know its value, nor would its aroma reach his nostrils."

The prince of the realm came and supped with him. But he thought, "It is too royal a wine for a mere princeling."

And even on the day when his own nephew was married, he said to himself, "No, not to these guests shall that jug be brought forth."

And the years passed by, and he died, an old man, and he was buried like unto every seed and acorn.

And upon the day that he was buried the ancient jug was brought out together with other jugs of wine, and it was shared by the peasants of the neighbourhood. And none knew its great age.

To them, all that is poured into a cup is only wine.

THE TWO POEMS

MANY CENTURIES AGO, on a road to Athens, two poets met, and they were glad to see one another.

And one poet asked the other saying, "What have you composed of late, and how goes it with your lyre?"

And the other poet answered and said with pride, "I have but now finished the greatest of my poems, perchance the greatest poem yet written in Greek. It is an invocation to Zeus the Supreme."

Then he took from beneath his cloak a parchment, saying, "Here, behold, I have it with me, and I would fain read it to you. Come, let us sit in the shade of that white cypress."

And the poet read his poem. And it was a long poem.

And the other poet said in kindliness, "This is a great poem. It will live through the ages, and in it you shall be glorified."

And the first poet said calmly, "And what have you been writing these late days?"

And the other answered, "I have written but little. Only eight lines in remembrance of a child playing in a garden." And he recited the lines.

The first poet said, "Not so bad; not so bad."

And they parted.

And now after two thousand years the eight lines of the one poet are read in every tongue, and are loved and cherished.

And though the other poem has indeed come down through the ages in libraries and in the cells of scholars, and though it is remembered, it is neither loved nor read.

LADY RUTH

THREE MEN ONCE looked from afar upon a white house that stood alone on a green hill. One of them said, "That is the house of Lady Ruth. She is an old witch."

The second man said, "You are wrong. Lady Ruth is a beautiful woman who lives there consecrated unto her dreams."

The third man said, "You are both wrong. Lady Ruth is the holder of this vast land, and she draws blood from her serfs."

And they walked on discussing Lady Ruth.

Then when they came to a crossroad they met an old man, and one of them asked him, saying, "Would you please tell us about Lady Ruth who lives in that white house upon the hill?"

And the old man raised his head and smiled upon them, and said, "I am ninety of years, and I remember Lady Ruth when I was but a boy. But Lady Ruth died eighty years ago, and now the house is empty. The owls hoot therein, sometimes, and people say the place is haunted."

THE MOUSE AND THE CAT

ONCE ON AN evening a poet met a peasant. The poet was distant and the peasant was shy, yet they conversed.

And the peasant said, "Let me tell you a little story which I heard of late. A mouse was caught in a trap, and while he was happily eating the cheese that lay therein, a cat stood by. The mouse trembled awhile, but he knew he was safe within the trap.

"Then the cat said, 'You are eating your last meal, my friend.'

"'Yes,' answered the mouse, 'one life have I, therefore one death. But what of you? They tell me you have nine lives. Doesn't that mean that you will have to die nine times?'"

And the peasant looked at the poet and he said, "Is not this a strange story?"

And the poet answered him not, but he walked away saying in his soul, "To be sure, nine lives have we, nine lives to be sure. And we shall die nine times, nine times shall we die. Perhaps it were better to have but one life, caught in a trap – the life of a peasant with a bit of cheese for the last meal. And yet, are we not kin unto the lions of the desert and the jungle?"

THE CURSE

AN OLD MAN of the sea once said to me, "It was thirty years ago that a sailor ran away with my daughter. And I cursed them both in my heart, for of all the world I loved but my daughter.

"Not long after that, the sailor youth went down with his ship to the bottom of the sea, and with him my lovely daughter was lost unto me.

"Now therefore behold in me the murderer of a youth and a maid. It was my curse that destroyed them. And now on my way to the grave I seek God's forgiveness."

This the old man said. But there was a tone of bragging in his words, and it seems that he is still proud of the power of his curse.

THE POMEGRANATES

THERE WAS ONCE a man who had many pomegranate trees in his orchard. And for many an autumn he would put his pomegranates on silvery trays outside of his dwelling, and upon the trays he would place signs upon which he himself had written, "Take one for aught. You are welcome."

But people passed by and no one took of the fruit.

Then the man bethought him, and one autumn he placed no pomegranates on silvery trays outside of his dwelling, but he raised this sign in large lettering: "Here we have the best pomegranates in the land, but we sell them for more silver than any other pomegranates."

And now behold, all the men and women of the neighbourhood came rushing to buy.

GOD AND MANY GODS

IN THE CITY of Kilafis a sophist stood on the steps of the Temple and preached many gods. And the people said in their hearts, "We know all this. Do they not live with us and follow us wherever we go?"

Not long after, another man stood in the market place and spoke unto the people and said, "There is no god." And many who heard him were glad of his tidings, for they were afraid of gods.

And upon another day there came a man of great eloquence, and he said, "There is but one God." And now the people were dismayed for in their hearts they feared the judgment of one God more than that of many gods.

That same season there came yet another man, and he said to the people, "There are three gods, and they dwell upon the wind as one, and they have a vast and gracious mother who is also their mate and their sister."

Then everyone was comforted, for they said in their secret, "Three gods in one must needs disagree over our failings, and besides, their gracious mother will surely be an advocate for us poor weaklings."

Yet even to this day there are those in the city of Kilafis who wrangle and argue with each other about many gods and no god, and one god and three gods in one, and a gracious mother of gods.

SHE WHO WAS DEAF

ONCE THERE LIVED a rich man who had a young wife, and she was stone deaf.

And upon a morning when they were breaking their fast, she spoke to him and she said, "Yesterday I visited the market place, and there were exhibited silken raiment from Damascus, and coverchiefs from India, necklaces from Persia, and bracelets from Yamman. It seems that the caravans had but just brought these things to our city. And now behold me, in rags, yet the wife of a rich man. I would have some of those beautiful things."

The husband, still busy with his morning coffee said, "My dear, there is *no* reason why you should not go down to the Street and buy all that your heart may desire."

And the deaf wife said, " '*No!*' You always say, 'No, no.' Must I needs appear in tatters among our friends to shame your wealth and my people?"

And the husband said, "I did not say, '*No.*' You may go forth freely to the market place and purchase the most beautiful apparel and jewels that have come to our city."

But again the wife mis-read his words, and she replied, "Of all rich men you are the most miserly. You would deny me everything of beauty and loveliness, while other women of my age walk the gardens of the city clothed in rich raiment."

And she began to weep. And as her tears fell upon her breast she cried out again, "You always say, 'Nay, nay' to me when I desire a garment or a jewel."

Then the husband was moved, and he stood up and took out of his purse a handful of gold and placed it before her, saying in a kindly voice, "Go down to the market place, my dear, and buy all that you will."

From that day onward the deaf young wife, whenever she desired anything, would appear before her husband with a pearly tear in her eye, and he in silence would take out a handful of gold and place it in her lap.

Now, it chanced that the young woman fell in love with a youth whose habit it was to make long journeys. And whenever he was away she would sit in her casement and weep.

When her husband found her thus weeping, he would say in his heart, "There must be some new caravan, and some silken garments and rare jewels in the Street."

And he would take a handful of gold and place it before her.

THE QUEST

A THOUSAND YEARS ago two philosophers met on a slope of Lebanon, and one said to the other, "Where goest thou?"

And the other answered, "I am seeking after the fountain of youth which I know wells out among these hills. I have found writings which tell of that fountain flowering toward the sun. And you, what are you seeking?"

The first man answered, "I am seeking after the mystery of death."

Then each of the two philosophers conceived that the other was lacking in his great science, and they began to wrangle, and to accuse each other of spiritual blindness.

Now while the two philosophers were loud upon the wind, a stranger, a man who was deemed a simpleton in his own village, passed by, and when he heard the two in hot dispute, he stood awhile and listened to their argument.

Then he came near to them and said, "My good men, it seems that you both really belong to the same school of philosophy, and that you are speaking of the same thing, only you speak in different words. One of you seeks the fountain of youth, and the other seeks the mystery of death. Yet indeed they are but one, and as one they dwell in you both."

Then the stranger turned away saying, "Farewell, sages." And as he departed he laughed a patient laughter.

The two philosophers looked at each other in silence for a moment, and then they laughed also. And one of them said, "Well now, shall we not walk and seek together?"

THE SCEPTRE

SAID A KING to his wife, "Madame, you are not truly a queen. You are too vulgar and ungracious to be my mate."

Said his wife, "Sir, you deem yourself king, but indeed you are only a poor soundling."

Now these words angered the king, and he took his sceptre with his hand, and struck the queen upon her forehead with his golden sceptre.

At that moment the lord chamberlain entered, and he said, "Well, well, Majesty! That sceptre was fashioned by the greatest artist of the land. Alas! Some day you and the queen shall be forgotten, but this sceptre shall be kept, a thing of beauty from generation to generation. And now that you have drawn blood from her Majesty's head, Sire, the sceptre shall be the more considered and remembered."

THE PATH

THERE LIVED AMONG the hills a woman and her son, and he was her first-born and her only child.

And the boy died of a fever whilst the physician stood by.

The mother was distraught with sorrow, and she cried to the physician and besought him saying, "Tell me, tell me, what was it that made quiet his striving and silent his song?"

And the physician said, "It was the fever."

And the mother said, "What is the fever?"

And the physician answered, "I cannot explain it. It is a thing infinitely small that visits the body, and we cannot see it with our human eye."

Then the physician left her. And she kept repeating to herself, "Something infinitely small. We cannot see it with our human eye."

And at evening the priest came to console her. And she wept and she cried out saying, "Oh, why have I lost my son, my only son, my first-born?"

And the priest answered, "My child, it is the will of God."

And the woman said, "What is God and where is God? I would see God that I may tear my bosom before Him, and pour the blood of my heart at His feet. Tell me where I shall find Him."

And the priest said, "God is infinitely vast. He is not to be seen with our human eye."

Then the woman cried out, "The infinitely small has slain my son through the will of the infinitely great! Then what are we? What are we?"

At that moment the woman's mother came into the room with the shroud for the dead boy, and she heard the words of the priest and also her daughter's cry. And she laid down the shroud, and took her daughter's hand in her own hand, and she said, "My daughter, we ourselves are the infinitely small and the infinitely great; and we are the path between the two."

THE WHALE AND THE BUTTERFLY

ONCE ON AN evening a man and a woman found themselves together in a stagecoach. They had met before.

The man was a poet, and as he sat beside the woman he sought to amuse her with stories, some that were of his own weaving, and some that were not his own.

But even while he was speaking the lady went to sleep. Then suddenly the coach lurched, and she awoke, and she said, "I admire your interpretation of the story of Jonah and the whale."

And the poet said, "But Madame, I have been telling you a story of mine own about a butterfly and a white rose, and how they behaved the one to the other!"

ONE BRANCH IN bloom said to his neighbouring branch, "This is a dull and empty day." And the other branch answered, "It is indeed empty and dull."

At that moment a sparrow alighted on one of the branches, and then another sparrow, nearby.

And one of the sparrows chirped and said, "My mate has left me."

And the other sparrow cried, "My mate has also gone, and she will not return. And what care I?"

Then the two began to twitter and scold, and soon they were fighting and making harsh noise upon the air.

All of a sudden two other sparrows came sailing from the sky, and they sat quietly beside the restless two. And there was calm, and there was peace.

Then the four flew away together in pairs.

And the first branch said to his neighbouring branch, "That was a mighty zig-zag of sound." And the other branch answered, "Call it what you will, it is now both peaceful and spacious. And if the upper air makes peace it seems to me that those who dwell in the lower might make peace also. Will you not wave in the wind a little nearer to me?"

And the first branch said, "Oh, perchance, for peace's sake, ere the Spring is over."

And then he waved himself with the strong wind to embrace her.

THE SHADOW

UPON A JUNE day the grass said to the shadow of an elm tree, "You move to right and left over-often, and you disturb my peace."

And the shadow answered and said, "Not I, not I. Look skyward. There is a tree that moves in the wind to the east and to the west, between the sun and the earth."

And the grass looked up, and for the first time beheld the tree. And it said in its heart, "Why, behold, there is a larger grass than myself."

And the grass was silent.

SEVENTY

THE POET YOUTH said to the princess, "I love you." And the princess answered, "And I love you too, my child."

"But I am not your child. I am a man and I love you."

And she said, "I am the mother of sons and daughters, and they are fathers and mothers of sons and daughters; and one of the sons of my sons is older than you."

And the poet youth said, "But I love you."

It was not long after that the princess died. But ere her last breath was received again by the greater breath of earth, she said within her soul, "My beloved, mine only son, my youth-poet, it may yet be that some day we shall meet again, and I shall not be seventy."

TWO MEN WERE walking in the valley, and one man pointed with his finger toward the mountain side, and said, "See you that hermitage? There lives a man who has long divorced the world. He seeks but after God, and naught else upon this earth."

And the other man said, "He shall not find God until he leaves his hermitage, and the aloneness of his hermitage, and returns to our world, to share our joy and pain, to dance with our dancers at the wedding feast, and to weep with those who weep around the coffins of our dead."

And the other man was convinced in his heart, though in spite of his conviction he answered, "I agree with all that you say, yet I believe the hermit is a good man. And may it not well be that one good man by his absence does better than the seeming goodness of these many men?"

THE RIVER

IN THE VALLEY of Kadisha where the mighty river flows, two little streams met and spoke to one another.

One stream said, "How came you, my friend, and how was your path?"

And the other answered, "My path was most encumbered. The wheel of the mill was broken, and the master farmer who used to conduct me from my channel to his plants, is dead. I struggled down oozing with the filth of those who do naught but sit and bake their laziness in the sun. But how was your path, my brother?"

And the other stream answered and said, "Mine was a different path. I came down the hills among fragrant flowers and shy willows; men and women drank of me with silvery cups, and little children paddled their rosy feet at my edges, and there was laughter all about me, and there were sweet songs. What a pity that your path was not so happy."

At that moment the river spoke with a loud voice and said, "Come in, come in, we are going to the sea. Come in, come in, speak no more. Be with me now. We are going to the sea. Come in, come in, for in me you shall forget your wanderings, sad or gay. Come in, come in. And you and I will forget all our ways when we reach the heart of our mother the sea."

THE TWO HUNTERS

UPON A DAY in May, Joy and Sorrow met beside a lake. They greeted one another, and they sat down near the quiet waters and conversed.

Joy spoke of the beauty which is upon the earth, and of the daily wonder of life in the forest and among the hills, and of the songs heard at dawn and eventide.

And Sorrow spoke, and agreed with all that Joy had said; for Sorrow knew the magic of the hour and the beauty thereof. And Sorrow was eloquent when he spoke of May in the fields and among the hills.

And Joy and Sorrow talked long together, and they agreed upon all things of which they knew.

Now there passed by on the other side of the lake two hunters. And as they looked across the water one of them said, "I wonder who are those two persons?" And the other said, "Did you say two? I see only one."

The first hunter said, "But there are two." And the second said, "There is only one that I can see, and the reflection in the lake is only one."

"Nay, there are two," said the first hunter, "and the reflection in the still water is of two persons."

But the second man said again, "Only one do I see." And again the other said, "But I see two so plainly."

And even to this day one hunter says that the other sees double; while the other says, "My friend is somewhat blind."

THE OTHER WANDERER

ONCE ON A time I met another man of the roads. He too was a little mad, and thus he spoke to me: "I am a wanderer. Oftentimes it seems that I walk the earth among pygmies. And because my head is seventy cubits farther from the earth than theirs, it creates higher and freer thoughts.

"But in truth I walk not among men but above them, and all they can see of me is my footprints in their open fields.

"And often have I heard them discuss and disagree over the shape and size of my footprints. For there are some who say, 'These are the tracks of a mammoth that roamed the earth in the far past.' And others say, 'Nay, these are places where meteors have fallen from the distant stars.'

"But you, my friend, you know full well that they are naught save the footprints of a wanderer."

THE GARDEN
OF THE PROPHET

ALMUSTAFA, THE CHOSEN and the beloved, who was a noon unto his own day, returned to the isle of his birth in the month of Tichreen, which is the month of remembrance.

And as his ship approached the harbour, he stood upon its prow, and his mariners were about him. And there was a homecoming in his heart.

And he spoke, and the sea was in his voice, and he said: "Behold, the isle of our birth. Even here the earth heaved us, a song and a riddle; a song unto the sky, a riddle unto the earth; and what is there between earth and sky that shall carry the song and solve the riddle save our own passion?

"The sea yields us once more to these shores. We are but another wave of her waves. She sends us forth to sound her speech, but how shall we do so unless we break the symmetry of our heart on rock and sand?

"For this is the law of mariners and the sea: If you would freedom, you must needs turn to mist. The formless is for ever seeking form, even as the countless nebulæ would become suns and moons; and we who have sought much and return now to this isle, rigid moulds, we must become mist once more and learn of the beginning. And what is there that shall live and rise unto the heights except it be broken unto passion and freedom?

"For ever shall we be in quest of the shores, that we may sing and be heard. But what of the wave that breaks where no ear shall hear? It is the unheard in us that nurses our deeper sorrow. Yet it is also the unheard which carves our soul to form and fashions our destiny."

Then one of his mariners came forth and said: "Master, you have captained our longing for this harbour, and behold, we have come. Yet you speak of sorrow, and of hearts that shall be broken."

And he answered him and said: "Did I not speak of freedom, and of the mist which is our greater freedom? Yet it is in pain I make pilgrimage to the isle where I was born, even like unto a ghost of one slain come to kneel before those who have slain him."

And another mariner spoke and said: "Behold, the multitudes on the sea-wall. In their silence they have foretold even the day and the hour of your coming, and they have gathered from their fields and vineyards in their loving need, to await you."

And Almustafa looked afar upon the multitudes, and his heart was mindful of their yearning, and he was silent.

Then a cry came from the people, and it was a cry of remembrance and of entreaty.

And he looked upon his mariners and said: "And what have I brought them? A hunter was I, in a distant land. With aim and might I have spent the golden arrows they gave me, but I have brought down no game. I followed not the arrows. Mayhap they are spreading now in the sun with the pinions of wounded eagles that would not fall to earth. And mayhap the arrow-heads have fallen into the hands of those who had need of them for bread and wine.

"I know not where they have spent their flight, but this I know: they have made their curve in the sky.

"Even so, love's hand is still upon me, and you, my mariners, still sail my vision, and I shall not be dumb. I shall cry out when the hand of the seasons is upon my throat, and I shall sing my words when my lips are burned with flames."

And they were troubled in their hearts because he spoke these things. And one said: "Master, teach us all, and mayhap because your blood flows in our veins, and our breath is of your fragrance, we shall understand."

Then he answered them, and the wind was in his voice, and he said: "Brought you me to the isle of my birth to be a teacher? Not yet have I been caged by wisdom. Too young am I and too verdant to speak of aught but self, which is for ever the deep calling upon the deep.

"Let him who would have wisdom seek it in the buttercup or in a pinch of red clay. I am still the singer. Still I shall sing the earth, and I shall sing your lost dreaming that walks the day between sleep and sleep. But I shall gaze upon the sea."

And now the ship entered the harbour and reached the sea-wall, and he came thus to the isle of his birth and stood once more amongst his own people. And a great cry arose from their hearts so that the loneliness of his home-coming was shaken within him.

And they were silent awaiting his word, but he answered them not, for the sadness of memory was upon him, and he said in his heart: "Have I said that I shall sing? Nay, I can but open my lips that the voice of life may come forth and go out to the wind for joy and support."

Then Karima, she who had played with him, a child, in the Garden of his mother, spoke and said: "Twelve years have you hidden your face from us, and for twelve years have we hungered and thirsted for your voice."

And he looked upon her with exceeding tenderness, for it was she who had closed the eyes of his mother when the white wings of death had gathered her.

And he answered and said: "Twelve years? Said you twelve years, Karima? I measured not my longing with the starry rod, nor did I sound the depth thereof. For love when love is home-sick exhausts time's measurements and time's soundings.

"There are moments that hold æons of separation. Yet parting is naught but an exhaustion of the mind. Perhaps we have not parted."

And Almustafa looked upon the people, and he saw them all, the youth and the aged, the stalwart and the puny, those who were ruddy with the touch of wind and sun, and those also who were of pallid countenance; and upon their face a light of longing and of questioning.

And one spoke and said: "Master, life has dealt bitterly with our hopes and our desires. Our hearts are troubled, and we do not understand. I pray you, comfort us, and open to us the meanings of our sorrows."

And his heart was moved with compassion, and he said: "Life is older than all things living; even as beauty was winged ere the

beautiful was born on earth, and even as truth was truth ere it was uttered.

"Life sings in our silences, and dreams in our slumber. Even when we are beaten and low, Life is enthroned and high. And when we weep, Life smiles upon the day, and is free even when we drag our chains.

"Oftentimes we call Life bitter names, but only when we ourselves are bitter and dark. And we deem her empty and unprofitable, but only when the soul goes wandering in desolate places, and the heart is drunken with overmindfulness of self.

"Life is deep and high and distant; and though only your vast vision can reach even her feet, yet she is near; and though only the breath of your breath reaches her heart, the shadow of your shadow crosses her face, and the echo of your faintest cry becomes a spring and an autumn in her breast.

"And Life is veiled and hidden, even as your greater self is hidden and veiled. Yet when Life speaks, all the winds become words; and when she speaks again, the smiles upon your lips and the tears in your eyes turn also into words. When she sings, the deaf hear and are held; and when she comes walking, the sightless behold her and are amazed and follow her in wonder and astonishment."

And he ceased from speaking, and a vast silence enfolded the people, and in the silence there was an unheard song, and they were comforted of their loneliness and their aching.

AND HE LEFT them straightway and followed the path which led to his Garden, which was the Garden of his mother and his father, wherein they lay asleep, they and their forefathers.

And there were those who would have followed after him, seeing that it was a home-coming, and he was alone, for there was not one left of all his kin to spread the feast of welcome, after the manner of his people.

But the captain of his ship counselled them saying: "Suffer him to go upon his way. For his bread is the bread of aloneness, and in his cup is the wine of remembrance, which he would drink alone."

And his mariners held their steps, for they knew it was even as the captain of the ship had told them. And all those who gathered upon the sea-wall restrained the feet of their desire.

Only Karima went after him, a little way, yearning over his aloneness and his memories. And she spoke not, but turned and went unto her own house, and in the garden under the almond-tree she wept, yet knew not wherefore.

AND ALMUSTAFA CAME and found the Garden of his mother and his father, and he entered in, and closed the gate that no man might come after him.

And for forty days and forty nights he dwelt alone in that house and that Garden, and none came, not even unto the gate, for it was closed, and all the people knew that he would be alone.

And when the forty days and nights were ended, Almustafa opened the gate that they might come in.

And there came nine men to be with him in the Garden; three mariners from his own ship; three who had served in the Temple; and three who had been his comrades in play when they were but children together. And these were his disciples.

And on a morning his disciples sat around him, and there were distances and remembrances in his eyes. And that disciple who was called Hafiz said unto him: "Master, tell us of the city of Orphalese, and of that land wherein you tarried those twelve years."

And Almustafa was silent, and he looked away toward the hills and toward the vast ether, and there was a battle in his silence.

Then he said: "My friends and my road-fellows, pity the nation that is full of beliefs and empty of religion.

"Pity the nation that wears a cloth it does not weave, eats a bread it does not harvest, and drinks a wine that flows not from its own winepress.

"Pity the nation that acclaims the bully as hero, and that deems the glittering conqueror bountiful.

"Pity a nation that despises a passion in its dream, yet submits in its awakening.

"Pity the nation that raises not its voice save when it walks in a funeral, boasts not except among its ruins, and will rebel not save when its neck is laid between the sword and the block.

"Pity the nation whose statesman is a fox, whose philosopher is a juggler, and whose art is the art of patching and mimicking.

"Pity the nation that welcomes its new ruler with trumpetings, and farewells him with hootings, only to welcome another with trumpetings again.

"Pity the nation whose sages are dumb with years and whose strong men are yet in the cradle.

"Pity the nation divided into fragments, each fragment deeming itself a nation."

AND ONE SAID: "Speak to us of that which is moving in your own heart even now."

And he looked upon that one, and there was in his voice a sound like a star singing, and he said: "In your waking dream, when you are hushed and listening to your deeper self, your thoughts, like snowflakes, fall and flutter and garment all the sounds of your spaces with white silence.

"And what are waking dreams but clouds that bud and blossom on the sky-tree of your heart? And what are your thoughts but the petals which the winds of your heart scatter upon the hills and its fields?

"And even as you wait for peace until the formless within you takes form, so shall the cloud gather and drift until the Blessed Fingers shape its grey desire to little crystal suns and moons and stars."

Then Sarkis, he who was the half-doubter, spoke and said: "But spring shall come, and all the snows of our dreams and our thoughts shall melt and be no more."

And he answered saying: "When Spring comes to seek His beloved among the slumbering groves and vineyards, the snows shall indeed melt and shall run in streams to seek the river in the valley, to be the cup-bearer to the myrtle-trees and laurel.

"So shall the snow of your heart melt when your Spring is come, and thus shall your secret run in streams to seek the river of life in the valley. And the river shall enfold your secret and carry it to the great sea.

"All things shall melt and turn into songs when Spring comes. Even the stars, the vast snow-flakes that fall slowly upon the larger fields, shall melt into singing streams. When the sun of His face shall arise above the wider horizon, then what frozen symmetry would not turn into liquid melody? And who among you would not be the cup-bearer to the myrtle and the laurel?

"It was but yesterday that you were moving with the moving sea, and you were shoreless and without a self. Then the wind, the breath of Life, wove you, a veil of light on her face; then her hand gathered you and gave you form, and with a head held high you sought the heights. But the sea followed after you, and her song is still with you. And though you have forgotten your parentage, she will for ever assert her motherhood, and for ever will she call you unto her.

"In your wanderings among the mountains and the desert you will always remember the depth of her cool heart. And though oftentimes you will not know for what you long, it is indeed for her vast and rhythmic peace.

"And how else can it be? In grove and in bower when the rain dances in leaves upon the hill, when snow falls, a blessing and a covenant; in the valley when you lead your flocks to the river; in your fields where brooks, like silver streams, join together the green garment; in your gardens when the early dews mirror the heavens; in your meadows when the mist of evening half veils your way; in all these the sea is with you, a witness to your heritage, and a claim upon your love.

"It is the snow-flake in you running down to the sea."

AND ON A morning as they walked in the Garden, there appeared before the gate a woman, and it was Karima, she whom Almustafa had loved even as a sister in his boyhood. And she stood without, asking nothing, nor knocking with her hand upon the gate, but only gazing with longing and sadness into the Garden.

And Almustafa saw the desire upon her eyelids, and with swift steps he came to the wall and the gate and opened unto her, and she came in and was made welcome.

And she spoke and said: "Wherefore have you withdrawn yourself from us altogether, that we may not live in the light of your countenance? For behold, these many years have we loved you and waited with longing for your safe return. And now the people cry for you and would have speech with you; and I am their messenger come to beseech you that you will show yourself to the people, and speak to them out of your wisdom, and comfort the broken of heart and instruct our foolishness.

And looking upon her, he said: "Call me not wise unless you call all men wise. A young fruit am I, still clinging to the branch, and it was only yesterday that I was but a blossom.

"And call none among you foolish, for in truth we are neither wise nor foolish. We are green leaves upon the tree of life, and life itself is beyond wisdom, and surely beyond foolishness."

"And have I indeed withdrawn myself from you? Know you not that there is no distance save that which the soul does not span in fancy? And when the soul shall span that distance, it becomes a rhythm in the soul.

"The space that lies between you and your near neighbour unbefriended is indeed greater than that which lies between you and your beloved who dwells beyond seven lands and seven seas.

"For in remembrance there are no distances; and only in

oblivion is there a gulf that neither your voice nor your eye can abridge.

"Between the shores of the oceans and the summit of the highest mountain there is a secret road which you must needs travel ere you become one with the sons of earth.

"And between your knowledge and your understanding there is a secret path which you must needs discover ere you become one with man, and therefore one with yourself.

"Between your right hand that gives and your left hand that receives there is a great space. Only by deeming them both giving and receiving can you bring them into spacelessness, for it is only in knowing that you have naught to give and naught to receive that you can overcome space.

"Verily the vastest distance is that which lies between your sleep-vision and your wakefulness; and between that which is but a deed and that which is a desire.

"And there is still another road which you must needs travel ere you become one with Life. But of that road I shall not speak now, seeing that you are weary already of travelling."

THEN HE WENT forth with the woman, he and the nine, even unto the market-place, and he spoke to the people, his friends and his neighbours, and there was joy in their hearts and upon their eyelids.

And he said: "You grow in sleep, and live your fuller life in your dreaming. For all your days are spent in thanksgiving for that which you have received in the stillness of the night.

"Oftentimes you think and speak of night as the season of rest, yet in truth night is the season of seeking and finding.

"The day gives unto you the power of knowledge and teaches your fingers to become versed in the art of receiving; but it is night that leads you to the treasure-house of Life.

"The sun teaches to all things that grow their longing for the light. But it is night that raises them to the stars.

"It is indeed the stillness of the night that weaves a wedding-veil over the trees in the forest, and the flowers in the garden, and then spreads the lavish feast and makes ready the nuptial chamber; and in that holy silence tomorrow is conceived in the womb of Time.

"Thus it is with you, and thus, in seeking, you find meat and fulfilment. And though at dawn your awakening erases the memory, the board of dreams is for ever spread, and the nuptial chamber waiting."

And he was silent for a space, and they also, awaiting his word. Then he spoke again, saying: "You are spirits though you move in bodies; and, like oil that burns in the dark, you are flames though held in lamps.

"If you were naught save bodies, then my standing before you and speaking unto you would be but emptiness, even as the dead calling unto the dead. But this is not so. All that is deathless in

you is free unto the day and the night and cannot be housed nor fettered, for this is the will of the Most High. You are His breath even as the wind that shall be neither caught nor caged. And I also am the breath of His breath."

And he went from their midst walking swiftly and entered again into the Garden.

And Sarkis, he who was the half-doubter, spoke and said: "And what of ugliness, Master? You speak never of ugliness."

And Almustafa answered him, and there was a whip in his words, and he said: "My friend, what man shall call you inhospitable if he shall pass by your house, yet would not knock at your door?

"And who shall deem you deaf and unmindful if he shall speak to you in a strange tongue of which you understand nothing?

"Is it not that which you have never striven to reach, into whose heart you have never desired to enter, that you deem ugliness?

"If ugliness is aught, indeed, it is but the scales upon our eyes, and the wax filling our ears.

"Call nothing ugly, my friend, save the fear of a soul in the presence of its own memories."

AND UPON A day as they sat in the long shadows of the white poplars, one spoke saying: "Master, I am afraid of time. It passes over us and robs us of our youth, and what does it give in return?"

And he answered and said: "Take up now a handful of good earth. Do you find in it a seed, and perhaps a worm? If your hand were spacious and enduring enough, the seed might become a forest, and the worm a flock of angels. And forget not that the years which turn seeds to forests, and worms to angels, belong to this *Now*, all of the years, this very *Now*.

"And what are the seasons of the years save your own thoughts changing? Spring is an awakening in your breast, and summer but a recognition of your own fruitfulness. Is not autumn the ancient in you singing a lullaby to that which is still a child in your being? And what, I ask you, is winter save sleep big with the dreams of all the other seasons."

And then Mannus, the inquisitive disciple, looked about him and he saw plants in flower cleaving unto the sycamore-tree. And he said: "Behold the parasites, Master. What say you of them? They are thieves with weary eyelids who steal the light from the steadfast children of the sun, and make fair of the sap that runneth into their branches and their leaves."

And he answered him saying: "My friend, we are all parasites. We who labour to turn the sod into pulsing life are not above those who receive life directly from the sod without knowing the sod.

"Shall a mother say to her child: 'I give you back to the forest, which is your greater mother, for you weary me, heart and hand'?

"Or shall the singer rebuke his own song, saying: 'Return now to the cave of echoes from whence you came, for your voice consumes my breath'?

"And shall the shepherd say to his yearling: 'I have no pasture whereunto I may lead you; therefore be cut off and become a sacrifice for this cause'?

"Nay, my friend, all these things are answered even before they are asked, and, like your dreams, are fulfilled ere you sleep.

"We live upon one another according to the law, ancient and timeless. Let us live thus in loving-kindness. We seek one another in our aloneness, and we walk the road when we have no hearth to sit beside.

"My friends and my brothers, the wider road is your fellow-man.

"These plants that live upon the tree draw the milk of the earth in the sweet stillness of night, and the earth in her tranquil dreaming sucks at the breast of the sun.

"And the sun, even as you and I and all there is, sits in equal honour at the banquet of the Prince whose door is always open and whose board is always spread.

"Mannus, my friend, all there is lives always upon all there is; and all there is lives in the faith, shoreless, upon the bounty of the Most High."

AND ON A morning when the sky was yet pale with dawn, they walked all together in the Garden and looked unto the East and were silent in the presence of the rising sun.

And after a while Almustafa pointed with his hand, and he said: "The image of the morning sun in a dewdrop is not less than the sun. The reflection of life in your soul is not less than life.

"The dewdrop mirrors the light because it is one with light, and you reflect life because you and life are one.

"When darkness is upon you, say: 'This darkness is dawn not yet born; and though night's travail be full upon me, yet shall dawn be born unto me even as unto the hills.'

"The dewdrop rounding its sphere in the dusk of the lily is not unlike yourself gathering your soul in the heart of God.

"Shall a dewdrop say: 'But once in a thousand years am I even a dewdrop,' speak you and answer it saying: 'Know you not that the light of all the years is shining in your circle?'"

AND ON AN evening a great storm visited the place, and Almustafa and his disciples, the nine, went within and sat about the fire and were still and silent.

Then one of the disciples said: "I am alone, Master, and the hoofs of the hours beat heavily upon my breast."

And Almustafa rose up and stood in their midst, and he said in a voice like unto the sound of a great wind: "Alone! And what of it? You came alone, and alone shall you pass into the mist.

"Therefore drink your cup alone and in silence. The autumn days have given other lips other cups and filled them with wine bitter and sweet, even as they have filled your cup.

"Drink your cup alone though it taste of your own blood and tears, and praise life for the gift of thirst. For without thirst your heart is but the shore of a barren sea, songless and without a tide.

"Drink your cup alone, and drink it with cheers.

"Raise it high above your head and drink deep to those who drink alone.

"Once I sought the company of men and sat with them at their banquet-tables and drank deep with them; but their wine did not rise to my head, nor did it flow into my bosom. It only descended to my feet. My wisdom was left dry and my heart was locked and sealed. Only my feet were with them in their fog.

"And I sought the company of men no more, nor drank wine with them at their board.

"Therefore I say unto you, though the hoofs of the hours beat heavily upon your bosom, what of it? It is well for you to drink your cup of sorrow alone, and your cup of joy shall you drink alone also."

AND ON A day, as Phardrous, the Greek, walked in the Garden, he struck his foot upon a stone and he was angered. And he turned and picked up the stone, saying in a low voice: "O dead thing in my path!" and he flung away the stone.

And Almustafa, the chosen and the beloved, said: "Why say you: 'O dead thing'? Have you been thus long in this Garden and know not that there is nothing dead here? All things live and glow in the knowledge of the day and the majesty of the night. You and the stone are one. There is a difference only in heart-beats. Your heart beats a little faster, does it, my friend? Ay, but it is not so tranquil.

"Its rhythm may be another rhythm, but I say unto you that if you sound the depths of your soul and scale the heights of space, you shall hear but one melody, and in that melody the stone and the star sing, the one with the other, in perfect unison.

"If my words reach not your understanding, then let be until another dawn. If you have cursed this stone because in your blindness you have stumbled upon it, then would you curse a star if so be your head should encounter it in the sky. But the day will come when you will gather stones and stars as a child plucks the valley-lilies, and then shall you know that all these things are living and fragrant."

AND ON THE first day of the week when the sounds of the temple bells sought their ears, one spoke and said: "Master, we hear much talk of God hereabout. What say you of God, and who is He in very truth?"

And he stood before them like a young tree, fearless of wind or tempest, and he answered saying: "Think now, my comrades and beloved, of a heart that contains all your hearts, a love that encompasses all your loves, a spirit that envelops all your spirits, a voice enfolding all your voices, and a silence deeper than all your silences, and timeless.

"Seek now to perceive in your selffulness a beauty more enchanting than all things beautiful, a song more vast than the songs of the sea and the forest, a majesty seated upon a throne for which Orion is but a footstool, holding a sceptre in which the Pleiades are naught save the glimmer of dewdrops.

"You have sought always only food and shelter, a garment and a staff; seek now One who is neither an aim for your arrows nor a stony cave to shield you from the elements.

"And if my words are a rock and a riddle, then seek, none the less, that your hearts may be broken, and that your questionings may bring you unto the love and the wisdom of the Most High, whom men call God."

And they were silent, every one, and they were perplexed in their heart; and Almustafa was moved with compassion for them, and he gazed with tenderness upon them and said: "Let us speak no more now of God the Father. Let us speak rather of the gods, your neighbours, and of your brothers, the elements that move about your houses and your fields.

"You would rise in fancy unto the cloud, and you deem it height; and you would pass over the vast sea and claim it to be distance. But I say unto you that when you sow a seed in the earth, you reach a greater height; and when you hail the beauty of the morning to your neighbour, you cross a greater sea.

"Too often do you sing God, the Infinite, and yet in truth you hear not the song. Would that you might listen to the song-birds, and to the leaves that forsake the branch when the wind passes by, and forget not, my friends, that these sing only when they are separated from the branch!

"Again I bid you to speak not so freely of God, who is your All, but speak rather and understand one another, neighbour unto neighbour, a god unto a god.

"For what shall feed the fledgling in the nest if the mother bird flies skyward? And what anemone in the field shall be fulfilled unless it be husbanded by a bee from another anemone?

"It is only when you are lost in your smaller selves that you seek the sky which you call God. Would that you might find paths into your vast selves; would that you might be less idle and pave the roads!

"My mariners and my friends, it were wiser to speak less of God, whom we cannot understand, and more of each other, whom we may understand. Yet I would have you know that we are the breath and the fragrance of God. We are God, in leaf, in flower, and oftentimes in fruit."

AND ON A morning when the sun was high, one of the disciples, one of those three who had played with him in childhood, approached him saying: "Master, my garment is worn, and I have no other. Give me leave to go unto the market-place and bargain that perchance I may procure me new raiment."

And Almustafa looked upon the young man, and he said: "Give me your garment." And he did so and stood naked in the noonday.

And Almustafa said in a voice that was like a young steed running upon a road: "Only the naked live in the sun. Only the artless ride the wind. And he alone who loses his way a thousand times shall have a home-coming.

"The angels are tired of the clever. And it was but yesterday that an angel said to me: 'We created hell for those who glitter. What else but fire can erase a shining surface and melt a thing to its core?'

"And I said: 'But in creating hell you created devils to govern hell.' But the angel answered: 'Nay, hell is governed by those who do not yield to fire.'

"Wise angel! He knows the ways of men and the ways of half-men. He is one of the seraphim who come to minister unto the prophets when they are tempted by the clever. And no doubt he smiles when the prophets smile, and weeps also when they weep.

"My friends and my mariners, only the naked live in the sun. Only the rudderless can sail the greater sea. Only he who is dark with the night shall wake with the dawn, and only he who sleeps with the roots under the snow shall reach the spring.

"For you are even like roots, and like roots are you simple, yet you have wisdom from the earth. And you are silent, yet you have within your unborn branches the choir of the four winds.

"You are frail and you are formless, yet you are the beginning of giant oaks, and of the half-pencilled pattern of the willows against the sky.

"Once more I say, you are but roots betwixt the dark sod and the moving heavens. And oftentimes have I seen you rising to dance with the light, but I have also seen you shy. All roots are shy. They have hidden their hearts so long that they know not what to do with their hearts.

"But May shall come, and May is a restless virgin, and she shall mother the hills and plains."

AND ONE WHO had served in the Temple besought him saying: "Teach us, Master, that our words may be even as your words, a chant and an incense unto the people."

And Almustafa answered and said: "You shall rise beyond your words, but your path shall remain, a rhythm and a fragrance; a rhythm for lovers and for all who are beloved, and a fragrance for those who would live life in a garden.

"But you shall rise beyond your words to a summit whereon the star-dust falls, and you shall open your hands until they are filled; then you shall lie down and sleep like a white fledgling in a white nest, and you shall dream of your tomorrow as white violets dream of spring.

"Ay, and you shall go down deeper than your words. You shall seek the lost fountain-heads of the streams, and you shall be a hidden cave echoing the faint voices of the depths which now you do not even hear.

"You shall go down deeper than your words, ay, deeper than all sounds, to the very heart of the earth, and there you shall be alone with Him who walks also upon the Milky Way."

And after a space one of the disciples asked him saying: "Master, speak to us of *being*. What is it to *be*?"

And Almustafa looked long upon him and loved him. And he stood up and walked a distance away from them; then returning, he said: "In this Garden my father and my mother lie, buried by the hands of the living; and in this Garden lie buried the seeds of yesteryear, brought hither upon the wings of the wind. A thousand times shall my mother and my father be buried here, and a thousand times shall the wind bury the seed; and a thousand years hence shall you and I and these flowers come together in this Garden even as now, and we shall *be*, loving life, and we shall *be*, dreaming of space, and we shall *be*, rising toward the sun.

"But now today to *be* is to be wise, though not a stranger to the foolish; it is to be strong, but not to the undoing of the weak; to play with young children, not as fathers, but rather as playmates who would learn their games;

"To be simple and guileless with old men and women, and to sit with them in the shade of the ancient oak-trees, though you are still walking with Spring;

"To seek a poet though he may live beyond the seven rivers, and to be at peace in his presence, nothing wanting, nothing doubting, and with no question upon your lips;

"To know that the saint and the sinner are twin brothers, whose father is our Gracious King, and that one was born but the moment before the other, wherefore we regard him as the Crowned Prince;

"To follow Beauty even when she shall lead you to the verge of the precipice; and though she is winged and you are wingless, and though she shall pass beyond the verge, follow her, for where Beauty is not, there is nothing;

"To be a garden without walls, a vineyard without a guardian, a treasure-house for ever open to passers-by;

"To be robbed, cheated, deceived, ay, misled and trapped and then mocked, yet with it all to look down from the height of your larger self and smile, knowing that there is a spring that will come to your garden to dance in your leaves, and an autumn to ripen your grapes; knowing that if but one of your windows is open to the East, you shall never be empty; knowing that all those deemed wrongdoers and robbers, cheaters and deceivers are your brothers in need, and that you are perchance all of these in the eyes of the blessed inhabitants of that City Invisible, above this city.

"And now, to you also whose hands fashion and find all things that are needful for the comfort of our days and our nights –

"To *be* is to be a weaver with seeing fingers, a builder mindful of light and space; to be a ploughman and feel that you are hiding a treasure with every seed you sow; to be a fisherman and a hunter with a pity for the fish and for the beast, yet a still greater pity for the hunger and need of man.

"And, above all, I say this: I would have you each and every one partners to the purpose of every man, for only so shall you hope to obtain your own good purpose.

"My comrades and my beloved, be bold and not meek; be spacious and not confined; and until my final hour and yours be indeed your greater self."

And he ceased from speaking and there fell a deep gloom upon the nine, and their heart was turned away from him, for they understood not his words.

And behold, the three men who were mariners longed for the sea; and they who head served in the Temple yearned for the consolation of her sanctuary; and they who had been his playfellows desired the market-place. They all were deaf to his words, so that the sound of them returned unto him like weary and homeless birds seeking refuge.

And Almustafa walked a distance from them in the Garden, saying nothing, nor looking upon them.

And they began to reason among themselves and to seek excuse for their longing to be gone.

And behold, they turned and went every man to his own place, so that Almustafa, the chosen and the beloved, was left alone.

AND WHEN THE night was fully come, he took his steps to the grave-side of his mother and sat beneath the cedar-tree which grew above the place. And there came the shadow of a great light upon the sky, and the Garden shone like a fair jewel upon the breast of earth.

And Almustafa cried out in the aloneness of his spirit, and he said:

"Heavy-laden is my soul with her own ripe fruit. Who is there would come and take and be satisfied? Is there not one who has fasted and who is kindly and generous in heart, to come and break his fast upon my first yieldings to the sun and thus ease me of the weight of mine own abundance?

"My soul is running over with the wine of the ages. Is there no thirsty one to come and drink?

"Behold, there was a man standing at the cross-roads with hands stretched forth unto the passers-by, and his hands were filled with jewels. And he called upon the passers-by, saying: 'Pity me, and take from me. In God's name, take out of my hands and console me.'

"But the passers-by only looked upon him, and none took out of his hand.

"Would rather that he were a beggar stretching forth his hand to receive – ay, a shivering hand, and brought back empty to his bosom – than to stretch it forth full of rich gifts and find none to receive.

"And behold, there was also the gracious prince who raised up his silken tents between the mountain and the desert and bade his servants to burn fire, a sign to the stranger and the wanderer; and who sent forth his slaves to watch the road that they might fetch a guest. But the roads and the paths of the desert were unyielding, and they found no one.

"Would rather that prince were a man of nowhere and nowhen, seeking food and shelter. Would that he were the wanderer with naught but his staff and an earthen vessel. For then at nightfall would he meet with his kind, and with the poets of nowhere and nowhen, and share their beggary and their remembrances and their dreaming.

"And behold, the daughter of the great king rose from sleep and put upon her her silken raiment and her pearls and rubies, and she scattered musk upon her hair and dipped her fingers in amber. Then she descended from her tower to her garden, where the dew of night found her golden sandals.

"In the stillness of the night the daughter of the great king sought love in the garden, but in all the vast kingdom of her father there was none who was her lover.

"Would rather that she were the daughter of a ploughman, tending his sheep in a field, and returning to her father's house at eventide with the dust of the curving roads upon her feet, and the fragrance of the vineyards in the folds of her garment. And when the night is come, and the angel of the night is upon the world, she would steal her steps to the river-valley where her lover waits.

"Would that she were a nun in a cloister burning her heart for incense, that her heart may rise to the wind, and exhausting her spirit, a candle, for a light arising toward the greater light, together with all those who worship and those who love and are beloved.

"Would rather that she were a woman ancient of years, sitting in the sun and remembering who had shared her youth."

And the night waxed deep, and Almustafa was dark with the night, and his spirit was as a cloud unspent. And he cried again:

"Heavy-laden is my soul with her own ripe fruit;
Heavy-laden is my soul with her fruit.
Who now will come and eat and be fulfilled?
My soul is overflowing with her wine.
Who now will pour and drink and be cooled of the desert heat?
"Would that I were a tree flowerless and fruitless,

For the pain of abundance is more bitter than barrenness,
And the sorrow of the rich from whom no one will take
Is greater than the grief of the beggar to whom none
    would give.

"Would that I were a well, dry and parched, and men
    throwing stones into me;
For this were better and easier to be borne than to be a source
    of living water
When men pass by and will not drink.

"Would that I were a reed trodden under foot,
For that were better than to be a lyre of silvery strings
In a house whose lord has no fingers
And whose children are deaf."

NOW, FOR SEVEN days and seven nights no man came nigh the Garden, and he was alone with his memories and his pain; for even those who had heard his words with love and patience had turned away to the pursuits of other days.

Only Karima came, with silence upon her face like a veil; and with cup and plate within her hand, drink and meat for his aloneness and his hunger. And after setting these before him, she walked her way.

And Almustafa came again to the company of the white poplars within the gate, and he sat looking upon the road. And after a while he beheld as it were a cloud of dust blown above the road and coming toward him. And from out the cloud came the nine, and before them Karima guiding them.

And Almustafa advanced and met them upon the road, and they passed through the gate, and all was well, as though they had gone their path but an hour ago.

They came in and supped with him at his frugal board, after that Karima had laid upon it the bread and the fish and poured the last of the wine into the cups. And as she poured, she besought the Master saying: "Give me leave that I go into the city and fetch wine to replenish your cups, for this is spent."

And he looked upon her, and in his eyes were a journey and a far country, and he said: "Nay, for it is sufficient unto the hour."

And they ate and drank and were satisfied. And when it was finished, Almustafa spoke in a vast voice, deep as the sea and full as a great tide under the moon, and he said: "My comrades and my road-fellows, we must needs part this day. Long have we sailed the perilous seas, and we have climbed the steepest mountains and we have wrestled with the storms. We have known hunger, but we have also sat at wedding-feasts. Oftentimes have we been naked, but we have also worn kingly raiment. We have indeed travelled far, but now we part. Together you shall go your way, and alone must I go mine.

"And though the seas and the vast lands shall separate us, still we shall be companions upon our journey to the Holy Mountain.

"But before we go our severed roads, I would give unto you the harvest and the gleaning of my heart:

"Go you upon your way with singing, but let each song be brief, for only the songs that die young upon your lips shall live in human hearts.

"Tell a lovely truth in little words, but never an ugly truth in any words. Tell the maiden whose hair shines in the sun that she is the daughter of the morning. But if you shall behold the sightless, say not to him that he is one with night.

"Listen to the flute-player as it were listening to April, but if you shall hear the critic and the fault-finder speak, be deaf as your own bones and as distant as your fancy.

"My comrades and my beloved, upon your way you shall meet men with hoofs; give them of your wings. And men with horns; give them wreaths of laurel. And men with claws; give them petals for fingers. And men with forked tongues; give them honey for words.

"Ay, you shall meet all these and more; you shall meet the lame selling crutches; and the blind, mirrors. And you shall meet the rich men begging at the gate of the Temple.

"To the lame give of your swiftness, to the blind of your vision; and see that you give of yourself to the rich beggars; they are the most needy of all, for surely no man would stretch a hand for alms unless he be poor indeed, though of great possessions.

"My comrades and my friends, I charge you by our love that you be countless paths which cross one another in the desert, where the lions and the rabbits walk, and also the wolves and the sheep.

"And remember this of me: I teach you not giving, but receiving; not denial, but fulfilment; and not yielding, but understanding, with the smile upon the lips.

"I teach you not silence, but rather a song not over-loud.

"I teach you your larger self, which contains all men."

And he rose from the board and went out straightway into the Garden and walked under the shadow of the cypress-trees as the day waned. And they followed him, at a little distance, for their heart was heavy, and their tongue clave to the roof of their mouth.

Only Karima, after she had put by the fragments, came unto him and said: "Master, I would that you suffer me to prepare food against the morrow and your journey."

And he looked upon her with eyes that saw other worlds than this, and he said: "My sister, and my beloved, it is done, even from the beginning of time. The food and the drink is ready, for the morrow, even as for our yesterday and our today.

"I go, but if I go with a truth not yet voiced, that very truth will again seek me and gather me, though my elements be scattered throughout the silences of eternity, and again shall I come before you that I may speak with a voice born anew out of the heart of those boundless silences.

"And if there be aught of beauty that I have declared not unto you, then once again shall I be called, ay, even by mine own name, Almustafa, and I shall give you a sign, that you may know I have come back to speak all that is lacking, for God will not suffer Himself to be hidden from man, nor His word to lie covered in the abyss of the heart of man.

"I shall live beyond death, and I shall sing in your ears
Even after the vast sea-wave carries me back
To the vast sea-depth.
I shall sit at your board though without a body,
And I shall go with you to your fields, a spirit invisible.
I shall come to you at your fireside, a guest unseen.
Death changes nothing but the masks that cover our faces.
The woodsman shall be still a woodsman,
The ploughman, a ploughman,
And he who sang his song to the wind shall sing it also to the
    moving spheres."

And the disciples were as still as stones, and grieved in their heart for that he had said: "I go." But no man put out his hand to stay the Master, nor did any follow after his footsteps.

And Almustafa went out from the Garden of his mother, and his feet were swift and they were soundless; and in a moment, like a blown leaf in a strong wind, he was far gone from them, and they saw, as it were, a pale light moving up to the heights.

And the nine walked their ways down the road. But the woman still stood in the gathering night, and she beheld how the light and the twilight were become one; and she comforted her desolation and her aloneness with his words: "I go, but if I go with a truth not yet voiced, that very truth will seek me and gather me, and again shall I come."

AND NOW IT was eventide.

And he had reached the hills. His steps had led him to the mist, and he stood among the rocks and the white cypress-trees hidden from all things, and he spoke and said:

"O Mist, my sister, white breath not yet held in a mould,
I return to you, a breath white and voiceless,
A word not yet uttered.

"O Mist, my wingèd sister mist, we are together now,
And together we shall be till life's second day,
Whose dawn shall lay you, dewdrops in a garden,
And me a babe upon the breast of a woman,
And we shall remember.

"O Mist, my sister, I come back, a heart listening in its depths,
Even as your heart,
A desire throbbing and aimless even as your desire,
A thought not yet gathered, even as your thought.

"O Mist, my sister, first-born of my mother,
My hands still hold the green seeds you bade me scatter,
And my lips are sealed upon the song you bade me sing;
And I bring you no fruit, and I bring you no echoes
For my hands were blind, and my lips unyielding.

"O Mist, my sister, much did I love the world, and the world
    loved me,
For all my smiles were upon her lips, and all her tears were in
    my eyes.

Yet there was between us a gulf of silence which she would
   not abridge
And I could not overstep.

"O Mist, my sister, my deathless sister Mist,
I sang the ancient songs unto my little children,
And they listened, and there was wondering upon their face;
But tomorrow perchance they will forget the song,
And I know not to whom the wind will carry the song.
And though it was not mine own, yet it came to my heart
And dwelt for a moment upon my lips.

"O Mist, my sister, though all this came to pass,
I am at peace.
It was enough to sing to those already born.
And though the singing is indeed not mine,
Yet it is of my heart's deepest desire.

"O Mist, my sister, my sister Mist,
I am one with you now.
No longer am I a self.
The walls have fallen,
And the chains have broken;
I rise to you, a mist,
And together we shall float upon the sea until life's second day,
When dawn shall lay you, dewdrops in a garden,
And me a babe upon the breast of a woman."

PROSE POEMS

Translated by Andrew Ghareeb

CONTENTS

AT THE DOOR OF THE TEMPLE

I PURIFIED MY lips with the sacred fire to speak of love,
But when I opened my lips I found myself speechless.
Before I knew love, I was wont to chant the songs of love,
But when I learned to know, the words in my mouth became
     naught save breath,
And the tunes within my breast fell into deep silence.
In the past, when you would question me concerning the
     secrets and the mysteries of love,
I would speak and answer you with assurance.
But now that love has adorned me with vestments,
I come, in my turn, to question you of all the ways of love,
     and all its wonders.
Who among you can answer me?
I come to question you about my self and that which is in me.
Who among you can reveal my heart to my heart,
And disclose my self to my self?
Tell me now, what flame is this that burns within my bosom,
Consuming my strength, and melting my hopes and my
     desires?
What hands are these, light, gentle, and alluring,
Which enfold my spirit in its hours of loneliness
And pour into the vessel of my heart a wine mixed of the
     bitterness of joy
And the sweetness of pain?
What wings are these beating around my bed in the long
     silence of the night,
So that I am wakeful, watching – I know not what;
Listening to that I do not hear, and gazing upon that I do
     not see;
Meditating on that I do not comprehend, and possessing that
     I have not attained.

Ay, wakeful am I, sighing,
For to me sighs and griefs are lovelier than the ring of joy and
    laughter;
Wakeful am I in the hand of an unseen power that slays me
    and then quickens me,
Even until the day dawns and fills the corners of my house
    with light.
Then do I sleep, while between my withered eyelids the
    shadows of my wakefulness still quiver,
And above my bed of stone hovers the figure of a dream.

*

And what is this that we call love?
Tell me, what is this mystic secret hiding behind the
    semblance of our life,
And living in the heart of our existence?
What is this vast release coming as a cause to all effects, and as
    an effect unto all causes?
What is this quickening that gathers death and life and from
    them creates a dream
More strange than life, and deeper far than death?
Tell me, my brothers, tell me, which of you would not awake
    from this sleep of life
When your spirit feels the touch of love's white fingers?
Which of you would not forsake his father and his mother and
    his birthplace
When the maiden his heart loves calls out to him?
Which of you would not cross the desert and climb the
    mountain and sail the seas
To seek her to whom your spirit yearns?
What youth, indeed, would not follow to the earth's
    uttermost bounds,
If one awaits him there whose breath and voice and touch he
    shall find sweet and wholesome?
What man would not thus burn his soul as incense
Before a god who regards his craving and grants him his
    petition?

*

It was but yesterday that I stood at the door of the temple
Questioning the passers-by concerning the mysteries and the
    benefits of love.
And a man passed by, of middle age, wasted and with a
    scowling countenance, and he said:
"Love is an inborn weakness which we have inherited from
    the first man."
Then a youth, strong and stalwart of body and arm, came
    chanting:
"Love is a resolution which accompanies our being, and binds
    this present with the ages past and future."
And now a sad-faced woman, passing, sighed and said:
"Love is a deadly venom which dark and fearful vipers diffuse
    in space from the abyss of hell,
So that it descends in dew upon the thirsty soul,
And the soul therefrom becomes for a moment drunken, then
    sobered for a year, and dead an æon."
But a young maiden, rosy, and with laughing lips, said:
"See, love is a nectar which the brides of dawn pour for
    the strong
So that they rise glorified before the stars of night, and joyous
    before the sun of day."
Thereafter came a man in a garment of sombre black, and a
    loose beard that fell upon his breast, and he said sternly:
"Love is a stupidity which comes with the dawn of youth and
    is gone with its eventide."
And one followed him with face radiant and serene, saying in
    tranquil joy:
"Love is a heavenly wisdom that lights our inner and outer eye
So that we may behold all things even as the gods."
Then passed by a blind man questioning the ground with his
    old staff, and there was a wailing in his voice as he said:
"Love is a dense fog to enshroud the soul, and veil from it the
    shows of life,
So that the soul sees naught but the shadows of its desires
Lost among rocky steeps,
And hears naught but the echo of its voice shouting from the
    valleys of desolation."

Then passed by a young man playing upon a lyre and singing:
"Love is a celestial light shining from the innermost of the
    sensitive self to illumine all about it,
That it may behold the worlds as a procession moving in green
    meadows,
And life as a dream of beauty between awakening and
    awakening."
And after the young man followed one decrepit, and with
    dragging feet, trembling, and he said:
"Love is the repose of the sad body in the silent grave,
And it is the security of the soul in the fastnesses of eternity."
Then came a young child whose years were but five, and he
    ran and shouted:
"Love is my father, and love is my mother,
And no one knows of love but my mother and my father."

*

And now the day was done and all the people were passed by
    before the temple,
And each and every one had spoken of love,
And in each word he had revealed his own longing and desire
And had disclosed the secret mysteries of life.

When evening was fully come, and the moving throng had
    gone their ways,
And all was hushed,
I heard a voice within the temple saying:
"All life is twain, the one a frozen stream, the other a burning
    flame,
And the burning flame is love."

Thereupon I entered into the temple and bowed myself,
    kneeling in supplication
And chanting a prayer in my secret heart:
"Make me, O Lord, food for the burning flame,
And make me, O God, fuel for the sacred fire.
Amen."

REVELATION

WHEN THE NIGHT waxed deep and slumber cast its cloak upon
    the face of the earth,
I left my bed and sought the sea, saying to myself:
"The sea never sleeps, and the wakefulness of the sea brings
    comfort to a sleepless soul."
When I reached the shore, the mist had already descended
    from the mountain tops
And covered the world as a veil adorns the face of a maiden.

There I stood gazing at the waves, listening to their singing,
    and considering the power that lies behind them –
The power that travels with the storm, and rages with the
    volcano, that smiles with smiling flowers and makes melody
    with murmuring brooks.

After a while I turned, and lo,
I beheld three figures sitting upon a rock near by,
And I saw that the mist veiled them, and yet it veiled them not.

Slowly I walked toward the rock whereon they sat, drawn by
    some power which I know not.
A few paces off I stood and gazed upon them, for there was
    magic in the place
Which crystallized my purpose and be stirred my fancy.
And at that moment one of the three arose, and with a voice
    that seemed to come from the sea depths he said:
"Life without love is like a tree without blossoms or fruit.
And love without beauty is like flowers without fragrance, and
    fruit without seeds.
Life, Love, and Beauty are three entities in one self, free and
    boundless,

Which know neither change nor separation."
This he said, and sat again in his place.

Then the second figure arose, and with a voice like the roar of
    rushing waters he said:
"Life without rebellion is like the seasons without a spring.
And rebellion without right is like spring in an arid and barren
    desert.
Life, Rebellion, and Right are three entities in one self,
And in them is neither change nor separation."
This he said, and sat again in his place.

Then the third figure arose, and spoke with a voice like the
    peal of the thunder, saying:
"Life without freedom is like a body without a spirit.
And freedom without thought is like a spirit confounded.
Life, Freedom, and Thought are three entities in one eternal
    self,
Which neither vanish nor pass away."

Then the three arose and with voices of majesty and awe
    they spoke:
"Love and all that it begets,
Rebellion and all that it creates,
Freedom and all that it generates,
These three are aspects of God . . .
And God is the infinite mind of the finite and conscious
    world."

Then silence followed, filled with the stirring of invisible
    wings and the tremor of the ethereal bodies.
And I closed my eyes, listening to the echo of the saying
    which I heard.

When I opened my eyes, I beheld naught but the sea hidden
    beneath a blanket of mist;
And I moved closer toward that rock
And I beheld naught but a pillar of incense rising unto the sky.

THE SOUL

. . . AND THE GOD of Gods created the soul, fashioning it
    for beauty.
He gave unto it the gentleness of a breeze at dawn, the scent
    of flowers, the loveliness of moonlight.
He gave unto it also the cup of joy, and He said:
"You shall not drink of this cup save that you have forgotten
    the past and renounced the future."
He gave unto it also the cup of sorrow, saying:
"Drink that you may understand the meaning of joy."

Then God bestowed within the soul love that would depart
    with the first sigh of content,
And sweetness that would flee from the first word of arrogance.
He made a heavenly sign to guide it in the path of truth.
He placed in its depths an eye that would behold the unseen.
He created within it a fancy to flow like a river with phantoms
    and moving figures.
He clothed it in garments of longing woven by angels, from
    the rainbow.
Within it He placed also the darkness of bewilderment, which
    is the shadow of light.
And God took fire from the forge of anger,
Wind blowing from the desert of ignorance;
Sand He gathered from the seashore of selffulness
And dust from beneath the feet of the ages;
Thus He fashioned man.
And unto man He gave blind strength that leaps into a flame
    in moments of mad passion, and lies down before desire.
God gave him life which is the shadow of death.
And the God of Gods smiled and wept, and He knew a love
    which hath no bound nor end;
Thus He united man and his soul.

SONG OF THE NIGHT

THE NIGHT IS hushed,
And the dreams hide in silence.
The moon is rising –
She has eyes to watch the day.

Come, daughter of the fields,
And let us go
Into the vineyards
Where the lovers meet.
For it may be
That there we, too, may quench
With love's good vintage
The drouth of our desire.

Hearken, the nightingale
Pours forth his song
Into the valleys
Which the hills have filled
With the green scent of mint.

Fear not, beloved,
The stars will keep the secret of our meeting,
And the soft mist of night
Veil our embrace.

Fear not –
The young bride of the djinns
In her enchanted cave
Lies sleeping, drunk with love,
And well-nigh hidden
From the houri's eyes.

And even should the king of the djinns pass by,
Then love will turn him back.
For is he not a lover as I am,
And shall he disclose
That which his own heart suffers?

MY SOUL COUNSELLED ME

MY SOUL SPOKE unto me and counselled me to love all that
    others hate,
And to befriend those whom others defame.
My soul counselled me and revealed unto me that love
    dignifies not alone the one who loves, but also the beloved.
Unto that day love was for me a thread of cobweb between
    two flowers, close to one another;
But now it has become a halo with neither beginning nor end,
Encircling all that has been, and waxing eternally to embrace
    all that shall be.

                *

My soul counselled me and taught me to see beauty veiled by
    form and colour.
My soul charged me to gaze steadfastly upon all that is deemed
    ugly until it appears lovely.
Before my soul had thus charged and counselled me,
I had seemed to see beauty like unto wavering torches
    between pillars of smoke;
But now the smoke has dispersed and vanished and I see
    naught but the burning.

                *

My soul counselled me and charged me to listen for voices
    that rise neither from the tongue nor the throat.
Before that day I heard but dully, and naught save clamour and
    loud cries came to my ears;
But now I have learned to listen to silence,
To hear its choirs singing the songs of ages,
Chanting the hymns of space, and disclosing the secrets of
    eternity.

                *

My soul spoke unto me and counselled me to quench my
   thirst with that wine which may not be poured into cups,
Nor lifted by hands, nor touched by lips.
Unto that day my thirst was like a dim spark laid in ashes
To be put out by a draught from any spring;
But now my strong yearning has become my cup,
Love has become my wine, and loneliness my joy.

*

My soul counselled me and charged me to seek that which is
   unseen;
And my soul revealed unto me that the thing we grasp is the
   thing we desire.
In other days I was content with warmth in winter, and with a
   cooling zephyr in the summer season;
But now my fingers are become as mist,
Letting fall all that they have held, to mingle with the unseen
   that I now desire.

*

My soul spoke to me and invited me to breathe the fragrance
   from a plant
That has neither root nor stalk nor blossom, and that no eye
   has seen.
Before my soul counselled me thus, I sought perfumes in the
   gardens,
In jars of sweet-smelling herbs and vessels of incense;
But now I am aware only of an incense that may not be
   burned,
I breathe an air more fragrant than all earth's gardens and all
   the winds of space.

*

My soul counselled me and charged me to answer and say:
   "I follow," when the unknown and the adventurous call
   unto me.
Hitherto I had answered naught but the voice of the crier in
   the market-place,
Nor did I pursue aught save roads charted and well trodden;
But now the known has become a steed that I mount to seek
   the unknown,

And the road has become a ladder by which I may climb to
    the perilous summit.

*

My soul counselled me and admonished me to measure time
    with this saying:
"There was a yesterday and there shall be a tomorrow."
Unto that hour I deemed the past an epoch that is lost and
    shall be forgotten,
And the future I deemed an era that I may not attain;
But now I have learned this:
That in the brief present all time, with all that is in time,
Is achieved and come true.

*

My soul spoke and revealed unto me that I am not bound in
    space by the words:
"Here, there, and over there."
Hitherto I stood upon my hill, and every other hill seemed
    distant and far away;
But now I know that the hill whereon I dwell is indeed all
    hills,
And the valley whereunto I descend comprehends all valleys.

*

My soul counselled me and besought me to watch while
    others sleep
And to seek my pillow while they are wakeful,
For in all my years I had not perceived their dreams, nor they
    mine.
But now I am winged by day in my dreaming,
And when they sleep I behold them free upon the night,
And I rejoice in their freedom.

*

My soul counselled me and charged me lest I be exalted
    because of overpraise
And lest I be distressed for fear of blame.
Until that day I doubted the worth of my own handiwork;
But now I have learned this:
That the trees blossom in spring, and bear fruit in summer,

575

And drop their leaves in autumn to become utterly naked in
    winter
Without exaltation and without fear or shame.

*

My soul counselled me and assured me
That I am neither higher than the pygmy nor lower than the
    giant.
Before that day I beheld mankind as two men,
The one a weakling whom I derided or pitied,
And the other a mighty man whom I would either follow, or
    oppose in rebellion.
But now I know that I was formed even from the same dust of
    which all men are created,
That my elements are their elements, and my inner self is their
    inner self.
My struggle is their struggle, and their pilgrimage is mine own.
If they transgress, I am also the transgressor,
And if they do well, then I have a share in their well-doing.
If they arise, I too arise with them; if they stay behind, I also,
    to company them.

*

My soul counselled me and instructed me to see that the light
    which I carry is not my light,
That my song was not created within me;
For though I travel with the light, I am not the light,
And though I am a lute fastened with strings,
I am not the lute-player.

*

My soul counselled me, my brother, and enlightened me.
And oftentimes has your soul counselled and enlightened you.
For you are like me, and there is no difference between us
Save that I speak of what is within me in words that I have
    heard in my silence,
And you guard what is within you, and your guardianship is as
    goodly as my much speaking.

MY BIRTHDAY
(Written while studying art in Paris, 6 January 1908)

ON THE DAY my mother gave me birth,
On that day five-and-twenty years ago,
Silence placed me in the vast hands of life, abounding with
    struggle and conflict.
Lo, five-and-twenty times have I journeyed round the sun.
How many times the moon has journeyed round me I do not
    know.
But this I know, that I have not yet learned the secrets of light,
Nor have I understood the mysteries of darkness.

Five-and-twenty times have I journeyed with the earth, the
    moon, the sun and stars encircling the universe.
Lo, now my soul whispers the names of cosmic systems
Even as the caverns of the sea resound to the waves,
For the soul exists, a current in the cosmos, but does not
    know its power.
And the soul chants the cosmic rhythm, high and low,
Yet attains not the fullness of its harmonies.

Five-and-twenty years ago Time wrote me down in the book
    of this strange and awful life.
Lo, a word am I, signifying now nothing and now many
    things.
On that day of every year what thoughts and what memories
    throng my soul!
They halt before me – the procession of the days gone by,
The parade of the phantoms of the night –
Then are they swept away, even as the wind sweeps clouds
    from the horizon;
They vanish in the darkness of my house as the songs of the
    rivulets in desolate and distant valleys.

On that day, every year, those spirits which have shaped my
    spirit
Come seeking me from the far ends of the worlds,
And chanting words of sorrowful remembrance.
Then they are gone, to hide behind the semblance of this life,
Even as birds descending to a threshing floor and finding no
    seeds to feast upon,
Hover but a moment and fly hence to seek another place.

Ever upon that day the meanings of my past life stand before
    me, like dim mirrors
Wherein I look for a while and see naught but the pallid
    corpse-like faces of the years,
Naught but the wrinkled and aged visages of hopes and
    dreams long lost.
Once more I look upon those mirrors, and there behold only
    my own still face.
I gaze thereon beholding naught but sadness.
I question sadness and I find it has no speech;
Yet could sadness speak, methinks it would utter a sweeter
    word than joy.

For five-and-twenty years I have loved much,
And oftentimes have I loved what others hate.
Yet what I loved as a child I love now,
And what I now love I shall love unto the end of life;
For love is all I have, and none shall make me lose it.

Oftentimes have I loved death,
Called death sweet names and spoken of it in loving words
    both openly and secretly.
Yet though I have not forgotten, nor broken the vows of death,
I have learned to love life also.
For death and life have become equal to me in beauty and
    in joy;
They have shared in the growth of my yearning and desire,
And they have divided my love and tenderness.

Freedom also have I loved, even as life and death.
And as my love grew, so grew also my knowledge of men's
  slavery to tyranny and contempt,
The while I beheld their submission to idols hewn by the
  dark ages,
Reared in ignorance and polished by the lips of slaves.
But I loved these slaves as I loved freedom, and I pitied them,
  for they are blind men
Kissing the jaws of foul bloodthirsty beasts, and seeing not;
Sucking the venom of malignant vipers, and feeling not;
Digging their graves with their own hands, and knowing not.
Freedom have I loved more than aught else,
For I have found freedom like unto a maiden wasted from
  privation and seclusion
Till she became a ghost that moves among the houses in the
  lonely streets,
And when she calls out to the passers-by, they neither hear
  nor look.

Like all men, during these five-and-twenty years I have loved
  happiness;
I have learned to awake at every dawn and seek it, even
  as they.
But never have I found it in their ways,
Nor seen the trace of the footsteps of happiness on the sand
  near their mansions,
Nor have I heard the echo of its voice from the windows of
  their temples.
I sought alone to find it.
I heard my soul whisper in my ear:
"Happiness is a maiden born and reared in the fastness of the
  heart;
She comes never from beyond its walls."
Yet when I opened the portal of my heart to find happiness,
I saw therein her mirror and her bed and her garments, but
  herself I could not find.

Mankind have I loved. Ay, much have I loved men,
And men in my opinion are three:
The one who curses life, the one who blesses it, and the one
    who contemplates it.
The first I have loved for his misery, the second for his
    beneficence, and the third for his wisdom.

*

Thus passed the five–and–twenty years,
And thus my days and nights, pursuing each other down my life
As the leaves of trees scatter before the winds of autumn.
And today I pause remembering, even as a weary climber
    half-way to the summit,
And I look backward, and to right and left, but I see no
    treasure anywhere
Which I may claim and say: "This is mine own."

Nor do I find in the seasons of my years any harvest
Save only sheets of fair white paper traced over with markings
    of black ink,
And strange and fragmentary canvases filled in with lines and
    colours, both harmonious and inharmonious.
In these have I shrouded and buried the loveliness and the
    freedom that I have thought and dreamed,
Even as the ploughman who goes to the field to sow his seeds
    in furrows
Returns to his house at eventide hoping and waiting.
But I, though I have sowed well the seeds of my heart,
Yet I have neither hoped nor waited.
And now that I have reached this season of my life,
The past seems hidden behind a mist of sighs and grief,
And the future revealed through the veil of the past.

I pause and gaze at life from my small window;
I behold the faces of men, and I hear their shouting rise into
    the sky.
I heed their footsteps falling among the streets of houses,
And I perceive the communion of their spirits, the eagerness
    of their desires, the yearning of their hearts.

I pause and behold the children throwing dust upon each
    other with laughter and loud cries.
I behold boys with their faces upward lifted as though they
    were reading an ode to youth written upon the margins of
    a cloud
Lined with the gleaming radiance of the sun.
I behold young maidens swaying to and fro, like branches of
    a tree,
Smiling like flowers, and gazing at the youths from behind
    eyelids
Quivering with love and soft desire.
I behold the aged walking slowly, with their low-bent backs,
Leaning upon their staffs and gazing fixedly at the earth
As if their old dim eyes were searching in the dust for lost
    bright jewels.
I pause beside my window and I gaze at all these shapes and
    shadows
Moving and creeping silently about the city.

Then I look afar beyond the city to the wilderness,
And I behold all that is therein of dreadful beauty and of
    calling silence,
Its lofty mounds and little valleys, its springing trees and
    tremulous grasses,
Its flowers with perfume laden, and its whispering rivers,
Its wild birds singing, and all its humming wingèd life.

I gaze beyond the wilderness, and there, behold, the ocean –
With its deep wonders and mysterious secrets, its hid
    treasures;
There I behold all that is upon the face of the raging, rushing,
    foaming waters,
And the spray that rises and the vapours that descend.

I peer far beyond the ocean and behold the infinity of space,
The drifting worlds, the glimmering constellations, the suns
    and moons, the fixed and the shooting stars;
And I behold the evidence of forces forever attracting and

repelling, the wars of elements, creating, changing, and
withal held prisoned within a law of no beginning and
no end.

These things I contemplate through my small window, and
I forget my five-and-twenty years,
And all the centuries which have preceded them,
And all the ages that shall follow.
Then my life, with its revelations and its mysteries, seems to
me like the sighing of a child
That trembles in the void of the eternal depths and heights.
Yet this atom, this self that I call *I*, makes ever a stirring and
a clamour,
Lifting its wings toward the vast firmament,
Reaching its hands toward the four corners of the earth,
Its being poised upon the point of time which gave it
conscious life.

Then from the holy of holies where this living spark abides,
a voice arises crying:
"Peace be with you, life!
Peace be with you, awakening!
Peace be with you, realization!
Peace be with you, day, whose abundant light enfolds the
darkness of earth!
Peace be with you, night, whose darkness reveals the light of
heaven!
Peace be with you, seasons!
Peace be with you, spring, that renews the youth of the earth!
Peace be with you, summer, that enriches the glory of the sun!
Peace be with you, autumn, that bestows the fruits of labour
and the harvest of toil!
Peace be with you, winter, that restores with tempests the
wasted strength of nature!
Peace be with you, years, which disclose what the years have
hidden!
Peace be with you, ages, which restore what the centuries
have destroyed!

Peace be with you, time, which moves with us unto the
    perfect day!
Peace be with you, spirit, that guards with prudence the reins
    of life, hidden from us by the sun!
Peace be with you, heart, that you are moved to acclaim peace
The while you bathe in tears!
Peace be with you, lips, that you utter peace
The while you taste the bread of bitterness!"

BE STILL, MY HEART

BE STILL, MY heart. Space does not hear you.
Be still, my heart. The ether, heavy with mourning and with
  lamentation, will not bear your songs.
Be still, for the phantoms of night will not heed the whisper of
  your mysteries,
And the procession of darkness will not halt before your
  dreams.
Be still, my heart, be still until dawn.
For whoso waits the morning patiently will greet the morning
  with strength,
And whoso loves the light, by light shall he be loved.
Be still, my heart, and listen to my words.

In dreams I heard a blackbird singing above the mouth of a
  raging volcano,
And saw a lily lifting its head above the snow;
I saw a naked houri dancing among tombstones,
And a babe laughing the while it played with skulls.
All this I saw in a dream.

When I waked and looked about me, lo, I saw the volcano
  pouring forth its fury,
But I could not hear the blackbird singing.
I saw the heavens scattering snow over the hills and valleys,
Garmenting with its white shroud the silent lilies.
I saw the graves, row upon row, standing before the tranquillity
  of ages, but none amongst them dancing or praying.

Then I beheld hills of skulls, but no laughter was there save
  the laughing wind.
Waking I saw naught but grief and sorrow.
Where, then, have the joys of dreams departed?

Where hides the splendour of our sleep,
And how has its image vanished?
How can the soul bear patiently until the shadow of its
    yearning shall return with sleep?

*

Be still, my heart, and attend unto my words.
It was but yesterday that my soul was a tree, old and strong,
Whose roots penetrated to the depths of the earth and whose
    branches reached toward the infinite, blooming in spring
    and bearing fruit in summer.
When autumn was come, I gathered the fruit on trays of silver
    and placed them at the cross-roads,
And the passers-by reached for the fruit and ate of it and
    walked their way.

When autumn was passed and its song was turned to wailing
    and a dirge,
I looked upon my trays and saw that men had left there but a
    single fruit;
And when I tasted, I found it bitter as aloes and sour as a green
    grape.
Then I said to myself:
"Woe unto me, for I have placed a curse upon the lips of men,
    and hostility in their bowels.
What then, my soul, have you done with the sweetness that
    your roots had sucked from the bosom of earth,
And with fragrance that your boughs had drunk from the light
    of the sun?"

Thereupon I uprooted the old and strong tree of my soul.
I severed it from its past and dismantled it of the memories of
    a thousand springs and a thousand autumns.

And I planted the tree of my soul in another place.
I set it in a field far from the roads of time, and I passed the
    night in wakefulness beside it, giving it to drink of my tears
    and my blood, and saying:
"There is a savour in blood, and a sweetness in tears."

586

When spring returned, the tree of my soul bloomed again, and
bore fruit in the summer season.

And when the autumn was come, I gathered the ripe fruit
once more, and I placed it upon trays of gold at the
meeting-place of the roads.

And men passed by, but no one reached to take of the fruit.

Then I took and ate, and I found the fruit as sweet as honey,
as luscious as nectar, perfumed as the breath of jasmine,
and mellow as the wine of Babylon.

And I cried aloud, saying:

"Men do not desire blessedness upon their lips, nor truth in
their bowels;

For blessedness is the daughter of tears, and truth is but the
son of pain."

Then I returned and sat down under the shade of the lonely
tree of my soul, and in the field far from the roads of time.

*

Be still, my heart, be still until dawn.

Be still, for space is heavy with the odour of dead things and
cannot inhale your living breath.

Be still, my heart, and listen to my voice.

It was but yesterday that my thought was like a ship, rocked
upon the waves of the sea, and moving with the winds from
shore to shore.

And the ship of my thought was empty save only for seven
phials filled to the brim with seven colours, even the seven
colours of the rainbow.

There came a time when I grew weary of drifting upon the
face of the waters, and I said:

"I will return with the empty ship of my thought to the
harbour of the town where I was born."

And as I sailed, I began to paint the sides of my ship with the
seven colours;

And it shone yellow as the sunset, azure like the sky, and red as
a blood-red anemone;

And upon its sails and rudder I traced sketches to allure and
    delight the eye.
And when it was done, the ship of my thought appeared like
    the vision of a prophet
Floating betwixt the two infinities, the sea and the sky.

Now, when my ship reached port, behold, all the people came
    to meet me;
With shout and joy they welcomed me and they took me into
    the city,
Beating their tambourines and blowing upon their reed flutes.
All this they did because my ship appeared enchanting to
    their eyes;
But none boarded the ship of my thought,
Nor did any perceive that I had brought my ship empty
    into port.

Then I said to myself:
"I have misled the people, and with seven phials of colours
    have I deceived their inner and their outer eye."

And when a year was passed, again I boarded the ship of my
    thought and put out to sea.
I sailed to the isles of the East, and there I gathered myrrh and
    frankincense and sandalwood and brought them to my ship.
I sailed to the isles of the South, and from thence I brought
    gold, jade, and emerald, and every precious stone;
To the isles of the North I sailed, and found rare silks and
    velvets and broideries of every kind;
Thence to the isles of the West and got me coats of mail, and
    spears and swords, and divers weapons.
Thus I filled the ship of my thought with the costly and
    strange things of the earth,
And I turned back to the harbour of my own city, saying in
    my heart:
"Now shall my people praise me as a man worthy of praise.
And now shall they indeed lead me into the market-place with
    singing and piping."

But, behold, when I reached the port, no man came to meet
and welcome me.
Alone I entered the streets of my city, but no man looked
upon me.
Even in the market-squares I stood, telling of all that I had
brought of the earth's fruit and goodly things.
But the people looked upon me with laughter on their faces,
and derision on their lips.
And they turned from me.
Thus was I troubled and cast down, and I turned me to the
harbour.

No sooner did my eyes fall upon my ship than I became aware
of a certain thing to which, in my voyaging and seeking for
good cargoes, I had paid no heed;
So I cried out in humiliation:
"Behold, the waves of the sea have washed the seven colours
from my ship
And now it appears but as a skeleton of bones.
And the winds and the storms and the heat of the sun have
effaced from the sails the images of wonder and delight,
And they seem now but as a faded and tattered garment.
Truly I have gathered the earth's costly treasures in a casket
floating upon the surface of the waters,
And returned unto my people, but they turn from me,
For their eyes see naught but outward show."

At that very moment I abandoned the ship of my thought and
sought the city of the dead,
Where I sat amid the whitened graves and pondered their
secrets.
Be still, my heart. Be still until dawn.
Be still, though the tempest mock the whispering of your
depths.
Be still, my heart, until dawn.
For whoso awaits the morning patiently,
The morning shall embrace him tenderly.

Behold, my heart, the dawn is come;
Speak, then, if you have yet the power of words.
Behold, my heart, the procession of the morning.
Did not the silence of the night stir in your depths a song
    wherewith to greet the morn?

Behold, the flight of doves and blackbirds above the valley;
Did not the awe of night strengthen your wings to fly with
    them?
Behold, the shepherds leading their flocks from the folds.
Did not the shadows of night urge your desire to follow also
    into the green meadows?
Behold, the young men and the maidens hastening toward the
    vineyard.
Would you not rise and join them?

Arise, my heart. Arise and move with the dawn.
For night is passed and the fears of night have vanished with
    their black dreams.
Arise, my heart, and lift your voice in song;
For he who joins not the dawn with his singing is but a child
    of darkness.

NIGHT

O NIGHT, ABIDING-PLACE of poets and of lovers and of
    singers,
O Night, where shadows dwell with spirits and with visions,
O Night, enfolder of our longing, our desire, our memory,
Vast giant standing betwixt the dwarfed evening clouds and
    the brides of dawn,
Girt with the sword of awe, crowned with the moon, and
    garmented with silence;
Who gazes with a thousand eyes into the depths of life,
And listens with a thousand ears to the sighs of desolation and
    of death!

*

It is your darkness that reveals to us the light of heaven,
For the light of day has enshrouded us with the darkness of
    earth.
It is your promise that opens our eyes to eternity,
For the vanity of day had held us like blind men in the world
    of time and space.
It is your tranquil silence that unveils the secret of ever
    wakeful, ever restless spirits;
For day is a turbulent clamour wherein souls lie beneath the
    sharp hooves of ambition and desire.
O Night, you are a shepherd who gathers unto the fold of
    sleep the dreams of the weak and the hopes of the strong.
You are a seer who closes with his mystic fingers the eyelids of
    the wretched and lifts their hearts to a world more kindly
    than this world.
In the folds of your grey garments lovers have found their
    bower,
And upon your feet, wet with the dew of heaven, have the
    lonely-hearted wept their tears;

In the palms of your hands, fragrant with the scent of field and
    vineyard, strangers have laid down their longing and despair;
To lovers you are a friend; to the lonely, a comforter; to the
    desolate, a host.
In your deep shade the poet's fancies stir; on your bosom the
    prophetic heart awakes; upon your brow imagination
    writes.
For to the poet you are a sovereign, to the prophet a vision,
    and to the thinker an intimate.

*

When my soul became weary of man, and my eyes were tired
    of gazing upon the face of the day,
I sought the distant fields where the shadows of bygone ages
    sleep.
There I stood before a dark and silent being moving with a
    thousand feet over the mountain, and over the valley and
    the plain.
There I gazed into the eyes of darkness and listened to the
    murmuring of invisible wings.
There I felt the touch of formless garments and was shaken by
    the terrors of the unseen.

There I saw you, Night, tragic and beautiful and awesome,
Standing between the heaven and the earth, with clouds for
    your garment, girdled with the fog,
Laughing at the light of the sun and mocking the supremacy
    of the day,
Deriding the multitude of slaves who kneel sleepless before
    their idols, and contemptuous of kings who lie asleep and
    dreaming in their beds of silk;
There I beheld you gazing into the eyes of thieves, and
    I beheld you keeping guard above the babe in slumber;
I saw you weeping before the smiles of prostitutes, and smiling
    at the tears of lovers,
And lifting with your right hand the great-hearted, and with
    your feet trampling the mean-spirited.

There I saw you, Night, and you saw me;
You, in your awful beauty, were to me a father, and I, in my
    dreams, was a son;
For the curtains of being were drawn away, and the veil of
    doubt was rent;
You revealed your secret purposes unto me, and I told you all
    my hopes and my desires.
Then was your majesty turned into melody more beautiful
    than the gentle whisper of flowers,
And my fears were transformed into trust more than the trust
    of birds;
And you lifted me and placed me on your shoulders,
And you taught my eyes to see, my ears to hear, my lips to
    speak, and my heart to love;
With your magic fingers you touched my thought,
And my thought poured forth like a flowing, singing stream,
    bearing away all that was withered grass.
And with your lips you kissed my spirit, and it kindled into
    flames
Devouring every dead and dying thing.

*

I followed you, O Night, until I became like unto you;
I went as your companion until your desires became mine;
I loved you until my whole being was indeed a lesser image of
    your own.
For within my dark self are glowing stars which passion
    scatters at evening and doubt gathers at dawn;
And within my heart is a moon that struggles, now with
    thick clouds, and now with a procession of dreams that
    fills all space.
Now within my awakened soul dwells a peace that reveals the
    lover's secret and the worshipper's prayer;
And upon my head rests a veil of mystery which the agony of
    death may rend, but the songs of youth shall weave again.

I am like you, O Night, and if men shall deem me boastful,
Do they not boast of their resemblance to the day?

I am like you, and like you I am accused of much that I am not.

I am like you with all my dreams and all my hopes and being.

I am like you, even though dusk does not crown me with its golden fleece.

I am like you, though morn does not adorn my trailing raiment with pearl and rose.

I am like you, though I am not yet belted with the milky way.

I too am a night, vast and calm, yet fettered and rebellious.

There is no beginning to my darkness and no end to my depths.

When the souls of the departed rise to pride themselves upon the light of joy,

My night soul shall descend glorified by the darkness of its sorrow.

I am like you, O Night, and when my dawn comes, then also shall come my end.

IN THE CITY OF THE DEAD

IT WAS BUT yesterday I escaped the tumult of the city
And went forth to walk in the silent fields;
And I came unto a lofty hill
Where nature had bestowed the gifts of her bountiful hand.
I ascended the hill and looked back upon the city.
And lo, the city appeared, with all its towers and temples,
To lie beneath a cloud of thick dark smoke that rose up from
    its forges and its factories.

As I sat contemplating from afar the works of man,
It seemed that most of them are vain and futile.
And heartily I turned my mind away from all that the sons of
    Adam have wrought,
And looked upon the fields, the seat of God's great glory.
And in their midst I beheld a graveyard with tombstones of
    fair marble, and with cypress trees.

There, between the city of the living and the city of the dead,
    I sat
And mused upon the endless struggle and the ceaseless
    turbulence in life,
And the enveloping silence and vast dignity in death.
On the one side I beheld hope and despair, love and hate,
    riches and poverty, belief and unbelief;
And on the other, dust in dust which nature intermingles,
Fashioning therefrom its world of green and growing things
    that thrive in the deep silence of the night.
While thus I pondered, behold, a great crowd, marching
    slowly, caught my vision,
And I heard music filling the air with dreary tunes.

Before my eyes passed a procession of the great and the lowly
    of mankind,
Walking together in procession at the funeral of a man who
    had been rich and powerful,
The dead followed by the living.
And these wept and cried aloud, filling the day with their
    wailings and their lamentations,
Even unto the burial-place.
And here the priests offered up prayers and swung their
    censers,
And the pipers blew mournfully upon their pipes.
The orators stood forth with sounding words of eulogy,
And the poets, bemoaning with their studied verses,
Until all had come unto a weary end.
And then the crowd dispersed, revealing a proud tombstone
    which the stone-cutters had vied in making,
And many wreaths of flowers, and garlands woven by deft and
    skilful fingers.
Then the procession returned toward the city, while I sat
    watching from afar, and musing.

And now the sun was sinking toward the west, and the
    shadows of the rocks and trees began to lengthen and
    discard their raiment of light.
At that moment I looked, and lo, two men bearing upon their
    shoulders a coffin of plain wood;
And after them a woman came in ragged garments,
A babe at her breast, and at her feet a dog that looked now to
    the woman, now to the wooden casket.
Only these, in the procession at the funeral of a man who had
    been poor and humble –
The wife whose silent tears bespoke her sorrow,
A baby crying because his mother wept, and a faithful beast
    who would follow also in his dumb grief.
And when these reached the place of graves,
They lowered the coffin down into a pit in the far corner, well
    removed from the lofty marble tombs.
Then they turned back in silence and in desolation,

And the dog's eyes looked oftentimes toward the last
   dwelling-place of his friend and master,
Until they had disappeared from sight behind the trees.

Thereupon I bent my eyes first upon the city of the living, and
   said to myself:
"This is for the rich and powerful men";
Then I looked upon the city of the dead, saying:
"And this is for the rich and powerful men."
And I cried aloud: "Where, then, is the abiding-place of those
   who are weak and poor, O Lord?"
This I said, and gazed up toward the heaven of clouds,
   glorious with the golden rays of the great sun.
And I heard a voice within me saying: "It is there!"

THE POET

AN EXILE AM I in this world.

An exile am I and alone, tormented by my aloneness, which
  ever directs my thought to a magic and unknown realm
And fills my dreams with shadows of a region distant and
  unseen.

An exile am I from my kinsmen and my countrymen, and
  should I meet one of them, I would say to myself:
"Who, then, is this one? Where is it I have known him?
What bond unites me to him, and why do I draw near to sit
  beside him?"

An exile am I from myself, and should I hear my own tongue
  speak, my ear finds the voice strange.
Sometimes I look within and behold my secret self, a hidden
  self that laughs and weeps, that dares and fears.
Then my being marvels at my being, and my spirit questions
  mine own spirit.
Yet I remain an exile, unknown, lost in the mist, clothed with
  the silence.

An exile am I from my body; and when I pause before a
  mirror, behold, in my face is that which my soul has not
  conceived, and in my eyes that which my depths do not
  contain.
When I walk upon the streets of the city, the children follow
  after me, shouting:
"Behold the blind man! Let us give him a staff to lean upon."
And in haste I flee from them.
If I meet a bevy of maidens, they cleave to my garments,
  singing:

"He is deaf as a rock! Let us fill his ears with harmonies of
love and passion."
And from them I flee also.
Whenever I approach the middle-aged in the market-place,
they gather about me, crying:
"He is as mute as a tomb! Let us straighten his twisted
tongue."
And I hasten from them in fear.
And if I pass by a company of elders, they point their
trembling fingers toward me, saying:
"He is a madman who has lost his reason in the land of the
Djinns and Ghouls!"

*

An exile am I in this world.
An exile am I, for I have traversed the earth both East and West,
Yet I found not my birthplace, nor one who knew me or had
heard my name.
In the morning I awake to find myself imprisoned in a
darkened cavern
Where vipers threaten from above, and every crawling thing
infests the walls and ground.
When I seek the outer light, the shadows of my body march
ahead of me –
Whereto I know not, seeking that I do not understand,
grasping that for which I have no need.
When eventide is come and I return and lie upon my bed of
thorn and feather,
Strange thoughts beguile me, both fearsome and joyous, and
desires besiege me with their pains and their delights.
When it is midnight, the shades of bygone ages fall upon me,
and spirits of forgotten regions visit me and look upon me,
And I gaze also upon them, and speak to them and ask of
ancient things,
And with kindliness and smiles they answer me.
But when I would hold them and keep them, they escape me
And fade as they were but smoke upon the air.

*

An exile am I in this world.
An exile am I, and no man understands the language of my
    soul.
I pace the wilderness and I behold the rivulets climbing from
    the depths of the valley to the mountain top;
Before my eyes the naked trees come into bloom and bear
    their fruit and scatter their dead leaves, all in one moment.
And before my eyes their boughs fall to the lowland and are
    turned into dark serpents.

Ay, strange are my visions, like unto the visions of no man,
For I see birds lifting their wings unto the morning with
    songs, and then with lamentation;
I see them alight and change before my eyes into nude women
    with long, loosened hair
Who gaze at me from behind eyelids painted for love, and
    who smile upon me with lips dipped in honey,
And who stretch white hands to me, perfumed with
    frankincense and myrrh.
And even as I gaze, they vanish like a shaken mist,
Leaving in space the echo of their mocking laughter.

*

An exile am I in this world.
A poet am I who gathers in verse what life scatters in prose;
And scatters in prose what life gathers in verse.
And hence an exile am I, and an exile I shall remain until
    death lifts me up and bears me even unto my country.

FAME

I WALKED UPON the sand at ebb-tide.
And bending down, I wrote a line upon the sand.
And in that line I wrote what my mind thought
And what my soul desired.

And when the tide was high,
I returned to that very shore,
And of that which I had written I found naught.
I found only the staff-marks of one who had walked blindly.

EARTH

WITH MIGHT AND power earth springs forth out of earth;
Then earth moves over earth with dignity and pride;
And earth from earth builds palaces for kings,
And lofty towers and goodly temples for all people,
And weaves strange myths, strict laws, and subtle dogmas.

When all these things are done, earth wearies of earth's labour,
And from its light and darkness it creates grey shadows, and
    soft drowsy fancies, and enchanting dreams.
Earth's slumber then beguiles earth's heavy eyelids,
And they close upon all things in deep and quiet slumber.

And earth calls out unto earth, saying:
"Behold, a womb am I, and I am a tomb;
A womb and a tomb I shall remain forever,
Ay, even until the stars are no more,
And until the suns are turned into dead ashes."

SPIRITS REBELLIOUS

Translated from the Arabic by H. M. Nahmad

To the spirit that did embrace my spirit. To the heart that did pour out its secrets into my heart. To the hand that did kindle the flame of my love.

CONTENTS

WARDÉ AL-HANI

I

UNHAPPY IS THE man who loves a maiden and takes her for his
lifemate, pouring out at her feet the sweat of his brow and
his heart's blood, placing in her hands the fruits of his labour
and the yield of his toil, and then learns, suddenly, that her
heart, which he sought to buy with exertion by day and watch-
fulness by night, is given as a gift to another that he may take
pleasure in its hidden things and rejoice in the secrets of its love.

Unhappy the woman who awakens from youth's ignorance
to find herself in the house of a man who overwhelms her
with his gifts and riches and clothes her with generosity and
kindliness, yet is not able to touch her heart with the living
flame of love nor yet satisfy her spirit with the divine wine that
God makes to flow from a man's eyes into a woman's heart.

From the days of my youth had I known Rashid bey Nu'man.
He was Lebanese by origin, Beiruti by birth and residence. He
came of an old and wealthy family known for its attachment
to the memory of ancient glories. He was fond of recounting
tales of his ancestors' nobility. In his daily life he clung to their
customs and traditions and took refuge therein amidst the West-
ern ways and fashions that filled the atmosphere of the East like
flights of birds.

Rashid bey was a man of good heart and generous instinct,
but like many men of Syria he saw the surface of things alone
and not that which lay concealed beneath. He did not hear the
singing in his spirit, but used his feelings only to listen to the
voices around him. He amused himself with things of no import,
things that blind one to life's secrets and take the spirit from its
understanding of creation's hidden things to pursue ephemeral
pleasures. He was of those who quickly show their love or hatred

of people and things only to repent of their haste after a while, by which time repentance has become a cause of mocking and scorn instead of pardon and forgiveness. It was these things in his nature that joined Rashid bey Nu'man with Wardé Al-Hani before her spirit could embrace his in the shade of a love that makes married life a bliss.

For a number of years I was away from Beirut, and on my return I went to see Rashid. I found him feeble in body and pale in colour. On his drawn face played shadows of sadness, and from his sorrowful eyes grief spoke silently of a heart broken and a breast oppressed. I sought the cause of his sickness and distress from the things around him, but without finding it. So I asked of him and said: "What is the cause of your suffering, my friend, and where is the joy that once shone from your face like a light? Where is the happiness that was your youth? Has death parted you from a loved one? Or has the darkness of night robbed you of what you garnered by the light of day? Tell me, then, by the right of friendship, what this grief is that holds your spirit in embrace and this sickness that possesses your body."

He looked at me with the look of a grief-stricken person to whom remembrance first brings back the echoes of happier days and then silences them. In a voice whose very utterance was misery and despair he said:

"If a man loses a dear friend, he looks around him and finds many others and is comforted and solaced. When a person loses his wealth he thinks on the matter a little, knowing that the efforts that brought him riches before will again come to his aid, and so he forgets. But if a man loses his peace of mind, where shall he find it and how shall he be requited? Death stretches forth its hand and strikes you with violence and you are hurt, but after the passing of a day and a night you feel the caress of Life's fingers and you laugh and rejoice. Destiny comes upon you unawares and looks at you with big frightening eyes, grips you by the throat and throws you to the ground, trampling upon you with feet of iron, and then departs laughing. But soon Destiny returns, seeking your forgiveness, raises you up with fingers of silken touch, and sings to you a song of hope.

The shades of night bring with them all manner of affliction and vexation, which fade into nothingness with the coming of morning. And then you feel your resolve and hold fast to your hopes. But if your lot in life be a bird that you love and feed with grain from your heart, whose drink is the light of your glances, whose cage is your ribs, and whose nest your soul; and if, whilst you are looking at your bird caressing his feathers tenderly, he suddenly leaves your hand and flies away high in the sky only to alight in another's cage never to return, what shall you do then, my friend? How shall you find patience and consolation and how shall hope be revived?"

Rashid bey spoke these last words in a voice strangled by pain and stood shaking like a reed in the path of the wind. He stretched forth his hands as though he would seize on a thing with his distorted fingers and tear it piece by piece. The blood rose in his face and dyed his wrinkled flesh a dark colour; his eyes grew big and his eyelids became rigid. He appeared as one seeing before him an evil spirit conjured out of nothingness come to take his life. Then he turned his gaze on me; his expression changed at once and the rage and anger in his enfeebled body gave place to agony and pain. Weeping, he said:

"She is the woman. She is the woman I delivered from penury and slavery and opened up to her my treasures and made her envied of all women for her fine clothes and priceless jewels and carriages and thoroughbred horses. The woman my heart loved, at whose feet it poured out its affection; toward whom my soul inclined and showered with gifts and offerings. The woman to whom I was a loving friend and a sincere companion and a faithful husband has betrayed me. She has left me and gone to another's house to live with him in the shadow of poverty and share with him bread kneaded with shame and drink with him of water mixed with dishonour and disgrace. She is the woman whom I loved. The graceful bird whom I fed from my heart and gave to drink from the light of my eyes. The bird to whom my ribs were a cage and my soul a nest has fled from my hand and flown to another nest, a nest woven from thorns, to eat therein of worms and thistles and drink of poison and gall. The angel I put to dwell in the paradise of my love and affection is become a frightening demon descending into the blackness to torment itself with its sins and torment me with its crime."

The man became silent and covered his face with his hands as though he would protect his one self from the other. Then he sighed and said: "This is all that I can tell to you, do not ask more of me. Do not give utterance to my misfortune, but let it be voiceless, that perchance it may grow in quietude and grant me peace and the grave."

I rose from my place, and tears filled my eyes and compassion rent my heart. In silence I took leave of him, for I could find naught in speech as a balm to his wounded heart nor in wisdom a light to illumine the gloom of his spirit.

II

A few days later I met with Wardé Al-Hani, for the first time, in a poor house surrounded by trees and flowers. She had heard my name mentioned in the house of Rashid bey, the man whose heart she had trodden under foot and abandoned for dead beneath the hoofs of existence. And when I saw her shining eyes and heard the soft tones of her voice, I said to myself: "Can this woman be evil? Is it possible that this transparent face should conceal an ugly soul and an evil heart? Is this, then, the treacherous wife? Is this the woman whom I ofttimes accused and pictured in my mind as a serpent concealed in the body of some bird of rare beauty?" But I returned and murmured to myself: "What, then, has caused that man his misery if not this comely face? Have we not heard and known that seeming beauty is a cause of hidden and terrible calamity and deep and painful grief? Is not the moon that illumines the imagination of poets with light the same moon that disturbs the tranquillity of the waters with ebb and flow?"

I sat down near her. As though she had heard my thinking and did not wish to prolong the struggle between my perplexity and my thoughts, she rested her beautiful head on her white hand, and in a voice in which were the clear notes of a flute she said: "I have not met with you before, my friend, but the echo of your thoughts and dreams has come to me by the mouths of people and I know you for one with pity for an oppressed woman, who has mercy on her weakness and is sensible of her feelings and emotions. Because of this I lay before you my heart and open to you my breast so that you may see what is hidden therein and, if you would, tell people that Wardé Al-Hani was never a woman evil and treacherous. I was eighteen years of age when destiny led me to Rashid Nu'man and he was near to forty years. He loved me with passion and, in the idiom of people, his intentions to me were honourable. Then he made me his wife and set me mistress over his fine house with many servants and clothed my body in silk and adorned my head and neck and wrists with jewels and precious stones. He showed me, as one exhibits a strange and rare object, in the homes of his friends and acquaintances. He smiled the smile of a conqueror whenever he saw their eyes resting on me with admiration and wonder. If he heard the wives of his friends speak of me with affection, he would lift high his head in pride. But when one asked: 'Is this the wife of Rashid bey or a girl he has adopted?' he did not hear. Neither did he pay heed when another remarked: 'Had Rashid bey married in his youth, his first-born would now be older in years than Wardé Al-Hani!'

"All this happened before my life had awakened from the deep sleep of childhood and ere the gods had kindled in my heart love's flame; ere the seeds of affection and feeling had flowered in my breast. Yes, all this took place at a time when I thought that the greatest happiness was in fine garments to adorn my body, and an elegant carriage to draw me, and priceless rugs to surround me. But when I awoke and my eyes opened to the light and I felt tongues of sacred fire reaching out in me and burning, and a hunger of the spirit overcoming me and hurting; when I awoke to see my wings moving now right, now left to bear me aloft into the regions of love and then quiver and droop powerless by the side of the shackles of custom binding my body ere I knew the meaning of those bonds or the portent of that custom; when I awoke and felt all these things, I knew that a woman's happiness is not in the glory and lordship of a man. Neither is it in his generosity or clemency; it is in a love that binds her spirit to his spirit, pouring out her love into his heart and making them a single member in the body of Life and one word on the lips of God. When this wounding truth revealed itself to my sight, I saw myself a thief in Rashid Nu'man's house who eats the owner's bread and then hides himself in the dark caves of night. I knew that each day passed near him was a lie that shame would brand on my forehead in letters of fire before heaven and earth. For I could not give him my heart's love against his generosity, neither could I grant him affection in exchange for his goodness and piety. I tried to love him, but in vain; for love is a force that makes our hearts; our hearts cannot create that force. I prayed and besought, but in vain. I prayed into the silences of the nights before Heaven, asking it to create in my depths a spiritual affinity that would draw near to me the man who had been chosen for my husband. But Heaven did not so, for love descends on our spirits on God's command and not on man's asking. And thus did I remain two full years in that man's house, where I envied the birds of the fields their liberty while the daughters of my kind envied me my captivity. Like a woman bereaved of her only-born I wept for my heart that was born of knowledge and sickened of custom and law and died each day of hunger and thirst. Then one black day I looked to beyond the darkness and saw a soft light shining from the eyes of a youth who walked the highways of life alone and who dwelt alone among his books and papers in this poor house. I closed my eyes that I might not see those rays, and said within myself: 'Thy lot, O spirit, is the blackness of the tomb; covet not, therefore, the light!' Then I listened and heard a divine melody the sweetness of which made a trembling in my limbs, whose purity possessed my being. Thereupon I closed my ears and said: 'Thy lot, O spirit, is the howling of the pit; covet not, therefore, song.' I closed my eyelids that I might not see and my ears that I might not hear. But my eyes saw the light while they were yet closed and my ears heard the melody even though they were stopped. At first I was afraid, like a pauper who finds a jewel outside the King's palace and dares not pick it up out of fear and yet is not able to leave it because of his poverty. I wept the tears of a thirsty man who sees a well of sweet water surrounded by wild beasts of the forest and throws himself on the ground, watching fearfully."

Wardé grew silent for a while. She closed her big eyes as though the past was standing before her and she had not the courage to look on it face to face. Then she continued:

"Those who come forth from out of the infinite and return thereto and have tasted naught of life's truths know not the meaning of a woman's agony when her spirit stands between the man whom Heaven has willed to love and the man to whom the laws of his fellows have bound her. It is a tragedy writ in the blood and tears of womanhood, which a man reads and laughs at because he understands nothing of it. Does he understand, then his laughter becomes harshness and.sneering, and in his wrath he heaps coals of fire on the woman's head and fills her ears with blasphemy and cursing. It is tragedy played out by the black nights in the heart of every woman who finds her body fettered to the bed of a man whom she knows as a husband ere she knows what is marriage. She sees her spirit fluttering around another whom she loves with all her soul, with all the beauty and purity of love. It is a harsh struggle that began with the birth of weakness in a woman and strength in a man, and it will not cease until the day wherein weakness ceases to be a slave to strength. It is a destructive war between the corrupt laws of men and the sacred emotions of the heart. Yesterday was I cast into the arena, and fear nigh destroyed me and weeping put an end to me. But I rose up and cast away from me the cowardice of the daughters of my kind and set free my wings from the bonds of weakness and submission. I flew aloft into the spacious airs of love and freedom. And now I rejoice by the side of the man with whom I left the hand of God as a single burning flame before the beginning of time. There is no force in this world that can rob me of my happiness, for it springs from the embrace of two souls held together by understanding and sheltered by love."

Wardé looked at me with a look that held a meaning as though she would pierce my breast with her eyes to see the effect of her words in my heart and hear the echo of her voice in my bones. But I remained silent lest I stop her from speaking. Then she spoke in a voice in which was the bitterness of remembrance and sweetness of freedom and delivery, and said:

"People will say to you that Wardé Al-Hani is a treacherous

and faithless woman who has followed her lusting heart and abandoned the man who raised her to him and put her mistress over his household. They will say to you that she is shameless, a whore who has defiled the holy crown of marriage with her unclean hands and taken in its stead a foul crown made from the thorns of hell. And cast from her body the garments of virtue to put on garments of shame and sin. They will tell to you all that and more, for the ghosts of their ancestors cease not living in their bodies. They are like the deserted caves of the valleys that throw back voices in echo without understanding of their meaning. They know naught of God's sacred law in His creatures; neither are they knowing of the true faith. They know not when a man is guilty and when he is innocent, but rather do they look only on outward things, their weak-sighted eyes not seeing what is concealed. They pass judgment in ignorance, and guilty and innocent and good and bad are as one to them. Woe to them who would judge and weigh! I was a harlot and a faithless woman in the house of Rashid Nu'man because he made me the sharer of his bed by virtue of tradition and custom rather than as a wife before Heaven, bound to him by the sacred law of love and the spirit. I was as one filthy and unclean in my own eyes and before God when I took of his property, that he might take of my body. But now I am pure and clean, for the law of love has set me free. I am become faithful and good because I have ceased to trade my body for bread and my days for clothes. Yes, I was a whore whilst people thought me a virtuous wife. Yet today, when I am pure and honourable, they think me a whore and unclean, for they judge souls according to their bodies and measure the spirit with the measements of matter."

Wardé ceased speaking and looked toward the window. With her right hand she pointed in the direction of the town. In a raised voice filled with loathing and contempt as though she saw in the streets and doorways and on the roofs shadows of corruption and baseness, she said: "Look toward those fine dwellings and noble mansions where dwell the rich and powerful of mankind. Between walls hung with woven silk lives treachery with hypocrisy, and beneath ceilings of beaten gold

stay lies and falseness. Look well at those buildings that speak to you of glory and power and good fortune. They are naught save caverns concealing wretchedness and misery. They are plaster tombs where a weak woman's deceit takes refuge behind the mascara of her eyes and the reddening of her lips; in whose corners are hidden the selfishness and brutality of a man behind the glitter of gold and silver. These are the palaces that raise high their walls in pride and splendour; yet could they feel the breath of trickery and deceit breathing over them, they would crack and crumble and fall to the ground. These are the houses to which the poor villager looks with tear-filled eyes, yet did he but know that in the hearts of their dwellers was not one grain of the love and sweetness that filled the heart of his companion he would smile in scorn and go back to his field with pity."

She took hold of my hand and led me to a corner of the window that looked out on those houses and mansions and said:

"Come and I shall show to you the secrets of these people whom I did not wish to be like. Look at that palace with the marble columns and the glass windowpanes. In it lives a rich man who inherited the wealth of his avaricious father and learned his way of life in corruption-infested streets. Two years ago he wed a woman of whom he knew little save that her father was of noble line and high standing among the aristocracy of the town. Their honeymoon was hardly ended before he tired of her and went back to the companionship of women of pleasure and left her in that palace as a drunkard leaves an empty wine jar. At first she wept in her agony; then she took patience and consoled herself as one who admits an error. She learned that her tears were too precious to shed upon a man such as her husband. Now she busies herself with the passion of a young man with a handsome face and a sweet tongue into whose hands she pours her heart's love and whose pockets she fills with her husband's gold – the husband who will have no affair with her because she will have naught with him. Look at that house surrounded by a luxuriant garden. It is the residence of a man whose descent goes back to an illustrious family who once ruled his country over a long period of time. Today, through the dissipation of its wealth and the idleness and sloth of its sons, it has fallen in esteem. Many years ago this man wedded a girl of great wealth and ugliness, and after he had acquired her riches he forgot her existence and took to him a mistress of much beauty. The other he left to bite her nails in repentance and dissolve in yearning and longing. Now she spends the hours in curling her hair and blackening her eyes and colouring her face with powders and unguents. She adorns her body with satins and silks that she may find favour in the sight of one of those who visit her, but she finds nothing except the glances of her reflection in the mirror. That house of paintings and statues is the house of a woman comely of face and ugly of soul. When her first husband died, she got his wealth and property. Then she chose a man weak in will and body and made him her husband in order to shelter behind his name against people's tongues and make his presence a defence for her wrongful actions. Now she is among those who desire her like a bee that sucks up from the flowers the sweet and the pleasant. Look you now at yonder house, the one with the spacious doorways and the cunningly built arches. In it lives a man, a lover of things material, busy and ambitious. He has a wife in whose body is beauty and delight and of sweet and tender spirit. In her the spirit and the body are harmonized as the fall of a metrical verse is companion to its delicacy of meaning. She was created to live by love and die for it. But like the daughters of her kind she was condemned by her father before her eighteenth year, and the yoke of a corrupt marriage was fastened upon her neck. Today she is sick in body and melting like a wax candle in the heat of her imprisoned affection. She is fading slowly as a perfumed breeze before a storm. She is being destroyed through love of a thing she feels but cannot see. She longs and yearns for the embrace of Death to deliver her from her sterile state and free her from the thrall of a man who passes his days in amassing wealth and his nights in counting money the while he curses the hour in which he took to himself a barren woman who bore him no son to inherit his riches and perpetuate his name. . . . Look again to that house standing alone amidst gardens. It is the dwelling of a gifted poet of lofty thought and spiritual belief. He has a wife dull of intellect and coarse-minded. She mocks at his verse because she understands naught of it, and scorns his works because they are strange. But now he has gone from her to the love of another, a married woman sensitive and wise, who by her love creates light in his heart, and whose glance and smile inspire him to immortal utterance."

Wardé grew silent again for a while. She sat down by the window as though her spirit had tired of its wanderings in the hidden chambers of those dwellings. Then she spoke again and said quickly:

"Those are the places wherein I did not want to live. Those are the graves in which I did not want to be buried alive. Those people from whose ways I freed myself and whose yoke I cast away from me, they are those who mate and come together in their bodies, but in spirit contend one with the other. There is nothing to intercede for them before God save their ignorance of His laws. I judge them not, but pity them; neither do I hate them, but only their surrender to lies and hypocrisy. I have revealed to you their secrets and shown you what is in their hearts, not out of love of slander and backbiting, but that you should know the truth about a people whose like I was yesterday and from whom I have escaped. And to reveal to you the way of a people who speak only evil of me because I forfeited their friendship to gain my soul and abandoned their deceitful ways to turn my eyes to the light where are sincerity and truth and justice. They have driven me away from them, but I am content, for it is those whose spirits rebel against falsehood and oppression whom the multitude drives from its midst. Who does not prefer exile to slavery is not free in that freedom which is truth and duty. Yesterday I was a richly laden table that Rashid bey approached when he felt the need of food. But our two spirits remained apart like humble servants standing at a distance. When knowledge came to me, I loathed this servitude and I tried to submit myself to my lot, but I was not able, for my spirit forbade me to pass my days in prostration before an idol raised by the dark eyes and called Law. I broke my chains asunder, yet did not know how to throw them from me until

I heard Love summoning and saw the Spirit girded for departure. I went out from the house of Rashid Nu'man as a prisoner from his prison and left behind me the jewels and the servants and carriages and came to the abode of my love, which is empty of fine furnishings but full with the things of the spirit. I know that I have done naught save what was right, for it was not the will of Heaven that I should cut off my wings and prostrate myself in the dust, hiding my head in my arms while I spilled my life blood from my eyes, saying: 'This is my lot in life.' Heaven did not decree that I pass my days crying out in agony in the night, saying: 'When will come the dawn?' and when the dawn came, asking: 'When will end this day?' It was not decreed that man should be unhappy and wretched, for in his depths is created the desire for happiness, because in a man's happiness God is glorified. This, then, is my story and this is my protest before heaven and earth. I shall sing it and tell it, but people will close their ears and hear not, for they fear the revolt of their spirits and they are afraid lest the foundations of their society be shaken and fall about their heads. This is the rough and uneven path I have trodden ere attaining the summit of my happiness. If Death should come now and bear me away, my spirit would stand before the throne on high without fear or trembling, but with hope and rejoicing; and the coverings of my secret thoughts would fall away before the great Judge and reveal them white as snow. For I have done naught save the will of the spirit, which God did separate from Himself. I have followed the cry of the heart and the echo of celestial melodies. This, then, is my story, which the inhabitants of Beirut count as a curse on the lips of Life and a sore in the body of society. But they shall repent when the days awaken in their clouded hearts the love of Love as the sun brings forth flowers from the depths of the earth, which is full with remains of the dead. Then will the passer-by stand by my grave and greet it, saying: 'Here sleeps Wardé Al-Hani, who freed her love from the bondage of the corrupt laws of men that she might live by the laws of love; who lifted her face to the sun that she might not see the shadow of her body among skulls and thorns.' "

Hardly had Wardé ceased from speaking when the door

opened and a young man entered. He was handsome and slim of build, from his eyes shone a light, and on his lips played a soft smile. Wardé stood up and took his arm with affection. She presented him to me, mentioning my name with a kind word. When she uttered his name she glanced at me with a glance that told that this was the youth for whom she had denied the world and set at naught its laws and customs.

We sat down. Each was silent, asking in his mind the thought of the other toward him. A minute passed, a minute filled with a silence that inclined all spirits to the dwelling on high. I looked at them both sitting side by side and saw what I had not seen before. Then I knew at once the meaning of Wardé's story and understood the secret of her protest against a society that persecutes the rebel against its edicts before knowing the cause of his rebellion. I saw before me a single divine spirit in the two human bodies made beautiful by youth and clothed in unison. Between them stood the god of love, his wings spread to protect them from the anger and blame of people. I felt a complete and perfect understanding arising from the two transparent faces lighted by purity. For the first time in my life I saw the image of happiness standing between a man and a woman whom dogma had condemned and law rejected.

I rose after a while and bade them farewell, a silent witness to the moving of my spirit.

I went out from that humble dwelling which affection had made a sanctuary of love and harmony, and made my way among those houses and mansions whose secrets Wardé had laid bare to me. I thought on her words and their underlying truth, but I had hardly reached the outskirts of the quarter when I remembered Rashid bey Nu'man. I saw again his misery and anguish and I said to myself: "He is unhappy and oppressed, yet would Heaven hearken to him if he stood before it grieving and blaming Wardé Al-Hani? Did that woman wrong him when she left him to follow her free spirit, or was it he that wronged her when he forced her body to yield to marriage ere her spirit was inclined toward love? Which of them is the oppressor and which the oppressed? Indeed, who is the guilty and who the innocent?"

I continued to soliloquize, probing into the strange events of the times, and again said to myself: "Ofttimes has vanity led women to abandon their husbands who are poor to follow rich men, for a woman's passion for fine clothes and a life of ease blinds her and leads her into shame and downfall. Was Wardé Al-Hani ignorant and lusting after the body when she proclaimed her independence over the heads of people and embraced a young man spiritually inclined? Whilst yet she was in her husband's house it was within her power to satisfy her senses in secret with the passions of young men who would have died to become slaves of her beauty and martyrs for love of her. Wardé Al-Hani was an unhappy woman; she sought happiness and found it and embraced it. And so this is a truth that human society despises and that the law exiles."

I murmured these words into the air and then said, whilst I groped for understanding: "But is a woman permitted to purchase her happiness with her man's misery?" And my innermost self answered: "Is then a husband free to make a slave of his wife's affections so that he may remain happy?"

I continued on my way, the while Wardé's voice filled my ears, until I reached the outskirts of the town. The sun was inclining toward the west, and the fields and gardens were putting on their veils of stillness and quiet and the birds were intoning the evening prayer. I stood in contemplation and, sighing, said:

"Before the throne of freedom do these trees rejoice in the breeze's caress and before its majesty do they glory in the rays of the sun and the moon. Into the ears of freedom do the birds speak and about her skirts flutter by the streams. Into the air of freedom do these flowers spill the fragance of their breath and before her eyes smile at the coming of morning. All that is on earth lives by the law of its nature, and by the nature of its law are spread the glories and joys of liberty. But man alone is forbidden this bliss, for he makes earthly laws binding to his mortal spirit, and on his body and soul passes harsh judgment, and raises up about his love and yearning dark prison walls, and for his heart and mind digs a deep grave. If one of his fellows rises and cuts himself off from society and law, the people say that such and such a one is a rebel and an evil one deserving of expulsion from their midst; one fallen and unclean and fit only for death. . . . Must man remain eternally a slave of his own corrupt laws or shall the days free him to live in the Spirit for the Spirit? Must he remain looking ever on the ground or shall he lift his eyes to the sun lest he see the shadow of his body among thorns and skulls?"

THE CRY OF THE GRAVES

I

THE AMEER SAT cross-legged upon the judgment seat, and on each side of him sat the wise ones of the country, in whose wrinkled faces were reflected the pages of tomes and books. About the Ameer stood soldiers grasping swords and holding aloft lances. The people stood before him. Some, sightseers come out of love of a spectacle; others, anxious watchers awaiting the passing of judgment on a kinsman. But they all stood with bowed heads and bated breath and humble eyes as though a glance from the Ameer were a force instilling fear and terror in their hearts and souls.

After the assembly had seated itself and judgment time was at hand the Ameer raised his hand and shouted: "Bring forth the criminals one by one and acquaint me with their misdeeds and crimes." So the prison door was opened and its dark walls were revealed like the throat of a wild beast when he opens his jaws to yawn. From all corners arose the sound of rattling chains and shackles to the accompaniment of the sighing and moaning of the imprisoned. The crowd shifted its gaze and craned its neck as though it would gain over the law in the spectacle of death's prey rising from out of the depths of the tomb.

After a few moments two soldiers came out of the prison leading a young man whose arms were pinioned. His grim face and taut features told of a strong spirit and a stout heart. They stood him before the court, then withdrew to the rear. The Ameer looked at him for a minute and said: "What is the crime of this man who stands before us with raised head like one in a place of honour rather than one in the grip of justice?" A member of the court answered: "He is a murderer who yesterday attacked one of the Ameer's officers and struck him to the ground as he was passing through the villages on his lawful occasions. When this man was seized, the bloodstained sword was yet in his hand."

The Ameer moved angrily on his high seat, and from his eyes darted glances of rage. In a loud voice he cried: "Take him back to the darkness and weight his body with chains. When dawn comes on the morrow strike off his head with the edge of his own sword and cast his body to the wilderness so that the vultures and prowling beasts may pick it clean and the winds carry the stench of its rottenness to the nostrils of his kith and kin."

They thereupon led the youth back to the prison house, and the multitude followed him with their pitying glances and deep sighs, for he was a young man in the spring of his life, handsome and strong of build.

The soldiers appeared a second time, leading from the dungeon a frail-looking girl of great beauty. The pallor of sorrow and misery was upon her face; tears filled her eyes, and her head was bowed in repentance and regret. The Ameer looked at her and said: "And what has she done, this sickly woman who stands before us like the shadow by the side of truth?" One of the soldiers answered him and said: "She is an adulteress. Her lord came upon her one night and found her in her lover's embrace, so he delivered her up to the police after her companion had fled."

The Ameer looked at her closely, the while she looked on the ground in her shame. Then he said harshly: "Return her to the darkness and stretch her out upon a bed of thorns; mayhap she will remember the bed she has fouled with her shame. Give her to drink vinegar with calocynth that she may taste again of the forbidden kiss. And when the dawn comes, drag her out in her nakedness and take her outside the city and stone her with stones. Leave there her body so that the wolves may enjoy her flesh and worms and insects gnaw at her bones." The girl was returned to the blackness of her prison and the crowd stared at her with wonder at the Ameer's justice and with sorrow at her sad beauty and wistful glances.

A third time the soldiers appeared, leading a feeble man of middle age who dragged along his trembling legs as if they were but tatters hanging from his ragged garments. He looked this way and that in his fright, and from his agonized glances leaped spectres of poverty and despair and wretchedness. The Ameer turned toward him and said in a scornful voice: "What is the crime of this foul creature who stands like the dead among the living?" One of his soldiers answered: "He is a thief, a robber, who entered the monastery one night. He was seized by the pious monks and they found in the folds of his garments a sacred vessel of the sanctuary."

The Ameer looked at him with the look of a hungry vulture about to seize a wounded sparrow and shouted: "Throw him into the dark depths and fetter him with iron. At the break of dawn take him out and hang him from a high tree with a rope of flax and leave his corpse suspended to swing between heaven and earth. Let the elements make his thieving fingers drop off like leaves from a tree and the winds scatter as dust his members."

And so they took the thief back to his cell while the people murmured one to another: "How does this weakling heathen dare to rob the monastery of its sacred vessels?"

The Ameer got down from the judgment seat, and the wise men and the lawmakers followed after him. Before and behind him went the soldiers, and the watching people dispersed. Soon the place was empty of all save the mournful cries of the imprisoned and the sobbing and sighing of these miserable wretches flitting like shadows across the walls.

I was there during all that took place. I stood there like a mirror in front of moving forms, thinking on the laws that men make for their fellows; pondering on what passes for justice with the people; probing into life's secrets and the meaning of existence. So I did till my thoughts grew vague and faint like the light in the evening sky behind a mist. As I went out from that place I said to myself: "Plants suck up the elements of the soil; sheep feed off the plants, and the wolf preys upon the sheep. The unicorn slays the wolf, the lion hunts the unicorn, and death in its turn destroys the lion. Is there a force mightier than death to forge this chain of cruelties with an enduring justice? Is there a power that will turn these hateful things to good ends? Is there a power that will gather up all life's elements in its hand and merge them smiling in itself as the ocean gathers back to its depths all the streams in song? Is there a power to make stand the slayer and the slain, the adulteress and her lover, the robber and the robbed, before a court higher than the court of the Anew?''

II

And on the second day I went outside the city and walked in the fields, wherein quietude showed to the spirit what the spirit had concealed, and the air in its purity killed the seeds of misery and despair born of narrow streets and dark dwellings.

When I reached the edge of the valley, I beheld there bands of eagles and vultures and crows soaring upwards into space and descending low to earth. The air was filled with their shrieking and croaking and the fluttering of their wings. I went forward to discover the cause of all this. Before me I saw the corpse of a man hanging from a high tree. Then I beheld the naked body of a woman lying on the ground amidst the stones that had stoned her. And the body of a youth caked with blood-soaked earth, his head severed from his body.

There I stood overpowered by the horror of the scene, blinded by a thick veil of blackness. I looked but saw naught save the terrifying spectre of death standing above the bloody corpses. I listened but I heard naught except the wail of annihilation merging into the "caw-caw" of the crows hovering and wheeling about these victims of man's laws.

Three human creatures. Yesterday they were in Life's embrace; today they are in Death's grasp. Three creatures did wrong according to the customs of men. And the Law in its blindness stretched forth a hand and crushed them. Three creatures whom ignorance made wrongdoers because they were weak; whom Law destroyed beause it was strong.

When a man destroys his fellow, people say that such a one is a murderer. When one set in authority destroys, it is said that this one is a faithful judge. And when a man would rob the monastery they call him a thief; but when the Ameer would rob him of his life, then they say that the Ameer is a virtuous prince.

A woman is unfaithful to her lord and master, so the people say that she is an adulteress and whore. But when the Ameer drives her out in her nakedness and has her stoned by the multitude, they say that this is a noble Ameer.

The shedding of blood is forbidden. Who, then, has sanctioned it to the ruler? To steal property is a crime. But who has made a virtue of the stealing of souls? The faithlessness of women is an abomination. But who has made the stoning of bodies a pleasantness?

Shall we meet evil with greater evil and say: this is the law; and fight corruption with more corruption and proclaim it moral? Shall we overcome a crime with one greater and call it justice?

Has the Ameer never struck down a foe in his life or robbed the weaker among his followers of lands and goods? Has he never beguiled a beautiful woman? Is he innocent of all wrongdoing that it is allowed him to condemn to death the murderer and hang the thief and stone the harlot?

Who are they that raised this thief upon a tree? Are they angels come down from heaven or men who violate and rape all that comes to their hand? Who cut off this man's head? Were they prophets descended from above or soldiers who kill and spill blood wherever they be? Who were those that stoned the harlot? The pious and the godly come from their cells or men who commit crime and do all manner of evil things in the blackness of the night? And the law – what is law? Who has seen it descend with the sunlight from the heavens? What human being has seen the heart of God and known His will in mankind? In what age have angels walked among men, saying: "Deny to the weak the light of existence and destroy the fallen with the edge of the sword and trample upon the sinner with feet of iron"?

These thoughts were still troubling my mind and heart when I heard footfalls nearby. I looked around and beheld a girl, who had appeared from among the trees, approaching the three corpses. As she walked she was looking furtively in all directions as though afraid. As soon as her eyes fell upon the beheaded youth she gave a shriek of terror and fell on her knees by his side, embracing him with trembling arms. Tears filled her eyes; with her fingers she stroked his curling hair, moaning the while in a low deep voice that seemed to rise up from her depths.

Then she set to work quickly, digging into the soil with her hands until she had made a wide grave. She dragged the murdered youth to it and laid him out slowly, placing the blood-matted head between the shoulders. After covering him with earth she planted the sword that had beheaded him on his grave. As she made to go I approached her. She took fright and began to tremble in her fear; she looked on the ground, while the hot tears fell from her eyes like rain. Then sighing, she said: "Go then, if you wish, and tell the Ameer, for it were better that I die and follow him that delivered me from shame than that I abandon his body as food for the vultures and beasts of prey."

"Do not fear me," I answered, "for I mourned the fate of this young man before you. Tell me how he saved you from shame."

"An officer of the Ameer came to our field to assess the tax and collect the tribute. When he saw me he looked at me with favour and I was afraid, and he levied an extortionate tax on my father's field – a tax so great as to be beyond even a rich man's purse. Then he seized me and carried me off by force to the palace of the Ameer in place of gold. I begged him with weeping to have pity on me, but he heeded not. I adjured him by my father's years, but he showed no mercy. I cried out for help to the men of the village, and this youth, my betrothed, came to my aid and saved me. The officer in his anger was about to strike him down, but the youth forestalled him and, seizing an old sword that hung from the wall of his house, slew the officer. This he did in defence of his own life and my honour. And because of his greatness of spirit he forbore to flee like a murderer but remined standing by the dead body until soldiers came and drove him in fetters to the prison house."

Having spoken, she looked up at me with a look that melted my heart and stirred me to grief. Then, suddenly, she turned and ran from me. The sad cadences of her voice still rippled and disturbed the surface of the air.

After a while I looked up and saw a young man approaching, his face partly concealed by his cloak. He went up to the corpse of the harlot and, standing there, took off his cloak and covered with it the woman's nakedness. Then he fell to digging the soil with a dagger, after which he moved the body gently and covered it with earth and with each clod was a tear. His task completed, he gathered up some flowers which grew in that place and put them on the grave. As he was about to go I stopped him and said: "What is this fallen woman to you that you would dare oppose the Ameer's will and put in danger your life to protect her broken body against the birds of the air?" He looked at me through eyes red with weeping and sleeplessness, eyes that spoke deep grief and sorrow. In a voice broken by sobs he said:

"I am that wretched man for whom this woman was stoned. We had loved each other from the days of our childhood, when we played together among the houses. We grew and with us love grew and developed until it became a mighty master whom we served with our hearts. Our secret souls stood in awe before this love and it took us in its embrace. One day when I was far from the town the father of the girl joined her by force to a man she hated. I returned, and when I heard of this my day became a night without end and my life a long and bitter death. I wrestled with my love and fought my heart's desire until they, in the end, overcame me and led me as the seeing the sightless. One day I went in secret to my beloved. My greatest desire was not more than to behold the light of her eyes and hear the music of her voice. I found her alone, bewailing her lot and mourning her days. We sat together and our speech was silence and our companion chasteness. An hour had not passed when her husband entered. When he saw me his baseness got the better of him and he gripped her slender neck in his rough hands and cried in a loud voice: 'Come you all and see the harlot with her lover!' The neighbours came running, and then soldiers, inquiring of the matter. The man gave her into their hands and they led her away with her hair loose and her clothes torn. As for me, nobody did me harm or hurt, for blind law and corrupt tradition punish the fallen woman but look tolerantly upon the man."

Having thus spoken, the youth walked back toward the town, his features once more concealed in his cloak.

I remained behind in reflection and thought, sorrowing. The hanging corpse of the thief swung a little when the wind blew through the branches of the tree as though, by its movement, to entreat the spirits of the air to cut it down and lay it out upon the earth with the martyr to courage and the sacrifice to love.

An hour passed and then there came a sickly-looking woman clothed in rags. She stood by the swinging corpse beating her breast and weeping. She climbed the tree and gnawed at the rope with her teeth until the body fell, striking the ground like a bundle of wet clothes. She thereupon descended and, digging a grave by the side of the other two, buried in it the body. After covering it with earth, she took two pieces of wood and fashioned a cross out of them and planted it over the grave. As she was about to return whence she had come I stopped her and said: "How come you to bury a thief?"

She looked at me through eyes made dark with the shadows of sorrow and misery and said: "He is my faithful husband and kindly companion and father of my children. I have five children crying out in their hunger. The eldest of them is eight years and the youngest is yet suckling. My man was not a thief; he was a peasant who farmed the monastery's land. But he received naught from the monks save a loaf of bread, which we divided up when evening came, leaving nothing for the morning. Since the days of his youth has he watered the fields of the monastery with the sweat of his brow, and with the strength of his arms made its gardens grow. When he grew feeble and his strength diminished through years of toil, he fell sick and the monks sent him away, saying that the monastery had no longer need of him. They told him to go and send his children to take his place in the fields as soon as they were of age. He wept and I wept and he implored them to have pity on him for Jesus' sake and entreated them by the angels and saints. But they had neither compassion nor pity for him or for our children, naked and hungry. So he went to the city and sought work there, only to return empty-handed, for the dwellers in those mansions would not employ save strong young men. In the end he sat by the wayside and begged. But people would not give him alms; they said: 'Charity is not for those given to sloth and idleness,' and passed him by. One night need so possessed us that our children lay prostrate with hunger and the suckling sucked at my breasts and found there no milk. A change grew over my husband and he went out hidden by the darkness of the night and entered a vault of the monastery. There the monks stored the crops from the fields and the yield of the vineyards. As he was about to return to us carrying with him a basket of flour, the monks awoke from their sleep and seized hold of him ere he had taken a few steps. They struck at him and reviled him. When morning came they delivered him up to the soldiers, saying: 'Behold a thief come to plunder the monastery of its gold vessels.' Then they led him away to the prison and thence to the scaffold, to fill the bellies of the vultures because he had tried to fill the bellies of starving children with grain his own sweat had garnered when he served the monastery."

Having also spoken, the wretched woman went her way, and from out of her broken words shadowy forms of grief rose up and swirled about like columns of smoke in a wind.

I stood in the midst of the three graves like a mourner who is dazed and tongue-tied by grief, whose tears alone speak of his innermost feelings. I tried to think and reflect, but my spirit rebelled, for the spirit is a flower that folds its petals against darkness and gives not of its fragrance to the shades of night.

I stood, what time from each particle of earth covering the graves arose the cry of oppression like a mist rising from the emptiness of the valley, and it lapped like waves about my ears that it might inspire in me words.

I stood there silent. Did people understand the language of silence, then they were nearer to the gods than to wild beasts of the forest.

I stood there and sighed. And could the fires of my sighing touch the trees of that field, they would bestir themselves and leave their places and march in their battalions to wage war with their branches against the Ameer and his soldiers and bring down with their trunks the walls of the monastery upon the heads of those within it.

I stood and looked, and out of my looking flowed pity's sweetness and sorrow's bitterness over those fresh graves. The grave of a youth who defended a girl's innocence with his life and saved her from the grasp of a wolf; him they beheaded in reward for his courage. And the girl came and sheathed his sword in the earth as a sign and symbol before the sun of the way of men in the kingdom of shame and ignorance. And there another grave. The grave of a girl whose being love had touched ere lust ravished her body. They stoned her because her heart was faithful even unto death. Her lover placed over her still body a garland of flowers of the field, which told, as they withered and decayed, of the lot of those souls whom love sanctified among a people rendered blind by dross and muted by ignorance. Yonder the grave of a poor wretch whose arms were broken by the fields of the monastery. Him the monks cast out and put others in his stead. He sought bread for his young through labour but found not; he asked for it as alms but no person gave him. When despair drove him to seek a return for his sweat and toil, they seized him and destroyed him. His widow came and set over him a cross to call in the stillness of night on the stars of heaven to bear witness to the tyranny of the monks who turn the teachings of the Nazarene into swords that behead and cut with sharp edges the bodies of the weak and lowly.

Soon the sun sank low and disappeared beyond the twilight as though weary of men's strivings and hating their tyranny. The evening came on, weaving from the threads of darkness and stillness a fine veil to draw across the body of nature.

I lifted up my eyes to the heights and spread out my hands toward the graves with their signs and symbols and cried out: "This, then, is thy sword, O Courage, and it is sheathed in the earth. And those are thy flowers, O Love, they are scorched by fires. That is Thy cross, Jesus of Nazareth, and the blackness of night submerges it."

THE BRIDAL COUCH[1]

THE BRIDE AND the bridegroom came out of the church preceded by lamps and torches and followed by rejoicing guests. Around them and about them moved the young men and maidens, trilling and singing songs of joy.

The procession reached the house of the bridegroom, which was adorned with costly carpets and gleaming vessels and sweet-smelling myrtle plants. The groom and his bride mounted a dais and the guests seated themselves on silken rugs and velvet-covered chairs. Soon the spacious room overflowed with the bodies of men and women. The servants moved hither and thither, serving out wine, and the tinkle of glass against glass rose up and became one with the sound of general rejoicing and merrymaking. Then the musicians came and took their places. They played airs that rendered drunk the listeners with their haunting refrains and filled their breasts with melodies woven with the whisper of a lute string and the sighing of men and the throbbing of drums.

Then the maidens rose to their feet and danced. They swayed gently back and forth to each rhythmic beat of the music as slender boughs sway to the movement of the gentle breeze. The folds of their soft garments rippled and shimmered like white clouds when the moonlight plays on them. All eyes were turned as one toward them and heads were bowed, and the spirits of the young men embraced them and those of the old wavered before their beauty. All gave themselves up to drinking and drowned their desires in wine. Movement grew lively and voices shouted and freedom reigned supreme. Sobriety took flight and

---

1 This happening took place in North Lebanon in the later half of the nineteenth century. It was related to the author by a woman from those parts who was a kinswoman of one of the people in this story.

minds became confused; spirits grew inflamed and hearts excited until that house and all in it became as a harp with broken strings in the hands of a daughter of the jinn, who plucked at it roughly, drawing from it sounds in which were both discord and harmony.

Here was a youth revealing his hidden love for a girl whom beauty had made to fascinate and excite. There a young man made to speak to a beautiful woman, hunting his memory for sweet words and subtle phrases. Yonder was a man in middle age drinking cup after cup, demanding with insistence that the musicians play old tunes to bring back to him his youth. In a corner a woman sat making eyes at a man who looked with love upon another. In that corner sat a woman white with age, looking and smiling at the maidens, picking out from among them a bride for her only son. By a window sat a wife who made her husband's drunkenness the opportunity to draw near to her lover. And so all submerged themselves in a sea of wine and dalliance, surrendering to the swift current of joy and gladness, forgetful of yesterday and fleeing from the morrow, intent only on the harvesting of the minutes of the present.

Through all these happenings the comely bride gazed upon the scene with sad eyes in the manner of a hopeless prisoner gazing on the sombre walls of his cell. Now and then she looked toward a corner of the room where a boy of twenty years sat alone, apart from the merrymakers, like an injured bird separated from his fellows. His arms were locked upon his breast as though standing between his heart and its flight, and his eyes were fixed upon some invisible thing in that room. It was as though his spiritual self had separated from his earthly being to cleave the air in pursuit of phantoms of the darkness.

Midnight struck and the merriment of the wedding guests grew apace until it became a rioting. Then senses grew hazy with wine fumes and they stammered and stuttered in speech. Soon the bridegroom rose from his place. He was a man in middle age and coarse in appearance. Drunkenness had taken possession of his senses and he moved among his guests dispensing good humour and kindly feeling.

At that very moment the bride made a sign to a girl among

the crowd to come up to her. The girl came and sat beside her. The bride, after glancing about like one anxious and impatient to divulge a fearful secret, leaned toward the girl and in a tremulous voice whispered into her ear these words:

"I entreat you, my dearest friend, by the affection that has bound us together since our childhood, by all that is dear to you in life, and by all that lies hidden in your heart. I entreat you by the love that caresses our spirits and illumines them, by the gladness in your heart and the agony in mine. I entreat you to go now to Selim and ask him to go down into the garden in secret and there await me beneath the willow trees. Plead for me, plead for me, Susan, until he does so. Call to his memory days gone by; implore him in love's name; say to him that his beloved is a foolish and unhappy woman, tell him that she is near to dying and would open to him her heart ere darkness comes; that she is already lost and despairing and would see the light of his eyes before the fires of hell consume her. Tell him that she has sinned and would confess her guilt and implore his forgiveness. Hurry now to him. Speak for me before him and heed not the glances of these swine, for the wine has stopped their ears and blinded their eyes."

Susan rose from her place by the bride and sat beside Selim, sad in his aloneness. She whispered in his ears the words of her companion, seeking his pity. Love and sincerity lighted up her features. He inclined his head, listening, but answered no word. When she had ceased from talking, he looked at her like a thirsty man seeing a cup high up in the sky. Then, in a voice so low that it might have risen from the bowels of the earth, he said: "I will await her in the garden among the willow trees." So saying, he rose from his seat and went out into the garden.

After the passing of a few minutes the bride likewise rose and followed him. She picked her way among men long ago seduced by the daughter of the vine and women whose hearts were given to lovemaking with the young men there. On gaining the garden, now cloaked by night, she quickened her pace. She ran like a frightened gazelle fleeing for cover from prowling wolves until she reached the willow trees where the youth awaited her. She threw herself upon him and encircled his neck with her arms. She looked into his eyes and spoke, the words pouring out from her lips with the falling of tears from her eyes, and said:

"Listen to me, my beloved; listen to me. I have repented of my folly and haste. I have repented, Selim, until repentance has crushed my very heart. I love you as I love no other and I shall love you to the end of my days. They told me that you had forgotten me and abandoned me out of love for another. They poisoned my heart with their tongues and rent my breast with their claws and filled my soul with their lying. Najibé said that you had forgotten me, that you hated me and were enslaved by her passion. She persecuted me, that evil woman, and played upon my feelings so that I might be satisfied with her kinsman as a husband; and it was so. But for me there is no bridegroom save you, Selim. And now, now the scales have fallen from my eyes and I have come to you. I have gone out from that house and I shall not return to it. I have come to take you in my arms, for there is no power in this world that can send me back to the embrace of a man whom I wedded in despair. I have left the bridegroom whom lies and deceit chose for me as a husband and the father whom fate made a guardian. I have left behind me the flowers that the priest plaited into a crown for the bride and the laws that tradition made as fetters. I have left all in a house full with drunkenness and vice and am come to follow you to a far-off land; to the very ends of the earth; to the hiding-places of the jinn – yea, into the clutches of Death itself. Come you, Selim, let us hasten from this place under cover of the night. Let us go down to the shore and take a ship that will bear us to a distant and unknown land. Come, let us go; let not the dawn come except we be in safety from the hands of the foe. Look, do you see these gold adornments and these precious rings and necklaces and jewels? They will be a security for us against the future and we will live by them like princes. . . . Why do you speak not, Selim? Why do you not look on me? Why do you not kiss me? Do you not hear my heart's cry and my spirit's travail? Do you no more believe that I have abandoned my husband and father and mother and come in my bridal gown to flee with you? Speak you, Selim, or let us hasten now, for these minutes are more precious than diamonds and their value is above the crowns of kings."

So spoke the bride, and in her voice was a music sweeter than the murmur of life and bitterer than the howl of death; lighter than the flutter of wings and deeper than the sigh of the waves. A melody whose beats hovered between hope and despair, and pleasure and pain, and joy and sorrow. In it were all the desires and longings in a woman's breast.

The youth stood and listened, the while love and honour struggled for mastery within him. The love that makes the jungle a plain and darkness light. The honour that stands before the spirit, turning it from its longing and desire. The love that God reveals to the heart and the honour with which the traditions of man flood the mind.

After an age silent and terrifying like the ages of obscurity and darkness in which nations totter between birth and decay, the youth raised his head. Honour had put his spirit victor over its desires. He turned his eyes from the frightened watching girl and said in a quiet voice: "Return, woman, to your husband, for all is over and awakening has erased that which dreams imagined. Go, go quickly back to the merrymaking lest prying eyes see you and people say that she has betrayed her husband on her wedding night as she betrayed her lover in days gone by."

The bride trembled at these words and shook like a withered flower in the path of the wind. In agony she cried: "I shall not return to this house even though I be at my last breath of life. I have left it forever; I have left it and all in it as a captive leaves the land of his exile. You shall not cast me from you, neither shall you say that I am faithless, for the hand of love that has made one our souls is more powerful than the hand of the priest that has delivered my body to the bridegroom's will. Behold my arms around your neck: no force shall lift them. My spirit has drawn near to your spirit, and death shall not them part."

The youth tried to set himself free of her arms. Aversion and abhorrence showed on his face, and he said: "Go from me, woman, for I have already forgotten you, for I love another. People have spoken naught but the truth. Do you hear what I say? I have banished you from my mind and existence. My hatred of you turns you from my very sight. Go then and leave me to tread my path. Return now to your husband and to him be faithful."

Overcome with grief, she said: "No, no; I do not believe that, for you love me. I have read the meaning of love in your eyes and felt its touch as I caressed your body. You love me, yea, even as I love you. Never will I leave this place except you be with me; neither will I enter this house while there is yet strength within me. Whither you go I will go; I shall follow you to the very end of the earth. Go you then before me, lift then your hand to spill my blood."

The youth raised his voice again and said: "Leave me, woman, lest I call out at the top of my voice and cause the guests at this feast to gather around us in the garden. Leave me, lest I show them your shame and make you a bitter taste in their mouths and a loathing on their tongues; lest I bring Najibé, my beloved, before you to scoff at you, rejoicing in her victory and mocking at your defeat."

As he spoke thus, he seized her arms to thrust her from him. Her expression changed and a light came into her eyes, and her bearing turned from that of pleading and pain to that of anger and harshness. She became like a lioness bereaved of her cubs, like a sea, its depths disturbed and angered by the storm. She cried out: "Who shall delight in your love after me? What heart will drink of the kisses of your life except my heart?"

Having uttered these words, she drew from out of her clothes a dagger and buried it in his heart with the speed of lightning. He stumbled, then fell to the earth like a branch cut down by the tempest. She dropped to her knees and leaned over him while the knife in her hand yet dripped blood. He opened his eyes, over which death was drawing a shadow; his lips trembled and with his failing breath came forth these words: "Draw near to me, my beloved, draw near to me, O Laila, and do not leave me. Death is stronger than life, but love is stronger than death. Hearken, hearken to the laughing and the merrymaking of the guests at your marriage feast. Hearken, my love, to the sound of cup against cup. You have delivered me, Laila, from the harshness of that discord and the bitterness of those cups. Let me kiss the hand that has broken my bonds. Kiss my lips; the lips that did take upon them lies and conceal the secrets of my heart. Close these withering eyelids with your fingers, on which is my blood. After my spirit has taken flight into space, put the knife in my right hand and say to them that he killed himself out of envy and despair. I have loved you, Laila, above all others, but I saw in the sacrifice of my heart and my happiness and life a thing worthier than my fleeing with you on your wedding night. Kiss me, beloved of my spirit, ere people look on my dead body. Kiss me, O Laila." And the stricken youth placed his hand over his pierced heart, his head fell to one side, and his spirit departed.

The bride raised her head and looked toward the house, crying in a terrible voice: "Come nigh, O people, and behold here the wedding and the bridegroom. Come that we may show to you the nuptial couch. Awaken, all you sleeping; arise, all you drunken, and hasten, for we shall reveal to you the secrets of love and death and life."

The cry of the bride found every corner of that house and carried its words to the ears of the rejoicing guests and filled their souls with trembling. They remained listening for a few second as though clarity had penetrated their intoxicated state. Then they ran hurrying out from the house and stumbled on, looking to the right and left of them until they came upon the dead body and the bride kneeling beside it. They drew back in terror, and no one of them dared to investigate the matter, for it was as though the sight of the blood flowing from the slain man's breast and the flash of the blade in the bride's hand had locked their tongues and frozen the life in their bodies.

The bride turned and looked up at them, her face sad and awe-inspiring. She cried out to them:

"Draw near, all you cowardly ones. Fear not the spectre of death, for death is a great thing and has naught of your littleness. Draw near and tremble not because of this knife, for it is a sacred instrument that will not touch your unclean bodies and your black hearts. Gaze awhile on this comely youth adorned with the adornments of marriage. He is my beloved and I have slain him because he is my beloved. He is my groom and I am his bride. We sought a couch fitting to our embrace, but found it not in this world which you have made straitened with your traditions and dark with your ignorance and corrupt with your lusting. It were better that we go to another land beyond the clouds. Come near, you who are afraid, and look; perchance you see God's face reflected in our faces and hear His sweet voice rising up from our hearts.... Where is that evil and envious woman who slandered me to my beloved and said that he was enamoured of her and had abandoned me and clove to her love that he might forget me? When the priest raised his hand above my head and the head of her kinsman, that wicked one bethought herself victor. Where is Najibé the traitress, that viper from hell? Call her, let her now come near and see how she has gathered you together to rejoice in the marriage of my loved one and not that of the man whom she chose for me. You understand naught of my words, for the depths are not able to hear the song of the stars, but you shall tell to your children of the woman who slew her lover on her wedding night. You shall remember me and curse me with foul lips. But your children's children will bless me, for truth and the spirit will abide with the morrow. And you, O foolish man, who used wiles and riches and treachery to make of me a wife, you are a symbol of a despairing people seeking light in darkness and awaiting the coming of water from out of a rock and looking for the rose from out of stony ground. You are a symbol of this land which is delivered up to its own folly like a blind man in the hands of a blind leader. You are a symbol of the false manhood that would sever a wrist and a neck to reach their adornments. I forgive you in your smallness, for the spirit rejoicing in its departure from the world pardons the sins of the world."

In that instant the bride lifted up the dagger heavenward, and with the look of one athirst lifting the cup to his lips she plunged the knife into her breast and fell by the side of her lover like a lily whose head is severed by the scythe. The women cried out in fear and pain and fainted and fell one upon another. The shouts and confusion of the men rose from all sides as they gathered about the two victims in fear and awe.

The departing bride looked up at them, the while the blood

flowed freely from her breast, and said: "You shall not come near us, reproachful ones, neither shall you separate us lest the spirit hovering above your heads seize you by the throat and put an end to you. Let this hungry earth consume our bodies in one mouthful. Let it conceal and protect us within its heart even as seeds are protected from winter snows against the coming of spring."

The bride pressed herself against her lover and touched his cold lips with her lips, and with her last breath came forth these broken words:

"Look, my beloved – look, bridegroom of my soul, see in what manner the envious stand about our bed. See their eyes upon us and hearken to the grinding of their teeth and the crunching of their bones. You have waited for me long, Selim. Behold me here. I have broken the bonds and loosed the chains. Let us not tarry, but hasten toward the sun, for our sojourn in the shadows has been long. All things have become blotted out and concealed and never again will I look upon anything save you, my beloved. Behold my lips, my last breath approaches. Come, Selim, let us go, for Love has lifted his wings and soars before us to the circle of light."

The bride then fell upon her lover's breast and her blood mingled with his and she laid her head upon his neck the while her eyes remained looking into his eyes.

The people stood silent awhile. Their faces were pale and their knees weak as though the majesty of death had robbed them of strength and movement.

At that moment there came forward the priest, the same who had joined the two in marriage. He waved his right hand toward the slain couple and, looking at the frightened people, spoke to them harshly, saying:

"Accursed the hands that stretch out to those two bodies defiled by the blood of shame and guilt. Accursed the eyes that would shed tears of grief over two damned ones whose souls are borne to hell by the Devil. Let the bodies of this son of Sodom and that daughter of Gomorrah remain abandoned on this soil polluted by their blood until the dogs have divided among themselves their flesh and the winds scattered their bones. Return now to your dwellings and flee from the stench of hearts created out of sin and destroyed by corruption. Go your ways, all you who stand by these two stinking corpses. Make haste ere the tongues of hell-fire begin to lick you. He that remains here shall be rejected and cast out and shall not enter into the church wherein the faithful kneel, neither shall he have part in the prayers and offerings of Christians."

Susan then came forward, the girl whom the bride had sent as emissary to her lover. She stood before the priest and looked at him with tear-filled eyes and spoke with courage and said:

"I will remain here, blind heathen, and watch over them till the coming of dawn and dig for them a grave under these hanging boughs. If you deny me that, I will tear the earth apart with my fingers. If you bind my hands I will dig with my teeth. Get you away from this place which is filled with the smoke of frankincense, for swine turn away from the fragrance of fine perfumes, and thieves fear the master of the house and are afraid at the coming of morning. Make haste to your beds of darkness, for the heavenly melodies that float in the air above the martyrs of love cannot enter ears closed with earth."

And the people dispersed and went away from the frowning face of the priest. But the girl remained by the still bodies like a mother watching over her children in the silence of the night. When the people had gone from that place, she gave herself to weeping and lament.

KHALIL THE HERETIC

I

AMONG THE DWELLERS of that village hidden away in the
northern Lebanon the Shaikh Abbas was as a prince among his
subjects. And his house, standing in the midst of their poor dwell-
ings, was like a giant standing among dwarfs. His way of life was
as far removed from theirs as is sufficiency from dearth, and his
habits differed from their habits as strength and weakness differ.

Did the Shaikh Abbas utter a word among those peasants,
they bowed their heads in affirmation as though a higher intelli-
gence had put him its agent and made him its spokesman. Was
he angry, then they trembled in terror and scattered before him
like autumn leaves before the winds. If he slapped one of them
on the cheek, that one became tongue-tied as though the blow
had descended from heaven. It was a sacrilege to dare raise the
eyes to see the one who had granted it. If he smiled at another,
the multitude declared him a fortunate fellow indeed to merit
thus the Shaikh's pleasure.

The submission of these unfortunates to the Shaikh Abbas
and their fear of his harshness did not come only from his
strength and their weakness, but it came from their poverty and
reliance upon him. The fields they tilled and the hovels in which
they dwelt belonged to him; they were a heritage from his father
and grandfather as the people's heritage from their forefathers
was poverty and wretchedness. They farmed the land and sowed
and reaped under his ever watchful eye, but their toil brought
no reward save a portion of the yield so small as would hardly
deliver them from the pangs of hunger. Most of them were in
need of bread before the long winter was out and so, one by
one, each would go to the Shaikh and stand before him and
entreat him with weeping for a loan of a dinar piece or a measure
of wheat. Shaikh Abbas answered their needs gladly, for he knew

that for each dinar he would receive in return two dinars and for each measure of wheat two measures when the days of the threshing came. And so lived those unfortunate people, burdened with debt to Shaikh Abbas and shackled by their reliance on him, fearing his anger and seeking his pleasure.

II

Winter came with its snows and storms, and the fields and valleys were empty save for the croaking ravens and the naked trees. The villagers took to their dwellings after they had filled the bins of the Shaikh Abbas with the yield and his vessels with produce of the vineyards. They were without work and passed their time by the hearth reciting tales of bygone ages and retailing to one another stories of the days and nights.

December drew to a close. The old year sighed and breathed its last minutes into the grey skies; then came night, wherein the new year was a child crowned by destiny and placed on the throne of existence.

The feeble light waned and darkness descended on the valleys and torrents. Snow began to fall heavily and the wind whistled and raced down from the mountain heights into the abyss, carrying with it the snow to store up in the valley. The trees trembled in terror and the earth shook before it. The wind gathered together the snowfall of that day and the snow that fell during the night until the fields and knolls and passes were like a white page on which death wrote obscure lines and then erased them. The mist separated the villages scattered over the edge of the valley, and the feeble lights that glimmered in the windows of the houses and poor huts were blotted out. Terror took hold of the peasants, the beasts crouched by their fodder, and the dogs hid themselves in corners. No thing remained save the wind, which spoke and shouted into the grottos and caves. Now its terrible voice rose from out of the depths of the valley; now it swooped down from the mountain heights. It was as though Nature waxed wrathful at the death of the old year and was avenging herself on the hidden life in those huts and fighting it with cold and bleakness.

On that terrible night beneath wild skies a youth of twenty and two years made his way along the road that rose gradually from the monastery of Kizhaya[1] to the village of the Shaikh Abbas. The cold had dried up his very bones, and hunger and fear had sucked away his strength. Snow covered his black cloak as though wishing to make for him a shroud ere killing him. He took a step forward, but the wind pushed him back as if it objected to seeing him in the houses of the living. The rugged path seized hold of his feet and he fell. He called out for help, then was silenced by the cold. He rose to his feet and stood still, silent and shivering. It was as though, standing amidst the battling elements, he was faint hope standing between violent despair and deep sorrow. Or like a bird with broken wings that falls into the river and is carried along with the current to the deep sea.

The youth resumed his way with death at his heels until in the end his strength and will failed him; the blood froze in his veins and he fell down in the snow. With the remnant of life in his body he cried out in a terrible voice – the voice of one afraid who sees the spectre of death face to face. The voice of one struggling and in despair whom the darkness is destroying, whom the tempest seizes that it may hurl him into the abyss. The voice of the love of life in the formless void.

III

To the north of that village was a small hut standing alone among the fields. In it lived a woman whose name was Rahel and her daughter Maryam, a girl of under eighteen years. This woman was the widow of Sam'an Al-Rami, who had been found murdered in the wilderness five years before. His murderer no one knew.

Rahel, like all poor widows of her kind, lived by her labour and toil, ever fearful of death and ruin. During the days of the

---

1 This is the richest and most famous of the monasteries in Lebanon. Its income from its produce is reckoned in thousands of dinars and it houses scores of monks well known in the two villages. – Author's note.

harvest she went out into the field and gleaned the ears of corn after the reapers. In the autumn she gathered rejected scraps of fruit in the orchards and in winter busied herself with the spinning of wool and the sewing of garments for a few coins or a measure of maize. She did all with care and patience and skill. Her daughter Maryam was a comely girl, quiet and placid, who shared with her mother the toil and housework.

On that wild night already described, Rahel and her daughter were sitting by a fire whose heat was lost in the cold and whose embers were grey. Above their heads hung a lamp, which sent forth its feeble yellow rays into the gloom like a prayer that sends forth consolation into the hearts of the bereaved.

Midnight came and the two women still sat listening to the howling of the wind without. From time to time the girl rose, opened the little window and gazed into the darkness, and then returned to her seat shaken and frightened by the fury of the elements.

At that moment the girl suddenly stirred as though awakened from a deep sleep. She looked at her mother in fear and said quickly: "Did you hear it, Mother? Did you hear a voice calling out?"

The mother lifted up her head and listened. "No," she replied, "I hear nothing but the howling of the wind."

"I heard something," the girl rejoined. "I heard a voice deeper than the noise of the wind and bitterer than the cry of the storm."

As she gave mouth to these words she stood up and opened the window. She listened for a minute and then said: "Mother, I heard the cry again."

Her mother hurried over to the window.

"I also heard something. Come, let us open the door and look. Close the window before the wind puts out the lamp."

While speaking, she wrapped a long cloak around her. She opened the door and went out with firm steps. Maryam stood by the door, the wind playing through her hair.

Rahel walked a few steps, digging up the snow with her feet as she went. She stopped and called out: "Who is there? Who cries out for help?" But no voice answered her. She repeated her cry two and three times. Hearing nothing but the shrieking of the storm, she went forward with courage, peering in every direction and covering her face against the gusts of harsh wind. She had not gone an arrow's distance before she saw footprints in the snow, now nearly obliterated by the wind. She followed them quickly, watching and fearful, until she beheld before her a body prostrate on the ground like a black patch on a fleecy white garment. She knelt down, brushed the snow from it, and cradled the head in her lap. She placed her hand on the youth's breast, and as she felt the feeble beatings of his heart she cried out in the direction of the hut: "Come you, Maryam, and help me, for I have found him."

Maryam came out of the hut. She followed her mother's footprints, trembling and shivering with fear and cold. When she reached that spot and saw the youth laid out on the snow and without movement, she moaned and cried out in pain at what she beheld. The mother put her hands beneath his armpits and said to the daughter: "Have no fear, for he lives. Take hold of the ends of his garments and let us carry him to the house."

The two women bore him away while the wind in its violence pushed and buffeted them and the thick snow on the ground caught at their feet. When they reached the hut, they laid him down by the fire. The mother began to rub his frozen limbs and the daughter to dry his wet hair and cold hands with her skirt. Many minutes had not passed before life returned to him. He stirred a little, his eyelids quivered, and he drew a deep sigh, which planted hope in the breasts of the two compassionate women. Said Maryam as she loosed the thongs of his broken shoes and stripped him of his wet cloak: "Look, Mother, look at his clothes; they look like a monk's habit." Rahel, who had made up the fire with dried twigs, looked at her and said in wonderment: "The monks do not leave the monastery on a night such as this night. What, then, has made this poor youth place his life in hazard?"

"But he is beardless, Mother, and monks grow thick beards," remarked the girl wonderingly. Her mother looked down at him and in her eyes was a mother's compassion. She sighed and said: "Dry his feet well, daughter, monk or criminal be he."

Then Rahel opened a wooden chest and drew from it a small wine jar and poured a quantity of the liquid into a vessel.

"Lift up his head, Maryam, and let him swallow the wine so that it may refresh him and bring back warmth to his body."

Rahel put the edge of the cup to the boy's lips and let him swallow a drop of the wine. He opened his big eyes and looked on his deliverers for the first time, a soft sad look, a look that sprang forth with tears of gratitude; the look of one who feels the caress of life after the grasp of death. The look of hope after despair. Then he turned his head and from between trembling lips came the words: "May God bless you both."

Rahel put her hand on his shoulder and said: "Do not burden yourself with speech, my brother; rather remain in silence until strength returns to you." And Maryam said: "Recline on this cushion and draw near the fire."

The youth leaned against the cushion with a sigh and Rahel filled the cup with wine a second time and to her daughter said: "Put his cloak by the fire to dry." Maryam did as she was bade and then sat back and looked at him with tenderness and compassion as if she would by her very look instil warmth and strength into his wasted body.

Rahel set before him two loaves of bread and a bowl of honey with a platter of dried fruit. She sat down by him and fed him out of her hand morsel by morsel, as a mother feeds her child, until he was satisfied. He felt stronger, so he sat up on the rug, and the ruddy glow from the fire lighted up his pale drawn features and gave to his sad eyes a brilliance. Then he shook his head gently and said: "Mercy and cruelty forever wage war in the hearts of men like the battle of the elements in this black night. But mercy shall vanquish cruelty, for mercy is a divine thing, while the terror of this night will pass with the coming of morning." He fell silent for a while, then continued in a low voice that was hardly heard: "Human hands they were that forced me into degradation and human hands they were that delivered me. How strong is man's cruelty, yet how abundant is his pity!" And Rahel said in a voice in which were a mother's sweet tenderness and serenity: "How then, my brother, did you dare to leave the monastery on a night such as even the wolves fear and from which they hide in caves; from which the eagles in their awe conceal themselves among the rocks?"

The youth closed his eyes as though with the lids he would return his tears to the depths of his heart. He answered: "The foxes have holes, and the birds of the air have nests; but the Son of man hath not where to lay His head." And Rahel said: "So spoke Jesus the Nazarene of Himself when one of the scribes asked that he might follow Him whither He did go." And the youth added: "And so say all who would follow the spirit and the truth in this age of lying and corruption and deceit."

Rahel fell silent, thinking on the meaning of his words, and then said, hesitant: "But in the monastery are many spacious rooms and chests of gold and silver and vaults filled with wheat and wine, and enclosures housing fatted calves and sheep. How come you, then, to leave all these things and go out into the night?"

"I left all these things because I was driven by force from the monastery," he replied, sighing.

Said Rahel: "A monk in a monastery is like a soldier on the field of battle. His commander rebukes him and he bears in silence; he gives him an order and the soldier obeys immediately. I have heard tell that a man cannot become a monk except that he banish from him all resolve and desire and thought and all that has to do with self. But a good master does not seek of his servants things beyond their power. How then does the head of Deir Kizhaya demand of you that you deliver up your life to the tempest and snows?" And the youth answered: "A man cannot become a monk in the eyes of the Superior unless he be as an instrument blind and dumb and bereft of strength and feeling. I left the monastery because I was not a blind and dumb being, but a man hearing and seeing."

Rahel and Maryam looked at him as though they had just seen in his face a secret that he would conceal. After a little while the mother spoke in a wondering voice and asked: "Does a man who hears and sees go forth into a night that blinds the eyes and deafens the ears?"

The youth, with a sigh, let his head droop on his breast and said in a deep voice: "I was driven out from the monastery."

"Driven out?" exclaimed Rahel in astonishment. Maryam repeated the words softly.

The youth raised his head, already repenting of his having told the truth to the two women. For he feared that their compassion for him would turn into contumely and scorn. But when he looked up he saw in their eyes only the light of tenderness and a seeking to understand. Then he spoke, and in a choking voice, said: "Yes, I was driven from the monastery because I could not dig my grave with my hands; because my heart was sick within me of the existence of lying and deceit. Because my spirit refused to live in comfort on the poor and the wretched. And my soul turned away from joys bought with the chattels of a people sunk in ignorance. I was driven forth because my body no longer found rest in the spacious rooms built by those who dwelt in hovels. Because my stomach no more accepted bread kneaded with the tears of the widow and orphan. Because my tongue ceased to move in prayer, prayer that the Superior sold for the money of the simple and the faithful. I was cast forth like a leper because I recited to the monks and priests those passages from the Book that had put them as monks and priests."

He fell silent again, the while Rahel and Maryam looked at him wondering at his words. They gazed on the sad beauty of his face and looked at each other as though asking silently what strange thing had led him to them. The mother was filled with a desire to know. She looked toward him with kindliness and asked: "Where are your father and mother? Are they living?" "No," returned the youth in a broken voice; "I have neither father nor mother nor home."

Rahel drew a deep sigh and Maryam turned her face to the wall to hide the hot tears that pity wrung from her eyes. He looked at the two women the look of the conquered to their liberator, and his spirit was refreshed by their kindness as a flower among the rocks is refreshed by the morning dew.

He raised his head and continued: "My father and mother died before I was seven years, so the priest in the village where I was born took me to the Deir Kizhaya. The monks were pleased with me, and they made me a cowherd. When I became fifteen years of age they clothed me in these ugly black garments and, making me stand before the altar, said to me: 'Swear before God and His saints that you now take the vow of poverty, obedience, and continence.' I repeated these words even before I understood their burden or knew the meaning of poverty, obedience, and continence; before I could see the narrow way on which they set me. My name was Khalil, but from that day the monks called me Brother Mubarak;[1] but never did they treat me as a brother. While they enjoyed rich food and meats they gave me to eat of dry bread and beans. They drank good wines but made me to drink of water mixed with tears. They laid them down on soft beds but me they put to sleep on a stone bench in a cold dark room with the swine. 'When I am a monk,' I would say to myself, 'I will also join them in their merrymaking and have title to their pleasures. No more will my stomach be tormented by the abundance of wines or my heart rent by the goodly smell of food; neither will my spirit tremble at the Superior's voice.' But in vain did I hope and dream, for I remained a cowherd and ceased not carrying heavy stones on my back and digging the earth with my arms. So I did in exchange for a piece of crust and a roof, for I knew not that there were places other than the monastery wherein I might live. The monks taught me to have no belief except in their way of life. They poisoned my soul with submission and despair until I reckoned the world an ocean of sorrow and misfortune and the monastery a port of salvation."

Khalil sat up and his haggard features expanded and he looked as though he saw something beautiful standing before him in that hut. Rahel and Maryam watched him in silence. After a little while he took up his tale. "Heaven, whose will it was to take away my father and banish me as an orphan to the monastery, did not will that I should pass my days as a blind man on perilous paths; neither did it will that I should remain an abject slave to the end of my life. So my eyes and ears were opened and I saw the light shining and I heard truth speaking." Whereupon Rahel shook her head, saying: "Is there, then, light other than the light of the sun given to all men? Is it in the power of men

1 An Arabic word meaning "blessed".

to know the truth?" Answered Khalil: "True light is that which radiates from within a man. It reveals the secrets of the soul to the soul and lets it rejoice in life, singing in the name of the Spirit. Truth is like the stars, which cannot be seen except beyond the darkness of night. Truth is like all beautiful things in existence: it does not reveal its beauties save to those who have felt the weight of falsehood. Truth is a hidden feeling which teaches us to rejoice in our days and wish to all mankind that rejoicing." Then said Rahel: "Many are they that live according to this feeling in their hearts, and many are those who believe it to be the law that God has given to mankind. But they rejoice not in their days; rather do they remain in misery until death."

Khalil answered her and said: "Without worth are the teachings and beliefs that make man wretched in his existence. And false are the feelings that lead him only to sorrow and despair. For it is a duty that man has to be happy in the world and know the roads to happiness and preach in its name wheresoever he be. Who sees not the kingdom of heaven in this world will not see it in the hereafter. We come not to this world as outcasts, but as ignorant children, that we may learn from life's beauties and secrets the worship of the everlasting and universal spirit and the search after the hidden things of the soul. This is the truth as I knew it when I read the teachings of Jesus the Nazarene, and this the light that emanated from within me and showed me the monastery and all in it as a black pit from whose depths rose frightening phantoms and images to destroy me. This is the hidden secret the wild places in their beauty showed to me as I sat hungry and weeping in the shade of the trees. And on the day when my spirit became drunk of the divine wine I grew bold and stood before the monks as they sat in the monastery garden like cows chewing the cud. I took upon me to reveal my thoughts and recite to them passages from the Book to show them their backsliding and sinfulness. I said: 'Why pass we our days in this separateness in the enjoyment of the charity of the poor, eating of bread kneaded with their sweat and tears, rejoicing in the bounty of land stolen from them? Why do we live in sloth and idleness far away from those in need of knowledge, denying the land our spiritual and bodily strength? Jesus of

Nazareth sent you as sheep among wolves, but what teaching has made you as wolves among sheep? Why do you put yourselves apart from men since God has created you men? If you are the most virtuous of those who walk in life's procession, then go you and teach them. How do you pledge yourselves to poverty and yet live as princes, and take the vow of obedience yet rebel against the gospel, and swear chastity, yet fill your hearts with lust? You make to scourge your bodies, but you achieve naught save the destruction of your souls. You make pretence that you are above all worldly things, but of all people you are the most covetous. You hold yourselves up as ascetic and celibate, but you are as cattle, whose care is only with the best of the pasture. Come then, let us give back to the needy dwellers of this village the monastery's spacious lands and return to their pockets the wealth we have taken. Let us disperse like birds over the land and serve this enfeebled people who is the source of our power and put to rights the country on whose bounty we live. Let us teach this despairing nation to smile in the sunlight and rejoice in heaven's gifts and life's freedom and glory. For the toiling of the people is finer and nobler than the ease to which we are given in this place. And pity in the heart of a neighbour is a finer thing than virtue concealed in a corner of the monastery. A word of comfort in the ears of the feeble and the criminal and the harlot is worthier than prayers recited in the temple.' "

Khalil paused to regain his breath; then he raised his eyes to Rahel and Maryam and resumed his words in a low voice:

"As I was speaking in this wise before the monks, astonishment and surprise spread over their faces as though they were loath to believe that a youth of my kind stood boldly addressing them in such words. When I had finished, one of them approached me and, baring his teeth, said: 'Do you thus dare, miserable wretch, to stand before us and speak these words?' And another laughed scornfully and said: 'Have you learned this wisdom from the cows and pigs with which you have consorted all your life?' Still another came forward and threatened me, saying: 'You will surely see what is to befall you, heretic.' Then they all rose and withdrew from me like the healthy shunning

the leper. Some of them went before the Superior and com-
plained against me, and he had me brought before him at sunset.
After rebuking me severely in the presence of the rejoicing
monks, he ordered me to be flogged. Having had me flogged
with rope ends he pronounced a month's imprisonment on me.
Whereupon, amidst much laughing and shouting, the monks
led me to a dank and gloomy cell. And so I passed one month
in that dungeon; no light did I see, neither was I conscious of
anything save the creeping and crawling of insects. I felt no
touch except that of the earthen floor, neither did I know the
night's ending from the day's beginning. I heard naught but the
footsteps of him who came and placed before me a morsel of
dry bread and a cup of water and vinegar. When I came out
from the prison and the monks beheld my wasted body and
yellow face, they imagined that my spirit's yearning had died
within me and that hunger and thirst and torture had destroyed
the feeling that God had awakened in my heart. Night followed
day and in my solitude I fell to thinking in what manner could
those monks be brought to see the light and hearken to life's
song. But in vain was my thinking, for the thick veil that the
long ages had woven across their eyes was not to be torn apart
by a few days. And the clay with which ignorance had stopped
their ears could not be moved by the soft touch of fingers."

After a silence full with sighing Maryam turned to her mother
as though seeking leave to speak and, looking sadly at Khalil,
said: "Did you speak these words a second time before the
monks so that they drove you out into this night of terror that
should teach men to be merciful even unto their enemies?"

The youth answered: "During the evening, as the tempest
increased in violence and the elements joined in battle, I sat
apart from the monks. They were then gathered around the
fire warming themselves and telling stories and humorous tales.
I opened the Gospel, contemplating those words wherein the
spirit finds comfort, forgetful of the wrath of nature and the
anger of the elements. When the monks saw that I sat alone
apart from them, they made it an occasion to jest and mock at
me. Some of them came over to me laughing and winking their
eyes and making scornful gestures. I paid them no heed but

closed the Book and remained gazing out of the window. This action stirred them to anger and they looked at me with hostility because my silence had put them in ill humour. Then one of them said: 'What are you reading, mighty reformer?' I did not look at the speaker, but I opened again the Gospel and read in a loud voice this passage: 'And he said unto the multitude that had come to his baptism; O children of vipers, who hath warned you to flee from the wrath to come? Bring forth therefore fruits for repentance; and think not to say within yourselves: We have Abraham to our father; for I say unto you that God is able of these stones to raise up children unto Abraham. And now also the axe is raised unto the roots of the trees; therefore every tree which bringeth not forth good fruit is hewn down and cast into the fire. And the multitude asked of him saying: What then shall we do? And he answered them saying: He that hath two garments let him give to him that hath none; and let him that hath food give likewise.' When I read these words spoken by John the Baptist, the monks withdrew into silence for a while as if a hidden hand had laid hold of their spirits. But soon they returned to their laughing and chattering and one among them said: 'We have ofttimes heard these words and we are in no need of cowherds to recite them.' Whereupon I said: 'Did you but read and understand these words, then in truth the people of these snow-covered villages were not now shivering from cold and crying in hunger the while you enjoy their bounty and drink the wine of their vineyards and eat the flesh of their cattle.' Hardly had the words left my lips ere a monk struck me across the face as if I were speaking naught but the words of an idiot. Another kicked me, while yet a third one snatched the Book from my hand. One called for the Superior and he came in haste. When they apprised him of what had taken place, he rose to his full height, his brows contracted, and trembling with rage, he shouted: 'Seize hold of this rebellious sinner; drag him out from the monastery and leave the wrathful elements to teach him obedience. Cast him forth into the cold and darkness and let nature do with him as God wills her. Then cleanse your hands of the poison of heresy that is on his garments. And if he return beseeching you and feigning repentance, open not the door to him, for the viper imprisoned in a cage does not become a dove, neither does the thicket planted in a vineyard bring forth fruit.' Thereupon the monks seized me and dragged me outside the monastery. They went back laughing. Before they closed the doors upon me I heard one of them say with scorn: 'Yesterday were you king over the cows and pigs; and today have we dethroned you, O reforming one, for you have managed your affairs ill. Go you now and be king over the ravening wolves and carrion birds and teach them how to live in their caves and lairs!' "

He ceased from speaking and sighed deeply. He turned his face to the fire and watched the flickering flames. When he spoke again, his voice had in it a wounding sweetness. "And so was I driven from the monastery. So did the monks deliver me into the hands of death. I took to the road, which was already hidden by mist. The violent wind tore at my clothes, and the snow piled up about my knees. Soon my strength gave out and I fell down crying out for help the cry of one in despair who feels that no one will hear him save terrifying death and the dark valleys. But from beyond the winds and the snows and the darkness and the clouds, from beyond the ether and the stars a Power, all-knowing and all-merciful, heard my cry. It was not its will that I should die ere I had learned what remained of life's secrets, and thus did it send you both to bring me back from the depths of the abyss and annihilation."

The two women continued to look at him with wonder and affection as though they within their hearts understood the hidden things in his heart and were at one with it in its knowing and feeling. Then Rahel stretched forth her hand, unprompted by her will, and touched his hand softly and, with tears glistening in her eyes, said to him: "Whom Heaven has chosen to defend right no oppression can destroy nor snows and tempests kill." And Maryam added, murmuring: "The snow and the storm destroy the flower, but its seed they cannot kill."

The drawn face of Khalil was illumined by these words of comfort as the horizon is lighted by the first rays of dawn. Said he: "If you reckon me not a rebel and a heretic as do those monks, then the persecution I have borne in the monastery is naught but a symbol of the harshness a people suffers ere attaining to knowledge. This night, which came near to destroying me, is as the revolt that precedes freedom and equality. For out of the sensitive heart of a woman comes forth the happiness of mankind, and in the sentiments of her noble spirit are born the sentiments of their spirits."

Having thus spoken, he laid his head on the pillow. The women were loath to continue the conversation, for they saw in his eyes that sleep, brought on by warmth and rest after his perilous wanderings, was already overtaking him. And soon Khalil closed his eyes and slept the sleep of a child safe in its mother's arms. Rahel rose quietly and Maryam followed her. They sat on their bed looking at him as though in his lean face was a power that inclined their spirits and drew them near. Then the mother whispered, like one talking to himself, and said: "In his closed eyes is a strange force that speaks with silence, awakening the longings of the spirit." And the daughter added: "His hands, Mother, are like the hands of Jesus in the picture in the church." And the mother murmured: "In his sad face is seen a woman's tenderness and a man's strength."

After a while the two women were borne on the wings of sleep away to the land of dreams. The fire on the hearth grew cold and became ashes, and the oil in the lamp dried up and the light grew weaker and faint till it was no more. The howling storm without abated nothing of its anger, and the black skies sent forth their snow, which the wind in its violence took and scattered in all directions.

IV

Two weeks had passed since that night. The cloud-filled sky was now tranquil, now turbulent, veiling the valleys in mist and burying the hillocks beneath snow. Three times did Khalil decide upon following his way to the coast, and each time did Rahel with gentleness prevent him, saying: "Put not your life a second time at the mercy of the blind elements, but remain here with us. For the bread that satisfies two will suffice for a third, and the fire on this hearth will remain alight after your going as it was before your coming. We are poor, my brother, but we exist under the sun as do all, for God gives to us our daily bread."

Maryam besought him with tender glances and gentle murmurs to wait upon his going, for since his coming to them between life and death she felt the existence of a divine force within him that sent life and light into her being, awakening in the holy of holies of her spirit feelings sweet and unwonted. For the first time in her life she felt an awareness of that strange sense which makes the pure heart of a maiden as a white rose drinking of dew drops and exhaling a delicate fragrance. There is no emotion in a human creature purer or sweeter than the hidden feeling that awakens to life unawares in the heart of a maiden to fill the emptinesses of her breast with enchanting melodies and make her days like the poet's dream and her nights like the prophet's vision. There is no mystery among nature's mysteries stronger or more beautiful than the desire that turns the stillness of the virgin's spirit into a continual awakening, obliterating with its force the memory of days gone by and breathing life, with its sweetness, into the hopes of days to come.

The Lebanese woman is distinguished from the woman of other nations in the strength of her affections and simplicity of feeling. For her simple upbringing and education, which is a hindrance to the development of her mind and an obstacle in the way of her advancement, leads her to explore the things of her spirit and her heart in quest of their mysteries. The Lebanese girl is as a spring issuing from the heart of the earth in low ground and, finding no path through which to go down as a river to the sea, becomes a placid lake reflecting on its surface the light of the moon and stars.

Khalil felt the waves of Maryam's being lapping the shores of his being, and he knew that the sacred flame enveloping his heart had touched her heart. And he rejoiced, for the first time – the rejoicing of a lost child who finds its mother. Yet he chided his spirit for its haste and its passion, thinking therefrom that this spiritual understanding would fade like the mist when the days should separate him from that village. He said within himself: "What things are these mysterious forces that make playthings of us in our ignorance? What are these laws that lead us

now by rough paths and now stand us up before the sun rejoic-
ing; now raising us to the summit of a mountain when we are
glad and exult, now casting us down to the depths of the valley
so that we cry out in our agony? What thing is this life that
embraces us as a friend today and shuns us as a foe on the
morrow? Was I not but yesterday hated and despised among the
monks of the monastery? Did I not accept mocking and torment
for the sake of that truth which Heaven awoke in my heart?
And did I not tell the monks that happiness is the will of God
in man? Then what is this fear, and why close I my eyes and
turn my head away from the light that shines in the eyes of this
maiden? I am an outcast and she is poor, but does man live by
bread alone? Is not life a debt and a fulfilment, and stand we not
between want and plenty as stands the tree between winter and
summer? And what would Rahel say did she know that the spirit
of an outcast youth and the spirit of her daughter had attained
understanding in silence and drawn near to the circle of light
on high? And that the youth she had delivered from out of the
jaws of death wished to take her daughter to wife? How would
speak the simple people of the village when they learned that a
boy reared in a monastery and driven away from it was come to
their village to live side by side with a comely woman? Would
they close not their ears if I said to them that the one who had
left the monastery to live in their midst was like a bird leaving
the darkness of its cage for light and liberty? And what, then,
should the Shaikh Abbas, dwelling among the poor peasants as
a prince among slaves, hear my story? What will the village
priest do when he hears of those things which were the cause
of my expulsion from the monastery?"

And as Khalil sat by the hearth in communion with his self,
looking into the tongues of flame so kin to his own feelings,
now and then Maryam stole glances at him, reading in his
features dreams, listening to the echoes of thoughts leaving his
breast, feeling in her awareness the presence of his innermost
secrets.

One evening when Khalil was standing by the window that
overlooked the valley, where the trees and rocks were still
covered with snow like corpses in burial shrouds, Maryam

appeared and stood by his side and looked through the window at the sky. He turned to her, and when his eyes met her eyes he sighed deeply and averted his face and closed his eyes as though his spirit had taken leave of him to soar upwards into the infinite in search of a word to utter. After a little while Maryam took courage and said: "Where are you going when the snow is melted and the roads are free?" He opened his big eyes and looked toward the distant horizon before replying. "I shall follow the road to where I know not." And the spirit of Maryam trembled within her and she said: "Why do you not dwell in this village and remain near to us? Is not life here better than a far-off exile?"

Her softly spoken words and her melodious voice caused a tumult to rise within him. He answered: "The people of the village will not accept as their neighbour an outcast from the monastery. Neither will they permit him to breathe the air that sustains them, for they hold that an enemy of the monks is a blasphemer before God and His saints."

Maryam gave a little moan and was silent, for the cutting truth had silenced her. Khalil leaned his head on his hand and continued: "The people of these villages, Maryam, have learned from the monks and priests to hate those who think for themselves. They are taught to remain apart from all those who pass their lives in seeking and not following. If I remained in this village and said to the people: 'Come, brethren, and let us worship God according to the dictates of our spirits and not as the priests will it, for God wants not the adoration of the ignorant in their imitation of others,' they would say that this one is a heretic who rebels against the authority placed by God in the hands of His priests. And if I said to them: 'Hearken, my brethren, to the voice of your hearts, and do the will of the spirit deep within you,' they would say that this one is evil and wishes us to be unfaithful to whom God has put between heaven and earth to intercede."

He looked into the eyes of Maryam, and when he again spoke, there was in his voice the dulcet note of silver strings: "Yet in the village, Maryam, is an unearthly force possessing me and laying hold on my soul; a higher power making me forgetful of my persecution by the monks and causing me to love their harshness. In this village I met death face to face, and in it the spirit of God embraced my spirit. In this village is a flower growing among thorns, for whose beauty my soul longs and whose fragrance fills my heart. Shall I then leave this flower to go forth proclaiming those principles for which I was cast out from the monastery, or shall I remain by the side of this flower to dig for my thoughts and dreams a grave among the thorns that surround it?"

When Maryam heard this, her body trembled like the trembling of a lily before the breeze of daybreak. The light in her heart overflowed from her eyes, and shyness fought with her tongue for mastery, and she said: "We are both of us between the hands of a hidden force, a just and merciful force; let it do with us as it will."

V

From distant times down to our own days the privileged of society have ever allied themselves with the clergy and leaders of religion against the body of society. It will not be cured save by the banishment of ignorance from the world when the mind of every man shall become a sovereign and the heart of every woman a priestess.

The son of the privileged builds his mansion with the bodies of the weak and the underprivileged, and the priest sets up his sanctuary on the graves of the faithful and the humble. The ruler lays hold of the arms of the wretched peasant, and the priest stretches forth his hand to his pocket. The governor looks at these children of the fields with a frown, and the priest moves among them smiling. Between the tiger's frown and the wolf's smile the flock perishes. The governor embodies law, and the priest religion, and betwixt the twain bodies are destroyed and spirits die.

Now in Lebanon, that mountain rich in sunlight but poor in the light of knowledge, the nobleman and the clergyman have united against the weak and indigent peasant who tills the soil and gets from it what he can to protect his body against the sword of the one and the curses of the other. The child of privilege stands by his palace in Lebanon calling out to his fellow countrymen: "The Sultan has put me as guardian over your bodies."[1] And the priest stands before the pulpit shouting: "And God has appointed me keeper of your souls." But the people of Lebanon stay silent, for hearts deep in earth do not break and the dead do not weep.

The Shaikh Abbas, who was governor prince and sovereign in that village, had a great love for the monks in the monastery. He followed faithfully their teachings and traditions, for they shared with him the killing of knowledge and the keeping alive of obedience among the labourers in his fields and vineyards. And on that very evening, the while Khalil and Maryam stood before the throne of love with Rahel watching them, seeking to know the secret within them, Father Ilyas, the village priest, betook himself to the Shaikh Abbas and related to him how the pious monks had driven out from their midst a rebellious and wicked youth. He told him, moreover, that this heretic and blasphemer was come to the village these two weeks past and was living in the house of Rahel, widow of Sam'an Al-Rami. Father Ilyas was not content with retailing to the Shaikh these simple tidings but must needs add: "The Devil who is driven out from the monastery does not become an angel in the village; and the sod that the keeper of the field cuts and throws on the flames does not yield fruit in the fire. If we would that this village remain whole and clean from the germs of a foul disease, then let us cast out this youth from our dwellings and fields as the good monks did drive him forth from the monastery."

"And what has told you that this youth will be as a foul disease in the village?" asked the Shaikh Abbas. "Were it not better to make him a cowherd or keeper of the vineyards? We are in sore need of labourers. The road did not bring us a strong-armed youth for naught."

The priest smiled a subtle smile, caressed his thick beard with his fingers, and said: "Were this young man a good worker,

[1] This was written in the days when Syria and Lebanon were under Ottoman Turkish domination. – Translator.

the monks had not expelled him, for the monastery's lands are spacious and its herds without number. A muleteer from the monastery who sojourned the night with me recounted to me how this youth had uttered blasphemous passages and spoke words of rebellion in the hearing of the monks – words that revealed the evil in him. In his boldness he said: 'Give back to the poor of this village the fields of the monastery and its vine-yards and properties and disperse their ownership over all parts, for that is better than prayer and worship.' And the muleteer told likewise that chastisement and flogging and the darkness of the prison cell availed naught to restore reason to this heretic: rather was the Devil within him nourished as are flies multiply-ing around a dunghill."

At these words the Shaikh Abbas stood upright, then retreated a little in the manner of a panther about to spring. For a second he was silent, grinding his teeth and trembling in his anger. He walked to the door of the hall and called for his servants. Three came and stood before him awaiting his commands. He addressed them thus: "In the house of Rahel the widow is a criminal youth clad in a monk's habit. Go you now and bring him before me bound. If the woman opposes you, seize her like-wise and drag her by the hair across the snow, for he that assists evildoers is himself evil."

The servants inclined their heads and hurried out to do their master's bidding. The priest and the Shaikh Abbas remained in conversation, discussing the manner in which they would deal with the youth and the widow Rahel.

VI

The day waned and night came on, sending forth its phantoms among the snow-shrouded huts. The stars shone in the cold dark sky like symbols of immortal hope beyond the agonies of separation and death. The peasants closed tight doors and win-dows and lighted the lamps and sat by their fires for warmth, unmindful of the shades of night around their dwellings.

It was in that very hour, as Rahel and Maryam and Khalil were seated at the wooden table at their evening meal, that a knock came at the door and the three servants of the Shaikh Abbas entered. Rahel stared at them in terror and Maryam shouted out in fright. But Khalil stayed silent and unmoved. It was as though his great spirit had been forewarned and was apprised of the men's coming even before their coming. Then one of the men advanced and laid his hand roughly on Khalil's shoulder, saying in a harsh voice: "Are you not the youth whom they drove from the monastery?" Khalil replied, speaking slowly: "I am he. What do you want of me?" Said the man: "We are to take you bound to the house of the Shaikh Abbas. If you resist, then we will drag you through the snow like a lamb to the slaughter."

Rahel stood the while, her face white and her brow wrinkled. Then she said in a trembling voice: "What crime brings him before the Shaikh Abbas, and why do you drag him away bound?" and Maryam added: "He is one and you are three. It is a coward's doing so to abase and punish him." She spoke with hope, beseeching them. But the servant was angry and in his rage shouted: "Do you find in this village, then, a woman who would rebel against the will of the Shaikh Abbas?" Having delivered himself of these words, he took from around his waist a stout rope and fell to binding Khalil's arms. The boy said naught and his demeanour did not change; his head was raised high like a tower in the face of a storm. On his lips was a sad smile. Then he spoke: "I have only pity for you, brothers, for you are the instruments of a blind force in the hands of a person sighted yet feeble who oppresses you and with your strength grinds the weak. You are the bondsmen of ignorance, and ignorance is blacker than the Negro's skin and more submissive to cruelty and shame. Yesterday I was as you are this day; on the morrow will you be as I am now. But today there stretches between you and me a vast dark gulf sucking up my cry and concealing my truth from you. You hear not, neither do you see. Here am I. Bind my arms and do what you will."

When the men heard these words, their eyes stared and their bodies shook. They were bereft of strength by the youth the space of a minute, as though the sweetness in his voice prevented them from movement and brought to awakening nobler desires slumbering in their depths. But they returned to their senses as though the Shaikh's voice still echoed in their ears, reminding them of the task for which he had sent them. They bound the boy's arms and led him out in silence, and they felt within their innermost selves the stirring of an agony. Rahel and Maryam followed in their steps like the daughters of Jerusalem when they followed Jesus to Mount Calvary. So did the two women walk in the wake of Khalil to the house of the Shaikh Abbas.

VII

In the small villages news, be it of great import or little, travels among the peasants with the quickness of thought, for their remoteness from the general activities of society gives them opportunity to investigate in detail all that goes on in their limited environment. During the winter days when the fields and orchards are covered with their blankets of snow and when all life huddles fearfully round the fires for warmth, the villagers are eager for news of events so that they may fill their empty days with discussion and pass the cold nights with the how and wherefore of things and people.

And so the serving men of the Shaikh Abbas had hardly laid hands on Khalil that night before the news spread like a contagious disease among the inhabitants of that village. The desire to satisfy their curiosity seized hold of them, and they came tumbling out of their huts in all directions like a company of troops deploying over a field. No sooner had the pinioned youth reached the house of the Shaikh than the spacious hall was filled with a multitude of men and women, young and old. They stretched their necks in their anxiety to have one glimpse of the blasphemer driven from the monastery, and the widow Rahel and her daughter Maryam, who were partners with the evil spirits in their spreading of fiendish poisons and diseases into the air of the village.

The Shaikh Abbas sat on a raised seat, and by his side sat Father Ilyas. The peasants and servants stood and gazed on the bound youth, who stood among them with head raised high like a lofty mountain among plains. Behind him stood Rahel and Maryam with hearts held in the grip of fear and spirits tortured by the hard glances of the multitude. But what can fear do with the spirit of a woman who has seen the truth and follows it, and what can hard looks do to the heart of a maiden who has heard love's summoning and is awakened?

The Shaikh Abbas then looked at the youth and in a voice of thunder asked:

"What is your name?"

"Khalil."

"What are your people and your kin, and where is your birthplace?"

Khalil turned his face to the peasants, who looked at him with eyes of hate and scorn, and replied: "The poor and downtrodden are my people and my tribe, and this vast land is my birthplace."

The Shaikh smiled a mocking smile. "Those whom you claim as kin seek your punishment, and the land that you call a home rejects you as of its people," said he.

Khalil felt within himself a disturbance as he said: "Nations in their ignorance seize their noblest sons and deliver them up to the tyrant's cruelty; and countries prey to disgrace and dishonour persecute those who would love them and deliver them. Yet does the good son abandon his mother in the time of her illness? Does the compassionate brother deny the brother who is in despair? These poor wretches who delivered me to you bound today are the selfsame that did deliver their necks to you yesterday. And those who brought me dishonoured before you are those very ones who sow the seeds of their hearts in your fields and pour out their life blood at your feet. And this land which rejects me is that same country which will not open its mouth to swallow the tyrant and the covetous."

The Shaikh Abbas laughed loudly as though he would submerge with his coarse laughter the youth's spirit and prevent its way to the simple souls of his listeners. Said he: "Were you not, young man, a shepherd in the service of the monastery? Why, then, did you leave your charge and have yourself expelled? Think you, perchance, that the people will be more merciful toward a heretic and a madman than the pious monks?" And Khalil said: "I was a shepherd and not a butcher. I used to lead

my beasts to green meadows and fresh pastures, and never did
I lead them to bare and stony ground. I took them down to
the springs of sweet water and not to the swamps. At eventide
I returned with them to the enclosures and did not leave them
in the valley as a prey to wolves and wild beasts. Thus did I with
those animals. Did you do so with this emaciated flock now
gathered about us, then you were not at this moment inhabiting
a palace while these people perish through hunger in dark and
gloomy hovels. Did you take pity on these simple children of
God as I had pity on the beasts of the monastery, you were not
now sitting on this silken seat while they stand before you like
naked branches before the north wind."

The Shaikh Abbas moved on his seat in disquiet. On his fore-
head stood out beads of cold sweat, and his merriment turned
to anger. But he controlled himself again lest he appear anxious
and concerned before his men and followers. He made a motion
with his hand and said: "We have not brought you here bound,
unbeliever, to hearken to your raving talk. You are here before
us that we may pass judgment on you as an evildoer. Know, then,
that you stand before the lord of this village and doer of the will
of the Ameer Ameen Al-Shehabi[1] – may God strengthen him!
And before Father Ilyas, embodiment of the holy Church, against
which you have transgressed. Defend yourself, then, against your
accusers or bend your knee in repentance before us and before
this mocking crowd, and we shall pardon you and make you
cowherd as you were in the monastery."

In a quiet voice the youth said: "The criminal is not judged
by criminals, neither does the backslider defend himself before
sinners."

Having thus spoken these words, he turned to the crowd in
that hall, and in a voice ringing and clear like a silver bell he
continued: "O brethren, the man whom your submission and
obedience made lord over your fields has brought me bound to
try me before you in this palace built on the remains of your
fathers and forefathers. And the man whom your faith made

1 Son of the great Ameer Basheer. He ruled Mount Lebanon after his
father's death.

priest in your church is come to judge me and assist at my degradation and abasement. And you, you have come running from all parts to look upon my agony and listen to my pleading and beseeching. You have left your warm hearths to see your brother and son bound and reviled. You have made haste to behold the writhing prey in the hold of the wild beast. You are come to look on the criminal and blasphemer standing before his judges. I am the criminal. It is I who am the heretic, cast forth from the monastery and carried by the tempest to your village. I am that wrongdoer. Then hear you my case and show not pity, but be just, for pity is only for the guilty; the innocent seek only justice. I have chosen you my judges, for the will of the people is God's will. Let your hearts be awakened and hear me well, then judge me according to your conscience. It is said that I am an evil person and an unbeliever, but you know not what my crime is. You have beheld me bound like a thief and murderer, but you have not heard of my wrongdoing because crimes and transgressions in this land remain hidden in the mist, but their punishment is manifest to all, like flashes of lightning on a dark night. My crime, O men, is in my knowledge of your despair and my feeling for the weight of your fetters. And my sin, O women, is in my compassion for you and your children, who suck in life from your breasts with the sting of death. I am your kin, for my forefathers lived in these valleys that exhaust your strength and died under this yoke which bends your necks. I believe in God, who hears the cry of your tormented spirits and sees into your broken hearts. I believe in the Book that makes us all brothers equal before the sun. I believe in the teachings that free you and me from bondage and place us unfettered upon the earth, the stepping-place of the feet of God. I was a cowherd in the monastery, but my solitude with the dumb beasts in quiet places did not blind me to the tragedy that you play out against your will in the fields. And my ear was not deaf to the cry of despair rising up from the huts. I looked and beheld me in the monastery and you in the fields as a flock of sheep following a wolf to his lair. I stood in the middle of the way crying out for help, whereupon the wolf fell on me and bore me away so that my cry might not move the spirit of the flock to rebel and scatter in fright in all directions, leaving him alone and hungry in the dark night. I have borne imprisonment and hunger and thirst for the sake of the truth that I see writ in blood in your faces; and torture and flogging and mockery because to your sighing I put voice, which filled the monastery from end to end. But I feared not and my heart weakened not, for your cry and your agony followed me and renewed my strength, and persecution and despising and death became dear to me. And now you ask yourselves saying: 'When did we cry out for help and who among us makes bold to open his lips?' I say unto you that every day your spirits cry out and in the night do your hearts in their anguish call for succour. But you do not hearken to your spirits and your hearts, for a dying man cannot hear the rattle of death within him, but those who sit by his bed hear. The slaughtered bird dances his fantastic dance without direction of will and knows not; but the beholders know. At what hour of the day sigh not your spirits in agony? Is it in the morning hour, when the love of existence calls you and tears from off your eyes the veil of sleep and leads you to the fields as slaves? Is it at noon, when you would sit in the shade of a tree to protect yourselves against the burning sun, yet cannot? Or at eventide, when you return hungry to your dwellings and find naught save dry bread and clouded water? Or at nightfall, when weariness throws you upon your stone couch and gives you fretful slumber; when you close your eyes in sleep only to awake in fright imagining the voice of the Shaikh still ringing in your ears? In what season of the year do your hearts not weep in sorrow? Is it in spring, when nature puts on her new garments and you go out to meet her in your tattered raggedness? Or is it in the summer, when you reap the harvest and gather in the yield to the threshing-floor and fill the bins of your lord and master with plenty and receive as your reward only straw and tares? Or in the autumn, when you gather the fruit and press the grapes in the winepress and receive naught of it except vinegar and acorns? Or yet in winter, when the elements oppress you and the cold drives you into your snow-covered huts, while you sit within on the hearth crouching and fearful of the raging storms? This is then your life, my poor

brethren. This is the night drawing over your souls, unfortunate ones. These are the shadows of your wretchedness and misery. This the cry of anguish which I heard arising out of your depths so that I awoke and rebelled against the monks and their way of life, and stood alone, complaining in your name and in the name of justice, which suffers your sufferings. And they reckoned me an unbeliever and drove me forth from the monastery. So did I come to share your wretchedness and dwell in your midst and mix my blood with your blood. But you delivered me in bonds up to your powerful foe, to one who has plundered your bounty, who lives in ease on your wealth and fills his capacious belly with the fruits of your toil. Are there not among you elders who know well that the soil you till and whose yield is denied you is yours and that the father of Shaikh Abbas took it by force from your father when law was writ on the edge of the sword? Have you not heard that the monks dispossessed your forebears of their lands and vineyards when the sacred verses were recorded on the lips of the priest? Know you not that the clergy and the privileged conspire together in your submission and abasement and the shedding of your heart's blood? Is there a man among you whom the priest has not made to bend his neck before the master of the field? Or a woman whom the master of the field has not rebuked and obliged to follow the will of the priest?

"You have heard how the Lord said to the first man: 'In the sweat of thy face shalt thou eat bread.' Then how does eat the Shaikh Abbas his bread kneaded with the sweat of your face and drink wine watered with your tears? Did God set aside this man and make him master whilst yet he was in his mother's womb? Did He visit His anger upon you for sins unknown, and send you as slaves into this life to gather the fruits of the field, yet eat not save of the thorns and thistles of the valleys? Or raise up fine palaces, yet have not where to live except in ruined hovels? You have heard Jesus the Nazarene when He spake to His disciples saying: 'Freely ye have received, freely give. Provide neither gold, nor silver, nor brass in your purse.' Then what teaching allows to the monks and priests the selling of their prayers for gold and silver? You pray in the silences of the night, saying: 'Give us this day our daily bread, O Lord.' So the Lord gave

677

unto you this land to sustain you with bread and sufficiency. But gave He to the heads of the monasteries the power to steal from between your hands this bread? You do curse Judas because he sold his Master for silver, but what makes you to bless those that sell Him every day of their lives? Judas in his wickedness repented of his sin and hanged himself; but those walk before you with heads held high in fine raiment and costly rings and gold adornments. You teach your children to love the Nazarene; then how do you teach them obeisance before those who hate Him and transgress against His laws and teachings? You have known that the apostles of Christ were stoned to death that the Holy Spirit might live within you; but know you that the priests and the monks are killing your spirits that they may live in enjoyment of your bounty. What thing tempts you in an existence full of lowliness and abjection and holds you prostrate before a terrifying image reared by lying and falsehood upon the graves of your fathers? And what priceless treasure do you guard by your submission to leave as a heritage to your sons?

"Your souls are in the grasp of the priest, and your bodies in the hold of the governor, and your hearts in the darkness of sorrow and despair. What thing can you point to in life and say: 'This is to us'? Know you, O feeble captives, who is the priest whom you fear and set up as a guardian over the holy secrets of your souls? Hearken unto me and I shall reveal to you that which you feel but are afeared to lay bare. He is a betrayer to whom the followers of Christ gave a holy Book that he made a net to catch that which belongs to them; a hypocrite whom the faithful girded with a fine crucifix, which he held aloft above their heads as a sharp sword; an oppressor to whom the weak delivered up their necks, which he bound with a halter and held with an iron hand and gave not up till they were broken like earthen pots and scattered as dust. He is a ravening wolf who enters the enclosure, and the shepherd thinks him a sheep and sleeps in peace. And when darkness descends, he falls upon the flock one by one. He is a glutton who reveres the well-laden table more than the altar; and a covetous one who pursues a farthing piece even to the caves of the jinn. He sucks the blood of his congregants as the desert sands suck up drops of rain. He is avaricious and watches after his own needs and stores up wealth. He is a trickster who enters through the cracks in the wall and goes out only when the house falls. A thief hard of heart who steals the widow's mite and the orphan's piece. He is a creature strange in his creation, with a vulture's beak and a panther's claws and a hyena's fangs and a viper's touch. Take you his book, rend his garments, pluck his beard. Do with him as you will, then return and place in his palm a coin and he will pardon you and smile on you with love. Smite him on the cheek, spit in his face, trample him underfoot, then seat him at your table and he will forget and be happy and loose his belt, the better to fill his belly of your food and drink. Blaspheme against the name of his Lord, defame his religion, mock at his faith, then send to him a jar of wine or a basket of fruit and he will forgive you and justify you before God and man. Does he see a woman but he averts his face, crying: 'Get thee hence, daughter of Babylon,' the while saying within himself: 'Marriage is better than burning'? Does he behold youths and maidens marching in love's procession without lifting up his eyes to heaven, crying out: 'Vanity of vanities, all is vanity'? But when he is alone he sighs, saying: 'Let be as naught the customs and traditions that have exiled me from the joys of life and denied me the delights of existence.' He counsels people that they judge not lest they be judged, but he judges harshly those who laugh at his loathsomeness and condemns their souls to hell before death and lifts his eyes heavenward, but his thoughts coil like vipers about your pockets. He calls you 'my children', but he feels not fatherly love, neither do his lips smile at a suckling infant nor does he carry a child on his shoulders. He says to you, inclining his head reverently: 'Let us lift ourselves above worldly affairs, for our lives fade away as the mist, and our days, like a shadow, are not.' But did you look well, then you saw him grasping the tale of existence and holding fast to the garments of life; grieving at yesterday's going; fearful of today's quickness; ever watching for the morrow's coming. He demands of you charity, but he is richer than you in wealth. And if you bring him he will bless you before people; if you deny him he will curse you in secret. In the temple he commends to you the poor and the needy, but around his house the hungry cry and before his face is stretched forth the hand of the helpless, but he sees not, neither does he hear. He sells for gain his prayers, and he who does not buy is an enemy of God and His prophets, denied heavenly bliss. This, then, followers of the Anointed, is the creature who frightens you. This is the good monk who sucks your blood. This is the priest who makes the Sign with his right hand and clutches at your heart with his left. This is the man of the Church whom you make servant and he becomes master; you beatify him as a saint and he turns into devil. You raise him up as guardian and he becomes a heavy yoke. This is the shadow ever following your spirit from the time of its entry into the world till its return to the infinite. This is the man who has come this night to pass judgment on me and revile me because my soul rebelled against the enemies of Jesus the Nazarene, who loved you and called you His brothers and sisters and was crucified for your sake."

The face of the youth was illumined and he felt a spiritual awakening in the breasts of his listeners and he saw on their faces the impression of his words. He lifted up his voice and continued: "You have heard, O brothers and sisters, that the Ameer Ameen Al-Shehabi did put the Shaikh Abbas lord over this village, and the sovereign did appoint the Ameer ruler over this mountain. But have you beheld the Power that did make the sovereign ruler over this land? You see not that Power as a body, neither do you hear it speak; but you feel its existence deep down in your souls, and you bow down before it in prayer and you call on it when you say: 'Our Father which art in heaven.' Yea, your heavenly Father it is that sets up kings and princes, for He is able of all things. Believe you then that your Father, who loves you and who has taught you the ways of truth through His prophets, would that you were wronged and oppressed? Believe you that God, who causes the rain to descend and makes the seed to bring forth the crop, and the flowers to blossom, would that you were hungry and despised so that one among you may be satisfied and puffed up? Believe you that the eternal Spirit who inspires within you love for a wife, tenderness to children, compassion on a kinsman, does set over you a harsh master to oppress you and place in servitude your days? That the Eternal Law that makes you love the light of existence does send to you one who would make you love instead the darkness of death? Believe you that nature has given you strength of body to humble it before weakness? You believe not these things, for did you so, then indeed would you be denying God's justice and unbelieving of the light of truth that shines on every one of us. Then what stirs you to assist the thing hateful to your spirits? Why fear you God's will, which has sent you as free men to this world, and become slaves to those who rebel against His law? Why do you lift up your eyes to the All-Powerful and call him 'Father' and then bend your necks before a weak man and call him 'Master'? How come God's children to be slaves of men? Did not Jesus call you brothers and sisters? Yet the Shaikh Abbas calls you servants. Did not Jesus make you free men in spirit and truth? Yet does the Ameer make you slaves to shame and corruption. Did not Jesus raise up your heads heavenward? Yet you lower them to the earth. Did He not pour the light into your hearts? Yet you submerge it in darkness. God has surely sent your souls into this life to be as a lighted torch growing in knowledge and increasing in beauty in their search after the secrets of the days and the nights. Yet you cover it with ashes and it is extinguished. God has given to your spirits wings to soar aloft into the realms of love and freedom. Then why do you cut them off with your own hands and crawl on the earth like insects? God has planted in your hearts the seeds of happiness, yet do you pull them out and throw them down on the shores for the ravens to pick and the winds to scatter. God has granted you sons and daughters so that you might show them the ways of truth and fill their hearts with the melody of life and leave to them the joy of living as an inheritance without price. Yet do you slumber and leave them for dead in the hands of fortune; strangers in the land that bore them; creatures of despair in the face of the sun. Is not the father who abandons his free-born son as a slave that same one who gives his son a stone when he asks for bread? Have you not seen the birds of the field teach their young to fly? Yet why do you teach your young ones to drag shackles and chains? Have you not seen how the flowers of the valley store their seeds in the sun-warmed earth? Yet do you deliver up your children to the darkness and cold."

Khalil became silent as though his thoughts and his feelings had expanded and grown and his words no longer wore garments. Then he resumed in a low voice:

"The words to which you have hearkened this night are those for which I was driven from the monastery. And the spirit whose stirrings you have felt in your hearts is that spirit which has delivered me bound before you. Should the lord of your fields and the preacher of your Church strike me down, then will I die rejoicing. For in my revealing to you of the truth, which is judged a crime by these tyrants, is the will of the Creator fulfilled."

In Khalil's clear voice was a mystic quality that excited the hearts of the men to wonder and amazement as though they were blind men who saw suddenly. The spirits of the watching women trembled to its sweetness, and their eyes filled with tears. But the Shaikh Abbas and Father Ilyas shook with anger. They tried to prevent the youth from speech, but they were not able, for he addressed that multitude with a divine force like to the tempest in its strength and to the breeze in its softness.

When Khalil had ceased from speaking he drew back a little and stood by the side of Rahel and Maryam. A deep silence descended, for it was as if his spirit, hovering above that spacious hall, were turning the eyes of the villagers toward a far-off place and drawing all power of thought and will from the spirits of the Shaikh and the priest, to make each stand trembling before his own troubled conscience.

Then the Shaikh Abbas stood up, his face drawn and yellow, and berated soundly the men standing about him. In a hoarse voice he shouted: "What ails you, dogs? Are your hearts poisoned and the life in your bodies stopped that you are no longer able to rend this mocking infidel? Has the spirit of this evil one bound your souls and his sorcery shackled your arms that you cannot destroy him?"

Having spoken these words, he seized hold of a sword by his side and advanced upon the pinioned youth to strike him with it. Upon this, one of the crowd, a man of strong build, came between them and said quietly:

"Sheath your sword, master, for he that draws the sword shall by the sword perish."

The Shaikh Abbas trembled and dropped the sword, shouting: "Does a servant oppose his master and benefactor?" And the man answered: "A faithful servant does not join with his master in evil deeds. This youth said only the truth before the people." Another came forward saying: "This youth has spoken naught to merit judgment and persecution." And a woman lifted up her voice and said: "He has not forsworn his faith, neither has he blasphemed the name of God. Why, then, do you call him a heretic?" Then Rahel took courage and came to the front and said: "In truth does this youth speak with our tongues and complain in our name. He is our enemy who wishes the boy evil." The Shaikh Abbas ground his teeth and shouted: "And you, fallen widow, do you likewise rebel? Have you forgotten, then, what thing befell your husband when he rebelled against me five years ago?"

When Rahel heard these words she cried out in pain, trembling like one who happens upon an awful secret. She turned her face to the people and cried out: "Do you hear now the murderer confessing his crime in his anger? Do you remember that my husband was found murdered in the field and you sought his murderer but found him not because he was in hiding behind these walls? My husband was a courageous man. Did you not hear him speak of the Shaikh's evil ways, condemning his actions, rebelling against his cruelty? Now has Heaven revealed to you the slayer of your neighbour and brother and brought him before you. Look you well at him and read the crime writ in his yellowed face. See how he is frightened and uneasy. Observe you all how he hides his face between his hands lest he see your eyes looking on him. Behold the powerful master shaking like a broken reed. The mighty man afraid in your presence like an erring slave. At this moment has God laid bare this killer whom you fear, and rendered naked the evil spirit that has made me a widow among your women and left my daughter an orphan among your children."

Whilst Rahel was thus uttering words that broke over the head of the Shaikh Abbas like a thunderbolt, and the shouting of the men and the screaming of the women descended like firebrands around him, the priest stood up and, taking him by the arm, sat him down on his seat. Then in a voice that trembled he shouted out to the servants: "Seize you this woman who would thus falsely accuse your master and drag her out with this heretic to a dark cell. Who stands in your way is their partner in evil and shall be excommunicated as he is from the holy Church."

But the servants did not move from their places, neither did they heed the command of the priest. They stood still, looking at the pinioned Khalil and Rahel and Maryam. The women stood, the one at his right hand, the other at his left, like two wings spread to fly aloft and cleave the air.

The beard of the priest quivered in his anger and he said: "Do you deny your master's generosity and his beneficence, shameless ones, for the sake of this infidel youth and this lying adulterous woman?" And the oldest among the servants answered him, saying: "We have served the Shaikh Abbas for the sake of food and shelter, but never shall we be his slaves." So saying, he took off his headdress and cloak and threw them at the feet of the Shaikh. "I no longer wish the favour of these garments lest my spirit remain forever in torment in this place of bloodshed." The other servants did likewise and joined the throng, and on their faces was the light of liberty and freedom.

When Father Ilyas saw what they had done he knew that his authority was no more, and he went out from that house cursing the hour that had brought Khalil to the village.

One of the men in the crowd then came forward and loosed Khalil's bonds. He looked at the Shaikh Abbas, who had fallen across his seat like a corpse, and in a strong and purposeful voice addressed him, saying: "This youth whom you had brought bound before us to be tried as a criminal has lighted the darkness of our hearts and turned our eyes in the way of truth and know-ledge. And this wretched widow woman whom you called shameless and lying has revealed to us the awful secret that lay hidden these six years. We came hither in our haste to see the trial of the innocent and the persecution of the just, but our eyes have been opened and Heaven has laid bare your guilt and your injustice. We will abandon you to your loneliness, and no person shall come near you. We will turn aside from you and ask Heaven to do its will with you."

From all parts of the spacious hall rose the voices of men and women. Said one person: "Come, let us leave this place of sin and crime." Another cried: "Let us follow the youth to the house of Rahel and hear his consoling wisdom and sweet sayings." Yet another shouted: "Let us do Khalil's will, for more than we he knows our needs." This one said: "If we want justice, let us go this morrow to the Ameer Ameen and acquaint him with the misdeeds of the Shaikh Abbas and demand his punishment." And that one called: "We must beg the Ameer to appoint Khalil as our master in this village." Yet another said: "We must complain to the Bishop that Father Ilyas joined with the Shaikh in all he did."

As these voices rose from all sides and fell like sharp arrows on the fluttering breast of the Shaikh, Khalil raised his hand, bidding the crowd to be silent, and exhorted them, saying: "Seek not haste, my brothers and sisters, but rather see and hear. In the name of my love for you I beseech you to go not to the Ameer; he will not give you justice against the Shaikh, for the wild beast does not bite his like. Lay not any complaint against the priest with his superior, for he knows that a house divided against itself falls. Neither seek the Ameer to appoint me as lord of the village, for the faithful servant wants not to be an aid to an evil master. If I be worthy of your love and affection, then let me live among you and let your joys be my joys and your sorrows my sorrows. Let me share your work in the fields and your rest in your dwellings, for if I be not like one of you I shall be naught save as one that preaches virtue but practises evil. And now I have laid the axe to the root of the tree. Therefore let us depart and leave the Shaikh Abbas standing in the courtroom of his conscience before the throne of God, whose sun sets on good and bad alike." Thus having spoken, he left that place, and the multitude followed him, for it was as if there were in him a force that directed their vision.

The Shaikh remained in his place alone like a tower in ruins, as a sorrowing commander in defeat. And when the multitude reached the churchyard, what time the moon was risen and pouring its silvery rays over the heavens, Khalil turned and beheld the faces of men and women looking towards him like a flock that looks up at its shepherd. And his spirit was moved within him and it was as though he found in those poor villagers a symbol of oppressed peoples and saw in those poor huts buried under the snow the symbol of a land submerged in misery and abjection. He stood like a prophet listening to the cry of the ages, and his expression changed and his eyes opened wide as though through his spirit he looked upon all the peoples of the East marching and dragging behind them their chains of servitude across those valleys. He raised his hands heavenward and in a voice in which was the roar of ocean waves cried: "From the depths of these depths do we call thee, O Liberty! Give ear to us. From out of this darkness we lift up our hands to thee. Then look upon us. Upon these snows do we prostrate ourselves before thee. Have mercy upon us. Before thine awful throne we stand and on our bodies the garments of our forefathers stained with their blood; covering our heads with the dust of graves mixed with their remains; bearing the swords that were plunged into their hearts; holding aloft the lances that pierced their breasts; dragging along the chains that slowed their steps; crying the cry that wounded their throats; lamenting their laments, which filled the darkness of their prison; uttering the prayers that rose out of hearts in torment. Give ear, O Liberty, and hear us! From the source of the Nile to the mouth of the Euphrates arises the wailing of souls in unison with the cry of the abyss. From the farthest ends of Arabia to the mountains of Lebanon hands trembling in the agony of death reach out to thee. From the shores of the gulf to the fringe of the desert, eyes brimming with the heart's tears are lifted up to thee. Turn, O Liberty, and behold us.

"In those huts standing in the shadow of poverty and degradation they bare their breasts before thee. In the emptinesses of houses sunk in the darkness of ignorance hearts are laid before thee. In the corners of dwellings obscured by the mist of falsehood and tyranny souls incline toward thee. Look thou upon us, O Liberty, and have mercy. In the schools and places of learning despairing youth speaks to thee, and in the churches and mosques the Book cast aside turns to thee. In the court-houses the law, long neglected, calls upon thee. Have pity, O Liberty, and deliver us. In our narrow streets the merchant bar-ters his days, and their price he gives to thieves of the West, and none gives him counsel. In our barren fields the peasant digs the soil with his fingernails and sows it with seeds of his heart and waters it with his tears, but reaps naught of it save thorns, and none teaches him. In our arid plains the Bedouin walks barefoot and naked and hungry, and none takes pity on him. Speak thou, O Liberty, and teach us.

"Our lambs graze off thorns and thistles instead of grass and herbs, and our calves gnaw at tree roots instead of grain, and our horses feed off dried plants for lack of barley. Come thou, O Liberty, and save us. Since the beginning has the darkness of night lain over our souls. When will come the dawn? From prison cell to prison cell are our bodies moved while the ages pass us by and mock. Until when must we endure the mocking of the ages? From one heavy yoke to another yet heavier move our necks while the peoples of the earth look from afar and laugh. For how long must we suffer the laughing of the peoples? From shackle to shackle do our legs drag. Our shackles are not destroyed, nor yet do we perish. For how long yet must we live?

"From the bondage of Egypt to the Babylonian exile; to the cruelty of Persia and the servitude of Greece; to the tyranny of Rome and Mongol oppression and the greed of Europe. Whither do we go now? When shall we reach the end of this mountain road? Yea, from the grip of the Pharaoh into the clutch of Nebuchadnezzar; to the hands of Alexander and Herod's swords and the talons of Nero and the teeth of the Devil. Into whose hands must we fall, and when will Death take us so that we may find rest in annihilation?

"By the strength of our arms were raised the columns of temples and places of worship to the glory of their gods; and on our backs were carried the mortar and stones to build walls and towers to make strong their defence; and by the strength of our bodies were the pyramids set up to make their names everlasting. Until when shall we build palaces and mansions and yet dwell in huts and caves? And fill the bins and storehouses while yet we eat of garlic and leeks? Until when shall we weave cloths of silk and wool and yet clothe ourselves in rags and tatters? Because of their wickedness and guile family was set against family; community against community; tribe against tribe. For how long shall we be scattered like dust before this cruel storm and quarrel like hungry whelps around this stinking corpse? The better to keep their thrones and ease of mind did they arm the Druse against the Arab and stir up the Shiite against the Sunnite and encourage the Kurd to slaughter the Bedouin and put Moslem to dispute with Christian. Until when will brother continue to slay brother on his mother's bosom? Until when will neighbour threaten neighbour by the grave of the beloved? Until when will the Cross be separated from the Crescent before the face of God?

"Give ear, O Liberty. Hear us, O mother of all people, and look to us. Speak now in the tongue of but one person, for one spark suffices to kindle dry straw. Awaken with the rustle of thy wings the spirit of one man among us, for from one cloud alone comes the lightning, which lights up with a single flash the spaces of the valleys and the mountaintops. Scatter with thy power these black clouds and descend like the thunderstorm and bring down as with a catapult those thrones raised upon bones and skulls, gilded with the gold of tribute and bribery, covered over with blood and tears. Hear us, O Liberty. Have mercy, O daughter of Athens. Save us, O sister of Rome; deliver us, O companion of Moses. Succour us, O beloved of Muhammad; teach us, O bride of Jesus. Strengthen our hearts that we may live or harden the arms of our enemies that we may perish and rest eternally in peace."

As Khalil was thus exhorting the heavens, the eyes of the peasants were upon him, and their love burst forth with the melody of his voice; their spirits soared with his spirit and their hearts beat in rhythm with his heart. And it was as though he were to them as is the soul to the body in that hour. After he had ceased from speaking he looked toward the multitude and in a quiet voice said: "Night has gathered us together in the house of the Shaikh Abbas that we might see the light of day;

and oppression has brought us before this cold clearness that we might understand one another and gather as young fowl beneath the wings of the eternal Spirit. Let us go now, each to his bed, and each one ready to meet with his brother on the morrow."

Having spoken, he walked away, following the steps of Rahel and Maryam to their hut. The people dispersed, every one going his way, pondering on what he had heard and seen and feeling the caress of a new life within him.

An hour had not passed before the lights in those huts were extinguished. Silence drew its veil over the village, and dreams carried away the spirits of the peasants. Only the spirit of Shaikh Abbas remained awake with the phantoms of the night, trembling before his crimes, tormented by his thoughts.

VIII

Two months had passed and Khalil continued to pour out the secrets of his spirit into the hearts of the villagers; speaking to them every day of the usurping of their rights and showing to them the life of the ambitious monks, relating to them stories of their harsh rulers, forging between him and them a strong link like to those eternal laws which bind together many bodies. They listened to him with joy as the parched land rejoices in the rainfall. They repeated his words in solitude, clothing the souls of their meaning with a body of love. They paid no heed to Father Ilyas, who took to fawning upon them since the uncovering of the crimes of his companion the Shaikh. Now he approached them pliable as a candle where once he was as hard as granite.

As for the Shaikh Abbas, he had become afflicted by an ill of the spirit, like a madness. He walked back and forth through the halls of his dwelling like an imprisoned tiger. He called on his servants in a loud voice, but none answered him save the walls. He shouted for his men to assist him, but none came except his wretched wife, who had borne his cruelty as had the peasants his tyranny. And when Lent came, and with it Heaven's heralding the coming of spring, the days of the Shaikh were ended with the passing of winter. He died in agony and terror, and his soul went its way, borne off upon the carpet of his deeds to stand in its nakedness before that throne whose existence we feel but see not.

Many and differing were the opinions of the peasants on the manner of his death. Some said that he lost his reason and died insane. Others that despair poisoned his life when his authority fell and drove him to die at his own hand. But the women who went to console his wife told their men that he died from fear and terror because the ghost of Sam'an Al-Rami used to appear before him in garments covered in blood and lead him by force at the midnight hour to the place where he had been found slain five years before.

And the month of Nisan came and announced to the people of the village the hidden love between Khalil and Maryam, daughter of Rahel. Their faces were lighted with joy and their hearts danced with happiness, for they no more feared that the youth who had awakened their hearts to a higher and wider realm would go from them. They went round, each one rejoicing with the other in his becoming a beloved neighbour to each one of them.

And when the days of the harvest came, the peasants went out to the fields and gathered in the yield to the threshing-floors. The Shaikh Abbas was not there to seize the crop and have it carried away to his bins and store-houses. Each peasant reaped what he had sown, and those huts were full with corn and maize and wine and oil. And Khalil was their partner in their toil and joy. He helped them gather in the crops and press the grapes and pick the fruits. He did not set apart himself from them save in his love and endeavor. From that year to our days each peasant in that village has reaped in joy that which he sowed in tears; and gathered up with rejoicing the fruits of the orchard which he planted with toil and labour. And the land became the land of him that tilled it and the vineyards the portion of him that cultivated them.

Half a century has now passed since these happenings, and an awakening has come to the people of Lebanon. As the wayfarer

goes his way toward the forest of the Cedars he stops and con-
templates the beauty of that village sitting like a bride on the
side of the valley. He sees the huts that were, as fine houses deep
in the fertile fields and blossoming orchards. And should that
wayfarer ask a villager concerning the Shaikh Abbas, he would
answer, pointing to a heap of stones and ruined walls, saying:
"This is his palace and this is the history of his life." And should
he be asked about Khalil, he would raise his hand toward heaven,
saying: "Yonder dwells our good friend Khalil; the history of
his life have our fathers inscribed in shining letters upon the
leaves of our hearts, and the days and nights shall not efface
them."

NYMPHS OF THE VALLEY

Translated from the Arabic by H. M. Nahmad

CONTENTS

MARTHA

I

HER FATHER DIED whilst she was still in the cradle, and her mother before she was ten years old. She was left an orphan in the house of a poor neighbour who lived with his wife and children and existed on the fruits of the soil in a small isolated hamlet amidst the beautiful valleys of Lebanon.

Her father died and bequeathed to her nothing save his name and a poor hut standing among the nut trees and poplars. From her mother she inherited only tears of grief and her orphan state. She sojourned a stranger in the land of her birth; alone among the intertwining trees and towering rocks. Each morning she walked barefooted in a tattered dress behind a milch cow to a part of the valley where the pasture was rich, and sat in the shade of a tree. She sang with the birds and wept with the brook while she envied the cow its abundance of food. She looked at the flowers and watched the fluttering butterflies. When the sun sank below the horizon and hunger overtook her she returned to the hut and sat beside her guardian's daughter and ate greedily of the maize bread with a little dried fruit and beans dipped in vinegar and olive oil. After the meal she spread some dry straw on the ground and laid herself down, her head resting on her arms. She slept and sighed, wishing that life were one long deep sleep undisturbed by dreams or awakening. At the approach of dawn her guardian roused her roughly to attend to his needs and she awoke from her slumbers afraid and trembling at his harshness and anger. Thus passed the years for Martha, the unfortunate, amongst those distant hills and valleys.

Soon she began to feel in her heart the stirring of emotions she had never before known; it was like becoming aware of the perfume in the heart of a flower. Dreams and strange thoughts crowded upon her like a flock that comes across a watercourse.

She became a woman, and she likened herself in some vague manner to fresh virgin soil that is yet to be planted with the seeds of knowledge and feel upon it the imprints of experience. A girl profound and pure of soul whom a decree of fate had exiled to that farmstead where life passed through its appointed phases with the seasons of the year. It was as though she were a shadow of an unknown god residing between the earth and the sun.

Those of us who have spent the greater part of our existence in crowded cities know little of the life of the inhabitants of the villages and hamlets tucked away in Lebanon. We are carried along on the current of modern civilization. We have forgotten – or so we tell ourselves – the philosophy of that beautiful and simple life of purity and spiritual cleanliness. If we turned and looked we would see it smiling in the spring; drowsing with the summer sun; harvesting in the autumn, and in the winter at rest; like our mother Nature in all her moods. We are richer in material wealth than those villagers; but their spirit is a nobler spirit than ours. We sow much but reap nothing. But what they sow they also reap. We are the slaves of our appetites; they, the children of their contentment. We drink the cup of life, a liquid clouded with bitterness, despair, fear, weariness. They drink of it clear.

Martha reached the age of sixteen years. Her soul was a polished mirror reflecting all the loveliness of the fields, and her heart was like the wide valleys which threw back voices in echo.

One autumn day when nature seemed filled with sadness she sat by a spring, freed from its earthly prison like thoughts from the imagination of a poet, looking at the fluttering of yellowed leaves as they fell from the trees. She watched the wind playing with them as Death plays with the souls of men. She gazed on the flowers and saw that they were withered and their hearts dried up and broken into little pieces. They were storing their seeds in the earth as women their trinkets and jewellery during times of war and disturbance.

While she sat thus looking at the flowers and trees and sharing with them their pain at the passing of summer, she heard the sounds of hoofs on the broken stones of the valley. She turned round and beheld a horseman riding slowly toward her; his bearing and dress told of ease and wealth. He dismounted from his horse and greeted her gently, in a manner no man had ever used to her before.

"I have strayed from the road leading down to the coast. Could you direct me to it?" he asked.

She stood upright by the edge of the spring, straight like a young branch, and answered him: "I do not know, my master, but I will go and ask my guardian; for he knows." She uttered these words, at the same time feeling a little afraid, with a shyness and modesty that heightened her tenderness and beauty. She was about to go when the man stopped her. The red wine of his youth coursed strongly through his veins. His look toward her changed as he said: "No, do not go." She remained standing and wondering, for she felt in his voice a force that prevented her from movement. She stole a glance at him. He was looking at her carefully; a look whose meaning she could not understand. Then he smiled at her in so bewitching a manner as to make her want to weep at its very sweetness. He let his eye rest with affection on her bare feet, her pretty wrists, her smooth neck, her soft thick hair. He noted, with a rising passion, her gleaming skin given her by the sun, and her arms, which nature had made strong. But she stayed silent and ashamed. She did not want to go away, nor, for reasons she was unable to divine, could she find power to speak.

The milch cow returned that evening to the enclosure without her mistress; for Martha did not go back. When her guardian came home from the fields, he sought her in all the hollows but did not find her. He called her by name but there came no answer save echoes from the cave and the soughing of the wind in the trees. He returned sorrowing to his hut and told his wife. She wept silently throughout that night, saying within herself: "I have seen her in a dream in the claws of a wild beast, who tore her body to pieces the while she smiled and wept."

That is what I gleaned of the life of Martha in that pretty hamlet. I learned it of an old villager who had known her since the days of her childhood. She had disappeared from those places leaving nothing behind her save a few tears in the eyes of the guardian's woman, and a pathetic memory that rode on the morning breeze over the valley and then, like the breath of a child on a windowpane, faded.

II

I returned to Beirut in the autumn of 1900 after having passed my college vacation in North Lebanon. Before returning to my studies I spent a week wandering around in the town with some of my fellow students, savouring with them the delights of freedom, for which youth hungers and which is denied it at home and within the four walls of a classroom. It is like a bird that, finding its cage door open, flies to and fro, its heart swelling with song and the joy of escape.

Youth is a beautiful dream, but its sweetness is enslaved by the dullness of books and its awakening is a harsh one.

Shall there come a day when wise men are able to unite the dreams of youth and the delights of learning as reproach brings together hearts in conflict? Shall there come a day when man's teacher is nature, and humanity is his book and life his school? Will that day be?

We know not, but we feel the urgency that moves us ever upwards toward a spiritual progress, and that progress is an understanding of the beauty of all creation through the kindness of ourselves and the dissemination of happiness through our love of that beauty.

That evening as I sat in the porch of my lodgings watching the moving crowds and listening to the cries of the street vendors, each extolling the excellence of his wares and foods, a boy came up to me. He was about five years of age and clad in rags and tatters, and on his shoulder he carried a tray filled with bunches of flowers. In a voice broken and feeble, as though handed down to him as a heritage of long suffering, he asked me to buy a flower from him.

I looked into his small pale face and remarked his eyes, dark with the shadows of weariness and poverty; his mouth, open a little like a wound in a scarred breast; his emaciated bare arms and his puny little body bent over the tray of flowers like a rose-plant yellowed and withered among fresh green plants. I saw all these things as it were at one glance, and in my pity I smiled, a smile in which was something of tears. Those smiles that break forth from the depths of our hearts and rise to our lips. Should we heed them not, they find outlet through our eyes.

I bought some of his flowers, but it was his speech that I wished to buy, for I felt that behind his wistful looks was curtained off the act of a tragedy – a tragedy of the poor, playing perpetually upon the stage of the days. An act seldom seen because it is a tragedy. When I spoke to him with kind words, he grew friendly as though having found a body in whom he could seek protection and safety. He gazed at me in wonder, for he and his like are accustomed only to rough words from those other boys who look upon boys of the streets as things defiled and of no account and not as little souls wounded by the arrows of fortune. I then asked him his name.

"Fouad," he answered, with his eyes averted to the ground.

"The son of whom, and where are your people?"

"I am the son of Martha, woman of Ban."

"And your father?" I asked.

He shook his small head as one who knows not what a father is.

"Then where is your mother, Fouad?"

"At home, ill."

These few words from the boy's lips smote my ears, and out of them my inmost feelings fashioned strange and melancholy forms and figures for I knew, at once, that the unfortunate Martha whose story I had heard from the villager was now ill in Beirut. That girl who yesterday was among the trees and valleys away from harm was today suffering the harshness of hunger and pain in a city. The orphan girl who passed the days of her childhood with nature, tending her cows in the beautiful fields, had been carried away on the tide of corrupt civilization to become a prey in the grasp of misery and misfortune.

As these things passed through my mind the boy continued to gaze at me as though he saw with the eye of his innocent spirit my broken heart.

He made as if to go away but I seized his hand and said: "Take me to your mother; I want to see her."

He led the way, walking before me silent and wondering. From time to time he looked back to see if in truth I was following behind him. With feelings of fear and dread I walked on through dirty streets wherein the air was leavened with the breath of death, past tumbledown houses wherein evil men practised their evil deeds behind the curtains of night. Through winding alleyways that twisted and writhed like vipers I walked behind that boy of tender years and innocent heart and unvoiced courage. The courage of those acquainted with the wiles and tricks of the dregs in the midst of a city known to the East as the "Bride of Syria" and the pearl in the crown of kings. We reached the outskirts of the quarter at last, and the boy entered a mean dwelling to which the passage of years had left only a crumbling side.

I went in after him, my heart beating rapidly as I approached the room. I found myself in the middle of a room the air of which was damp. It possessed no furniture save a lamp whose feeble light cut the gloom with its yellow rays, and a couch whose appearance spoke of dire poverty and destitution and want. Upon the couch was a sleeping woman with her face turned to the wall as though taking refuge in it from the cruelties of the world; or mayhap seeing in its stones a heart more tender and compassionate than the hearts of men. The boy went up to her crying: "Mother, Mother." She turned round and saw him pointing at me. At this she made a movement beneath the tattered bed-coverings and, in a voice rendered bitter by the sufferings of a spirit in agony, cried:

"What do you want, O man? Do you come to purchase the last shreds of my life so that you might defile it with your lust? Go from me, for the streets are filled with women ready to sell their bodies and souls cheaply. But I, I have naught for sale save a few gasps of breath, and those will Death soon buy with the peace of the grave."

I moved near to the bed. Her words moved me to the depths of my heart for they were the epitome or her tale of sorrow. I spoke to her and wished that my feelings might flow with my words.

"Be not afraid of me, Martha. I come not to you as a ravening beast but as a sorrowing man. I am of Lebanon and long have I dwelt in the midst of those valleys and villages by the forest of the cedars. Fear not, then, Martha."

She listened to my words and knew in her being that they rose from the deepnesses of a spirit that wept with her, for she shook and trembled upon her bed like a naked branch before the winter wind. She put her hands over her face as though she would hide herself from that memory, frightening in its sweetness, bitter in its beauty. After a silence in which was a sighing her face reappeared between her trembling shoulders. I saw her sunken eyes gaze at an unseen thing standing in the emptiness of the room, and her dry lips quiver with the quiver of despair. In her throat the approach of death rattled and with it a deep and broken moaning. Then she spoke. Entreaty and supplication gave her utterance, and weakness and pain brought back her voice:

"You have come here from kindness and compassion, and if pity for the sinful be deemed a pious deed, and compassion on those who have gone astray a meritorious act, then shall Heaven reward you for me. I pray you go from here and return whence you come, for your presence in this place will earn for you shame, and your pity for me will bring insult and contempt upon you. Go, go ere anybody see you in this foul room, filthy with the filth of swine. Walk swiftly and cover your face with your cloak so that no passer-by may know you. The compassion that fills you will not bring back my purity, neither will it wipe out my sin, nor stay the strong hand of Death from me. My wretchedness and guilt have banished me to these dark depths. Let not your pity bring you near to blemish. I am a leper dwelling amidst graves. Do not approach me lest people hold you unclean and draw away from you. Return now, but mention not my name in those sacred valleys, for the shepherd will deny the diseased lamb in fear for his flock. If you should make mention of me say that Martha, woman of Ban, is dead; say naught else."

She then took her son's two small hands and kissed them sadly. She sighed and spoke again:

"People will look upon my child with contempt and a mocking, saying this one is the offshoot of sin; this is the son of Martha, the harlot; this is the child of shame, of chance. They will say of him more than that, for they are blind and will not see and know not that his mother has purified his childhood with her agony and tears and atoned for his life with her sorrow and misfortune. I shall die leaving him an orphan among the children of the streets, alone in this pitiless existence, bequeathing to him naught save a terrible memory. If he be a coward and a weakling, he will be ashamed before this memory; if he be courageous and just, then will his blood be stirred. If Heaven should perchance preserve him and let him grow to be a man in strength, then will he be helped by Heaven against those who have wronged him and his mother. If he should die and be delivered from the snare of years, he shall find me beyond, where all is light and rest, awaiting his coming."

My heart inspired me to speak:

"You are no leper, Martha, even if you dwelt among graves. You are not unclean even if life has put you in the hands of the unclean. The dross of the flesh cannot reach out its hand to the pure spirit, and the masses of snow cannot kill the living seeds. What is this life except a threshing-floor of sorrows upon which the sheaves of souls are trodden ere giving up their yield? But woe to those ears that are left without the threshing-floor, for the ants of the earth shall carry them away and the birds of the sky shall take them up and they shall not enter into the storehouses of the master of the field.

"You are oppressed, Martha, and he who has oppressed you is a child of the palaces, great of wealth and little of soul. You are persecuted and despised, but it were better that a person should be the oppressed than that he should be the oppressor; and fitter that he should be a victim to the frailty of human instincts than that he should be powerful and crush the flowers of life and disfigure the beauties of feeling with his desire. The soul is a link in the divine chain. The fiery heat may twist and distort this link and destroy the beauty of its roundness, but it cannot transmute its gold to another metal; rather will it become even more glittering. But woe to the bruised and the weak when the fire shall consume him and make him ashes to be blown by the winds and scattered over the face of the desert! Ay, Martha, you are a flower crushed beneath the feet of the animal that is concealed in a human being. Heavy-shod feet have trodden you down, but they have not destroyed that fragrance which goes up with the widow's lament and the orphan's cry and the poor man's sigh toward Heaven, the fount of justice and mercy. Take comfort, Martha, in that you are the flower crushed and not the foot that has crushed it."

She listened with intentness as I spoke, and her face was lighted up with solace as the clouds are illuminated by the soft rays of the setting sun. She motioned me to sit beside her. I did so, seeking to learn from her eloquent features of the hidden things of her sad spirit. She had the look of one who knows that he is about to die. It was the look of a girl yet in the springtime of life who felt the footfalls of Death by her broken-down bed. The look of a woman forsaken who yesteryear stood in the beautiful valleys of Lebanon filled with life and strength, but now exhausted and awaiting deliverance from the bonds of existence.

After a moving silence she gathered together the remnants of her strength. She started to speak, her tears adding meaning to the words, her very soul in every breath she took:

"Yes, I am oppressed. I am the prey to the animal in men. I am a flower trodden underfoot.... I was sitting by the edge of the spring as he rode by. He spoke kindly to me and said that I was beautiful, that he loved me and would not forsake me. He said that the wide spaces were places of desolation and the valleys the abode of birds and jackals.... He took me and drew me to his breast and kissed me. Until then I knew not the taste of kisses, for I was an orphan and outcast. He mounted me behind him on the back of his horse and took me to a fine house standing alone. There he gave me garments of silk and perfumes and rich food and drink.... All this did he do, smiling, and behind soft words and loving gestures did he conceal his lust and animal desires. After he had satisfied himself of my body and brought low my spirit in humility he went away, leaving inside me a living flame fed by my liver, and it grew in swiftness. Then I went out into this darkness from between the embers of pain and the bitterness of weeping. . . . So was life cut into two parts; one weak and grieving, and the other small and crying into the silences of the night, seeking return to the vast emptiness. In that lonely house my oppressor left me and my suckling child to endure the cruelties of hunger and cold and aloneness. No companion had we save fear and haunting; neither had we helper save weeping and lament. His friends came to learn of my place and know of my need and weakness. They came to me, one following upon another. They wanted to buy me with wealth and give me bread against my honour. . . . Ah, many times did my own hand determine to set free my spirit. But I turned from that, for my life belonged not to me alone; my child had part in it. My child, whom Heaven had thrust aside from it into this life as it had exiled me from life and cast me into the depths of the abyss. . . . Behold now, the hour is at hand and my bridegroom Death is come after long absence to lead me to his soft bed."

After a deep silence that was like the presence of spirits in flight, she lifted up eyes veiled by the shadows of death and in a gentle voice said:

"O Justice who are hidden, concealed behind these terrifying images, you, and you alone, hear the cry of my departing spirit and the call of my neglected heart. You alone do I pray and beseech to have mercy on me and guard with your right hand my child and with your left receive my spirit."

Her strength ebbed and her sighing grew weak. She looked toward her son with grief and tenderness, then lowered her eyes slowly and in a voice that was almost a silence recited:

"Our Father which art in heaven, hallowed be Thy name. . . . Thy kingdom come. Thy will be done on earth as it is in heaven. . . . Forgive us our transgressions. . . ."

Her voice ceased, but her lips still moved for a while. When they grew still, all movement left her body. A shudder ran through her and she sighed and her face became pale. Her spirit departed and her eyes remained gazing at the unseen.

With the coming of dawn Martha's body was laid in a wooden coffin and carried on the shoulders of two poor persons. We

buried her in a deserted field far out from the town, for the priests would not pray over her remains, neither would they let her bones rest in the cemetery, wherein the cross stood guard over the graves. No mourners went to that distant burial-ground save her son and another boy whom the adversities of existence had taught compassion.

DUST OF THE AGES AND
THE ETERNAL FIRE

I

[Autumn, 116 B.C.]

THE NIGHT WAS still and all life slept in the City of the Sun.[1]
The lamps in the houses scattered around the great temples in
the midst of olive and laurel trees had long been extinguished.
The rising moon spilled its rays over the whiteness of the tall
marble columns which stood upright like giant sentinels in the
tranquil night over the shrines of the gods. They looked in
wonder and awe toward the towers of Lebanon, dwelling in
rugged places on distant heights.

At that magic hour poised between the spirits of the sleeping
and dreams of the infinite, Nathan, son of the priest, entered
the temple of Astarte.[2] He carried in his trembling hand a torch
and kindled with it the lamps and the censers. The sweet smell
of frankincense and myrrh rose in the air, and the image of the
goddess was adorned with a delicate veil like the veil of desire
and longing that enshrines the human heart. He prostrated him-
self before an altar overlaid with ivory and gold, raised his hands
in supplication, and lifted eyes filled with tears to the heavens.
In a voice strangled with grief and broken by harsh sobs, he
cried:

"Mercy, O great Astarte. Mercy, O goddess of love and
beauty. Have pity on me and lift the hand of death from off my
beloved, whom my soul has chosen to do your will. The potions
and powders of the physicians have availed nothing, and the

1 I.e., Baalbek, city of Baal, the sun god. The ancients knew it as
Heliopolis; it was one of the loveliest cities of Syria, and its ruins still stand.
2 Goddess of love and beauty among the ancient Phœnicians, who wor-
shipped her in Tyre, Sidon, Byblos, and Baalbek. The Greek Aphrodite
and the Roman Venus.

charms of the priests and wise men are in vain. There remains but your sacred name to help and succour me. Answer, then, my prayer; look to my contrite heart and agony of spirit, and let her that is the part of my soul live so that we may rejoice in the secrets of your love and exult in the beauty of youth, which proclaims your glory. . . . From the depths do I cry unto you, sacred Astarte. From out of the darkness of this night do I seek the protection of your mercy. . . . Hear my cry! I am your servant Nathan, son of Hiram the priest, who has dedicated his life to the service of your altar. I love a maiden and have taken her for my own, but the brides of the Jinn have breathed upon her beautiful body the breath of a strange disease. They have sent the messenger of death to lead her to their enchanted caves. He now lies like a roaring hungry beast by her couch, spreading his black wings over her and stretching out his defiled hands to wrest her from me. Because of this have I come to you. Take pity on me and let her live. She is a flower that has not lived to enjoy the summer of its life; a bird whose joyful song greeting the dawn is cut off. Save her from the clutches of death and we will sing praises and make burnt offerings to the glory of your name. We will bring sacrifices to your altar and fill your vessels with wine and sweet scented oil and spread your tabernacle with roses and jasmine. We will burn incense and sweet-smelling aloe wood before your image. . . . Save her, O goddess of miracles, and let love conquer death, for you are the mistress of love and death."

He stopped speaking, weeping and sighing in his agony. Then he continued: "Alas, sacred Astarte, my dreams are shattered and the last breath of my life is fast ebbing; my heart is dying within me and my eyes are burned with tears. Sustain me through your compassion and let my beloved remain with me."

At that moment one of his slaves entered, came slowly toward him, and whispered in his ear: "She has opened her eyes, my lord, and looks around her couch but does not see you. I come to call you, for she cries for you continually."

Nathan rose and went out quickly, the slave following. On reaching his palace he entered the room of the sick girl and stood over her bed. He took her thin hand in his and kissed her lips repeatedly as though he would breathe new life into her emaciated body. She turned her face, which had been hidden among the silken pillows, toward him and opened her eyes a little. Upon her lips appeared the shadow of a smile – all that remained of life in her beautiful body; the last ray of light from a departing spirit; the echo from the cry of a heart fast approaching its end. She spoke, and her breath came in short gasps like that of a starveling child.

"The gods call me, betrothed of my soul, and Death has come to part us.... Grieve not, for the will of the gods is sacred and the demands of Death are just.... I am going now, but the twin cups of love and youth are still full in our hands and the ways of sweet life lie before us.... I am going, my beloved, to the meadows of the spirits, but I shall return to this world. Astarte brings back to this life the souls of lovers who have gone to the infinite before they have tasted of the delights of love and the joys of youth.... We shall meet again, Nathan, and together drink of the morning dew from the cups of the narcissus and rejoice in the sun with the birds of the fields.... Farewell, my beloved."

Her voice grew low and her lips began to tremble like the petals of a flower before the dawn breeze. Her lover clasped her to him, wetting her neck with his tears. When his lips touched her mouth they found it cold like ice. He gave a terrible cry, rent his garments, and threw himself upon her dead body, while his spirit in its agony hovered between the deep sea of life and the abyss of death.

In the stillness of that night the eyelids of those who slept trembled, and the women of the quarter grieved, and the souls of children were afraid, for the darkness was rent by loud cries of mourning and bitter weeping rising from the palace of Astarte's priest. When morning came the people sought Nathan to console him and soothe him in his affliction, but they did not find him.

Many days later, when the caravan from the east arrived, its leader related how he had seen Nathan far off in the wilderness wandering like a stricken soul with the gazelles of the deserts.

*

711

Centuries passed and the feet of time obliterated the work of the ages. The gods went from the land, and other gods came in their stead — gods of anger wedded to destruction and ruin. They razed the fine temple of the City of the Sun and destroyed its beautiful palaces. Its verdant gardens became dry, and drought overtook its fertile fields. Nothing remained in that valley except decaying ruins to haunt the memory with ghosts of yesterday and recall the faint echo of psalms chanted to a past glory. But the ages that pass on and sweep away the works of man cannot destroy his dreams, nor can they weaken his innermost feelings and emotions; for these endure as long as the immortal spirit. Here, perhaps, they are concealed; there they may go into hiding like the sun at eventide or the moon with the approach of the morning.

II

[Spring, A.D. 1890]

DAY WAS WANING and the light was fading as the sun gathered up her garments from the plains of Baalbek. Ali Al-Husaini[1] turned with his flock toward the ruins of the temple and sat down by the fallen pillars. They looked like ribs of a long-forgotten soldier that had been broken in battle and rendered naked by the elements. The sheep gathered around him brows-ing, lulled into safety by the melodies of his pipe.

Midnight came and the heavens cast the seeds of the morrow into its dark depths. The eyelids of Ali grew tired with the spectres of wakefulness. His mind became weary with the pass-ing of the processions of imagination marching through the awful silence amidst the ruined walls. He supported himself on his arm while sleep crept upon him and covered his wakefulness lightly with the folds of its veil as the fine mist touches the surface of a calm lake.

Forgotten was his earthly self as he met his spiritual self; his hidden self filled with dreams transcending the laws and teach-ings of men. A vision appeared before his eyes and things hidden revealed themselves to him. His spirit stood apart from the procession of time ever hurrying on toward nothingness. It stood alone before the serried ranks of thoughts and contending emotions. He knew, or he was about to know, for the first time in his life, the causes of this spiritual hunger overtaking his youth. A hunger uniting all the bitterness and sweetness in existence. A thirst bringing together a cry of yearning and the serenity of fulfilment. A longing that all the glory of this world cannot blot out nor the course of life conceal.

For the first time in his life Ali Al-Husaini felt a strange sensa-tion awakened in him by the ruins of the temple. A feeling without form of the remembrance of incense from the censers. A haunting feeling that played unceasingly upon his senses as the fingertips of a musician play upon the strings of his lute. A new feeling welled up from out of nothingness – or perhaps it

---

1 The Husainis are an Arab tribe dwelling in tents around Baalbek.

713

was from something. It grew and developed until it embraced the whole of his spiritual being. It filled his soul with an ecstasy near to death in its kindness, with a pain sweet in its bitterness, agreeable in its harshness. A feeling born of the vast spaces of a minute filled with sleepiness. A minute that gave birth to the patterns of the ages as the nations grow from one seed.

Ali looked toward the ruined shrine, and his weariness gave place to an awakening of the spirit. The ruined remains of the altar appeared to his sight and the places of the fallen pillars and the foundations of the crumbling walls grew clear and sharp. His eyes became glazed and his heart beat violently, and then suddenly, as with one who was till then sightless, the light returned to his eyes and he began to see – and he thought and reflected. And out of the chaos of thought and confusion of reflection were born the phantoms of memory, and he remembered. He remembered those pillars standing upright in greatness and pride. He recalled the silver lamps and censers surrounding the image of an awe-inspiring goddess. He recalled the venerable priests laying their offerings before an altar overlaid with ivory and gold. He recalled the maidens beating their tambourines and the youths chanting praises to the goddess of love and beauty. He remembered, and saw these figures becoming clear before his gaze. He felt the impressions of sleeping things stirring in the silences of his depths. But remembrance brings back naught save shadowy forms, which we see from the past of our lives; neither does it bring back to our ears except the echoes of voices that they once heard. What then was the link joining these haunting memories to the past life of a youth reared among the tents, who passed the springtime of his life tending his sheep in the wilderness?

Ali rose and walked among the ruins and broken stones. Those distant remembrances raised the covering of forgetfulness from his mind's eyes as a woman brushes away a cobweb from the glass of her mirror. And so it was until he reached the heart of the temple and then stood still as though a magnetic attraction in the earth were drawing his feet. And then he suddenly saw before him a broken statue lying on the ground. Involuntarily he prostrated himself before it. His feelings overflowed within him like the flowing of blood from an open wound; his heart-beats rose and fell, like the rise and fall of sea waves. He was humbled in its sight and he sighed a bitter sigh and wept in his grief, for he felt an aloneness that wounded and a distance that annihilated, separating his spirit from the beautiful spirit that was by his side ere he entered this life. He felt his very essence as naught save part of a burning flame that God had separated from his self before the beginning of time. He felt the light fluttering of wings in his burning bones, and around the relaxed cells of his brain a strong and mighty love taking possession of his heart and soul. A love that revealed the hidden things of the spirit to the spirit, and by its actions separated the mind from the regions of measurement and weight. A love that we hear speaking when the tongues of life are silent; that we behold standing as a pillar of fire when darkness hides all things. That love, that god, had fallen in this hour upon the spirit of Ali Al-Husaini and awakened in it feelings bitter and sweet as the sun brings forth the flowers side by side with thorns.

What thing is this love? Whence does it come? What does it want of a youth resting with his flock among the ruined shrines? What is this wine which courses through the veins of one whom maidens' glances left unmoved? What are these heavenly melodies that rise and fall upon the ears of a bedouin who heard not yet the sweet songs of women?

What thing is this love and whence does it come? What does it want of Ali, busied with his sheep and his flute away from men? Is it something sowed in his heart by man-wrought beauties without the awareness of his senses? Or is it a bright light veiled by the mist and now breaking forth to illumine the emptiness of his soul? Is it perchance a dream come in the stillness of the night to mock at him, or a truth that was and will be to the end of time?

Ali closed his tear-filled eyes and stretched out his hands like a beggar seeking pity. His spirit trembled within him, and out of its trembling came broken sobs in which were both whining complaint and the fire of longing. In a voice that only the faint sound of words lifted above a sigh he called:

"Who are you that are so close to my heart yet unseen by my

715

eyes, separating myself from my self, linking my present to distant and forgotten ages? Are you a nymph, a sprite, come from the world of immortals to speak to me of the vanity of life and the frailty of the flesh? Are you mayhap the spirit of the queen of the Jinn risen from the bowels of the earth to enslave my senses and make of me a laughing-stock among the young men of my tribe? Who are you and what thing is this temptation, quickening and destroying, which has seized hold of my heart? What feelings are these that fill me with fire and light? Who am I and what is this new self I call 'I' yet which is a stranger to me? Is the spring water of life swallowed up with the particles of air and I am become an angel that sees and hears all things secret? Am I drunk of the Devil's brew and become blinded to real things?"

He fell silent for a little while. His emotion grew in strength and his spirit grew in stature. He spoke again:

"O one whom the spirit reveals and brings near and whom the night conceals and makes distant, O beautiful spirit hovering in the spaces of my dreams, you have awakened within my being feelings that were aslumber like flower seeds hidden beneath the snow, and passed as the breeze, the bearer of the breath of the fields. And touched my senses so that they are shaken and disturbed as the leaves of a tree. Let me look upon you, if you be then of body and substance. Command sleep to close my eyelids that I might see you in my dreaming, if you be free of the earth. Let me touch you; let me hear your voice. Tear aside the veil that covers my whole being and destroy the fabric that conceals my divineness. Grant me wings that I might fly after you to the regions of the assembly on high, if you be of those that inhabit there. Touch with magic my eyelids and I shall follow you to the secret places of the Jinn, if you be one of their nymphs. Put your unseen hand upon my heart and possess me, if you be free to let follow whom you will."

So did Ali whisper into the ears of darkness words moving up from the echo of a melody in the depths of his heart. Between his vision and his surroundings flowed phantoms of the night as though they were incense rising out of his hot tears. Upon the walls of the temple appeared enchanted pictures in the colours of the rainbow.

So passed the hour. He rejoiced in his tears and was glad in his grief. He listened to the beating of his heart. He looked to beyond all things as though seeing the pattern of this life slowly fading and in its place a dream wonderful in its beauties, awful in its thought-images. As a prophet who looks to the stars of the heavens watching for divine inspiration, so he awaited the comings of the minutes. His quick sighing stopped his quiet breathing and his spirit forsook him to hover around him and then return as though it were seeking among those ruins a lost loved one.

The dawn broke and the silence trembled at the passing of the breeze. The vast spaces smiled the smiles of a sleeper who has seen in his sleep the image of his beloved. The birds appeared from out of clefts in the ruined walls and moved about among the pillars, singing and calling out one to the others and heralding the approach of day. Ali rose to his feet and put his hand to his hot brow. He looked about him with dull eyes. Then like Adam when his eyes were opened by the breath of God, he looked at all before him and wondered. He approached his sheep and called them; they rose and shook themselves and trotted quietly behind him toward the green pastures.

Ali walked on before his flock, his large eyes looking into the serene atmosphere. His inmost feelings took flight from reality to reveal to him the secrets and closed things of existence; to show him that which had passed with the ages and that which yet remained, as it were in one flash; and in one flash to make him forget it all and bring back to him his yearning and longing. And he found between himself and the spirit of his spirit a veil like a veil between the eye and the light. He sighed, and with his sigh was a flame stripped from his burning heart.

He came to the brook whose babblings proclaimed the secrets of the fields, and he sat him down on its bank beneath a willow tree whose boughs hung down into the water as though they would suck up its sweetness. The sheep cropped the grass with bent heads, the morning dew gleaming on the whiteness of their wool.

After the passing of a minute Ali began to feel the swift beating of his heart and the renewed quaking of his spirit. Like a sleeper whom the sun's rays have startled into wakefulness he moved and looked about him. He beheld a girl coming out from among the trees carrying a jar upon her shoulder. Slowly she walked toward the water; her bare feet were wet with dew. When she came to the edge of the stream and bent to fill her jar she looked toward the opposite bank and her eyes met the eyes of Ali. She gave a cry and threw the jar to the ground and drew back a little. It was the act of one who finds an acquaintance who has been lost.

A minute passed by and its seconds were as lamps lighting the way between their two hearts; creating from the silence strange melodies to bring back to these two the echo of vague remembrances, and show to each one the other in another place, surrounded by shadows and figures, far from that stream and those trees. The one looked at the other with imploring in the eyes of each; and each one found favour in the eyes of the other; each listened to the sighing of the other with ears of love.

They communed, the one with the other, in all the tongues of the spirit. And when full understanding and knowledge possessed their two souls, Ali crossed the stream, drawn thither by an invisible power. He drew nigh to the girl, embraced her, and kissed her lips and her neck and her eyes. She made no movement in his arms, as though the sweetness of the embrace had robbed her of her will and the lightness of touch taken from her all strength. She yielded as the fragrance of the jasmine gives itself up to the currents of air. She dropped her head upon his breast like one exhausted who has found rest, and sighed deeply. A sigh telling of the birth of contentment in a constricted heart and the stirring of life within that had been sleeping and was now awakened. She raised her head and looked into his eyes, the look of one who despises the speech customary among men by the side of silence – the language of the spirit; the look of one who is not content that love should be a soul in a body of words.

The two lovers walked among the willow trees, and the oneness of each was a language speaking of the oneness of both; and an ear listening in silence to the inspiration of love; and a seeing eye seeing the glory of happiness. The sheep followed them, eating the tops of flowers and herbs, and the birds met them from all sides with songs of enchantment.

When they came to the end of the valley, which time the sun had risen and cast upon the heights a golden mantle, they sat down by a rock that protected the violets with its shadow. After a time the girl looked into the black eyes of Ali while the breeze played in her hair as though it were invisible lips that would kiss her. She felt bewitched fingertips caressing her tongue and lips, and her will was a prisoner. She spoke and said in a voice of wounding sweetness:

"Astarte has brought back our souls to this life so that the delights of love and the glory of youth might not be forbidden us, my beloved."

Ali closed his eyes, for the music of her words had made clear the patterns of a dream that he saw ofttimes in his sleep. He felt that unseen wings were bearing him away from that place to a room of strange form. He was standing by the side of a couch on which lay the body of a beautiful woman whose beauty death had taken with the warmth of her lips. He cried out in his anguish at this terrible scene. Then he opened his eyes and found sitting beside him the maiden; upon her lips was a smile of love and in her glance the rays of life. His face lighted up and his spirit was refreshed, the visions were scattered, and he forgot both the past and the future. . . .

The lovers embraced and drank of the wine of kisses until they were satisfied. They slept each enfolded in the arms of the other until the shade moved away and the sun's heat awakened them.

YUHANNA THE MAD

I

AND IN THE summer Yuhanna went out every morning to the
field leading his oxen and his calves and carrying his plough over
his shoulder, the while listening to the songs of the thrushes
and the rustling of the leaves in the trees. At noontide he sat
beside the dancing stream that wound its way through the low-
land of the green meadows, where he ate his food, leaving un-
finished morsels of bread on the grass for the birds. In the
evening, when the setting sun took with it the light of day, he
returned to his humble dwelling, which looked out over the
villages and hamlets of North Lebanon. There, as he sat with
his aged parents and listened in silence to their conversation and
their talk about happenings of the times, a feeling of sleepiness
and restfulness gradually overtook him.

During the winter days he crouched by the fireside for
warmth and listened to the soughing of the wind and the cry of
the elements, pondering the way the seasons followed one upon
another. He looked out of the window toward the valleys under
their garment of snow, and the trees denuded of their leaves like
a crowd of poor people left outside to the mercy of the harsh
cold and the violent winds. Throughout the long nights he
stayed up until after his parents had gone to sleep. Then he
would open a wooden chest and take out of it the book of the
Gospels to read from it in secret by the feeble glow of a lamp,
looking stealthily from time to time in the direction of his
slumbering father, who had forbidden him to read the Book. It
was forbidden because the priests did not allow the simple in
mind to probe the secrets of the teachings of Jesus. If they did
so, then the church would excommunicate them. Thus did
Yuhanna pass the days of his youth between that field of wonder
and beauty and the book of Jesus, filled with the light and the

spirit. Whenever his father spoke he remained silent and in thought, listening to him, but never a word would he utter. Ofttimes he would sit with companions of his own age, silent and looking beyond them to where the evening twilight met the blue of the sky. Whenever he went to church he returned with a feeling of sorrow because the teachings that he heard from the pulpit and altar were not those that he read about in the Gospel. And the life led by the faithful and their leaders was not the beautiful life of which Jesus of Nazareth spoke in His book.

Spring returned to the fields and the meadows, and the snows melted away. On the mountaintops some snow still remained until it in turn melted and ran down the mountainsides and became streams twisting and winding in the valleys below. Soon they met and joined one another until they were swift-flowing rivers, their roaring announcing to all that Nature had awakened from her sleep. The apple and the walnut trees blossomed and the poplar and the willow bore new leaves; and on the heights appeared grass and flowers. Yuhanna grew weary of his existence by the fireside; his calves fretted in their narrow enclosure and hungered for the green pastures, for their store of barley and straw was almost consumed. So he set them free of their manger and led them out to the countryside. He carried his Bible under his cloak so that nobody should see it, until he reached the meadow that rested on the shoulder of the valley near the fields of a monastery which stood up grimly like a tower in the midst of the hillocks.[1] There his calves dispersed to pasture on the grass. Yuhanna sat him down against a rock, now looking across the valley in all its beauty, now reading the words in his book that spoke to him of the Kingdom of Heaven.

It was a day toward the end of Lent, when the villagers, who were abstaining from the eating of meats, awaited impatiently the coming of Easter. But Yuhanna, like all the poor farmers,

1 This is a wealthy monastery in North Lebanon, owning extensive lands. It is known as the Deir Elisha Al-Nabi (i.e., Monastery of the Prophet Elisha). – Author's note.

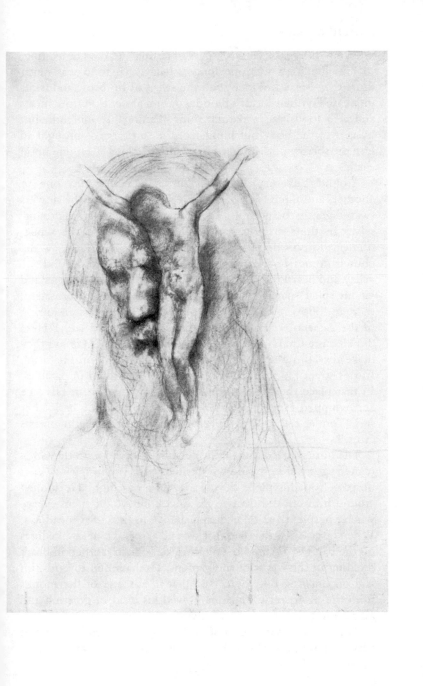

knew no difference between days of fasting and days of feasting; to him life itself was one long fast-day. His food was never more than bread kneaded with the sweat of his brow and fruits purchased with his heart's blood. For him abstention from meats and rich foods was a natural thing. Fasting brought him not hunger of the body but hunger of the spirit; for it brought to him the sorrow of the Son of Man and the close of His life upon earth.

Around Yuhanna the birds fluttered, calling out one to another, and flocks of doves flew swiftly overhead; the flowers swayed gently to and fro in the breeze as though bathing themselves in the warming rays of the sun. He read the while, immersed in his book, and then lifted up his head. He saw the church domes in the towns and villages scattered around the valley and heard the pealing of the bells. He closed his eyes and let his spirit soar high across the centuries to old Jerusalem, there to follow in the footsteps of Jesus in the streets, inquiring of the passers-by about Him. They answered and said: "Here did He cure the blind and make the halt to rise. There did they make for Him a crown of thorns and place it upon His head. In this street He stopped and addressed the crowd in parables. In that place they bound Him to a pillar and spat in His face and whipped Him. In this lane did He forgive the harlot her sins. Yonder fell He to the ground under the weight of His cross."

The hours passed, the while Yuhanna suffered with the God-man in agony of body and was exalted with Him in spirit. When he rose from his place the midday sun was high. He looked around him but did not see his calves; he sought them everywhere, perplexed at their disappearance in those flat meadows. When he reached the road that wound across the fields like lines on the palm of a hand, he saw from afar a man clothed in black standing in the midst of the gardens. He hastened toward him and on drawing near perceived that it was one of the monks from the monastery. Yuhanna bowed his head in greeting and asked him if he had seen his calves in the gardens.

The monk, trying to conceal his anger, looked at him and answered roughly: "Yes, I have seen them, they are yonder;

come, and thou shalt see them." Yuhanna followed the monk until they came to the monastery. There he saw his calves tethered by ropes within a wide enclosure and guarded by another monk. In his hand was a heavy stick with which he belaboured the beasts whenever they moved. When Yuhanna made as if to lead them away, the monk seized him by his cloak and, turning in the direction of the doorway of the monastery, shouted in a loud voice: "Here is the guilty shepherd boy; I have caught him." At his cry priests and monks ran from all directions toward him, led by their Superior, a man distinguished from his companions by his dress of fine material and his soured features. They surrounded Yuhanna like soldiers scrambling after loot. He looked at the Superior and in a gentle voice said: "What have I done that you call me a criminal and why have you seized me?" The Superior answered him in a voice that rasped like a saw: "Thou hast pastured these cattle on land that is the monastery's land and they have nibbled and gnawed at our vines. We have seized them because the shepherd is responsible for the damage wrought by his flock." His angry face grew hard as he spoke. Then spoke Yuhanna with pleading in his voice: "Father," he said, "they are but dumb creatures without intelligence, and I am a poor man and possess naught except the strength of my forearm and these beasts. Let me take them away and I shall promise not to come to these meadows again."

The Father Superior moved a step forward, raised his hand toward the heavens, and again spoke: "God has put us in this place and He has entrusted to us the guardianship of this land, the land of His chosen, the great Elisha. Day and night do we guard it with all our might, for it is sacred; those who approach it will it consume with fire. If thou refusest to render account to the monastery, then shall the very grass turn to poison in the bellies of thy beasts. There is no escape for thee for we shall keep the calves here in our enclosure until thou hast paid the last fils."[1]

---

1 Coin of fractional value.

The Superior was about to go when Yuhanna stopped him and said in a voice of supplication: "I entreat you, my lord, for the sake of these sacred days wherein Jesus suffered and Mary wept in sorrow, to let me go with my calves. Harden not your heart against me; I am poor and the monastery is rich and powerful. It will assuredly forgive my foolishness and have pity upon my father's years." The Superior looked at him, mocking, and said: "The monastery will not excuse thee, not even to the amount of one grain, stupid one; it matters not whether thou be rich or poor. Who art thou to adjure me by things sacred since it is we alone that know their secrets and hidden things? If thou wouldst take away the calves from these pastures, then shalt thou redeem them in the sum of three dinars to pay for what they have consumed of the crops." Said Yuhanna in a choking voice: "I have nothing, father, not even a para piece. Have compassion on me and my poverty."

The Superior caressed his thick beard with his fingers. "Then go thou and sell part of thy field and return with three dinars. Is it not better for thee to enter heaven and possess no field than to earn Elisha's wrath with thy ceaseless arguing before his altar and thus go down into hell, where all is eternal fire?"

Yuhanna remained silent for a while. From his eyes shone a light and his features expanded with joy. His bearing changed from one of entreaty and pleading to one of strength and resolve. When he spoke it was in a voice in which were knowledge and the determination of youth:

"Must the poor sell the fields that earn them their bread and maintain their existence in order to fill further the coffers of the monastery, heavy with gold and silver? Is it just that the poor should be yet poorer and the wretched die of hunger that great Elisha may forgive the sins of hungry beasts?" The Superior shook his head haughtily. "Jesus the Christ said: For unto everyone that hath shall be given and he shall have abundance; but from him that hath not shall be taken away even that which he hath."

As Yuhanna heard these words his heart beat faster in his breast, he grew in spirit and increased in stature. It was as though the earth were developing at his feet. From his pocket he drew out his Bible as the warrior draws his sword to defend himself, and cried: "Thus do you make a mockery of the teachings of this Book, O hypocrites, and use that which is most sacred in life to spread the evils therein. Woe to you when the Son of Man shall come a second time and lay in ruins your monasteries and scatter their stones across the valley and burn with fire your altars and images! Woe to you by the innocent blood of Jesus and the tears of His mother's weeping, for they shall overwhelm you as a flood and carry you down to the depths of the abyss! Woe to you who prostrate yourselves before the idols of your greed and conceal beneath your black raiment the blackness of your deeds! Woe to you who move your lips in prayer while your hearts are yet hard as rock; who bend low in humility before the altar yet in your souls rebel against your God! In your harshness you have brought me to this place and seized hold of me as a transgressor for the sake of a little pasture land that the sun has nourished for us equally. When I entreat you in the name of Jesus and adjure you by the days of His sorrow and pain, you scoff at me as one who speaks in ignorance. Take then this Book, look into it, and show me when Jesus was not forgiving. Read this divine tragedy and tell me where He speaks without mercy and compassion. Was it in His Sermon on the Mount or in His teachings in the temple before the persecutors of the wretched harlot or upon Golgotha as He opened wide His arms on the cross to embrace all mankind? Look down, all you hard of heart, upon these poor towns and villages in whose dwellings the sick writhe in agony on beds of pain; in whose prisons the unfortunate pass their days in despair; at whose gates the beggars beg; on whose highways the stranger makes his bed, and in whose cemeteries the widow and the orphan weep. But you are here living in sloth and idleness and comfort, enjoying the yield of the fields and the grapes of the vine. You visit not the sick and the imprisoned; nor do you feed the hungry or give refuge to the stranger or comfort to the mourner. Would that you were content with what you hold and that which you have plundered from our forefathers! You stretch out your hands as the viper its head and rob the widow of the labour of her hands and the peasant of his store against old age."

727

Yuhanna ceased from talking in order to regain his breath. Then he went on, his head lifted proudly and said in a gentle voice:

"You are many and I am one. Do to me as you wish. The ewe may fall as prey to the wolves in the darkness of the night, but her blood will stain the stones of the valley until the coming of dawn and the rising of the sun."

Yuhanna spoke these words, and in his voice was a strength inspired, a force that restrained the monks from all movement and caused anger and harshness to rise within them. They trembled in their rage and ground their teeth like caged and hungry lions, awaiting a sign from their chief to tear the youth to pieces. So they were until Yuhanna had ceased speaking and became silent like the calm after the storm has wrought destruction on the topmost branches of a tree and the strongest of plants. Then cried the Superior: "Seize this miserable sinner; take from him the Book and drag him away to a dark cell. Those who would curse God's elect shall receive pardon neither here nor in the hereafter." The monks fell upon Yuhanna as the lion falls upon his prey; they pinioned his arms and led him away to a narrow chamber. Before locking the door on him they belaboured his body with blows and kicks.

In that dark place stood Yuhanna, the victor whom fortune has given to the foe as captive. Through a small opening in the wall he looked out on the valley reposing in the sunlight. His face became illumined and his spirit felt the embrace of a divine content; a sweet tranquillity took possession of him. The narrow cell imprisoned his body, but his spirit was free to roam with the breeze among the meadows and ruins. The hands of the monks had bruised his limbs, but they had not touched his inmost feelings; in those he rested in safety with Jesus the Nazarene. Persecution harms not the just man nor does oppression destroy one who is on the side of truth. Socrates drank of the hemlock smiling; Paul was stoned rejoicing. When we oppose the hidden conscience, it does us hurt. When we betray it, it judges us.

The parents of Yuhanna came to know of what had befallen their only child. His mother came to the monastery walking with the aid of her stick and threw herself at the feet of the Superior. She wept and kissed his hands and beseeched him to have pity on her son and pardon his ignorance. The Superior lifted his eyes heavenwards like one raised above worldly affairs and said to the woman: "We can forgive the playfulness of thy son and show tolerance toward his foolishness, but the monastery possesses sacred rights to which account must be rendered. We in our humility forgive the transgressions of men, but great Elisha forgives not nor pardons the trespassers on his vineyards and those who put to pasture their beasts on his land."

The mother looked up at him while the tears ran down her withered old cheeks. Then from around her neck she took a silver collar and put it in his hand, saying: "I have naught except this collar, father. It is a gift of my mother, given me on the day of my marriage. Perchance the monastery will accept it as an atonement for the guilt of my only son."

The Superior took the collar and put it in his pocket and addressed the mother, the while she kissed his hands in gratitude and thankfulness: "Woe to this generation, for the verses of the Book have become contrariwise and the children have eaten of sour grapes and the fathers' teeth are set on edge! Go now, good woman, and pray for thy foolish son that Heaven may cure him and give back his reason."

Yuhanna went out from his prison and walked slowly before his calves by the side of his mother as she leaned on her staff, bowed down under the weight of her years. When he reached the hut, he left the calves to browse and sat beside the window in silence, looking at the fading light of day. After a little time he heard his father whisper these words into his mother's ear: "Many times have I told thee, Sarah, that our son is weak in mind, but never didst thou agree with me. Now thou dost no longer contradict me, for his actions have justified my words. What the reverend father told thee today have I been telling thee for years."

Yuhanna remained looking toward the west, where the rays of the setting sun put colour to the close-packed masses of cloud.

II

It was Easter-tide and fasting gave place to feasting. The building of the new church was completed and it rose above the houses of Besharry, in whose midst it stood, like the palace of a prince among the mean dwellings of his subjects. The people stood and watched for the coming of the bishop to dedicate their sanctuary and consecrate its altars. And when they felt that the time of his arrival was near they went out from the town in processions and he entered with them to songs of praise from the young men and the chanting of the priests, and the clashing of cymbals and ringing of bells. When he dismounted from his horse, adorned with decorated saddle and silver bridle, he was met by men of religion and notable persons who welcomed him with pomp and fitting words and verse and songs of praise. When he reached the new church he was invested with a priestly robe embroidered in gold, and a jewel-encrusted crown was put upon his head. Then he was girded with the shepherd's crook of cunning workmanship and precious stones. He made a circuit of the church, singing and chanting orisons with the priests, while around him rose and swirled goodly-smelling incense and the flickering flames of many candles.

At that hour Yuhanna was standing among the shepherds and tillers of the soil on a raised platform observing this spectacle through his sad eyes. He sighed bitterly in his pain and grief as he saw on the one side silken clothes and gold vessels, censers and costly silver lamps; and on the other, crowds of poor and wretched people who had come up from little villages and hamlets to assist at the rejoicings of this festival and the ceremony of consecration. On the one side, power in its velvets and satins; on the other, misery in its rags and tatters. Here wealth and power personifying the religion with its songs and chants; there an enfeebled people, humble and poor, rejoicing in its secret soul in the Resurrection. Praying in silence and sighing sighs that rose from the bottom of broken hearts to float on the ether and whisper into the ears of the air. Here the leaders and headmen to whom power gave life like the life of the evergreen cypress tree. There the peasants who submit, whose existence is a ship with Death for its captain; whose rudder is broken by the waves and whose sails are torn by the winds; now rising, now sinking between the anger of the deep and the terror of the storm. Here harsh tyranny; there blind obedience. Which one is parent to the other? Is tyranny a strong tree that grows not except on low ground? Or is submission an abandoned field in which naught lives but thorns?

With these sorrowful reflections and torturing thoughts did Yuhanna occupy himself. He pressed his arms against his breast as if his throat were closing in upon his breathing, in fear that his breast were being rent asunder to let go his breath. In this manner he remained until the ceremony of dedication was at an end, when the people dispersed and went their diverse ways.

Soon he began to feel as though there were a spirit in the air urging him to arise and speak in its name; and in the crowd a power moving him to come forth as a preacher before heaven and earth.

He came to the end of the platform and, lifting up his eyes, made a sign with his hand to the heavens. In a strong voice that compelled the ears and eyes to give attention he cried:

"Behold thou, O Jesus, Man of Nazareth, who sittest within the circle of light on high. Look down from beyond the blue dome of heaven upon this earth; whose elements Thou didst wear yesterday as a cloak. Look, O faithful Tiller, for the thorns of the thicket have strangled the flowers whose seeds did quicken into life by the sweat of Thy brow. Look, O good Shepherd, for the weak lamb Thou didst carry on Thy shoulder is torn to pieces by wild beasts. Thine innocent blood is sucked into the earth, and Thy hot tears are dried up in the hearts of men. The warmth of Thy breath is scattered before desert winds. This field hallowed by Thy feet is become a battleground where the feet of the strong grind the ribs of the outcast, where the hand of the oppressor blights the spirit of the weak. The persecuted cry out from the darkness, and those who sit upon thrones in Thy name heed not their cries. Neither is the weeping of the bereaved heard by those who preach Thy words from pulpits. The lamb that Thou didst send for the sake of the Lord of Life is become a rampaging beast tearing to pieces the wings of the Lamb

enfolded by Thine arms. The word of life that Thou didst bring down from the heart of God is concealed and hidden within the pages of books, and in its place is a terrible shouting, putting fear and dread into all hearts. These people, O Jesus, have raised temples and tabernacles to the glory of Thy name and adorned them with woven silk and molten gold. They have left naked the bodies of Thy chosen poor in the cold streets: yet do they fill the air with the smoke of incense and candles. Those who believe in Thy godlike state have they robbed of bread. Though the air echoes to their psalms and hymns, yet they hear not the orphan's cry, neither the widow's lamentation. Come then, O Jesus, a second time, and drive out from the temple those who trade in religion, for they have made of it a nest of vipers with their cunning and guile. Come, and do reckoning with these Cæsars who have wrested from the weak that which is theirs and God's. Behold the vine that Thy right hand did plant. The worms have eaten of its shoots, and its grapes are trampled beneath the feet of the passer-by. Consider those upon whom Thou didst enjoin peace and see how they are divided, contending among themselves. Our troubled souls and oppressed hearts have they made as victims of their wars. On their feast-days and holy days they lift up their voices saying glory to God in His heaven, peace upon earth, and joy to all men. Is Thy heavenly Father glorified when corrupt lips and lying tongues utter His name? Is there peace upon earth when the children of sorrow toil in the fields and see their strength ebbing away in the light of the sun to feed the mouth of the strong and fill the tyrant's belly? Is there rejoicing among men when the outcast look with their broken eyes toward death as the conquered looks to his deliverer? What is peace, gentle Jesus? Is it in the eyes of children at the breasts of hungry mothers in cold dark dwellings? Or in the bodies of the needy who sleep in their beds of stone wishing for the food that comes not to them but is thrown by the priests to their fattened swine? What is joy, O Jesus? Does it exist when a prince can buy the strength of men and the honour of women for a few pieces of silver? Is it in those silent ones that are slaves in body and soul to whosoever dazzles their eyes with the gleam of bejewelled orders and the flash of stones in rings and the silk of their garments? Is there rejoicing in the cries of the oppressed and downtrodden when tyrants fall upon them with the sword and crush the bodies of their women and young ones under horses' hoofs and make drunk the earth with their blood? Stretch forth Thy strong hand, Jesus, and save us, for the oppressor's hand is heavy upon us. Or send to us Death, that he might lead us to the grave, wherein we shall sleep in peace against the second coming, secure in the shadow of Thy cross. For verily our life is naught but a darkness whose inhabitants are evil spirits, and a valley wherein snakes and dragons make sport. What are our days except whetted swords concealed by night between our bed-coverings and revealed by the morning light hanging over our heads whenever the love of existence leads us to the fields? Have mercy, O Jesus, on these multitudes joined together as one by Thy name on the day of the Resurrection. Have compassion on their weakness and humility."

Thus did Yuhanna hold converse with the heavens while the people stood around him. Some were pleased and praised him; others were angry and reviled him. One shouted: "He says aright and speaks for us before Heaven, for we are oppressed." Another said: "He is possessed and speaks with the tongue of an evil spirit." That one cried: "We never heard such foolishness from our fathers before us; neither do we wish to hear it now." Yet another whispered into his neighbour's ear, saying: "At the sound of his voice I felt within me an awful trembling that shook my very heart, for he spoke with a strange power." Answered his friend: "It is so; but our leaders are more knowledgeable in these affairs than are we. It is wrong to doubt them."

As the cries rose from all sides and swelled into a roar like the sea only to be scattered and lost in the ether, a priest appeared, seized hold of Yuhanna, and delivered him up to the police. They led him away to the Governor's house. When they asked him questions he answered not a word, for he remembered that Jesus was silent too before His persecutors. So they threw him into the dark prison house and there he slept, gently leaning against the stone wall.

And on the morning of the following day came Yuhanna's father to testify before the Governor to his son's madness.

"My lord," he said, "often have I heard him babbling in his solitude and talking of strange things that have no existence. Night after night has he spoken into the silence in unknown words, calling upon the shadows of darkness in a terrible voice like that of sorcerers uttering incantations. Ask of the boys of the quarter who used to sit with him, for they know how his mind was attracted by another world beyond. When they spoke to him, seldom did he answer. And when he did speak, his words were confused and without relation to their conversation. Ask of his mother, for more than all others was she aware of a soul stripped of all its senses. Ofttimes did she see him looking toward the horizon with eyes staring and glazed, and hear him speaking with passion of the trees and brooks and flowers and stars in the way children prattle of trifles. Ask of the monks in the monastery with whom he contended yesterday, mocking at their godliness and scorning their sacred way of life. He is mad, my lord, but to his mother and me he is kind. He sustains us in our old age and fulfils our wants with the sweat of his brow. Show him mercy through your compassion upon us and forgive his foolishness for the sake of his parents."

Yuhanna was set free and the story of his madness spread abroad. The young men spoke of him with mocking. But the maidens looked at him with sad eyes and said: "For much that is strange in men are the heavens accountable. So in this youth is beauty united with madness, and the light of his beautiful eyes wedded to the darkness of his sick soul."

Between the meadows and the heights, clothed in their garments of flowers and plants, sat Yuhanna by the calves, who had fled from the stress and strife of men to the good pastures. He looked with tear-dimmed eyes toward the villages and hamlets scattered upon the shoulders of the valley and, sighing deeply, repeated these words:

"You are many and I am one. Say what you will of me and do to me as you wish. The ewe may fall as prey to the wolves in the darkness of the night, but her blood will stain the stones of the valley until the coming of the dawn and the rising of the sun."

A TEAR AND A SMILE

Translated from the Arabic by H. M. Nahmad

TO M.E.H.

I offer this book, the first breath in the tempest of my life,
to that noble spirit who loves with the breeze and walks
with the tempests.
GIBRAN

To Yvonne from the translator

CONTENTS

A TEAR AND A SMILE

I WOULD NOT exchange the sorrows of my heart for the joys of the multitude. And I would not have the tears that sadness makes to flow from my every part turn into laughter. I would that my life remain a tear and a smile.

A tear to purify my heart and give me understanding of life's secrets and hidden things. A smile to draw me nigh to the sons of my kind and to be a symbol of my glorification of the gods.

A tear to unite me with those of broken heart; a smile to be a sign of my joy in existence.

I would rather that I died in yearning and longing than that I lived weary and despairing.

I want the hunger for love and beauty to be in the depths of my spirit, for I have seen those who are satisfied the most wretched of people. I have heard the sigh of those in yearning and longing, and it is sweeter than the sweetest melody.

With evening's coming the flower folds her petals and sleeps, embracing her longing. At morning's approach she opens her lips to meet the sun's kiss.

The life of a flower is longing and fulfilment. A tear and a smile.

The waters of the sea become vapour and rise and come together and are a cloud.

And the cloud floats above the hills and valleys until it meets the gentle breeze, then falls weeping to the fields and joins with the brooks and rivers to return to the sea, its home.

The life of clouds is a parting and a meeting. A tear and a smile.

And so does the spirit become separated from the greater spirit to move in the world of matter and pass as a cloud over the mountain of sorrow and the plains of joy to meet the breeze of death and return whence it came.

To the ocean of Love and Beauty – to God.

THE LIFE OF LOVE

SPRING

COME, MY BELOVED, let us walk among the little hills, for the snows have melted and life is awakened from its sleep and wanders through the hills and valleys.

Come, let us follow the footsteps of spring in the far-off field;

Come and we will ascend the heights and look upon the waving greenness of the plains below.

The dawn of spring has unfolded the garment concealed by the winter night, and the peach tree and the apple wear it, adorned as brides on the Night of Power.

The vines are awakened, their tendrils entwined like the embrace of lovers.

The streams run and leap among the rocks singing songs of rejoicing.

The flowers are bursting forth from the heart of Nature as foam from the crest of sea waves.

Come, my beloved, let me drink of the last of rain's tears from narcissus cups and make full our spirits of the joyful songs of birds.

Let us breathe the scent of the breeze and sit by yonder rock where hides the violet, and give and take of Love's kisses.

SUMMER

Arise, my love, to the field, for the days of the harvest are come and the time of reaping is nigh.

The grain is ripened by the sun in the warmth of its love to Nature;

Come ere the birds reap the fruits of our labour, and the ants consume our land.

Come, let us garner the earth's yield as the spirit does grains of bliss from fulfilment's sowing in the depths of our hearts,

And fill our bins with Nature's bounty as Life does the storehouses of our souls.

Come, my mate, let us make the grass our couch and the heavens our coverlet.

Lay us down our heads on a pillow of soft hay and seek thereon repose from the toil of the day and hearken to the music of the murmur of the brook in the valley.

AUTUMN

Let us go to the vineyard, my love, and press the grapes and store the wine thereof in vessels as the spirit stores the wisdom of ages.

Let us gather the fruits and distil from the flowers their fragrance.

Let us return to the dwellings, for the leaves of the trees are become yellow and the winds have scattered them to make of them a burial shroud for flowers that died grieving at summer's passing.

Come, for the birds have taken flight to the seashore bearing upon their wings the good cheer of the gardens, bequeathing desolation to the jasmine and the myrtle, and the last tears have been shed upon the sod.

Come, let us go, for the brooks have ceased their flowing and the springs are no more, for the tears of their joy are dried up; and the hillocks have cast aside their fine garments.

Come, beloved. For Nature is overcome by sleep and bids farewell to wakefulness with sad and wishful melody.

WINTER

Draw nigh unto me, my soul-mate. Draw nigh and let not icy breath separate our bodies. Sit you with me by this fireside, for fire is winter's fruit.

Speak with me of things of the ages, for mine ears are wearied of the winds' sighing and the elements' lamenting.

Make fast door and window, for the angry face of Nature makes sad my spirit, and to look upon the city beneath the snows, sitting like a mother bereaved, causes my heart to bleed.

Fill you, then, the lamp with oil, for it is already dim. Put it beside you that I may see what the nights have writ on your face. Bring hither the wine-jar that we may drink and remember the days of the pressing.

Draw nigh to me, loved of my spirit, for the fire is dying and ashes conceal it.

Embrace me, for the lamp is dimmed and darkness has conquered it.

Heavy are our eyes with the wine of years.

Look on me with your sleep-darkened eyes. Embrace me ere slumber embrace us. Kiss me, for the snows have prevailed over all save your kiss.

Ah, my beloved one, how deep is the ocean of sleep! How distant the morning . . . in this night!

A TALE

ON THE BANKS of that river in the shade of the walnut and the willow sat a farmer's son, gazing quietly at the running water. A youth, he was reared among the meadows where everything spoke of love. Where the branches embraced and the flowers inclined one to another and the birds dallied. Where nature in its all preached the gospel of the Spirit.

A youth of twenty years he was, and yestereve he had seen sitting by the spring a maiden among other maidens and he loved her. But he heard tell that she was the daughter of a Prince and he blamed his heart and complained in his self. Yet blaming does not draw away the heart from love, neither does reproof drive away the spirit from the truth. For a man stands between his heart and his soul as a tender branch in the path of the south wind and the north wind.

The youth looked and saw the violet growing by the side of the daisy, and he heard the nightingale calling out to the black-bird, and he wept in his aloneness and his solitude. And so passed the hours of his love before his eyes like the passing of phantom forms. Then he spoke, his affection overflowing with his words and tears, and said:

"Thus does love mock and make jest of me and lead me whither hope is reckoned an error and longing a despised thing. Love, which I have adored, has lifted my heart to a Prince's palace and brought low my state to a peasant's hut and led my spirit to the beauty of a nymph of paradise guarded by men and protected by honour. . . .

"I am obedient, O Love. What then do you desire? I did follow you along fiery paths, and the flames consumed me. I did open mine eyes and saw naught save darkness; and loosed my tongue, but spoke not save in grief. Yearning embraced me, O Love, with a hunger of the spirit that will not cease except with the kiss of the beloved. I am enfeebled, O Love. Whyfor do you contend with me, you that are strong?

"Whyfor do you oppress me, you that are just? Whyfor do you abandon me, you that are my existence?

"If my blood flows not save by your willing, then pour it out. If my feet move save upon your path, then shrivel them. Do your will in this body, but let my soul rejoice in these meadows, safe in the shadow of your wings. . . .

"The stream goes to the sea, its lover, and the flower smiles at its impassioned, the light, and the cloud descends to its valley, its desired. But there is in me what the brook does not know nor the flower hear nor the cloud understand. Behold me alone in my love, separate in my passion, far off from her who wants me not, a soldier in her father's armies or a servant in her palace."

And the youth became silent for a while as though he would learn speech from the murmur of the river and the rustle of leaves on the boughs. Then he said:

"O you whose name I fear to pronounce, O one concealed from me behind coverings of might and walls of majesty, O being of another world whose meeting I dare not covet save in eternity, where all stand equal, O one to whom the strong show obeisance, before whom heads are bowed, to whom treasure-houses are opened:

"You have possessed a heart sanctified by love, and enslaved a soul ennobled by God, and captivated a mind that was yesterday free with the freedom of the fields. Today it has become a captive of passion.

"I have looked on you, O fair creature, and know now the reason of my coming into this world. And when I knew of your lofty state and saw my humbleness, I learned that the gods possess secrets unknown to men and ways wherein they lead spirits where love holds rule without the laws of mankind. When I looked into your eyes it was told me beyond all doubting that this life is but a paradise whose door is the human heart.

"I saw your grandeur and my lowliness locked in struggle and knew that this earth was no more a resting-place for me. When I did find you sitting among your women, as the rose among the myrtle plants, I bethought me that the bride of my dreams had taken body and was become flesh like myself. But on my knowing your father's glory I perceived beyond the rose thorns to prick the fingers. What dreams had united, awakening parted. . . ."

The youth rose to his feet and walked toward the spring, cast down in spirit and broken in heart. And in him despair and grief spoke these words:

"Come, O Death, and deliver me, for the earth, whose thorns do strangle its flowers, is no longer a habitable place. Arise now and save me from days that would wrest love from its seat of glory and put in its stead worldly might. Deliver me, O Death! For eternity is more sweet than the world for a trysting-place of lovers. Yonder shall I await my beloved; there shall I be joined with her."

He came to the spring, and evening was nigh and the sun was lifting her golden mantle from off the meadow. There he sat and wept tears that fell to the ground on which the feet of the Princess had trod. His head fell forward on his breast as though to prevent his heart's flight.

Upon that minute from beyond the willow trees a maiden appeared, dragging the ends of her garment on the grass. She stopped by the youth and put her soft hand on his head. He looked up at her like a sleeper awaked by the sun's rays. He saw standing before him the daughter of the Prince, upon which he fell on his knees and prostrated himself as did Moses before the burning bush. He wished to speak, but no words came, so his tear-filled eyes took the place of his tongue. Then the girl embraced him and kissed his lips and his eyes, sucking in their hot tears, and said in a voice of flute-like clearness:

"I have seen you, my love, in my dreaming and looked upon your face in my aloneness. You are my spirit's companion whom I did lose, and my beautiful half that was separated from it on my coming into this world. I have come in secret, my darling, to meet with you, and now do I behold you in my arms. Have not fear, for I have forsaken my father's glory to follow you to the very ends of the world and drink with you the cup of Life and Death.

747

"Arise my love and let us go to distant places away from mankind."

There on the outskirts of the land the scouts of the Prince happened upon two human skeletons. On the neck of one was a necklet of gold, and near them both was a stone upon which were written these words:

"Love has joined us; then who shall put us asunder? Death has taken us; and who shall bring us back?"

IN THE CITY OF THE DEAD

I FREED MYSELF yesterday from the clamour of the city and walked in the quiet fields until I gained the heights, which Nature had clothed in her choicest garments.

There I stood and beheld the city below, with its high buildings and fine mansions standing beneath dense clouds of smoke rising from factories. I sat myself down observing from afar the works of man and found them a trouble and a stress. I tried in my heart to forget what men had wrought and I turned my eyes toward the field, the throne of God's glory, and beheld in its midst a burial ground. Monuments of stone surrounded by cypress trees.

And so did I sit between the City of the Living and the City of the Dead. Yonder I sat thinking on the never ending strife and ceaseless movement in the one and the quiet that reigned over and the peace that dwelled in the other. Here, hope and despair and love and hate; poverty and riches, belief and unbelief. There, earth within earth that Nature turned over and in the stillness of night created therefrom first plant, then animal life.

Whilst I thus gave myself to these reflections my eyes were drawn to a knot of people walking along preceded by music whose sad refrains filled the air. A procession of pomp and circumstance wherein marched all manner of persons. The funeral of a rich and powerful one. The remains of the dead followed by the quick, who wept and wailed and filled the ether with crying and lament.

The procession reached the burial ground. The priests prayed and made incense, and the musicians blew upon their trumpets. Others spoke and praised the departed with fine words. Poets lamented him in their choicest verses. All this took a long and wearisome time. After a while the crowd dispersed and left the tombstone in whose fashioning sculptor had vied with mason. Around it were placed flowers arranged cunningly by artful hands. Then the cortege returned to the city, whilst I looked on from afar, thinking.

The sun inclined toward the west, and the shadow of rocks and trees lengthened and Nature began to shed her garments of light.

On that very moment I looked and beheld two men bearing a wooden casket. Behind them came a woman in rags carrying a suckling child. By her side trotted a dog, looking now at her, now at the casket. It was the funeral procession of a poor man, a humble man. There went a wife shedding tears of grief and a child who wept at his mother's weeping, and a faithful dog in whose steps were a pain and a sadness.

They came to the burial ground and laid the coffin in a grave dug in a corner far from those marble headstones. Then they returned in silence, the while the dog looked back at the last resting place of his good companion. And so till they vanished from my sight beyond the trees.

And I looked toward the City of the Living, saying within myself: "That belongs to the wealthy and the mighty." And toward the City of the Dead I said: "This too belongs to the wealthy and the mighty. Where then, O Lord, is the home of the poor and the weak?"

Having thus spoken, I lifted my eyes to the clouds, whose edges were coloured with gold by the rays of the setting sun. And a voice within me said: "Yonder."

THE POET'S DEATH IS HIS LIFE

NIGHT SPREAD ITS wings over the city, and the snow clothed it with a garment, and the cold drove men from the market places to take refuge in their dwellings. The wind rose sighing among the houses like a mourner who stands amidst tombstones lamenting the dead.

On the outskirts of that city was an old house with crumbling walls upon which the weight of the snows lay so that it was near falling. And in a corner of that house was a broken-down bed upon which lay a dying man, who watched the feeble light of a lamp battling with the darkness. He was a youth in the springtime of life who knew that the hour of his deliverance from the bonds of existence was at hand. So was he awaiting Death's coming. On his wan features was the light of hope and upon his lips a sad smile.

A poet he was who had come to rejoice the hearts of men with his beautiful sayings. Now he lay dying of hunger in the city of the living and the rich. A noble spirit that had descended by the grace of the gods to render life sweet was now bidding farewell to our world ere mankind had smiled on that spirit.

He was drawing his last breath and there was none by his side save the lamp, which was his companion in his aloneness, and scraps of paper on which were images to his gentle spirit.

The dying youth gathered together the remnants of his ebbing strength; he raised his hands heavenward and moved his withered eyelids as though his departing sight would pierce the roof of that broken-down hut so that he might look on the stars beyond the clouds. And he said:

"Come now, fair death, for my spirit yearns toward you. Come nigh and loose the fetters of matter, for I am become weary of their dragging. Come then, sweet death, and deliver me from men, who reckon me a stranger in their midst because

I did speak the tongue of the angels in the language of mankind. Hasten, for men have rejected me and cast me into the corners of forgetfulness because I coveted not wealth as did they, nor profited from him who was weaker than I. Come to me, sweet death, and take me, for those of my kind need me not. Clasp me to your breast, which is full with love; kiss my lips, the lips that tasted not of a mother's kiss, nor touched a sister's cheek, nor felt a sweetheart's mouth. Hasten and embrace me, death, my beloved."

Then at the bedside of that dying youth stood the image of a woman of unearthly beauty. She was clothed in a garment white as snow and in her hand was a crown of lilies from heavenly valleys.

She drew near to him and embraced him, and closed his eyes that he might behold her with eyes of his spirit. She kissed his lips with a kiss of love, a kiss that left upon his lips a smile of fulfilment. And on that moment the hut became empty save of earth and pieces of paper scattered in dark corners.

The ages passed and the people of that city remained in the stupor of ignorance and folly. When they awoke therefrom and their eyes beheld the dawn of knowledge, they set up in the centre of the town a great statue to the poet, and at an appointed time each year they held a festival in his honour.

How foolish are men!

DAUGHTERS OF THE SEA

IN THE DEPTHS of the ocean that surrounds the isles near the sun's rising-place was the dead body of a youth. Around him, among the coral plants, sat the golden-haired daughters of the sea gazing on him through their beautiful blue eyes. They spoke softly in tones of music, and their words were taken up by the deep and borne by the waves to the shore, whence the breeze carried them to my spirit's hearing.

Said the first one:

"This is a human who came down yesterday when the sea was angry."

And a second one said:

"Nay, the sea was not angry. But this man – such are called those descended from the gods – was in a war in which much blood was shed until the water became the colour of red. This human is a victim of that war."

Said a third:

"I know not what war means, but I know that man was not satisfied with his conquest of the dry land but coveted the lordship of the oceans and invented strange machines to cleave the waters. Then Neptune, god of the seas, came to know, and he was angry because of this enmity. And man was made to appease our sovereign with sacrifices and offerings. That which we beheld yesterday descending was man's latest offering to mighty Neptune."

A fourth one said:

"How great is Neptune, but how hard is his heart! If I were mistress of the seas I would not be pleased with bloody sacrifices. Come, let us look on this dead youth; mayhap we learn something of humankind."

Then the daughters of the sea drew near to the body and searched in the pockets of his garment. In the garment nearest his heart was a letter, which one of them took and read:

"My darling. Midnight has struck and I keep vigil sleepless, with no one to console me save my tears and nobody to comfort me but my hope in your return to me from the terrors of war. Well do I recall what you did tell me when we parted, that with every man are tears as a trust that must be returned one day.

"I know not, my love, what I write; rather shall I let my soul flow on to the paper. A soul tormented by misery and consoled by love, which makes suffering a delight and grief a joy.

"When love made one our two hearts and we awaited the union of two bodies within which was one spirit, war called you and you followed it, impelled by duty to your country. Yet what thing is this duty that separates lovers and makes of women widows and of children orphans? What thing is this patriotism which for little causes calls to war to lay in ruins the land? What is this duty that fastens itself upon the wretched villages, but is heeded not by the strong and privileged?

"If duty exiles peace from among nations, and patriotism makes havoc of man's tranquillity, then away with duty and patriotism! . . . No, my darling, heed not my words, but be brave and a lover of your land. Do not hearken to the words of a woman whom love has blinded, whom separation has robbed of seeing. . . . If love brings you not back to me in this life, then love will join me with you in the life to come."

The sea maidens put back the letter beneath the youth's garments and swam away in silent grief. And when they were gone a distance, one of them said:

"In truth man's heart is harder than Neptune's."

THE SPIRIT

AND THE GOD of gods separated a Spirit from Himself and created in it Beauty.

He gave to it the lightness of the breeze at dawn and the fragrance of the flowers of the field and the softness of moonlight.

Then He gave to it a cup of joy, saying:

"You shall not drink of it except that you forget the Past and heed not the Future."

And He gave to it a cup of sadness, saying:

"You shall drink and know therefrom the meaning of Life's rejoicing."

Then He put therein a Love that would forsake it with the first sigh of satisfaction; and a Sweetness that would go out therefrom with the first word uttered.

And He caused to descend upon it knowledge from the heavens to guide it in the way of Truth. And planted in its depths Sight, that it might see the unseen.

Therein He created Feeling to flow with images and phantom forms;

And clothed it with a garment of Yearning woven by angels from rainbow strands.

In it He did put the darkness of Confusion, which is Light's image.

And the God took Fire from Wrath's furnace, and a Wind from the desert of Ignorance, and Sand from the seashore of Selfishness, and Earth from beneath the feet of the ages, and He created man.

He gave to him unseeing Force to rise up in fury with madness and subside before lust.

And the God of gods smiled and wept and knew a Love boundless and without limit, and He mated Man with his Spirit.

A SMILE AND A TEAR

THE SUN GATHERED up its garments from over those verdant gardens, and the moon rose from beyond the horizon and spilled its soft light over all. I sat there beneath a tree watching the changing shades of evening. I looked beyond the boughs to the stars scattered like coins upon a carpet of blue colour, and I heard from afar the gentle murmur of the streams in the valley.

When the birds had made themselves safe in the leafy branches, and the flowers closed their eyes, and peace reigned, there came to my ears the fall of light footsteps on the grass. I turned my head and beheld a youth and a maid coming toward me. They stopped and sat them down at the foot of a tree.

The youth looked about him on all sides and said:

"Sit by me, beloved, and hear well my words. Smile, for your smiling is a sign to what is before us. Rejoice, for the very days rejoice for our sake. Yet does my soul tell me that your heart is full with doubting, and doubting in things of love is a sin.

"In days to come will you be mistress over these spacious lands which the moon lights up with its light; and lady of this palace which is likened to the palaces of kings. My fine horses will carry you to pleasure places, and my carriages will take you to merrymaking and dancing.

"Smile, my loved one, even as smiles the gold in my coffers. Look on me as do my father's precious stones. Hearken to me, my love, for my heart longs only to pour its secret before you. Before us lies one year of bliss; a year we shall pass with gold in the palaces of the Nile; beneath the cedars of Lebanon. You shall meet with daughters of princes and nobles and they shall envy you your dress and adornments. All that shall I give you. Does it not find favour in your sight? Ah, how sweet is your smiling; for it is as the smile of my destiny."

After a while they departed, walking slowly and treading

underfoot the flowers as the foot of the rich treads upon the heart of the poor. And so they vanished from my sight, the while I thought upon the place of riches in love; I thought upon riches, the source of men's evil; and love, the spring of light and happiness.

I fell to roaming the realms of thought, when of a sudden my eyes alighted on two figures that passed before me and sat them down on the grass. A youth and a maid who were come from a corner of the field where are the peasants' huts.

After a silence that was felt, I heard these words come forth with deep sighing from wounded lips:

"Dry your tears, my darling, for love, which has opened our eyes and made us its servants, will grant us the blessing of patience and forbearance. Dry your tears and be consoled, for we have made a covenant with love, and for that love shall we bear the torment of poverty and the bitterness of misfortune and the pain of separation.

"I shall not cease to contend with the days until I have wrested from them treasure worthy for your hands to receive. Love, which is God, will accept from us these tears and sighs as an offering, and we shall be rewarded in the measure of our due. Fare you well, my love, for I go ere the moon wanes."

Then I heard a soft voice in which was a sob; the voice of a virgin maid in which were the warmth of love and the bitterness of parting and the sweetness of patience, saying: "Farewell, beloved."

They separated, what time I remained sitting beneath that tree. And compassion's fingers drew me, and the secrets of this wondrous creation made me part. Upon that hour I looked toward Nature aslumber and pondered and found therein a thing boundless and without end. A thing not purchased with gold. I found a thing that is not effaced by autumn's tears nor destroyed by grief and wretchedness. A thing that endures and lives in the spring and comes to fruit in summer days. Therein I found Love.

A VISION

THERE IN THE midst of a field on the banks of a limpid stream I saw a cage whose bars were wrought by a cunning hand. In one corner of the cage was a dead bird and in another corner was a vessel wherein the water was dried up and a plate empty of seeds.

I stood, overcome by the silence, and listened humbly, as though in the dead bird and the voice of the stream were a sermon seeking out the heart and asking of the conscience. I pondered and considered and then I knew that the poor bird had died of thirst by the side of running water and perished of hunger in the midst of fields, the very cradle of life. Like a rich man locked in his treasury who dies of hunger in the midst of his gold.

And after a while I saw that the cage was become the dry skeleton of a man, and the dead bird was turned into a human heart; and in the heart a deep wound from which dripped blood. The edges of the wound were like to the lips of a grieving woman.

Then I heard a voice arising from the wound saying: "I am the human heart, the captive of matter and the slain of men's edicts. In the midst of this field of beauty on these banks of the source of life I am captive in this cage of laws fashioned by men for the feeling.

"In the cradle of Creation's beauties, between the hands of Love, I died neglected. For the bounty of those beauties and the fruits of this Love were forbidden to me. All that did awaken my desire was in man's conception shameful; and that for which I yearned did he judge a thing of scorn.

"I am the human heart, which is imprisoned in the darkness of the multitude's edicts and fettered by illusion until I am arrived at death's point.

"I am forsaken and abandoned in the corners of civilization and its seduction. The tongue of mankind is bound and its eyes are dry the while they smile."

These words did I hear and behold as they came out with the very drops of blood from that wounded heart.

Thereafter I saw no thing more, neither did I hear a voice, for I had returned to my reality.

LETTERS OF FIRE
"Here lies one whose name was writ in water."
JOHN KEATS

IS IT THAT the nights pass by us
And destiny treads us underfoot?
Is it thus the ages engulf us and remember us not save as a
    name upon a page writ in water in place of ink?
Is this life to be extinguished
And this love to vanish
And these hopes to fade?

Shall death destroy that which we build
And the winds scatter our words,
And darkness hide our deeds?

Is this then life?
A past that has gone and left no trace,
A present, pursuing the past?
Or a future, without meaning, save when it is present
    and past?
Shall all that is joy in our hearts
And all that saddens our spirit
Vanish ere we know their fruits?

Shall man be even as the foam
That sits an instant on the ocean's face
And is taken by the passing breeze –
And is no more?

No, in truth, for the verity of life is life;
Life whose birth is not in the womb
Nor its end in death.

What are these years if not an instant in eternity?

This earthly life and all therein
Is but a dream by the side of the awakening
We call by death and terror.
A dream, yet all we see and do therein
Endures with God's enduring.

The air bears every smile and every sigh
Arising from our hearts,
And stores away the voice of every kiss
Whose source and spring is love
And angels make account
Of every tear dropped by sadness from our eyes,
And fill the ears of wandering spirits
With song created by our hidden joys.

Yonder in the hereafter
We shall see the beating of our hearts
And comprehend the meaning of our godlike state,
That in this day we hold as nought
Because despair is ever at our heels.

The erring that today we call a weakness
Shall appear on the morrow
A link in man's existence.
The fret and toil that requite us not
Shall abide with us to tell our glory.
The afflictions that we bear
Shall be to us a crown of honour.

If that sweet singer Keats had known that his songs would never cease to plant the love of beauty in men's hearts, surely he had said:

"Write upon my gravestone: Here lie the remains of him who wrote his name on heaven's face in letters of fire."

AMIDST THE RUINS

THE MOON DREW a fine veil across the City of the Sun and stillness enveloped all creation. And the awesome ruins rose like giants mocking at nocturnal things.

In that hour two forms without substance appeared out of the void like mist ascending from the surface of a lake. They sat them on a marble column which time had wrenched from that wondrous edifice, and looked down upon a scene that spoke of enchanted places. After a while one of them lifted up his head and, in a voice likened to the echo thrown back by distant valleys, said:

"These are the remains of those shrines that I builded for you, my beloved; and there the ruins of a palace I raised for your pleasure. Now they are level with the earth, and naught remains save a trace to tell to the nations of the glory for whose renown I expended my life and the might for whose aggrandizement I did put to work the weak. Look well and ponder, beloved, for the elements have vanquished the city I builded, and the ages have made as naught the wisdom I knew, and forgetfulness has overtaken the kingdom I founded. No thing remains save the particles of love created by your beauty and the beauty your love brought to life.

"I builded a temple in Jerusalem to worship therein. The priests sanctified it, and the days brought it to dust. Then I builded to love a temple within me, and God sanctified it, and no thing shall prevail against it. I passed my days seeking to know things of matter and substance, and men said: 'How wise is he in things of the world!' And the angels said: 'How little of wisdom is he!' Then did I behold you, beloved, and sang the song of love and yearning, and the angels rejoiced thereat, but as for men, they did not heed.

"The days of my splendour were as fences between my

thirsting soul and the spirit that is in all creatures. And with my beholding you, love did awake and destroy the fences and I grieved over the days passed in submission to waves of despair, deeming all things under the sun a vanity. I put on my armour and took up my shield, and the tribes feared me. And when love lighted me I was humbled even before my kind. And when Death came, it put away that coat of mail and the earth and bore my love to God."

After a silence the other form spoke and said: "As the flower takes its fragrance and life from the soil, so in like measure does the spirit distil from the frailty of matter and its erring wisdom and strength."

Then the two forms were joined one with the other and became one and departed.

After a while the air spoke these words into those places:

"The Infinite keeps naught save Love, for it is in its own likeness."

A VISION

(To the Viscountess S. L. in answer to a letter she wrote me)

YOUTH WALKED BEFORE me and I followed in his steps until we came to a distant field. There he stopped and stood, looking at the clouds drifting across the evening sky like a flock of white lambs. He looked at the trees whose naked branches pointed heavenward as if they would ask of heaven the return of their verdant leaves. And I said: "Where are we, youth?"

He replied: "We are in the fields of perplexity. Take heed."

"Let us then return, for the desolation of this place makes me afraid and the sight of the clouds and the naked trees saddens my spirit."

And he said: "Wait awhile, for perplexity is the beginning of knowledge."

Then I looked and beheld a nymph drawing nigh to us like a vision, and in my astonishment I cried: "Who is this?"

"'Tis Melpomene, daughter of Jupiter, and goddess of tragedy," answered he.

"And what wants tragedy of me whilst you are yet by my side, happy youth?" And he answered me and said: "She has come to show you the world and its sorrows, for who has not seen sorrow cannot see joy."

Then the nymph put her hand over my eyes, and when she lifted it my youth was gone and I was naked of the garments of matter. And I said: "Where is youth, daughter of the gods?" She answered me not, but embraced me with her wings and took me in flight to the summit of a high mountain. And I saw the earth and all in it spread out before me like a page, and the secrets of its habitants appeared before my eyes like writings. And so did I stand in awe by the side of the nymph, gazing on Man's mysteries and striving to know life's symbols.

I saw, yea, I saw, yet would that I had been sightless. I saw

angels of happiness contending with devils of misfortune, between them Man, and in his perplexity was he drawn now to hope, now to despair. I beheld love and hate playing with the human heart. This one concealed his guilt and made him drunk of the wine of submission and loosed his tongue in eulogy and praise. That one excited his passions and blinded him to truth and closed his ears against right speech.

I beheld the city squatting like a daughter of the streets holding to the hem of Man's garment. And the beautiful wild parts I saw standing from afar and weeping for his sake.

I beheld priests, sly like foxes; and false messiahs dealing in trickery with the people. And men crying out, calling upon wisdom for deliverance, and Wisdom spurning them with anger because they heeded not when she called them in the streets before the multitude.

I saw heads of religion vying one with another in raising their eyes heavenward, the while their hearts were interred in the graves of lust. I saw young men showing love on their tongues and drawing near to the hopes of their boldness, their divineness a distant thing, and their affections aslumber.

I saw also lawmakers trading their garbled speech in the market of shame and deceit; and physicians making sport with the trusting souls of the simple. The ignorant sitting with the wise also did I see, raising his past upon a throne of glory and cushioning his present at ease upon a carpet of spaciousness and spreading for his future a bed of honour.

I saw the wretched poor sowing and the powerful rich harvesting and eating; and oppression standing there and the people calling it Law.

Thieves and robbers and darkness I beheld, stealing the treasures of the mind; and the custodians of light drowned in the sleep of sloth.

A woman I saw like a lute in the hands of one who cannot play upon it and is displeased with its sound.

I beheld those armies investing the city of privilege; and armies in retreat because they were few in number and not united. And true freedom walking alone in the streets, seeking shelter before doors and rejected by the people. Then I saw selffulness walking in a mighty procession and the multitude hailed it as freedom.

I saw religion buried within books and in its stead illusion. I saw men wearing patience as a cloak for cowardice and calling forbearance by the name of sloth; and gentleness they dubbed as fear. I saw the intruder at the banquet making claim while the guest remained silent. And wealth in the hands of a squanderer as a snare of evildoing, and in the hands of the miser as hatred of his fellows. In the hands of the sage I saw not any riches.

When I beheld all these things I cried out in agony: "Is this, then, the earth, daughter of the gods? Is this indeed man?"

And she answered in a still wounding voice: "This is the path of the spirit, paved with stones and thorns. This is man's shadow. This is the night, but morning will come."

Thereupon she put her hands on my eyes, and when they were lifted I beheld myself and my youth walking slowly. And hope ran before me.

TODAY AND YESTERDAY

THE RICH MAN walked in the garden of his palace, and in his footsteps followed care and above his head hovered disquiet like vultures that circle over a dead body. He came to a lake that men had wrought with art and cunning, and around it were images in alabaster. Then he sat him down and looked, now at the water pouring forth from the mouths of the stone figures as the pouring out of thoughts from the imagination of a lover; now at his fine palace, sitting on high ground like a mole on the cheek of a maiden.

There he sat, and remembrance sat beside him unfolding before his eyes pages that the past had written in the story of his life. And he fell to reading, the while tears concealed from his sight that which men had builded about him, and grief brought back to his heart the strands of days that the gods had woven, and his anguish overflowed in words and he said:

"Yesterday I pastured my sheep on the green heights and rejoiced in life and played on my pipe to tell of my rejoicing. Today I am the captive of greed, and riches are leading me to riches, and more riches to miserliness, and miserliness to despair. I was as a bird trilling its song and a butterfly fluttering hither and thither. No gentle breeze was lighter in step on the flower-tops than my footsteps upon those fields.

"Behold me now a prisoner of people's customs. See how I dissimulate in my dress and at my board and in all that I do for the sake of people's favour and approbation. Would that I were born to rejoice in existence! Riches have decreed me tread the paths of sorrow, and I am like to a camel heavy-laden with gold and dying beneath its burden.

"Where are the vast plains and the murmuring brooks? Where the washed air and nature's glory? Where is my Godlikeness? All these things are lost to me, and naught remains save the gold

I love ever mocking me, an abundance of slaves, and diminished joy; and a mansion I raised to bring down my happy state.

"Once I roamed with the Bedouin's daughter, with virtue as a third one and love as our companion and the moon our guardian. This day do I walk among women whose necks are outstretched, in whose eyes is dalliance, who sell for rings and girdles and bracelets their bodies.

"Once I played with young playmates and we ran among the trees like gazelles. We sang together songs of happiness and shared the pleasures of field and meadow. Today am I become a lamb in the midst of ravening beasts. Whensoever I walk in the streets eyes of hate are cast upon me and envious fingers point to me. And in the pleasure grounds I see but frowning faces and lifted heads.

"Yesterday was I granted life and nature's beauty; today I am plundered of them: yesterday was I rich in my joy; today I am become poor in my riches. Yesterday I was with my flock as a merciful ruler among his subjects; today I stand before gold as a cringing slave before a tyrannous master.

"I knew not that riches would efface the very essence of my spirit, nor did I know that wealth would lead it to the dark caves of ignorance. And I reckoned not that what people call glory is naught except torment and the pit."

And the man of riches rose from his place and walked slowly toward his palace, sighing the while, and saying again and again: "Are these, then, riches? Is this, then, the god whose priest I am become? Is this the thing we barter for life, yet cannot exchange it for a single grain of life? Who will sell me one beautiful thought for a measure of gold? Who will take from me a handful of gems for a particle of love? Who will give me an eye through which to behold beauty and take in its stead my treasury?"

And when he came to the gate of his palace he turned and looked toward the city as did Jeremiah to Jerusalem. He raised his hands toward it as though in lamentation and cried out in a loud voice: "O people who walk in darkness and sit in the shadow of death; who pursue woe and judge falsely and speak in ignorance! Till when will you eat of thistles and thorns and cast fruits and herbs into the abyss? Till when will you dwell in wild and desolate places and turn aside from the garden of life? Wherefore do you clothe yourselves in rags and tatters when garments of silk are fashioned for you?

"O people, the lamp of wisdom is extinguished; therefore replenish it with oil. And the wayfarer destroys the vineyard of good fortune; therefore watch over it. The robber plunders the coffers of your peace; therefore take heed."

In that minute a poor man stood before the rich man and stretched forth his hand for alms. The rich man looked on him, and his trembling lips became firm and his sad countenance expanded and from his eyes shone the light of kindliness. The yesterday he had lamented on the shore of the lake was come today to greet him. He drew near to the beggar and kissed him with a kiss of love and brotherliness and filled his hands with gold. Then he said with compassion in his words: "Take now, my brother, and return on the morrow with your companions and take you all of what is yours." And the poor man smiled the smile of a withered flower after the rain and departed hastily.

Then the man of riches entered into his palace, saying: "All things in life are good, even riches, for they teach man a lesson. Riches are as a musical instrument that gives off only discord to him who cannot play on it. Wealth is as love in that it destroys him who withholds it but grants life to him who gives freely of it."

HAVE MERCY, MY SOUL

HOW LONG, my soul, will you continue in lamenting
Whilst yet sensible of my weakness?
Until when will you cry out,
Whilst yet I have naught save the speech of men
To tell therein your dreams?

Consider, my soul,
How I did pass my days in hearkening to your teaching.
Look well, my tormentor, behold my body
Wasted and enfeebled in pursuit of you.
My heart was sovereign,
It is now become your slave;
My patience was a comforter,
It is now my chastiser.
My youth was to me a fellow,
Yet today is become my blamer.
This is the all the gods have granted.
What thing more do you desire!

I have denied myself
And abandoned life's joy,
And turned aside from the glory of my years.
Now naught remains to me save you.
Judge me, then, with justice,
For justice is your splendour,
Or summon Death, and free me
From the prison of your essence.

Have mercy, my soul,
For you have burdened me
With a love I cannot carry.
You and love are as one in strength,
And I and matter – weakness divided.
Shall the struggle between strong and weak be eternal?

Have mercy, my soul,
For you did show to me fortune from afar.
You and fortune are upon a high mountain;
I and misfortune in a deep valley.
Shall the high and the low meet?

Have mercy, my soul,
For you have revealed to me beauty –
And concealed it.
You and beauty are in the light;
I and ignorance in darkness.
Shall light and darkness merge?

You, O soul, rejoice in the hereafter –
Ere its coming.
This body despairs of life
Whilst yet in life.

You walk toward the Infinite, hastening;
This body falters in its step to destruction.
You tarry not, and it does not hasten.
This, O soul, is the summit of despair.
You are raised aloft by Heaven;
This body falls, descending with earth's pull.
You do not console it,
And it says you not: "Well done."
This, my soul, is hate.

You, O soul, are rich in your wisdom;
This body is poor in its understanding.
You deal not with leniency,
And it follows you not.
This, my soul, is the sum of wretchedness.

You walk in the still night
To the beloved,
And rejoice in his embrace and love.
This body remains
E'er the slain of separation and longing.
Have mercy on me, my soul.

THE WIDOW AND HER SON

NIGHT DESCENDED SWIFTLY upon northern Lebanon, over-
taking a day wherein much snow had fallen on the villages
around Wadi Kadisha.[1] It made of the fields and hillocks a white
page upon which the winds had inscribed lines and then erased
them. The tempest played with them, making the angry sky at
one with wrathful nature.

People took refuge in their houses and beasts in their stalls,
and no living thing moved. No thing remained without save the
bitter cold and the black terrifying night, and death, strong and
fearsome.

In a lonely cottage in one of those villages a woman sat before
the fire weaving a garment of wool. By her side sat her only
child, looking now into the fire, now up at the serene face of
his mother.

In that hour the storm grew in force and the winds increased
in violence until the walls of the house trembled and shook. The
boy became frightened and drew near to his mother, seeking in
her tenderness a protection against the enraged elements. She
held him to her breast and kissed him and seated him on her
lap, saying: "Be not afraid, my son, for it is naught save Nature
warning man of her might against his littleness, and her strength
by the side of his weakness. Fear not, my child, for beyond the
falling snows and thick clouds and the howling tempest is a Holy
Spirit who is knowing of the needs of the fields. Beyond all
things is a Power that looks upon the wretchedness of mankind
with mercy and compassion. Be not frightened, my precious
one, for Nature, who smiles with the spring and laughs on a

---

1 I.e., the Valley of the Saints. So called because it was a refuge of ascetics
and holy men seeking sanctuary from the world and its tribulations. –
Author's note.

summer's day and sighs with autumn's coming, now wants to weep. With her cold tears is watered sleeping life under the layers of earth.

"Sleep, then, my child, for your father looks down upon us from eternal pastures. Storm and snow bring near to us the remembrance of those immortal spirits.

"Sleep, my darling, for out of the warring elements will come forth beautiful flowers for you to gather in the mouth of Nisan.[1] So it is, my son, that men reap not love save after painful absence and bitter patience and black despair.

"Sleep, my little one, and sweet dreams shall come to your spirit, unafraid of the awe of night and the cold without."

The boy looked up at his mother with eyes darkened by sleepiness and said: "My eyes are sleepy, Mother, and I am afraid to go to sleep before saying my prayers."

The mother embraced him tenderly and, looking through her tears to his child's face, said:

"Say with me, my child: Have mercy, O Lord, upon the poor and guard them against the bitter cold and clothe their naked bodies with Thy hands. Look Thou to the orphans aslumber in huts, whose bodies are hurt by the snow's cold breath.

"Hearken, O Lord, to the cry of the widow standing in the street between death and cold. Stretch forth Thy hand to the rich man's heart and open Thou his eyes that he may see the wretchedness of the weak and the oppressed.

"Show pity, O Lord, to those ahunger outside doors on this dark night, and guide the stranger to a refuge of warmth, and have mercy on his strangeness.

"Look, O Lord, upon the fledgling and preserve with Thy right hand the tree fearful of the harsh wind. Be this so, O Lord."

And when sleep had gathered up the boy, his mother laid him upon the bed and kissed his brow with trembling lips. Then she returned to the fireside and there sat making for him a coat of wool.

1 April.

A PEOPLE AND DESTINY

AT THE FOOT of Mount Lebanon a shepherdess sat by a stream that wound its way among rocks like a silver thread. About her moved her flock of sheep, lean and sickly of body, feeding off the dried-up grass that grew amidst clumps of thistle and thorn. A maiden she was, looking into the twilight as though she would read in it of days to come on the pages of space. Tears stood in her eyes like dewdrops on the narcissus, and sorrow opened her lips that it might plunder her heart of sighs.

And when evening came and the heights were clothed in garments of black, there appeared unawares before the girl an old man whose white hair fell upon his shoulders and breast. In his right hand was a sharpened scythe. He spoke with a voice that had in it the sound of sea waves, saying: "Peace be upon Syria."

The girl rose to her feet, afraid, and said in a voice in which were fear and grief:

"What would you of me, Destiny? Behold the remnant of a flock that once filled these valleys; the remnant of your coveting. Are you come, then, to demand even more? These are the pastures your treading has rendered barren; once they were the source of sustenance and fertility. My lambs fed of the flower-tops and gave forth sweet milk. Now are their bellies empty and they gnaw thistles and tree roots out of fear that they might perish.

"Fear God, Destiny, and get you hence from me, for the remembrance of your oppression has made me to hate life, and the cruelty of your scythe has made death beloved of me.

"Leave me with my aloneness to drink of tears for wine and lift my nostrils to grief as a breeze. Go you to the places of the West wherein the people are at life's wedding feast and let me to mourn at burials you have determined."

The old man looked on her as a father looks on his child. Then he concealed his scythe in the folds of his cloak and said:

"Naught have I taken from you, O Syria, save of my gifts; neither have I plundered, but have borrowed to restore. Know that your sisters the nations have a portion in that splendour which was your handmaid, and title to wear the cloak that was yours. I and justice are the two elements of one being. It is not pleasing to me that I give not to your sisters that which I gave to you. I am not able to make you equal portions in my love, for love does not so divide itself. Your likeness is in your neighbours, Egypt and Persia and Greece, for their flocks are even as your flocks, and their pastures even as your pastures. That which you call by abasement, O Syria, is in my sight a needful slumber before the awakening to strength and deeds. No flower returns to life save by way of death, and love does not become a mighty thing except after separation."

The old man drew near to the girl and, stretching forth his hand, said: "Take you my hand, Daughter of the Prophets." And she took his hand and looked toward him through a veil of tears, saying: "Fare you well, Destiny, fare you well." And he returned: "Fare you well, Syria, for we shall meet again."

Whereupon the old man was gone with the quickness of lightning. The shepherdess called to her flock and went on her way, murmuring the while: "Shall there again be meeting?"

BEFORE THE THRONE OF BEAUTY

I FLED FROM the multitude and wandered in that wide valley, now following the course of the stream, now listening to the conversation of the birds, until I came to a place guarded by branches from the heat of the sun. There I sat and communed with my spirit and addressed my aloneness. A thirsty spirit that saw the visible as a mirage and the unseen as an oasis.

And when my mind had fled from the prison of matter to the realm of imagining, I turned my head and beheld, standing by my side, a maiden. It was a nymph of paradise. On her was neither garment nor adornment save a branch of the vine that concealed part of her, and a crown of poppies that bound her hair of gold. And when she perceived my glances of surprise and wonderment, she said: "I am a daughter of the forests. Fear me not."

And I asked her, saying: "Do those of your like dwell in a place inhabited by desolation and wild beasts? Tell me who you are and whence you come."

She sat down on the grass and said: "I am a symbol of Nature. I am the virgin whom your forefathers did adore; for whom they builded altars and shrines and temples in Baalbek and Aphaca and Byblos." And I said: "Those temples are destroyed and the bones of my forefathers lie level with the earth, and naught remains of their gods and their ways save a few pages between the covers of books."

Said she: "Many of their gods live in the life of their adorers and die in their death. Others of them live eternally and forever. My god-state is sustained by the beauty you behold wheresoever you lift your eyes; a beauty that is Nature in all her forms. A beauty that is the beginning of the shepherd's happiness as he stands among the hills; and of the villager's in his fields; and of the wandering tribes between mountain and plain. A beauty that is a stepping-stone for the wise to the throne of living truth."

Then I said, the while my heartbeats uttered things unknown of the tongue: "In truth, beauty is a terrible and awe-filling force." And on her lips was the smile of a flower and in her eyes the hidden things of life. She said: "You, children of the flesh, are afraid of all things, even yourselves do you fear. You fear heaven, the source of safety. Nature do you fear, yet it is a haven of rest. You fear the God of all gods, and attribute to Him envy and malice. Yet what is He if not love and compassion?"

After a silence, in which were gentle dreams, I asked of her: "What thing is this beauty? For people differ in its defining and their knowledge thereof as they contend one with another in praise and love of it."

And she answered: "It is that which draws your spirit. It is that which you see and makes you to give rather than receive. It is that thing you feel when hands are stretched forth from your depths to clasp it to your depths. It is that which the body reckons a trial and the spirit a bounty. It is the link between joy and sorrow. It is all that you perceive hidden and know unknown and hear silent. It is a force that begins in the holy of holies of your being and ends in that place beyond your visions...."

Then the daughter of the forests drew near to me and laid her fragrant hand on my eyelids. And when she lifted it, behold, I was alone in that valley.

I returned, the while my spirit recited: "In truth is beauty that which you see and makes you to give rather than receive."

A VISIT FROM WISDOM

IN THE STILLNESS of night Wisdom came and stood by my bed. She gazed upon me like a tender mother and wiped away my tears, and said: "I have heard the cry of your spirit and I am come to comfort it. Open your heart to me and I shall fill it with light. Ask of me and I shall show you the way of truth."

And I said: "Who am I, Wisdom, and how came I to this frightening place? What manner of things are these mighty hopes and these many books and strange patterns? What are these thoughts that pass as doves in flight? And these words composed by desire and sung by delight, what are they? What are these conclusions, grievous and joyous, that embrace my spirit and envelop my heart? And those eyes which look at me seeing into my depths and fleeing from my sorrows? And those voices mourning my days and chanting my littleness, what are they?

"What is this youth that plays with my desires and mocks at my longings, forgetful of yesterday's deeds, rejoicing in paltry things of the moment, scornful of the morrow's coming?

"What is this world that leads me whither I know not, standing with me in despising? And this earth that opens wide its mouth to swallow bodies and lets evil things to dwell on its breast? What is this creature that is satisfied with the love of fortune, whilst beyond its union is the pit? Who seeks Life's kiss whilst Death does smite him, and brings the pleasure of a minute with a year of repentance, and gives himself to slumber the while dreams call him? What is he who flows with the rivers of folly to the sea of darkness? O Wisdom, what manner of things are these?"

And she answered, saying:

"You would see, human creature, this world through the eyes of a god. And you would seek to know the secrets of the here-after with the thinking of men. Yet in truth is this the height of folly.

"Go you to the wild places and you shall find there the bee above the flowers and behold the eagle swooping down on his prey. Go you into your neighbour's house and see then the child blinking at the firelight and his mother busied at her household tasks. Be you like the bee and spend not the days of spring looking on the eagle's doing. Be as the child and rejoice in the firelight and heed not your mother's affairs. All that you see with your eyes was and is for your sake.

"The many books and the strange patterns and beautiful thoughts are the shades of those spirits that came ere you were come. The words that you do weave are a bond between you and your brothers. The conclusions, grievous and joyous, are the seeds that the past did scatter in the field of the spirit to be reaped by the future. That youth who plays with your desires is he who will open the door of your heart to let enter the light. This earth with the ever open mouth is the saviour of your spirit from the body's slavery. This world which walks with you is your heart; and your heart is all that you think that world. This creature whom you see as ignorant and small is the same who has come from God's side to learn pity through sadness, and knowledge by way of darkness."

Then Wisdom put her hand on my burning brow and said:

"Go then forward and do not tarry, for before walks perfection. Go, and have not fear of thorns on the path, for they deem naught lawful save corrupted blood."

THE TALE OF A FRIEND

I

I KNEW HIM as a young man lost on the road of Life, ruled by his youthful deeds, baiting Death in the pursuit of his desires. I knew him as a tender bloom borne by the winds of fancy to the fathomless sea of lust.

I knew him in that little village as a cruel boy whose fingers tore apart the nests of birds and slew their young. Who trampled flowers underfoot and destroyed their beauty. I knew him at school, as one in adolescence, scorning learning and an enemy of peace. I knew him in the city for a youth who traded his father's honour in the market place of loss, squandering his riches in places of shame and surrendering his mind to the daughter of the vine.

Withal, I loved him. Ay, I loved him with a love compounded of sorrow and kneaded with compassion. I loved him because his faults were not the fruits of a small spirit, but rather the acts of a spirit weak and despairing.

The spirit, O people, avoids the path of wisdom unwillingly, but returns thereto willingly. And in youth is a whirlwind that blows the dust and the sands and carries them along and fills the eye to close and blind it.

I loved that youth and felt for him a warmth, for I had seen the dove of his conscience contending with the vulture of his evil parts, and the dove was vanquished by her adversary's strength and not by cause of her cowardliness. The conscience is a judge, just and weak, and weakness stands in the way of its carrying out of judgment.

I have said that I loved him. But love comes in many guises. Sometimes it is as wisdom, other times justice, ofttimes hope. My love for him was my hope that the strong light of its sun might triumph over the darkness of transient sorrows. But

I knew not when and where a filthiness became a clean thing, and cruelty kindness, and ignorance wisdom. A man knows not in what manner the spirit is freed from matter until after it is freed. Neither knows he how a flower smiles save after the coming of morning.

II

The days followed on the heels of the nights, and I remembered that youth with pain and grief and I uttered his name with a sighing that rent the heart. Then yesterday came from him a letter, saying:

"Come to me, my friend, for I wish to take you to a young man. Your heart will rejoice at his meeting and your spirit will be refreshed at his knowing."

I said: "Alas! Does he seek to add to his sad friendship the companionship of another like him? Is he not in himself an example to point the words of error? Does he now seek to write in the margin of that example the words of his companions so that not even one letter in the book of matter shall pass me by?"

Again did I say: "I will go, and mayhap the spirit in its wisdom shall find for me a fig among the thistles, and the heart in its love draw light out of darkness."

And when night fell I betook myself thence and found the young man alone in a room reading from a book of verse. I greeted him and wondered at the book in his hands, and said:

"Where, then, is the new friend?"

"I am he, my friend, I am he," he returned. He sat with a quietness I had not known in him; then he looked at me. In his eyes was a strange light that pierced the breast. The eyes in which I had for so long seen no thing save harshness and cruelty now radiated a light that filled the heart with love. In a voice that seemed to come from another than him he said: "In truth, that one whom you knew as a child and whose playfellow you were and whom you accompanied in youth is dead, and out of his dying I am born. I am he, your new friend. Take, then, my hand."

I took his hand and felt in its touch a gentle spirit coursing with the blood; ay, that hard and cruel hand was become soft and tender. The fingers that yesterday were a panther's claws today caress the heart with their lightness.

Again I spoke (would that I remembered the strangeness of my words): "Who are you, what has befallen you, how are you become thus? Has the Spirit taken you as a sanctuary and sanctified you, or are you playing before me a poet's fancy?"

He answered: "Ay, my friend, the Spirit has in truth descended upon me and sanctified me. A mighty love has made my heart an altar of purity. It is woman; woman, whom yesterday I reckoned a plaything of men, has delivered me from the darkness of the pit and opened before me the gates of paradise and I have entered. The true woman has led me to the Jordan of her love and baptized me. She whose sister I did in my folly despise has lifted me to the throne of glory. She whose companion in my blindness I despoiled has cleansed me with her love. She whose kind I did enslave has liberated me with her beauty. She that did cast the first man from the Garden by the strength of her desire and his weakness has led me back to Eden by her compassion and my obedience."

I looked on him in that moment and beheld tears in his eyes and a smile on his lips and the light of love as a crown on his head. I drew near to him and kissed his brow in blessing as the priest kisses the face of the altar.

I bade him farewell, repeating the while his words: "She that did cast the first man from the Garden by the strength of her desire and his weakness has led me back to Eden by her compassion and my obedience."

FANTASY AND TRUTH

LIFE CARRIES US hither and thither and destiny moves us from one place to another. We see not save the obstacle set in our path; neither do we hear save a voice that makes us to fear.

Beauty appears before us seated on her throne of glory and we draw nigh. And in the name of longing do we defile her garment's hem and wrest from her the crown of purity.

Love passes by us clothed in a robe of gentleness, and we are afraid and hide us in dark caves, or follow her and do evil things in her name.

The wise man walks in our midst bearing his heavy yoke; yet is it softer than the breath of a flower and gentler than the breezes of Lebanon.

Wisdom stands on the street corner and calls to us above the multitude, but we deem her a thing without worth and despise them that follow her.

Wisdom summons us to her board that we may enjoy her food and drink; and we go thence and fill our bellies, and that table becomes an occasion for littleness and a place of self-abasement.

Nature stretches forth to us the hand of friendship and bids us take delight in her beauty; but we fear her stillness and take refuge in the city and tumble one upon another as a flock of sheep before the prowling wolf.

Truth visits us led by the smile of a child and a lover's kiss, and we close the door of our tenderness against her and abandon her as one unclean.

*

The human heart asks succour of us, and the spirit calls us, but we stand as one turned to stone, hearing not nor understanding.

And when one hears the cry of his heart and the call of his spirit, we say that such a one is possessed of a madness, and we cleanse ourselves of him.

Thus wise pass the nights and we are heedless of them. The days meet us, and we fear the days and the nights.

We are near to earth, yet the gods are our kin. We pass by the bread of life, and hunger feeds off our strength.

How sweet to us is life, and how far we are from life!

O MY POOR FRIEND

O YOU WHO were born on a bed of sorrow and reared in the lap of misfortune and brought to manhood in the houses of oppression, you who eat your crust of bread with a sigh and drink of your clouded water with tears and weeping.

O soldier who is sentenced by man's cruel law to forsake his mate and his little ones and kin to go out of the field of death for the sake of greed in its guise of duty.

And you, poet, who sojourn in the land of your birth, unknown among those who know you, satisfied with a morsel and fragments of ink and paper.

O captive, cast into the darkness for a small wrong made big by those who match evil with evil; banished by them that seek doing good by way of corruption.

And you, unfortunate woman, on whom God did bestow beauty; upon whom the eyes of the young men of the age fell, who pursued you and tempted you and conquered your poverty with gold. To them you did yield and were left as prey trembling in the hold of misery and shame.

You, my beloved weak, are the martyrs of men's law. You are in despair, and your despairing is the fruit of the iniquity of the strong and the ruler's deceit and the rich man's oppressing, and the selffulness of the lustful.

Despair not. For beyond the wrongs of the world, beyond matter and clouds and air, beyond all things is a Power that is justice and mercy and love and compassion.

You are as flowers that grow in the shade. Gentle breezes shall pass and bear your needs to the sunlight, and you shall live there a pleasant life.

You are like to naked trees bowed under heavy winter snows. But soon will spring come to clothe you with fresh green leaves.

Truth shall tear aside the veil of tears that conceals your smile. And I will greet you, my brothers, and humble your oppressors.

LAMENT OF THE FIELD

AT THE HOUR of dawn, before the sun's rising from beyond the horizon, I sat in the middle of a field communing with Nature. At that hour filled with purity and beauty I lay on the grass, what time men were yet wrapped in slumber, disturbed now by dreams, now by awakening. I lay there seeking to know from all that I looked upon the truth of Beauty and the beauty of Truth.

And when my reflecting had set me apart from the flesh, and my imaginings lifted the covering of matter from off my inner self, I felt my spirit growing, drawing me near to Nature and revealing to me her hidden things and teaching me the language of her wonders.

Thus I was as the breeze passed through the branches of the tree, sighing plaintively like an orphan child. I sought understanding and said: "Why do you sigh, gentle breeze?" And it answered: "Because I am going to the city away from the sun's warmth. To the city, where the germs of sickness and disease will cling to the hem of my clean garment, and the poisoned breath of flesh breathe on me. Because of this do you behold my sadness."

Then I looked toward the flowers and saw dewdrops falling like tears from their eyes. I said:

"Why weep you thus, fair flowers?" And one of them lifted up its head in reply and said:

"We weep because men will come and cut off our heads and take us to the city and sell us, who are free, as slaves. And when evening falls and we are withered they will cast us into the dust. How then should we weep not when men in their cruelty would separate us from our home the field?"

After a while I heard the brook lamenting like a bereaved mother over her lost ones, and I asked: "Why do you lament, sweet brook?" And it answered: "Because I am driven to the city, wherein men despise me and exchange me for the juice of grapes and make me to carry their dregs. How then should I not lament when soon my innocence will become guilt and my purity dross?"

And I heard the birds chanting a mournful chant like to a dirge and I said: "Wherefore do you mourn, comely birds?" Whereupon a small one among them approached me and said: "Tomorrow a man will come bearing in his hand a fearful instrument to destroy us, as the sickle cuts off the standing corn. We shall bid farewell one of the other, for we know not which among us will escape his doom. How then should we not mourn when death follows us wheresoever we go?"

The sun rose from behind a mountain and crowned the tree-tops with gold, the while I asked myself why men pull down what Nature has builded up.

THE PALACE AND THE HUT

I

NIGHT WAS FALLING and the lights in the mansion of the rich man shone brightly. The servants, clad in velvet, with buttons gleaming on their breasts, stood awaiting the guests. Music played and the lords and ladies descended on that palace from all parts, drawn in their carriages by fine horses. There they entered, trailing after them their rich garments and dragging the ends of pomp and pride.

Then the men rose from their places and took the ladies to dance. And that hall became a garden through which the breezes of melody passed, and its flowers inclined in awe and wonder.

Soon midnight approached and the table was laid with the choicest of fruits and the finest of foods. Cups were passed from one to another and wine played with the senses of all those there until they in turn took to play. And when morning was near they dispersed, for they were tired with merrymaking and bemused by wine and wearied of dancing and revelry. And everyone betook himself to his bed.

II

As the sun sank low beyond the horizon, a man dressed in the garb of a labourer stood at the door of a mean house and knocked thereon. It opened to him and he entered, greeting those within with a cheerful countenance, and sat down in the midst of his children by the fire.

After a while his wife prepared a meal and they seated themselves around a wooden table and ate their food. And after their repast was finished they rose and sat by the lamp, which sent the arrows of its feeble yellow rays into the heart of the darkness. When the first watch of night was passed they lay down in silence and gave themselves to sleep.

At dawn's approach that poor man rose from his bed and partook of a little bread and milk with his wife and little ones. Then he kissed them and went away with a heavy spade over his shoulder to the field, to water it with his sweat and make it fruitful that it might feed those mighty ones who yestereve made merry.

The sun rose from beyond the mountain and the heat was heavy on the head of the toiler, the while those with riches still slept in their mansions.

So is man's burden: a tragedy played on the stage of time. Many are the spectators that applaud; few are they that comprehend and know.

TWO INFANTS

A PRINCE STOOD on the balcony of his palace and hailed the multitude gathered in the palace garden and cried: "I bring you good tidings and felicitate our country, for the Princess has brought forth a boy to perpetuate the honour and glory of my line. He will be to you a pride and delight and the heir to the inheritance of my great forefathers. Rejoice then and give songs of praise, for your future now belongs to this scion of our house."

And the multitude raised its voice in shouting and filled the air with ululations of joy in honour of one to be reared in the cradle of plenty and raised in the seat of the mighty; to be supreme ruler over the necks of slaves and to drive with his strength the weak. To be free to enchain their bodies and destroy their souls. For such a thing were they rejoicing and singing songs and drinking out of cups of joy.

And that time the people of that town sang the praises of power and humbled themselves before an oppressor and made the angels to weep for their littleness, a woman lay prostrate on a bed of pain in an old and abandoned dwelling. To her burning breast she clasped an infant swaddled in rags. A girl she was to whom the days had allotted poverty and misery and whom men had forsaken. A wife whose man had the tyranny of the Prince destroyed. A woman alone to whom the gods that night had sent a little friend to shackle her hands against earning her substance by their labour.

When the noise of the multitude in the streets had died, the wretched woman placed the infant on her lap and looked into its shining eyes, and she wept a bitter weeping as though she would baptize the child with her tears. Then in a voice such as even would pierce a rock she said: "Why did you come, O flesh of my flesh, from the world of spirits? Was it out of desire to

793

share with me life's bitterness? Or out of compensation for my weakness? Why did you leave the angels and the spaceless firmament for this life, narrow and full with misery and lowliness? I have naught but tears, my only one. Will they nurture you in place of milk? And will my naked arms clothe you instead of woven stuffs? The smallest of animals pasture on sweet grasses and take shelter in safety at night. The tiniest of birds pick up grain and sleep rejoicing in the branches. But for you, my child, there is naught save my sighing and my weakness."

Thus saying, she clasped the child closely to her breast, as though she would make the two bodies one, and lifted her eyes heavenward and cried: "Have compassion on us, O Lord!"

And when the clouds scattered, revealing the moon's face, the gentle rays entered through the window of that poor house and spilled themselves over two cold bodies.

UNDER THE SUN

"I have seen all the works that are done under the sun;
and, behold, all is vanity and vexation of spirit."

ECCLESIASTES i, 14

O SPIRIT OF Solomon that floats in the vast spaces in the world of spirits, O you that have cast off the garments of matter, which we now do wear, you have left behind you these words born of weakness and despair which did create in the prisons of bodies weakness and despair.

Now is it known unto you that in this life is a meaning not concealed by death. Is it perchance that that knowledge, which is not understood until the spirit is freed from its earthly bonds, is withheld from mankind?

Now is it known unto you that life is not as a vexation of spirit, nor that all under the sun is in vain; but rather that all things were and are ever marching toward truth. Yet we have clung to your words and pondered deep on them and have not ceased to reckon them a shining wisdom. But they are a darkness that loses the mind and obscures hope, and you are knowing of that.

Now is it known unto you that ignorance and evil and tyranny have good causes. And we see not beauty save in manifestations of wisdom and the results of virtue and the fruits of justice.

Well do you know that poverty and grief purify the human heart, and that our bounded minds see no free thing in life save happiness and ease.

Well do you know that the spirit is going toward the light in face of the obstacles of life, yet do we still recite your words which tell that man is naught but a plaything in the hand of a Force unknown.

You did repent of your sending abroad a spirit to weaken love of this life and destroy the passion for the life to come. Yet did we continue to treasure your words.

O spirit of Solomon, who dwell in the region of the immortals, inspire those who love wisdom so that they take not the path of despair and disbelief; mayhap it shall be an atonement for a sin not intended.

A GLIMPSE INTO THE FUTURE

FROM BEYOND THE wall of the Present I heard the praises of mankind.

I heard the voices of bells that shook the very air, heralding the commencement of prayer in the sanctuary of Beauty. Bells wrought by strength from the metal of feeling and raised above that holy shrine – the human heart.

From beyond the Future I saw the multitudes prostrate on Nature's breast, turning toward the rising sun, awaiting the morning light – the morning of Truth.

I beheld the city razed low, naught remaining of it save its ruins telling of the flight of Darkness before Light.

I saw old men seated beneath the poplar and the willow tree; around them stood boys listening to their tales of the times.

I saw young men playing on stringed instruments and the pipe; and maidens with loosed hair dancing around them under jasmine boughs.

Likewise did I see those in middle age gathering the harvest, and women bearing away the yield with songs of gladness and joy;

And a woman too I did see who cast forth her unseemly garment for a crown of lilies and a girdle of verdant leaves from off the tree.

I saw a companionship between man and all creation;

And flights of birds and butterflies drawing nigh to him in safety,

And gazelles flocking to the pool, trusting.

*

I looked, and beheld not poverty, neither did I see anything above what suffices. Rather did I meet brotherhood and equality.

I saw not any physician, for each morrow is a healer unto itself by the law of knowledge and experience.

Neither did I see a priest, for conscience was become the High Priest.

No lawyer did I behold, for Nature was risen among them as a tribunal recording covenants of amity and fellowship.

I saw that Man was knowing of his place as the cornerstone of creation, lifted above smallness and raised above little things; tearing the veil of deception from off the eyes of the Spirit that it might read what the clouds had writ on heaven's face, and the breeze on the surface of the water; and know the manner of the flower's breathing and the meaning of the songs of the thrush and the nightingale.

*

From beyond the wall of the Present, on the stage of days to come –
I saw Beauty as the groom and the Spirit his bride
And Life, in its all, the Night of Power.[1]

1 The twenty-seventh night of Ramadan, the Moslem month of fasting, when the first revelation came to Muhammad. It is said that on this night the gates of paradise are open so that any demand made on God or the Prophet will go direct to them.

THE QUEEN OF FANTASY

I CAME TO the ruins of Palmyra and, wearied by my journey thereto, I cast myself down on the grass that grew among pillars and columns broken by time and brought level with the earth. And when night fell with the gathering together of scattered creation beneath a cloak of silence, I felt an awareness in the air about me of something that flowed, fragrant as incense and intoxicating as wine.I drank of it and felt hidden hands playing with my senses, and my eyelids grew heavy and my spirit was freed from its fetters. Then the earth opened and the firmament trembled and I leaped forward, impelled thither by an unearthly force. And I found myself in the midst of a garden whose like no human creature had imagined. About me was a company of virgins who were clothed in no garment save that of beauty. They walked around me, and as they walked, it was as though their feet touched not the ground. They chanted melodies woven from dreams of love and played upon lyres wrought of ivory and having strings of gold.

And I came to an opening and beheld in its midst a throne encrusted with precious stones. It was in a meadow from out of which flowed light and divers colours of the rainbow. On the right hand and the left stood the virgins. They lifted up their voices and looked toward a part wherefrom rose the smell of myrrh and frankincense. And lo, there came out from among the flowering branches a Queen, who walked slowly toward the throne and set herself upon it. Then a flight of doves, white as driven snow, descended, and they settled themselves about her feet in the form of a crescent.

The virgins chanted verses in praise of their Queen, and the incense ascended in columns to her glory. The while I stood and looked upon what no other man's eye had seen and heard what no human ear had heard.

Then the Queen made a sign with her hand, and all movement ceased. In a voice that made my spirit tremble as lute strings under the player's fingers, and moved everything in that enchanted place as though the things were ears and hearts, she said:

"I have called you hither, human, for I am the mistress of the regions of fantasy. I have granted you leave to stand before me, for I am Queen over the glade of dreams. Hearken, therefore, to my commands and proclaim them abroad among mankind. Say that the city of fantasy is a wedding feast, and its gate is guarded by a mighty man of valour, and no person may enter therein except he be clad in wedding garments. Say that it is a paradise whose overseer is the angel of Love, and no man may cast eyes thereon save him who has the sign of Love on his brow. It is a field of imaginings whose rivers are as good wine; whose birds cleave the air as angels; whose flowers are prodigious of their fragrance; whose ground none treads save the child of dreams.

"Speak with men and say that I granted them a cup brimful of joy, but they in their folly did pour it out and the angel of darkness came and filled it with a draught of grief. And this did they swallow up and were drunk of it. Say you that none can play upon the stringed instrument of Life save one whose finger tips have touched my girdle and whose eyes have looked upon my throne.

"Isaiah uttered verses of wisdom as a necklace of pearls strung on strands of my love. John related his vision in my tongue. And Dante trod not the pasture of souls except with my guidance. I am a symbol embracing reality; and a truth revealing the oneness of the spirit; a witness testifying to the deeds of the gods. Say: In truth, thought has a resting-place above the world of visible things, whose heaven is not obscured by the clouds of joy. And visions have form in the heaven of the gods and are reflected in the mirror of the soul so that its hope may be in all that is to be after its release from the world of matter."

Then the Queen of Fantasy drew me toward her with a look of enchanting and kissed my burning lips, saying: "Say that who passes not his days in the region of dreams is the slave of those days."

Thereupon the voices of the virgins ascended and the smoke of the incense receded and twisted upwards into the air and the vision departed. A second time the earth opened and the firmament trembled and I beheld myself back among the ruins.

The dawn broke smiling, and on my tongue and between my lips were the words: "Who passes not his days in the region of dreams is the slave of those days."

MY BLAMER

LEAVE ME, my blamer, in my solitude.
By the love that binds your spirit
To the beauty of the loved one,
I adjure you;
By the love that makes one your heart
With a mother's tenderness,
And holds you close to a child's affection,
I pray you, leave me;
Forsake me and my dreams.
I will wait upon the morrow
And it shall judge me as it will.

Advice and counsel you gave me,
But advice is naught save a spectre
Beckoning the spirit to confusion's abode
And leading it whither life is cold as earth.

I have a little heart;
I would free it from the darkness of my breast
To bear it in my palm,
Seeking its depths and asking its secrets.
Loose not your shafts at it, my blamer,
Lest you cause it to fear, and hide
Within its cage of ribs
Ere it pour out its secret's blood,
And do what the gods did will it
When they fashioned it of love and beauty.

The sun is risen
And the nightingale is trilling
And the spirit of the myrtle ascends.

I would be free of sleep's covering
To wander with the white lambs.
Frighten me not, my blamer,
With the lion of the forest
And the vipers of the valley,
For my spirit knows not fear
Nor is aware of evil ere its coming.

Leave me, my blamer,
Exhort me not,
For affliction has opened my eyes,
And tears given me sight.
Grief has taught me the language of hearts.

Cease this recital of things forbidden,
For my conscience is a tribunal
That will judge me with justice.
It will guard me from punishment if I am innocent,
And withhold from me favour when I am guilty.

The procession of love goes its way
And beauty walks with banner aloft;
And youth, too, sounding horns of joy.
Do not prevent me, my blamer,
But let me go;
For the way is strewn with roses and fragrant herbs.
And censers of musk have perfumed the air.

Free me from stories of riches and tales of glory,
For my spirit is satisfied
And busied with the glory of the gods.

Absolve me from things of pomp and state,
For the earth in its all is my land,
And all mankind my countrymen.

SOLILOQUY

WHERE ARE YOU, my love,
Are you in that little garden watering the flowers
That love you as infants love their mother's breast?
Or in your little room, wherein you have raised to innocence
    an altar
And sacrificed upon it my spirit and my heart?
Or mayhap amidst your books
Harvesting the wisdom of men –
You who are so rich in the wisdom of the gods?

Where are you, companion of my spirit?
Are you in the sanctuary praying for me?
Or in the meadow calling to Nature –
The haven of your wonder and dreams?
Or mayhap in the houses of the wretched
Consoling those of broken heart
With the sweetness of your self,
And giving of your bounty to fill their hands?
You are in all places, for you are the spirit of God,
And in all times, for you are greater and stronger than
    time itself.

Remember you the nights of our union
And the light of your spirit that was as a halo about us?
And the angels of love that hovered above us
Singing and chanting in the things of the spirit?

Remember you the days when we sat beneath the boughs
That cast o'er us a covering
And concealed us from the sight of men
As ribs conceal the sacred secrets of the heart?

And the paths and the slopes we trod, our fingers interwoven,
When we leaned our heads one against the other
As though to take refuge from ourselves within ourselves?

Remember you the hour I came to say farewell?
You embraced me and kissed me the kiss of Mary.
And I learned that where the lips embrace
They utter divine secrets the tongue knows not.
A kiss it was, the prelude to a sigh,
As the breath the Almighty breathed into clay –
And made it man.
Thus is the sigh that goes before us to the world of spirits,
Proclaiming the glory of our twin souls.
There shall it remain until we and it are joined
For eternity.

Again did you kiss and embrace me,
Saying, with tears flowing from your eyes:
"In truth have earthly bodies desires unbeknown
And must they ofttimes separate for earthly purpose,
And remain apart for worldly reason.
But all spirits abide in safety in love's hands
Till Death do come and bear them aloft to God.
Go, then, my darling, for Life has made you her delegate.
Go, obey her.
She is a comely woman, giving them that obey her
To drink from the limpid Poot[1] of joy in full.
As for me, your love has given me a waiting groom,
And your memory, an eternal wedding."

Where are you now, my companion?
Are you awake in the still night,
Waiting on a breeze
That shall carry my heartbeats and innermost thoughts
Toward you?
Or seeing the picture of your young love?

1 In Arabic, *Kauthar*, River of Paradise.

That picture is no more like the pictured,
For sadness has cast its shadow
Upon a face yesterday rejoicing in your presence,
And weeping has withered eyes your beauty did anoint.
Grief has parched a mouth moistened by your kisses.

Whither are you, beloved?
Do you hear my call and lament beyond the oceans?
See you my weakliness and abasement –
Know you of my patience and enduring?
Are there not in space spirits
To bear the last breath of a dying one?
Are there not between souls hidden strands
To carry the complaint of a lover in sickness?

Where are you, beloved?
Darkness enfolds me,
And mourning is victor.
Smile into the air and I shall be refreshed;
Breathe into the ether and I shall live.

Where are you, beloved, where . . . ?
Ah, how mighty is love,
How does it diminish me!

THE CRIMINAL

A YOUTH SAT on the roadside begging alms; a youth strong of body, made weak by hunger. There he sat with his hands stretched forth, asking of the passers-by, entreating the charitable and bewailing his lot, and crying out against the pangs of hunger.

Night fell; his lips were dry and his tongue heavy and his hands and stomach empty.

Soon he rose and went outside the city and sat him beneath the trees and wept a bitter weeping. He lifted up his tear-filled eyes and his hunger spoke, saying: "O Lord, I went to the wealthy seeking work and they turned me away because of my tattered garments. I knocked on the door of a school and they forbade me entry because my hands were empty. I sought to labour for my daily bread, but people rejected me because my star was against me. So did I come to beg.

"They that adore Thee, O Lord, beheld me and said this one is strong and able; charity is not for him given to sloth and idleness. My mother bore me at Thy willing; now by Thee do I exist. Wherefore do people deny to me the bread that I seek in Thy name?"

And on that very minute the countenance of that despairing man changed. He rose on his feet, and his eyes shone like a bright star. Then from the dried branches he fashioned for himself a stout club. He pointed with it toward the city and shouted: "I sought life with the sweat of my brow and found it not. Now shall I take it with the strength of my forearm. I begged for bread in love's name, but no man heard me. Now shall I seek it in the name of evil. . . ."

Many years passed and that youth severed necks for the sake of their adornment, and destroyed bodies to satisfy his appetite. He increased in riches and was renowned for his strength and violence. He was beloved among the plunderers of the people and feared by the law-abiding. One day the Amir appointed him deputy in that town, in the manner of all princes who chose those to speak in their name.

Thus do men in their greed make of the wretched criminals, and with their harshness drive the child of peace to kill.

THE BELOVED

'TIS THE MINUTE separating life's ecstasy from its awakening; and the first light to illumine the vast fields of the spirit.

The first enchanting note upon the first string of the heart's lyre;

The instant that brings back to the ear of the spirit the mention of bygone days, and reveals to its sight the happenings of nights past, and shows to its understanding deeds wrought by joy and grief in this world, and the secret of immortality in the world to come.

'Tis the seed that Astarte casts down from the heights to be sown by the eyes in the field of the heart, and nurtured by love and brought to fruit by the spirit.

The first glance from the beloved is like the Spirit that hovered over the face of the deep, out of which came heaven and earth;

The first glance from the companion of life's way is as the word of God when He said: "Be."

THE FIRST KISS

'Tis the first sip of a cup that the gods have filled from the limpid pool of Love. The dividing line between doubt that saddens the heart and certainty that makes it joyful.

The first line of the poem of unearthly life; the first chapter of the story of man in the spirit.

A link joining the wonder of the past with the future's splendour; uniting the silence of feeling with its song.

A word uttered by four lips making the heart a throne, and love a sovereign, and fulfilment a crown.

A soft touch like the fingertips of the breeze in their passing over the rose, bearing a sigh of gladness and a sweet moaning.

The beginning of disturbance and trembling that separate

lovers from the world of matter and transport them to the regions of inspiration and dreams.

And if the first glance is as the seed that the goddess of love sows in the field of the human heart, the first kiss is as the first blossom on the first branch of the tree of life.

UNION

Here, then, does love begin in making life's prose verse, creating from the mysteries of existence chapters chanted by the days and nights.

Thus does longing tear away the veil from the secrets of past years and fashion from the smallest joy happiness transcended only by the soul's bliss when it embraces its Lord.

Union is the fusion of two divinities to create a third on earth; the binding together of two strong in their love against an adversary weak in its hating.

'Tis the casting away by two spirits of discord and their oneness with unity.

The golden link in a chain whose first is a glance, whose last is the Infinite.

The fall of refreshing rains from heaven upon sanctified Nature to distil strength from the blessed fields.

And if the first glance from the eyes of a loved one is as the seed sown by Love in the field of the heart,

Then is the first kiss of her lips as the first blossom on the tree of life.

And in her union is the first fruit of that sowing.

THE ABODE OF HAPPINESS

MY HEART WAS weary within me and bade me farewell and repaired to the Abode of Happiness. And when it was come to that sanctuary which the spirit had sanctified, it stood in wonderment, for it saw not there things it had imagined.

It saw not there power or wealth, nor yet authority. It saw naught save the youth of Beauty and his companion the daughter of Love and their child Wisdom.

Then my heart spoke to the daughter of Love and said: "Where is contentment, O Love? I had heard that it shared with you this dwelling." And she answered: "Contentment is away preaching in the city, where is corruption and greed; we are not in need of it in this place. Happiness desires not contentment, for happiness is naught but a longing that union embraces; contentment is a diversion conquered by forgetfulness. The immortal soul is not contented, for it is ever desiring of perfection; and perfection is the Infinite."

And my heart spoke to the youth of Beauty and said: "Show to me the secret of woman, O Beauty, and enlighten me, for you are knowledge." He said: "She is you, human heart, and as you were, so was she. She is I, and wheresoever I be, there is she. She is as a religion when the ignorant profane it not; as a full moon when clouds do not hide it; as the breeze untouched by corruption and impurity."

Then my heart drew near to Wisdom, the daughter of Love and Beauty, saying: "Give me wisdom that I may carry it to humankind." She answered: "Say that happiness begins in the holy of holies of the spirit and comes not from without."

THE CITY OF THE PAST

LIFE STOOD WITH me at the foot of the mountain of youth and pointed to what was behind us. I looked, and beheld a city of strange form and pattern in the bosom of the plains, wherein were images and ascending smokes of divers colours. And the whole was veiled in a fine mist, almost obscured from sight.

I said: "What thing is this, Life?"

She answered: "It is the City of the Past. Observe it well."

And I observed and saw places of work sitting like great giants beneath the wings of slumber. And sanctuaries of words around which hovered souls crying out in despair – and singing in hope. I beheld temples of religion set up by faith and destroyed by doubting. And minarets of thoughts rising heavenward like hands uplifted for alms.

Streets of desires flowing like rivers between hills I saw. And storehouses of secrets guarded by silence and plundered by thieves of inquiring. Towers of progress builded by courage and overthrown by fear.

Palaces of dreams that the nights adorned and awakening spoiled. Dwellings of littleness inhabited by weakness; and places of aloneness wherein rose self-denial. Meeting-places of knowledge illumined by wisdom and darkened by folly. Wineshops of love wherein lovers drank, mocked by emptiness.

Stages of life whereon Life plays her piece; to which Death comes to end his tragedy.

That, then, is the City of the Past. A city far off, yet near; seen and unseen.

Then Life walked before me and said: "Follow me, for we have tarried long." And I asked: "Whither now, Life?" She answered: "To the City of the Future." Said I: "Have pity, for the journey has surely wearied me, and my feet have trodden stones, and obstacles have drunk my strength."

"Come, for only the coward tarries, and it is folly to look back on the City of the Past."

MEETING

WHEN THE NIGHT had completed its adornment of heaven's robe with the stars' jewels, there ascended from the Valley of the Nile a nymph having invisible wings. She sat upon a throne of clouds raised high above the Mediterranean Sea, which was made silver by the moonlight. Before her passed a heavenly host of spirits chanting, "Holy, holy, holy to the daughter of Egypt, whose glory filleth the earth."

And there rose from the mouth of a waterspout in the forest of the cedars the form of a youth borne by the hands of the seraphim, and he sat upon the throne by the side of the nymph. The spirits passed again, before them both, crying: "Holy, holy, holy to the youth of Lebanon, whose glory filleth the ages."

And when the lover took the hand of his beloved and looked into her eyes, the winds and the waves carried the communion of the one with the other to all the corners of the earth.

How perfect is thy splendour, O daughter of Isis, and how great my love for thee!

How comely art thou among the youths, O son of Astarte, and how great my longing for thee!

My love is like unto thy Pyramids, beloved, and the ages shall not destroy it.

My love is as thy Cedars, beloved, and the elements shall not conquer it.

The wise ones of the earth come from East and West to taste of thy wisdom and inquire of thy signs.

And the great ones of the earth come from many lands to drink the wine of thy beauty and the magic of thy mysteries.

In truth, beloved, are thy palms the source of abundance to fill the storehouses.

In truth, beloved, are thine arms the fount of sweet waters, and thy breath a refreshing breeze.

The palaces of the Nile and its temples proclaim thy glory, and Father of Terror[1] telleth of thy greatness, my love.

The cedars upon thy breast are a mark of nobleness, and the towers about thee chant thy might and valour, my love.

How goodly is thy love and how sweet is the hopeof thine exaltation, beloved!

How generous a companion art thou and how sufficient a spouse! How fine are thy gifts and how precious thine offerings! Thou sendest to me young men and they are as an awakening from deep sleep. Thou givest me a man of valour to overcome my people's feebleness; and a sage to raise them; a noble man to ennoble them.

I have sent to thee seeds and thou hast made them to flower; and young shoots and thou hast raised them as trees. For thou art the virgin field that giveth life to the rose and the lily and bringeth up the cypress tree and the cedar. . . .

1 I.e., the Sphinx.

IN A FINE palace standing in the dark night like Life in the shadow of Death a maiden sat in a chair of ivory. Her head was supported by her hand in the manner of a withered flower leaning upon its petals. She looked about her like a prisoner without hope who would pierce the prison wall with his eyes to look at life ever moving in the procession of freedom.

The hours passed as phantoms in the darkness, what time the maiden solaced herself with tears and took refuge in her solitude and grief. And when the violence of her feeling became heavy on her heart and unlocked the treasury of her secret thoughts, she took up a pen, and her tears flowed with the ink. And she wrote thus:

"Beloved sister: When the heart is straitened with that which it conceals and eyelids are oppressed with tears and ribs are nigh torn asunder with growing hidden things, what is there for man save speech and complaint? The saddened deems complaint a sweet thing, and the lover finds consolation in the fire of his youth, and the oppressed sees relief in supplication. . . . Now do I write to you thus because I am become a poet who beholds the beauty of all things and arranges the pattern of that beauty impelled by the power of his divineness. Or as a starveling child seeing succour, driven by the bitterness of its hunger, unmindful of its mother's poverty and destitution.

"Hearken to my pitiful tale, my sister, and weep for me. For weeping is like prayer, and the tears of compassion are as a good deed that goes not unrequited; they ascend from the depths of the spirit, a living thing. . . . My father joined me in marriage with a man of riches and station, the like of all fathers of possessions and honour who wish to propagate wealth by wealth; fearing poverty and embracing honour with honour as a refuge from the shame of days. And so I and my dreams and longings were sacrificed on an altar of gold that I held as naught; to high estate, which was hateful in my sight. I was a prey trembling in the grasp of matter which, if it be not made to serve the spirit, is harsher than death and bitterer than the grave. I hold in esteem my lord, for he is generous and honourable and strives in the way of my happiness and pursues riches for my delight. But I have found that all these things are not worth one moment of a true and sanctified love; that love which holds as naught all things and remains mighty.

"Do not mock at me, my sister, for I am now become the most knowing of people in the things of a woman's heart, that palpitating heart, that bird fluttering in the firmament of love. That vessel overflowing with the wine of ages prepared for the lips of the soul. That book wherein are writ chapters of joy and grief; happiness and misery; pleasure and pain. That book none shall read save the true companion, the half of woman that is created for her from the beginning to the end of time. . . .

"Ay, I have known women in their longings and desires since I saw that my lord's fine horses and carriages and his ever filled coffers and high estate were not the equal of one glance from the eyes of a poor youth who entered this existence for my sake and for whom I did come. A patient one waiting in grief and the wretchedness of separation. An oppressed one sacrificed to my father's will; imprisoned without guilt in the dungeons of time. . . . Seek not to console me, for out of my affliction is a consoler, the knowledge of my love's power and the honour of my yearning and longing. I look now from beyond my tears and behold my lot, day by day, drawing nigh to lead me whither I shall await the companion of my spirit and meet with him and embrace him a long and sacred embrace. Reproach me not, for I do as is proper to a faithful wife, submitting to the laws and customs of men with forbearance and enduring. I honour my lord and esteem him and laud him, but I am not able of giving him my all, for God has already granted that to my beloved ere I knew him. Heaven has willed in its hidden wisdom that I pass my days with a man other than for whom I was created, and I shall pass this existence in silence in accordance with Heaven's willing. And when the doors of eternity are open and I am joined with the half of my spirit, I shall look back upon the past – and the past is this very present – as does the spring on winter. I shall ponder on this life as one who has gained the summit considers the passes through which he has come ere attaining it."

Here the maid ceased from writing. She covered her face with her hands and gave herself to bitter weeping as though her great spirit rebelled against the committing to paper of the holiest of her secrets. She dried her tears quickly and they were gone to abide in the gentle air, the resting-place of the souls of lovers and flowers.

After a while she took up again her pen and wrote:

"Do you remember that youth, my sister? Do you remember the light shining from his eyes, and the sadness impressed upon his brow, and his smile that was like the tears of a bereaved woman? Do you recall his voice, which was as the echo of a far-off valley? Do you call him to memory when he would ponder on things with a long silent look, and speak of them in wonder, and incline his head and sigh as though in fear that speech would betray what was concealed in his depths? And his dreams and beliefs, those too do you remember? Ay, these many things in a youth whom other men thought their like, whom my father did despise because he was raised above dross and more honourable than that he should inherit honour from his forebears.

"Ay, my sister, well do you know that I am a martyr of the small things of this world and a sacrifice to folly. Show pity to your sister, who sits up in the silent watches of the night to uncover to you the secrets of her breast. Have compassion, for love did likewise visit your heart."

Morning came and the maiden rose from her writing and soon sleep overtook her. Mayhap she would find therein dreams sweeter than the dreams of awakening.

THE BLIND FORCE

SPRING CAME AND Nature spoke in the tongues of brooks and streams and made glad the heart. And she smiled on the lips of flowers and made rejoice the spirit.

Then she waxed wroth and razed the fine city and caused men to forget the sweetness of her words and the tenderness of her smile.

A blind and terrifying force destroying in a minute what the ages had builded. A merciless death clutching at throats with sharpened talons and crushing without ruth. A consuming fire swallowing sustenance and life. A black night concealing the beauty of life beneath a covering of obscurity.

Terrifying elements blowing from their resting-places to do battle with man in his weakness and destroy his dwelling-places, scattered in a second what he has gathered in an hour. A mighty earthquake, which the earth conceived, and in travail bore naught save destruction and despair.

And so it was, the while the grieving spirit looked on from afar, sorrowing and reflecting. It pondered upon the limited night of men before unseen forces, and sorrowed with the fleeing victims of fire and ruin. It reflected on the enmity of man hidden beneath layers of earth and in the very particles of the air.

It sorrowed with the lamenting mothers and the hungry children, and thought on the cruelty of matter and its belittlement of life. It shared likewise the suffering of those that yestereve did sleep in safety in their houses, who today are standing afar, mourning the fine city with broken sobs and bitter tears.

It saw how hope was become despair, and joy sorrow, and rest unrest. And it grieved with hearts trembling in the grasp of sadness and despair and torment.

Thus did stand the spirit betwixt sorrow and reflection. Now led to doubt the justice of those divine laws binding the forces one to the other; now turning back and murmuring into the ears of the stillness:

"In truth is there beyond creation an eternal wisdom born of calamities and scourges that we behold, but whose good fruits we see not. And the fires and earthquakes and tempests are to the earth's body as are hatred and envy and evil in the human heart. They rage and storm and then are still. And from out of their raging and storming and stillness create the gods a beautiful knowledge, which man purchases with his tears and his blood and gains.

"I stand in remembrance. The tragedy of this people fills the ears with sighing and lamenting. And before my eyes appear the tears and misfortunes that have crossed the stage of the days.

"I have seen man in all his generations set up on the earth's breast towers and palaces and temples, and the earth has taken them back to her heart.

"I have seen likewise the strong build firm buildings, and workers in stone create from the rock pictures and images. And tracers adorn walls and gates with painting and drawing. And I have seen this earth open wide its mouth and swallow up the creation of artful hands and profound minds. Blotting out in its harshness the pictures and images; destroying in its anger the tracings and the drawings; burying in its wrathfulness the noble walls and columns; making fine dwellings bare of the adornments with which men had adorned them; putting in the stead of the meadow's green garment stuff embroidered with gold of the sand and the jewellery of stones and pebbles."

Yet did I find among these wrongs and misfortunes the divinity of man standing upright as a giant mocking at earth's foolishness and the anger of the elements. And like a pillar of light standing out of the ruins of Babylon and Nineveh and Palmyra, and Bombay and San Francisco, it sang a hymn of immortality, saying: "Let the earth then take what is to it; for I am without end."

TWO WISHES

IN THE STILLNESS of the night Death descended from God on the sleeping city and abode upon the highest tower therein. He pierced the walls of the houses with his brilliant eyes and saw in them spirits borne away on the wings of dreams, and bodies given up to slumber.

And when the moon waned at the approach of dawn and the city was covered with an enchanted veil, Death walked with soft footsteps among those dwellings until he reached the mansion of the rich man. He entered therein and there was none to stop him. He stood by the bedside and touched the eyelids of the sleeper. The rich man woke in terror. And when he saw the spectre of Death before him, he cried out in a voice in which were fear and rage:

"Get you from me, terrible dream! Go, evil spirit! How did you enter, thief, and what do you want, snatcher? Go, then, for I am master of this house. Away with you, lest I call the slaves and the guards to tear you to pieces!"

Then Death drew near and in a voice of thunder roared: "I am Death; therefore take heed and be humble."

And the rich and powerful man asked: "What want you from me now, and what thing do you seek? Why have you come whilst yet my work is unfinished? What do you wish from the powerful like me? Go you to the sickly. Get you hence from me and show me not your whetted talons and hair that hangs like coiling snakes. Go, for the sight of your terrible wings and corrupt body is hateful to me." But after an uneasy silence he spoke again and said:

"No, no, kind Death, take no heed of what I said, for fear makes me speak words my heart would forbid. Take, then, a measure of my gold or the soul of one of my slaves and leave me. . . . I have account with life yet unfulfilled and wealth with people not yet gathered. I have on the seas ships not yet come to port, and in the earth produce not yet garnered. Take you of these things what you will and leave me. Concubines I have, fair as the morning, for your choosing, Death. Hearken further: I have an only son whom I love, the apple of my eye. Take him too, but leave me alone."

Then Death put his hand on the mouth of this slave of earthly life and took his reality and gave it up to the air.

Death proceeded on his way through the quarters of the poor until he reached a humble dwelling. He entered therein and approached a bed on which lay a young man. After gazing on his tranquil countenance he touched his eyes and the youth awoke. And when he saw Death standing above him he fell upon his knees and lifted his hands toward him and in a voice touched by the spirit's longing and love, said:

"Here I am, beautiful Death. Receive my spirit, reality of my dreams and substance of my hopes. Embrace me, beloved of my soul, for you are merciful and will not abandon me here. You are the messenger of the gods. You are the right hand of truth. Leave me not. How long have I sought you without finding, and called upon you and you hearkened not! But now have you heard me, therefore do not meet my love with shunning. Embrace my soul, my beloved Death."

Then Death put his gentle fingers upon the boy's lips and took his reality and put it beneath his wings.

And when Death cleft the air, he looked back at this world, and into the void blew these words:

"Who has not come from the Infinite shall not return to the Infinite."

THE PLAYGROUND OF LIFE

A MINUTE MOVING among the patterns of Beauty and the dreams of Love is greater and more precious than an age filled with splendour granted by the weak to the strong.

From that minute rises the god-state of man, and in that age it sleeps a deep sleep veiled by a veil of disturbing dreams;

In that minute is the spirit freed from the burdens of men's conflicting laws,

And in that age is it prisoned behind walls of neglect and weighted with chains of oppression.

That minute was the cradle of Solomon's song and the Sermon on the Mount and the lyrics of al-Farid. That age was blind force that destroyed the temples of Baalbek and razed the palaces of Palmyra and Babylon's towers.

A day spent by the soul in lamenting the death of the rights of the poor man and in weeping for the loss of justice is nobler than the age lost by a man in enjoyment of his appetite.

That day purifies the heart with its fire and fills it with its light; and that age envelops it with its dark wings and buries it 'neath layers of earth.

That day was the day of Sinai and of Calvary and the Flight.[1] That age did Nero pass in the market place of wrongs, and Korah set it up on the altar of lust, and Don Juan buried it in the grave of bodily desires.

And so is life. Played by the nights on the stage of destiny as a tragedy; sung by the days as a hymn. And in the end guarded by Eternity as a jewel.

1 The flight, or Hegira, of Muhammad to Medina.

MY FRIEND

IF YOU KNEW, my poor friend, that the poverty which condemns you to misery is that same thing which inspires in you the knowledge of justice and gives you understanding of life's meaning, you would be satisfied with God's ruling.

You would say: The knowledge of justice; for the rich man is buried in his treasury away from that knowledge. Life's meaning; for the powerful leave it aside in their pursuit of glory.

Rejoice, then, in justice, for you are its mouthpiece; and in life, for you are its book. Be glad, for you are the source of the merit of those who help you and the strong arm of the virtue of them that take your hand.

If you knew, my sad friend, that the misfortune that has overtaken you is the force that illumines the heart and raises up the spirit from mocking to esteem, you would be content with it for a heritage and praise it for a guidance. And from it you would know that life is a chain, its links taking hold one of another. And that grief is a golden link separating submission to the present from business with future's joy, as morning comes between sleep and awakening.

In truth, my friend, poverty manifests nobleness of spirit, and riches reveal its littleness.

Grief softens our feeling, and rejoicing hardens. For men have not ceased to use wealth and joy as a means to increasing, even as they do in the name of the Book evil of which the Book is innocent. And in the name of humanity that which humanity rejects.

Were poverty to be banished and grieving be no more, then were the spirit a page empty save of symbols showing selffulness and amassing, and words telling of earthly lusts.

For I have looked and have found a divineness, the unearthly self in man, that is not sold for riches or developed by the joys of the time. I have considered, and I have seen the rich man cast aside his godlikeness to covet his riches; and the young men of the age forsake it in pursuit of their pleasures.

The hour, my friend, that you pass with the companion of your days and your little ones on your return home from the fields is a symbol of the human family in ages to come: it is the sign of the happiness of future days. And the life that the rich man passes in the counting-house is in truth an existence likened to the existence of worms in the grave: the symbol of fear.

And the tears you shed, my grieving one, they are sweeter than the laughing of one seeking to forget, and pleasanter than loud voices in jest. Those tears shall cleanse the heart of hating and teach him that sheds them to be companion to those of broken heart. They are the tears of the Nazarene.

The strength you sow, poor one, which is reaped by the powerful, shall return to you, for all things return to their source in Nature's dispensation.

The grief you have borne shall be turned into gladness on Heaven's command. And coming ages shall learn equality from poverty, and love through grieving.

IN A LONELY house sat a youth in the morning of his life. He sat looking now through the window at the starry sky, now at the picture of a woman in his hand. A picture it was the line and colour of which were reflected in his face. The picture of a woman's face speaking to him and making his eyes ears; putting in him understanding of the language of the hovering spirits in that room; bringing to birth hearts lighted by love and filling with yearning.

So passed the hour as a minute of pleasant dreaming, or as a year from eternity. Then the youth set the picture before him and took up pen and paper and wrote:

"Beloved of my soul: Great and sublime truths pass not from one human creature to another by way of human speech; rather do they choose silence as a road between souls. I know that the stillness of this night is a messenger between our two spirits bearing messages even more tender than those the breeze writes upon the water's face; reciting the pages of our two hearts to each other. As God willed that our souls be placed in the prison of our bodies, so did love decree that I should be the prisoner of words.

"They say, my darling, that love through worship turns into an all-consuming fire. I have found that the hour of separation does not prevail against the joining of our unearthly selves, as I have known with the first meeting that my spirit was your companion for countless ages, and that your first glance was not, in truth, the first glance.

"Ah, my love, verily the hour that did join our two hearts exiled from another world was one among many that upheld my believing in the eternity of the spirit and its immortality. In such an hour does Nature tear away the veil from the face of timeless justice that people think injustice.

"Do you recall, beloved, the garden wherein we stood, each regarding the face of a loved one? And your glances told me your love for me sprang not from pity. Those glances taught me to proclaim to myself and to the world that the gift whose source is justice is greater than that which begins in charity. And love that is created of circumstance is like the waters of a swamp.

"Before me, my love, is a life I would to be great and beautiful. A life that will be dear to the memory of future men and evoke their love and esteem. A life whose beginning was your meeting, of whose immortality I was assured. For I believed that your being was able to bring back the strength that God had taken from me. Yea, even as the sun brings forth fragrant flowers of the field. And so does my love remain to me and to the ages and endure free from selffulness, that it may be spread abroad and be raised above small things in its devotion to you."

The youth rose and walked across the room slowly. Then he looked again from the window and saw that the moon was risen, filling the firmament with its gentle radiance. He returned to the letter and wrote:

"Forgive me, beloved, for I have spoken to you as another person, yet you are my half that I lost when we emerged from the hand of God on the same moment. Forgive me."

THE DUMB BEAST
"In the glance of a dumb beast is speech
understood by the souls of the wise."
AN INDIAN POET

ONE EVENING WHEN images took possession of my mind, I passed by the outskirts of the town and stood before a deserted house. Its walls were crumbling and its supports falling, and there remained of it naught save traces to show of its long abandonment and decay.

Then I perceived a dog lying down in the dust, his weak body overrun with sores and his meagre form emaciated by sickness. He was looking toward the setting sun with eyes veiled by the shadows of misery and despair. It was as though he knew that the sun was withdrawing its warm breath from that deserted place, far from the children who persecuted the helpless beast. He gazed at the setting sun with sorrow and a parting.

I drew near to him slowly, wishing that I knew his speech that I might console him in the extremity of his grief and show to him compassion in his despair. At my approach he took fright and moved with what remained to him of a life nearing its end, and sought escape with limbs withered by illness and watched by corruption. And since he was no more able to rise, he looked at me a look in which were the bitterness of imploring and the sweetness of supplication; a look in which were affection and reproach. A look that took the place of speech; which was clearer than the words of men and more eloquent than a woman's tears. When my eyes met his sad ones my feelings moved me and my emotions bestirred themselves, and his glances took body and became voiced speech customary among mankind. And this is what they said:

"Enough, such and such a one. Sufficient that which I have borne of men's cruelty and suffered of pain and ill. Pass you by and leave me and my silence. I shall ask succour of the warming rays of the sun. I have fled from the harshness and oppression of man and sought refuge in the dust, which is softer than his heart, and concealed myself in ruins less desolate than his soul. Get you hence, for what are you if not of the dwellers of an earth bereft of all justice? I am a lowly animal, but I have served the son of man. I have been to him an ever faithful companion and a comfort in his house. In his sorrow I was partner, and his joy was my joy. I remembered him in times of absence and welcomed him on his homecoming. I was satisfied when he threw me the scraps from his table and was happy with a bone his teeth had gnawed clean. But when I grew old and infirm with age, and illness took me, he cast me forth from his house and made me the plaything of cruel boys of the streets and a target for the slings and arrows of dirt and disease.

"I, human being, am a helpless animal, but I find a like thing between me and many of your brothers in kind when they are no longer strong enough to gain their sustenance. I am like the soldiers who fight for their land in their youth and make the earth fruitful in middle age, and when the winter of their lives draws near and their value is diminished, they are cast aside and forgotten. I am like a woman who was a lovely maiden that made rejoice the heart of youth and passed the nights as a wife to rear children and bring to being men of the future. A woman who in her old age is despised and forgotten. . . . How cruel you are, human, and how harsh!"

So did speak the glances of that beast. My heart understood whilst my spirit wavered between pity for him and thinking on the children of my kind. And when he closed his eyes I wished not to disturb him, so I went from that place.

THE STORM ABATED after having compelled all growing things to bend before it. Stars appeared in their semblance of shattered remnants of the lightning upon the sky's face. And the fields were still as though the battle of the elements had never been.

In that hour a maid entered her room and threw herself upon her couch and wept in bitterness. Her sobbing rose and her broken breaths became words.

"Bring him back to me, O Lord, for my tears are dried up and my bowels are turned to water. Return him to me, O Spirit that judgeth with a wisdom transcending men's prudence, for my spirit fails me and grief takes hold of me. Save him from the whetted fangs of war; deliver him from the hands of death and have pity on a frail youth wronged by the power of the strong and snatched from me.

"Conquer, O Love, and vanquish war, your enemy. Save my loved one, for he is of your sons. Get you hence, O Death, that he may see me, or come you and lead me to him."

On that very moment entered a youth whose head was swathed in white wrappings upon which battle had writ in crimson letters. He came near to the maiden and greeted her with a tear and a smile. Then he took her hand and put it against his lips, and in a voice in which were a wounding love and a joyous meeting said: "Have not fear, for he for whom you weep is come back. Rejoice, then, for peace has restored to you him whom war did take, and magnanimity has returned that which greed did plunder. Dry your tears, my loved one, and smile. Be not astonished at my return alive, for love has a sign before which death flees on beholding; the adversary perceives it and is confused.

"Yea, I am he. Do not think me a phantom come from the regions of darkness to visit a place wherein dwell your beauty and peace. Be not afraid, for I am a truth delivered from fire and sword to bear witness before all people to the victory of love over war. I am a word uttered by a man of peace as a foreword to the tale of your bliss."

With this utterance his tongue became tied and tears took the place of speech. Spirits of rejoicing filled that mean dwelling, and two hearts found that which was lost at their parting.

And when morning came, the two stood in a field and looked upon nature's beauty. After a silence in which was converse, the soldier looked toward the east and said to his beloved: "Behold the sun rising from out of darkness."

THE POET

A LINK
Between this world and the hereafter;
A pool of sweet water for the thirsty;
A tree planted
On the banks of the river of beauty,
Bearing ripe fruits for hungry hearts to seek.

A singing bird
Hopping along the branches of speech,
Trilling melodies to fill all bodies with sweetness and
    tenderness.
A white cloud in the sky at even,
Rising and expanding to fill the heavens,
And then pour out its bounty upon the flowers of the fields
    of Life.

An angel
Sent by the gods to teach man the ways of gods.
A shining light unconquered by the dark,
Unhidden by the bushel
Astarte did fill with oil;
And lighted by Apollo.

Alone,
He is clothed in simplicity
And nourished by tenderness;
He sits in Nature's lap learning to create,
And is awake in the stillness of night
In wait of the spirit's descent.
A husbandman who sows the seeds of his heart in the garden
    of feeling,

Where they bring forth yield
To sustain those that garner.

This is the Poet that is unheeded of men in his days,
And is known by them on his quitting the world to return to
    his heavenly abode.
This is he who seeks no thing of men save a little smile;
Whose breath rises and fills the firmament with living visions
    of beauty.
Yet do the people withhold from him sustenance and refuge.

Until when, O Man,
Until when, O Existence,
Will you build houses of honour
To them that knead the earth with blood
And shun those who give you peace and repose?
Until when will you exalt killing
And those who make bend the neck beneath the yoke of
    oppression?
And forget them that pour into the blackness of night
The light of their eyes to show you the day's splendour?
Those whose lives are passed in misery
That happiness and delight might not pass you by.

And you, O Poets,
Life of this life:
You have conquered the ages
Despite their tyranny,
And gained for you a laurel crown
In the face of delusion's thorns.
You are sovereign over hearts,
And your kingdom is without end.

MY BIRTHDAY
Written in Paris, 6 December 1908

ON THIS DAY my mother bore me.

On this day five and twenty years ago the silence put me between the hands of this existence, full with cries and battle and contending.

Thus have I walked round the sun twenty and five times. And I know not how many times the moon has encircled me. Yet I have not unveiled the secrets of life, neither have I known the hidden things of darkness.

I have walked five and twenty times with the earth and the moon and the sun and the planets around the Universal Law.

Behold now my spirit murmuring the names of that Law like caves echoing the voice of sea waves. Its being is in His being, but knows not His essence; it sings the songs of His ebb and flow, but comprehends Him not.

Twenty and five years ago the hand of time wrote me as a word in the book of this strange terrifying world. Behold me, then, a word vague and confused of meaning; now signifying no thing; now meaning many things.

On this day of the year thoughts and reflections and remembrance jostle one the other in my soul. They stand before me as processions of days gone by and show me phantoms of nights long departed. Then they are dispersed as the winds disperse straying clouds at twilight. They dwindle and become faint in the corners of my room like the songs of streams in far-off and empty valleys.

On this day every year come the spirits that have moulded my spirit, hastening toward me from all corners of the earth, encircling me with songs of sad remembrance.

Then gently they withdraw and hide behind visible things. They are like birds that descend upon an abandoned threshing-floor and, finding there no grain, flutter awhile ere flying off to another place.

On this day the meaning of my past life rises up before me as a faded mirror into which I look long and see therein naught except the pallid faces of the years like the faces of the dead; and the wrinkled features of hopes and dreams and passions like the features of old men.

Then I close my eyes and look a second time in the mirror and I see naught but my face;

And I look into my face and behold therein a sadness. I examine this sadness and find it dumb and giving not utterance. Yet could this sadness speak, it were sweeter than joy.

Much have I loved in these five and twenty years. And much that I have loved is hateful to people; and much that I have hated is by them admired. What I have loved as a boy I cease not now to love. And that which I now love I shall love to the end of my days. For love is the all I can attain, and no person shall deprive me thereof.

Many are the times I have loved death, and called it by sweet names and wooed it in secret and public places. Life also have I loved. For death and life are one to me in beauty, and equal in delight, and partners in the growth of my longing and yearning. They have shared alike my love and affection.

I have loved freedom, and my love has grown with the growth of my knowledge of the bondage of people to falsehood and deceit. And it has spread with my understanding of their sub-mission to idols created by dark ages and raised up by folly and polished by the touch of adoring lips.

But I have loved also those adorers with my unfettered love. Yea, I have had pity on them, for they are blind and kiss the bloody lips of a wild beast and see not; and suck up the venom of the viper and feel not. They dig their own graves with their fingernails and know not.

I have loved freedom because I have found it to be a maiden whom aloneness has made sickly and solitude rendered weak until she is become a phantom passing among houses, standing in the streets and calling on the passer-by, who hears not nor heeds her.

In five and twenty years have I loved happiness as have all

men. I have awakened each morning and sought it even as they have sought. But I have found it not in their way; neither have I seen its footprints on the sand outside their mansions; nor have I heard echo of its voice coming from within their temples.

But when I sought it in solitude, I heard my spirit thus whisper in my ear, saying: "Happiness is a child born and brought to life in the heart's depths; it comes not to it from without."

And when I opened my heart to see happiness, I found therein its mirror and its couch and garments. It I did not find.

I have loved all people – much have I loved them. In my sight people are of three kinds. One curses life; one blesses it; one observes it. I have loved the first for his despair; the second for his tolerance; the third for his understanding.

Thus have passed twenty and five years. So have gone my days and my nights, hastening on, one on the heels of another; falling from my life as leaves from a tree in the path of autumn winds.

And today, today I stand in remembrance as a tired wayfarer who stands midway on the ascending road, and I look on this side and that and see not in the past of my life any thing to which I can point before the sun and say: This is to me.

Neither do I find in the seasons of my years any harvest save leaves tinted with drops of ink, and strange scattered tracings full with line and colour, harmonious and discordant.

In these dispersed pages and drawings I have buried and interred my feelings and my thoughts and dreams as does the husbandman seeds in the earth.

But the peasant who goes out to the field and sows his seeds in the soil returns with hope to his house at eventide and awaits the season of harvesting and gathering. Not so I. For I have cast forth seeds of my heart and there is no hope, neither is there awaiting.

And now that I am come to this stage of my journey and see the past from beyond a mist of sighing and grieving, and the future from behind the veil of the past, I stand and gaze on existence from my window.

I behold the faces of people and hear their voices rising

upwards. I hear the fall of their footsteps among the dwellings and feel the touch of their spirits and the waves of their desires and the beating of their hearts.

I see children at play running and jumping and throwing bits of soil at one another, the while laughing with glee.

And the young men I see walking with firm step, their heads held high as though they would read a poem of youth writ on the margin of clouds lined with sun rays. And the maidens who walk and sway like young boughs and smile like flowers, the while they gaze upon the young men from under lids that flutter with love and desire.

I see old men walking slowly with bent backs, leaning on sticks and looking on the ground, as though seeking between the cracks precious stones they have lost.

So do I stand at my window and look and ponder on these images and shadows in their silent progress through the streets and byways of the city.

Then I look to that which is beyond the city and see the wild parts in their awful beauty and voiced silence, and rising hills and sloping valleys. The erect trees and gently swaying grass and fragrant flowers; the chanting rivers and singing birds.

I look to that which is beyond the wild places and I behold the sea and the wonders and marvels of its depths, its secrets and buried things. Its foaming waves in their anger and scorn; its spume and spray; its rise and its fall. All this do I see.

And I look then to that which is beyond the sea, and I perceive the limitless firmament with its worlds floating in space, and the brilliant stars and the suns and the moons. And the planets and the fixed stars, and all the contending and reconciled forces of attraction and repulsion do I see, created and borne by that Will, timeless and without limit. Submitting to a Universal Law whose beginning has no beginning and whose end is without end.

Through my window I look and ponder on these things and I am forgetful of the five and twenty years and the ages that preceded them and the centuries that will follow. And my being and my existence are manifest before me, the concealed and the revealed, as the ghost of a child's sigh trembling in the eternal

depths of space and its everlasting heights and endless bound-
aries. And I feel the existence of this ghost, this spirit, this
essence, this self I call "I". I feel its stirrings and hear its clamour.
Now does it lift its wings upwards and stretch forth its hands in
all directions, and sway trembling on this the day which showed
it to existence. Now in a voice rising from its holy of holies
does it cry:

"Peace, O Life. Peace, O awakening. Peace, O vision.

"Greeting, O day, whose light conquers the earth's darkness.
Greeting, O night, whose darkness reveals the light of the
firmament.

"Greeting to spring, which renews the earth's youth; to sum-
mer, which proclaims the sun's splendour. Greeting to autumn,
the giver of labour's fruits and toil's reward; to winter, which
brings back in its tempests nature's strength.

"To the years which reveal that which the years have hidden.
To the ages which have redressed the wrongs of ages: greeting.

"Peace, O time, who carry us onward to perfection. And
peace to you, guiding spirit, who are the reins of existence; who
are hidden from us behind the sun's veil.

"Peace and greeting to you, O heart, because you meditate
whilst yet overcome with weeping.

"And to you, O lips, greeting and peace, for verily do you
speak peace whilst yet tasting of bitterness."

THE CHILD JESUS

I WAS ALONE yesterday in this world, beloved; and my aloneness was as pitiless as death. I was alone as a flower growing in the shadow of mighty rocks, and Life heeded not my existence. And I heeded not the existence of Life.

Today my spirit is awakened and beholds you standing beside it, and its countenance is bright. It prostrates before you even as did the shepherd when he beheld the burning bush.

Yesterday the air's touch was hard and the sun's rays weakly. Mist concealed the earth's face, and the roar of sea waves was like to a howling tempest.

This way I looked and that, and saw not save my self in pain standing beside me. And the shadows of darkness rising and falling about me like hungry ravens.

Today the air is serene and all nature is bathed in light, and the sea waves are at peace and the clouds dispersed. Wheresoever I look do I behold you and see the secrets of life about you like the shimmering spray thrown up by a bird bathing on the lake's placid face.

Yestereve I was a voiceless word in the mind of the night. Today I am become a joyful song on the tongue of the days. And this did come to pass in a minute of time formed of a glance and a word, and a sigh and a kiss.

That minute, my beloved, did join my spirit's past with its future. It was as a white rose rising from the heart of the dark earth to the light of day.

That minute was to my life as was the birth of Jesus to the ages, for it was full with the spirit and purity and love. It made the darkness in my depths as light, and sorrow and despair as good fortune.

*

The fires of love fall from heaven in divers shapes and forms but they are one in their mark upon the earth.

The little flame that illumines the corners of one man's heart is as the great bright flame that descends from above to light the darkness of nations. For in the one soul are elements and desires and feelings that differ no whit from those within the soul of all mankind.

The Children of Judah, my beloved, awaited the promised coming of a Mighty One since the beginning of time to deliver them from the bondage of the nations.

The great spirit in Greece saw that the worship of Jupiter and Minerva was of no account; and no more was the spirit satisfied.

And in Rome sublime thought considered, and found that the divineness of Apollo was become far from human feeling. And the timeless beauty of Venus was near to old age.

The nations knew, without understanding of the cause thereof, a hunger of the spirit for instruction in affairs transcending matter. And they yearned for a freedom that is not of the body to teach man to rejoice with his neighbour in the light of the sun and the beauty of life.

For, in truth, it is that freedom which draws a man near to the unseen Force without fear or trembling.

All that did come to pass two thousand years before when the yearnings of the human heart were fluttering among visible things, fearing to come near the Immortal, the Universal Spirit. When Pan, god of the forests, was filling with dread the souls of shepherds, and Baal of the sun oppressing the breasts of the lowly and wretched with his priests.

And upon one night, nay, an hour, an instant separated from the ages – for it was stronger than the ages – the lips of the Spirit were opened and they sent forth the Word of Life, which was in the beginning with the Spirit.

And it descended with the light of the stars and the rays of the moon and took form and was a child in the arms of a woman. And it was in a humble place where shepherds guarded their flocks from the perils of the night.

It was a child that slept upon dry straw in a manger;

A sovereign who sat upon a throne fashioned of hearts heavy with the weight of bondage; and souls hungry for the Spirit; and thoughts thirsting for Wisdom.

A suckling child it was, swaddled in his mother's garments, who wrested with his gentleness the sceptre of power from the hands of Jupiter and delivered it unto the poor shepherd resting on the earth with his flock.

He it was who took wisdom from Minerva and put it on the tongue of the lowly fisherman sitting in his craft by the shores of the lake.

Who distilled joy through his own sorrow from Apollo and granted it to the brokenhearted standing in entreaty before the door. And poured forth beauty through his beauty from Venus and planted it in the soul of the fallen woman who was afraid of her oppressors.

He it was who brought Baal low from his seat of power and put in his stead the poor husbandman who sowed seeds in the field by the sweat of his brow.

Was not my suffering, beloved, the suffering of the tribes of Israel of yesteryear?

Did I not watch in the stillness of night for the coming of a Saviour to deliver me from the thrall of days?

Did I not know with the nations in days of yore that deep hunger of the spirit?

Did I not walk on the road of life as a child lost in strange places? And was not my soul as a seed cast on to a stone, which the birds took not up nor destroyed, and the elements cleft not nor brought to life?

All this did come to pass when my dreams sought a dark corner and feared to come near the light.

And upon a night, nay, an hour, an instant discarded from the years of my life, for it was fairer than all the years of my life, the Spirit descended upon me from the circle of light on high and looked upon me with your eyes, and spoke to me with your tongue. From that look and that word sprang love, and it found rest in my broken heart.

A mighty love it was, seated in the manger within my breast; a beautiful love swaddled in clothes of kindness. A gentle suckling lying upon the breast of the spirit, turning my grief into joy and my wretchedness to glory, and making my aloneness a pleasant thing.

A king raised high on the throne of unearthly essence, who brought back with his voice life to my dead days, and light to my weeping eyes with his touch; whose right hand snatched hope from the pit of despair.

The night has been long, my beloved, and now dawn is nigh; soon shall it be day. For the breath of the Child Jesus has filled the firmament and is merged with the air.

My life was a tale of woe; now it is become a joyful thing. And it will be turned to bliss, for the arms of the Child have enfolded my heart and embraced my soul.

COMMUNION OF SPIRITS

AWAKE, MY LOVE, awake!
For my soul calls to you from beyond the raging seas;
My spirit stretches forth her wings above the angry foaming
　　waves.

Awake, for all is still,
The beat of horse's hoof and the step of passer-by
Are quieted;
And sleep enfolds the souls of men.
But I alone remain awake,
For longing holds me when slumber would engulf me,
And love draws me nigh to you
When visions would plant me far.

I have left my couch, beloved,
For I fear the shades of comfort concealed beneath the
　　coverings.
I have cast aside the book,
For my sighs erased the lines upon its pages
So that they are white and empty before me.

Awake, awake, beloved, and hearken to me.

Behold me here, my love,
For I have heard your call across oceans
And felt the touch of your wings.
I have left my bed to walk upon the grass,
And the night dew has wetted my feet and my garment's hem.
Behold me standing before you 'neath the flowered almond
　　boughs
Hearkening to your call.

Speak then, my beloved,
And let your breath ride with the breeze that comes to me
    from the valleys of Lebanon.
Speak, and none save me shall hear your words,
For night has banished all creation to its rest,
And the dwellers in the city are drunk of sleep.
Alone am I in my wakefulness.

The heavens have woven a veil from moonbeams
And cast it o'er Lebanon's form.
The heavens have fashioned a cloak from the darkness of night
And lined it with the smoke of workshops and the breath
    of Death.
They have concealed within its folds the city's bones.

Those of the village are aslumber in their huts
Midst the willow and the walnut tree;
And their spirits make haste toward the land of dreams, my love.

Men are bowed down by the weight of gold,
And greed makes weak their knees.
Their eyes are heavy with trouble and fret,
And they are cast down upon their beds.
Tortured are their hearts, beloved, by spectres of misery and
    despair.

The phantoms of past ages walk in the valleys,
On the heights the spirits of kings and prophets wander.
My thoughts have turned toward the places of remembrance
And shown to me the might of Chaldea and the Assyrian's
    pride and Arabia's nobility.

In the narrow ways walk the dark ghosts of robbers
And in the crevices of walls vipers of lust rear their heads;
On street corners the breath of the sickly mingles with the
    pangs of death.
Memory has torn aside the curtains of forgetfulness
And revealed to me the abominations of Sodom and Gomorrah.

The boughs are swaying, my love,
And the rustling of their leaves
Merges with the murmur of the brook in the valley,
Bringing to our ears
Solomon's song, and the strains of David's lyre,
With the melodies Mausili[1] made.
The souls of children in the quarter tremble,
And hunger gnaws them.
Their mothers lie in anguish on their beds of misery and care,
And dreams of want make the hearts of idle men afraid.
I hear deep lament and bitter sighing
That fill the very bones with weeping and mourning.

The fragrance of lily and narcissus
Rises and kisses the jasmine's perfume,
And mingles with the sweet breath of cedar
Riding on the breeze above hillocks and winding paths;
Filling with love the spirit
And granting it longing
To take the air in flight.
Foul odours from the narrow ways arise,
Mixing with sickness and disease,
And like hidden arrows sharpened, wound
The senses, and the good air fill with poison.

The morning is come, beloved,
And fingers of wakefulness caress
The eyes of them that slumber.
The violet rays are rising from beyond the hills
To toss aside the covering of night
From off Life's splendour and power.
The villages resting in stillness and peace upon the shoulders
    of the valley
Are awakened.
Church bells ring out their praises,
And fill the air with pleasing sounds

1 Ishak al-Mausili (A.D. 767–850), celebrated Arabian musician.

Telling that the hour of prayer is nigh.
The caves throw back their chimes in echo
As though all Nature stood in prayer.

The calves have left their stalls,
And the sheep and goats their pens;
They are gone to the meadows to pasture
And eat of the dew-laden glistening grass.
Before them shepherds walk, playing on their pipes,
And behind them the maidens, greeting with the birds
     morning's coming.

The morning is come, beloved,
And upon the crowded dwellings
Day's heavy hand is laid.
Curtains are drawn back from windows,
And doors thrown open.
Tired eyes and troubled faces are revealed
And despairing souls betake themselves to toil.
Within their bodies Death dwells side by side with Life;
And the shadows of fear and misery stand astride their
     tightened features
As though they are driven to the shambles.

Behold the streets groaning with the press of hurrying
     covetous souls;
The air filled with clank of iron, the grinding of wheels, and
     whistle of steam.
The city is become a battlefield wherein the strong contend
     with the weak,
And the wealthy harvest the labour of the poor.

*

How beautiful is life, beloved!
'Tis like the heart of a poet,
Full with light and spirit.
How harsh is life, beloved!
'Tis like an evildoer's heart,
Full with guilt and fear.

846

O WIND

NOW SINGING AND rejoicing, now weeping and lamenting.

We hear, but behold you not; we feel your presence yet do not see you.

You were as a sea of love submerging our spirits, yet not drowning us; playing with our hearts in their stillness.

You ascend with the heights and descend with the valleys and are spread out upon fields and meadows.

In your ascending is there strength, and in your descending grace.

You were as a merciful ruler dealing justly with the weak and lowly and showing pride with the strong and mighty.

In autumn do you sigh in the valleys, and the trees weep with you, sighing;

In winter you do shout and roar, and all nature shouts with you.

In spring are you weak and sickly, and in your weakness the fields awake;

In summer you are shrouded in stillness and we take you for dead, slain by the sun's shafts and interred in its heat.

Were you mayhap lamenting in autumn's days, or laughing at the shame of the trees when you rendered them naked?

Were you angry in the days of winter, or dancing about the snow-covered graves of the night?

And in spring were you sickly, or were you a loved one sickened by absence, and come with sighing breath upon the beloved's cheek, the youth of the seasons, to rouse him from his slumber?

Were you perchance dead those summer days, or sleeping in the hearts of fruits, or among the vines or on the threshing-floor?

You bear the breath of illness from city streets, and from the heights the spirit of a flower;

Thus do the great spirits that carry life's agony in silence; and in silence shall we meet its joys.

You murmur wondrous secrets in the ear of the rose, and she understands. Ofttimes she is troubled; ofttimes she smiles. In like manner do the gods with the souls of men.

Here do you tarry; there do you hasten. Thither you run, but you abide not. So does a man's thought; it lives by movement and in repose dies.

On the water's face you inscribe verses – then erase them. Likewise do poets who recite.

From the south you come hot as love.
From the north cold as death;
From the east gentle as the caress of spirits.
From the west you come forth with violence as one hating.
Are you fickle as the ages, or are you an apostle come to give us of your faith?

You pass in anger across deserts and trample underfoot the caravans and bury them in graves of sand.

Are you that hidden flood flowing with the light of dawn through the leaves of trees?

Passing on like a dream in the valley, where flowers incline for love of you and the plants sway in ecstasy?

You fall upon the seas in assault and disturb the peace of their depths so that they rise against you in anger and open wide their mouths to swallow vessels and souls.

Are you, then, that gentle lover who plays with the locks of children running among the houses?

Whither are you hastening with our souls and our spirits and our sighs?

Whither do you carry the pattern of our smiles? What do you with the flaming brands of our hearts in flight?

Do you go with them to where is beyond the twilight –

beyond this life? Or drag them as prey to distant caves to blow them hither and thither till they grow faint and die?

In the stillness of night hearts reveal to you their secrets, and with the breaking of dawn the fluttering of lids darkens the eyes.

Are you mindful of what the hearts felt and what the eyes saw?

Between your wings is stored the cry of anguish from the poor man, and the orphan's cry and the mourning woman's lament.

In the folds of your garment the stranger puts his longing, and the forsaken his grief and the fallen woman the cry of her spirit.

Are you the keeper of these lowly ones' trust? Or are you as this earth that takes no thing except to put it to her own body?

Do you hear this cry and this clamour and this weeping? Or are you as the mighty among mankind who heed not the outstretched hand nor hear the voices rising to them?

THE LOVER'S RETURN

NIGHT HAD NOT fallen ere the enemy took to flight, their bodies sword-scarred and punctured by lances. The victors returned bearing aloft banners of glory. And chanting songs of victory to the time of their horses' hoofbeats, which fell upon the stones of the valley like hammer blows.

They looked down upon the ravine, and the moon rose from behind the mouth of the river. The mighty towering rocks, rising with the spirits of the people, appeared, and the forest of the cedars revealed itself as though it were a sign of honour that past ages had hung upon the breast of Lebanon.

They continued on their way, and the moonlight shone on their weapons, and the distant caves echoed their hymns, until they came to the foot of an ascent, when they were halted by the neighing of a horse. The beast stood among the grey-coloured rocks as though it were cut from them. The men approached it, seeking the cause of the neighing, and they stumbled across a dead body stubbed out on the ground whose blood mingled with the earth. Then the chief of the group shouted: "Show me the man's sword; I know its owner."

Some of the horsemen dismounted and surrounded the corpse. After a while one of them lifted his head and, looking toward the chief, said in a hoarse voice: "His fingers grasp the hilt of the sword tightly: it would be wrong to loose them."

Said another: "The weapon is sheathed with blood, and its metal cannot be seen."

A third one said: "The blood has congealed on hand and hilt and bound the blade to the arm and made them one."

Thereupon the leader dismounted and went over to the slain man and said: "Raise his head and let the moonlight show to us his face." The men hastened to do his bidding and the dead warrior's face was revealed from behind the veil of death. Its

features were strong and told of courage and boldness and endur-
ance; the face of a warrior speaking without voice of his man-
hood. The face of one sorrowing and rejoicing. The face of one
who faced the foe with valour and met death with a smile. The
face of a hero of Lebanon who was present that day in battle
and saw the vanguard of victory but lived not to sing songs of
triumph with his comrades.

And when they took off his head–cloth and wiped the dust of
battle from his pale face, the leader cried out in a voice of pain:
"'Tis the face of Al-Sa'abi's son. Ah, the pity of it!" And the men
echoed that name, sighing. Then they became silent as though
their hearts, drunk with the wine of victory, were become
sobered in an instant and had seen in the loss of a hero a thing
greater than the might and glory of victory.

There they stood like stone images before the awe of this
scene, and their tongues were dried up and they held their peace.
For so do the brave in spirit in the face of death. Weeping and
lament are for women; and crying and wailing are of children.
For men of the sword there is naught but to stand in silence and
awe. The silence that holds in grip strong spirits as the eagle's
talons grip the throat of its prey. That silence which rises above
weeping and lament; which in its sublimeness renders mis-
fortune more awesome and terrifying. A silence causing the
mighty spirit to descend from mountain heights to the depths
of the valley. A silence presaging the coming of the storm. And
when the storm comes not is yet greater and mightier than it.

They removed the garments of the slain youth to see whereon
death had placed its hand. On his breast were sword wounds
agape like mouths afoam, speaking in the stillness of that night
of the ambitions of men. The leader dropped on his knees by
the dead man and, looking closely at the body, saw that a kerchief
embroidered with gold thread was tied round the forearm. He
pondered on this, for he knew the hand that had spun the silk
and the fingers that had worked the thread. Then he hid it away
among the garments and withdrew a little, covering his own
drawn face with a trembling hand. That same hand which had
severed a head from a body now trembled and wiped away a
tear. For it had touched the edge of a kerchief that beloved

fingers had wound round the arm of a boy gone to do battle bravely. Now he was fallen and would return to her borne on the shoulders of his comrades.

And while the chieftain's spirit hovered thus between the horrors of death and mysteries of love, one of his men spoke and said:

"Come you, let us dig for him a grave under yonder oak tree. Its roots will drink from his blood, and its branches will flourish through his remains. 'Twill grow in strength and become immortal and will be a sign telling these knolls of his bravery and valour."

And another said: "Nay; let us carry him to the forest of the cedars and bring him by the church. There will his bones rest guarded by the shadow of the Cross against the Last Day."

And said another: "Bring you him here when his blood has fed the earth. And leave his sword in his right hand. Then plant his lance by his side and slay his beast over his grave. And let his weapon stay as a solace to him in his solitude."

"Bury not a sword stained with enemy blood, nor slay a yearling that has faced death. Do not abandon in the wilderness a weapon accustomed to an active hand and a strong forearm. Rather carry all back to his kinsman as a goodly inheritance." So spoke one.

Yet another raised his voice. "Let us kneel by his side and pray the prayers of the Nazarene, that Heaven might pardon him and bless our victory."

"Nay, let us raise him upon our shoulders and make our shields and lances as a bier to him; and encircle this valley, singing songs of victory. Let him look upon the slain of our foes, and the lips of his wounds shall smile ere they are closed by the earth of the grave."

"Let us lift him on to his steed and support him with the skulls of the killed and gird him with his lance and bring him into the quarters a victor. He submitted not to death till he had taken heavy count of the enemies' souls."

"Come, let us away and bid him farewell at the foot of this mountain. The echo from the caves shall be his companion and the ripple of the streams his comforter. His bones shall rest in the wilderness and hear the gentle tread of night's approach."

"Leave him not here, for in this place do dwell desolation and solitude. Rather do you carry him to the village burial place. There will he have the spirits of our fathers as comrades to speak with him in the still night and recount to him their battle stories and tales of glory."

In that wise did they all speak.

Then their chief rose among them and made a sign for their silence. He drew a sigh and said:

"Trouble him not with memories of war; neither let the ears of his soul in flight listen more to tales of lances and swords. Suffer us to bear him in peace and quiet back to his birthplace. For there one sits watching for his homecoming. The spirit of a maiden waits upon his return from the slaughter. Let us, then, take him back to her that she be not denied the sight of his face and the kissing of his brow."

So they lifted him to their shoulders and bore him away, their heads and their eyes downcast. Behind them walked his sorrowing horse, its halter trailing on the ground. From time to time it neighed, and it was answered by the caves in echo. It was as if those caves had hearts and could feel with the heart in the extremity of its grief.

And so down that valley bathed in moonlight went the Procession of Victory behind the Cortege of Death. The Ghost of Love led them, dragging along his broken wings.

THE BEAUTY OF DEATH
Dedicated to M. E. H.

LET ME SLEEP, for my soul is drunk of love;
Let me slumber, for my spirit is replete with the days and
    the nights.
Kindle the lights
And put fire to the censers about my couch;
Scatter around my body
Petals of the rose and narcissus,
And on my hair put pounded musk;
Pour out upon my feet
Goodly smelling perfumes.
Then behold, and read what is writ by death's hand upon
    my brow.

Leave me deep in the arms of slumber;
For mine eyelids are tired, and heavy with this wakefulness.
Strike upon the lyre and the lute
And let the echo of their silvered strings
Fall and sway upon mine ears.
Blow upon the pipe and flute
And weave from their limpid notes
A veil about my heart,
The heart that hastens to its end.
Sing to me songs of Ruha
And from their enchanting cadence
Spread wide a carpet for my spirit,
Then look, and in my eyes
Will you behold the light of hope.

Dry then your tears, my friends,
Raise aloft your heads
As flowers lift up their crowns at dawn's breaking,

And behold Death's bride standing as a pillar of light
Between my bed and the void.
Still your breath awhile and hearken with me
To the fluttering of her wings.

*

Come you, children of my mother, say me farewell;
Kiss my brow with smiling lips,
Embrace my lips with your eyes
And kiss my eyelids with your lips.
Bring nigh the children to my bed,
Suffer them to caress my head
With fingers soft as the petal of a rose.
Bring near the aged to bless my brow
With fingers gnarled and withered.
Let the daughters of the quarter come
And see God's image in my eyes,
And hearken to the echo of an everlasting melody hastening
    with my spirit.

PARTING

Now I am come to the mountaintop,
And my spirit soars in the upper regions of freedom and
    release.
I am become far, far away, sons of my mother,
And the hill's face is hidden from mine eyes beyond the mist.
The emptiness of the valley is submerged in a sea of silence,
And the ways and passes erased by fingers of forgetfulness.
The meadows and the forest are concealed behind phantoms,
    white like clouds in spring,
And yellow as the sun's rays,
Red as the cloak of evening.

The song of the sea waves is stilled,
The music of the brooks in the fields grows faint,
And voices rising from the multitude are silenced.
I hear not any more save the hymn of Eternity,
Merging with the soul's desire.

REST

Unwrap my body of its linen shroud
And clothe me in leaves of lily and jasmine.
Take my remains out of this ivory casket
And lay them on a couch of orange blossom.
Lament not over me, sons of my mother,
But sing you songs of youth and joy.
Shed not tears, O daughter of the fields,
But chant a poem of days of the harvest and the pressing.
Cover not my breast with weeping and sighing,
But write upon it with your fingers
The symbol of love and the sign of joy.
Disturb not the air's repose
With the chanting of priest and threnody,
But let your heart to exult with me
In praise of immortality and everlasting life.

Wear not the black of mourning,
But rejoice with me in white raiment.
Speak not in sorrow of my going,
But close your eyes and you shall see me among you,
Now and forevermore.
Lay me down upon leafy boughs,
Raise me high upon shoulders,
Then lead me slowly to the wild places.
Carry me not to a burying-place,
For the multitude's clamour disturbs my rest,
And the rattling of bones and skulls robs me of slumber.
Bear me to the forest of cypress trees
And on that place where the violet and anemone grow
Dig me a grave.
Dig my grave deep,
That the floods bear not my bones to the valley.
Dig my grave wide,
That the phantoms of night may come and sit beside me.

Cast aside these garments
And lead me naked to the earth's heart;
Lay me down softly
On my mother's breast.
Cover me with soft earth,
And with each sod
Sow the seeds of the wild rose and jasmine
That they may blossom upon my grave,
Nourished by the body's elements,
To grow and spread abroad
The fragrance of my heart;
And stand forth
Holding aloft in the sun's face
The secrets of my rest,
Swaying in the breeze
To tell the passer-by
Of my yearnings and my dreams that are gone.

Leave me now, sons of my mother –
Leave me in my aloneness.
Go hence with silent steps,
The going of the stillness in the empty valley.
Leave me in my solitude – and disperse
Like the almond and the apple blossom
Scattered by Nisan's[1] breath.
Return you to your dwelling-places
And there shall you find that which Death cannot take
From you and me.
Leave now this place,
Whom you seek is gone far from this world.

1 April's.

SONGS

A SONG

IN THE DEPTHS of my spirit is a song no words shall clothe;
A song living in a grain of my heart that will flow not as ink
    on paper.
It encompasses my feeling with a gossamer cloak,
And will not run as moisture on my tongue.
How shall I send it forth even as a sigh
Whilst I fear for it from the very air?
To whom shall I sing it that knows no dwelling
Save in my spirit?
I fear for it from the harshness of ears.

Did you look into my eyes, you had seen the image of its
    image;
Did you touch my fingertips, you had felt its trembling.

The works of my hand reveal it
Even as the lake mirrors the shining stars.
My tears disclose it
Even as dewdrops that proclaim the rose's secret as the warmth
    scatters them.

A song sent forth of silence,
Engulfed by clamour
And intoned by dreams.
A song concealed by awakening.

O people, 'tis the song of Love;
What Ishak[1] shall recite it?
Nay, what David shall sing it?

1 Ishak al-Mausili, celebrated Arabian musician (A.D. 767–850).

KAHLIL GIBRAN

Its fragrance is sweeter than the jasmine's;
What throat shall enslave it?
More precious is it than the virgin's secret;
What stringed instrument shall tell it?
Who shall unite the sea's mighty roar
With the nightingale's trilling?
And the sigh of a child with the howling tempest?
What human shall sing the song of the gods?

SONG OF THE WAVE

I AND THE shore are lovers:
The wind unites us and separates us.

I come from beyond the twilight
To merge the silver of my foam with the gold of its sand;
And I cool its burning heart with my moisture.

At dawn's coming I read passion's law to my beloved,
And he draws me to his breast.
At even I chant the prayer of longing,
And he embraces me.

I am fretful and without rest,
But my loved one is the friend of patience.
Comes the ebb and I embrace my love;
It flows, and I am fallen at his feet.

How I danced around the daughters of the sea
When they rose up from the depths
To sit upon the rocks
And behold the stars!
How I hearkened to the lover
Protesting his passion to a comely maid:
I did help him with sighing and moaning.
How I consorted with the rocks when they were cold
    and still,
And caressed them, laughing, when they smiled not!
How I delivered bodies from the deep
And brought them to the living!
In what measure did I steal from the depths
Pearls, and gave to the daughters of beauty!

863

*

In the still night when all created things embrace the phantom
of sleep, I alone am awake, now singing, now sighing.
Alas, wakefulness has destroyed me, but I am a lover and the
truth of Love is awakening.

Behold my life;
As I have lived, so shall I die.

SONG OF THE RAIN

I AM THE silver threads
The gods cast down from the heights,
And Nature takes me to adorn the valleys.

I am the precious pearls
Scattered from Astarte's crown,
And the daughter of morning stole me to beautify the fields.

I weep and the hillocks smile;
I am abased and the flowers are lifted.

The cloud and the field are two lovers
And I a messenger bringing one to the other;
Slaking with abundance this one's thirst
And healing that one's sickness.

The voice of thunder and lightning's blades
Herald my coming;
The rainbow proclaims my journey's end.
So is earthly life,
Entering between the feet of wrath,
Departing between the peaceful hands of Death.

I rise from the lake's heart
And glide upon wings of air
Until I am a verdant garden.
Thereon I descend
And kiss the lips of its flowers
And embrace its boughs.

KAHLIL GIBRAN

In the stillness, with my gentle fingers,
I tap upon window panes:
The sound thereof is a song known to feeling spirits.

I am created of the earth's heat
And I am its slayer –
So is the woman who prevails over a man by the force that she
    takes from him.

I am the sigh of the ocean
And heaven's tear,
And the smile of the field.
So is love –
A sign from the ocean of feeling;
A tear from the heaven of thought;
A smile from the field of the spirit.

SONG OF BEAUTY

I AM THE guide of love,
I am wine of the spirit,
I am food to the heart.

I am a rose;
I open my heart at daybreak; a maiden plucks me and kisses
    me and puts me to her breast.
I am the abode of happiness
And the source of joy.
I am the beginning of repose.

I am a gentle smile on the lips of a maid;
Youth beholds me, his toil is forgotten, and his life becomes a
    stage for sweet dreams.

I am the poet's imagination
And the artist's guide.
I am teacher to the music-maker.
I am the glance in the eye of a child
Beheld by a tender mother.
Before it does she pray and glorify God.

I appeared to Adam in Eve's image
And enslaved him.
I was revealed to Solomon in his beloved, and made him poet
    and sage.
I smiled on Helen,
And Troy was destroyed;
I crowned Cleopatra, and peace conquered the Nile.

I am as Destiny;
In this day I build,
On the morrow destroy.
I am God,
I quicken and make dead.

I am lighter than a sigh from the violet flower,
And mightier than the tempest.
I am a Truth, O people, yea, a Truth.

SONG OF HAPPINESS

MAN IS MY beloved and I am his. I yearn toward him and he has longing for me.

Woe is me, for in his loving is a sharer who troubles me and torments him. She is a cruel mistress called Matter. Wheresoever we go does she follow like a guardian to rive us apart.

I seek my beloved in the wild places beneath the trees and beside the pools, and I find him not. For Matter has seduced him and is gone with him to the city, wherein are the multitude and corruption and wretchedness.

I seek him in the seats of learning and the temples of wisdom. But I find him not, for Matter, who wears a garment of earth, has led him thither to the walled places of selffulness where dwell those busied in paltry things.

I seek him in the field of contentment, but find him not, for mine enemy has bound him in the caverns of coveting and greed.

I call to him at the hour of dawn, and he hears me not, for his eyes are heavy with the sleep of avarice.

I caress him at the fall of even, when silence is sovereign and the flowers are aslumber. But he heeds me not, for his love of things of the morrow has taken him.

My beloved loves me. He seeks me in his deeds, but he shall not find me save in the actions of God.

He seeks my union in a palace of glory builded on the skulls of the weakly, and among silver and gold.

I shall not be sufficient unto him save in the house of simplicity, which the gods have builded on the banks of the stream of love.

He would embrace me before slayers and oppressors, yet I shall not let him to kiss my mouth except in solitude among the flowers of innocence.

He would that trickery be a mean between him and me; but I seek no mediator save a deed free from evil.

My beloved has learned clamour and tumult from mine adversary, Matter. I will teach him to shed tears of beseeching from the eyes of his spirit and sigh a sigh of contentment.

My beloved is mine and I am his.

SONG OF THE FLOWER

I AM A WORD uttered by Nature,
Then taken back
And hidden in her heart,
And a second time uttered.
I am a star fallen from the blue sky
Upon a green carpet.

I am a daughter of the elements:
Carried in Winter,
Born of Spring,
Reared by Summer;
And Autumn lays me to rest.

I am a gift to lovers
And a nuptial crown.
I am the last offering of the quick to the dead.

With morning's coming
I and the breeze together
Proclaim the light.
At even the birds and I bid it farewell.

I sway upon the plains
And adorn them.
I breathe my fragrance to the air.
I embrace slumber,
And the manifold eyes of night look long upon me.
I seek awakening to look on the single eye of day.

I drink of the dew's intoxication
And hearken to the blackbird's song.

I dance to the rhythm of the grasses shouting;
I look ever heavenward to see the light,
Not to behold therein my image.
This is a wisdom man has not learned yet.

THE HYMN OF MAN

I WAS,
And I am.
So shall I be to the end of time,
For I am without end.

I have cleft the vast spaces of the infinite, and taken flight in the world of fantasy, and drawn nigh to the circle of light on high.

Yet behold me a captive of matter.

I have hearkened to the teachings of Confucius, and listened to the wisdom of Brahma, and sat beside the Buddha beneath the tree of knowledge.

Behold me now contending with ignorance and unbelieving.

I was upon Sinai when the Lord showed Himself to Moses. By the Jordan I beheld the Nazarene's miracles. In Medina I heard the words of the Apostle of Arabia.

Behold me now a prisoner of doubt.

I have seen Babylon's strength and Egypt's glory and the greatness of Greece. My eyes cease not upon the smallness and poverty of their works.

I have sat with the witch of Endor and the priests of Assyria and the prophets of Palestine, and I cease not to chant the truth.

I have learned the wisdom that descended on India, and gained mastery over poetry that welled from the Arabian's heart, and hearkened to the music of people from the West.

Yet am I blind and see not; my ears are stopped and I do not hear.

I have borne the harshness of unsatiable conquerors, and felt the oppression of tyrants and the bondage of the powerful.

Yet am I strong to do battle with the days.

All this have I heard and seen, and I am yet a child. In truth shall I hear and see the deeds of youth, and grow old and attain perfection and return to God.

I was,
And I am.
So shall I be to the end of time,
For I am without end.

A POET'S VOICE

I

STRENGTH SOWS WITHIN the depths of my heart and I harvest and gather ears of corn and give it in sheaves to the hungry.

The spirit revives this small vine and I press its grapes and give the thirsty to drink.

Heaven fills this lamp with oil and I kindle it and place it by the window of my house for those that pass by night.

I do these things because I live by them, and were the days to forbid me and the nights stay my hand, I would seek death; for death is more meet to a prophet cast out by his nation and a poet who is an exile in his own land.

Mankind is disturbed as the tempest, and I sigh in silence. For I have found that the anger of the storm abates and is swallowed by the gulf of time; but a sigh endures with God's enduring.

Mankind clings to matter cold as snow. I seek love's flame to clasp to my breast that it may consume my vitals and make weak my bowels. For I have found that matter slays a man without pain, and love resurrects him in agony.

Mankind is divided into sects and tribes, and belongs to countries and territories.

I see myself a stranger in one land, and an alien among one people. Yet all the earth is my homeland, and the human family is my tribe. For I have seen that man is weak and divided upon himself. And the earth is narrow and in its folly cuts itself into kingdoms and principalities.

Humankind is gathered upon the destruction of the shrine of the spirit and helps build up temples of the body.

I stand alone in mourning, listening. And I hear from within me a voice of hope, saying:

"As love gives life to the human heart in travail, so does folly teach it the ways of wisdom. Pain and folly lead to a great joy and a perfect knowledge, for the Eternal Wisdom has created no thing in vain under the sun."

II

I stand alone in mourning, listening. And I hear those that dwell thereon for their weariness.

But did my people take up the sword, saying it was out of love of their land, and fall upon my neighbour's land and plunder its goods and slay its men and render its children orphans and make its women widows, and water its soil with its sons' blood and feed to the prowling beast the flesh of its youth, I would hate my land and its people.

I am kindled when I remember the place of my birth, and I lean in longing toward the house wherein I grew;

But should a wayfarer seek food and shelter in that house and its inhabitants turn him away, then would my joy be turned to mourning and my longing become a consoling, and I would say:

"In truth, the house that refuses bread to the needy and a bed to the seeker is most meriting of destruction and ruin."

I love the place of my birth with some of the love for my land;

I love my country with a little of my love for the world, my homeland;

I love the world with my all, for it is the pastureland of Man, the spirit of divinity on earth.

Sacred humanity is the spirit of divinity on earth. That humanity which stands amidst ruins clothing her nakedness in ragged garments, and shedding abundant tears upon her withered cheeks; calling upon her sons in a voice that fills the air with lament and mourning.

The sons that hear her not for the chanting of their battle hymns; who flee from her tears in the flashing of gleaming swords.

Humanity, who sits in her aloneness crying out to the people for succour and is not heeded. But did one among them draw near and dry her tears and comfort her in her affliction, then the others would say: "Forsake her, for tears make only the weak to grieve."

Humanity is the spirit of divineness on earth. Divineness walks among the nations speaking of love and pointing to the way of life.

And the multitude laughs and jeers at its words and teachings, which yesterday the Nazarene heard and for which He was crucified. Socrates, too, heard, and they gave him poison to drink.

Those today among the people who hear and say with the Nazarene and Socrates, them the multitude cannot kill, but they mock them, saying: "Scorn is harsher than death and more bitter."

Jerusalem was not able of the Nazarene's killing, for He lives eternally. Athens could not destroy Socrates, for he likewise lives.

Mockery and scorning shall not prevail against those that hearken to humanity and follow in the steps of the gods. They shall live forevermore.

III

You are my brother and we are the children of one universal holy spirit.

You are my likeness, for we are prisoners of two bodies formed of one clay.

You are my companion on the road of life and my helper in the understanding of a truth concealed beyond the clouds. You are man, but I have loved you, my brother.

Say of me what you will and the morrow will judge you, and your words shall be a witness before its judging and a testimony before its justice.

Take from me what you will, but you shall not plunder save the portion to which you have title and those things I took in my greed. You are worthy of a sum thereof, if that sum satisfy you.

Do with me what you will, for you are not able to touch my reality.

Spill my blood and pierce my body, but you shall not do hurt to my soul, neither shall you destroy it. Bind my hands and feet with bonds and cast me into the blackness of a prison cell. Yet you shall not prison my thought, for it is free as the breeze that passes through timeless and boundless space.

You are my brother and I love you.

I love you when you prostrate yourself in your mosque, and kneel in your church, and pray in your synagogue.

You and I are sons of one faith – the Spirit. And those who are set up as heads over its many branches are as fingers on the hand of a divinity that points to the Spirit's perfection.

I love you for the love of your truth arising from the minds of all people. That truth I see not now because of my blindness, but I hold it sacred because it is of the things of the Spirit. The truth that shall meet with my truth in the hereafter and merge the one with the other like the fragrance of flowers, and become one all-embracing and immortal with the immortality of Love and Beauty.

I love you, for I have seen you weak before the strong and the cruel; and poor and needy before the palaces of the endowed and the coveting.

So did I weep for your sake, and through my tears did I behold you in the arms of a justice that smiled on you and mocked at your tormentors.

You are my brother and I love you.

IV

You are my brother. Why then do you contend with me?

Why come you to my land striving to humble me to satisfy them that would seek glory from your words and joy from your labouring?

Why do you forsake your wife and your young to pursue death to a far-off land for the sake of those that lead who would buy honour with your blood and high station with your mother's grief? Is it a noble thing that a man contend in battle with his brother?

Let us raise, then, an image to Cain and sing the praise of Hanan.

They do say, my brother, that the preserving of self is the first canon of nature. But I have seen those that covet privilege commend to you the abasement of self, the easier to enslave your brothers.

Likewise do they say that the love of existence makes incumbent the robbing of others of their right.

But I say that the protection of another's right is of the noblest and finest of men's acts.

And if my existence be the condition of another's destruction, then, say I, death were sweeter to me.

And if I found no honourable and loving person to kill me, then gladly by my own hand would I bear myself to eternity before its time.

Love of self, my brother, creates blind dispute, and disputing begets strife, and strife brings forth authority and power, and these are the cause of struggle and oppression.

The spirit deems the power of wisdom and justice above ignorance and tyranny. But it rejects that power which forges out of metal keen-edged swords to spread abroad ignorance and injustice.

That is the power which destroyed Babylon and razed Jerusalem to its foundations and brought low Rome;

The same that set up shedders of blood and slayers to whom the multitudes ascribed greatness; whose names writers glorified; whose battles books rejected not to mention, as the earth failed not to carry them on its back when they dyed its face with innocent blood.

What, my brother, made you enamoured of him that would deceive you, and made you crave him who did you hurt?

True power is a wisdom keeping guard over a just and natural law.

Where is the justice of sovereignty when it slays the slayer and imprisons the robber and then falls upon its neighbour and kills and plunders in its thousands?

What say the zealots of killers who punish murderers, and robbers who requite the plunderer?

You are my brother and I love you, and love is justice in its highest manifestation.

And if I be not just in my love for you in all lands, then I am naught save a deceiver concealing the evil of selffulness beneath love's fine raiment.

CONCLUSION

My spirit is to me a companion who comforts me when the days grow heavy upon me; who consoles me when the afflictions of life multiply.

Who is not a companion to his spirit is an enemy to people. And he who sees not in his self a friend dies despairing. For life springs from within a man and comes not from without him.

I came to say a word and I shall utter it. Should death take me ere I give voice, the morrow shall utter it. For the morrow leaves not a secret hidden in the book of the Infinite.

I came to live in the splendour of Love and the light of Beauty.

Behold me, then, in life; people cannot separate me from my life.

Should they put out my eyes I would listen to the songs of love and the melodies of beauty and gladness. Were they to stop my ears I would find joy in the caress of the breeze compounded of beauty's fragrance and the sweet breaths of lovers.

And if I am denied the air I will live with my spirit; for the spirit is the daughter of love and beauty.

I came to be for all and in all. That which alone I do today shall be proclaimed before the people in days to come.

And what I now say with one tongue, tomorrow will say with many.